NOT WHAT THE BUS PROMISED

What does the UK's exit from the EU mean for health and the NHS?

This book explains the legal and practical implications of Brexit on the NHS: its staffing; cross-border healthcare especially in Ireland; medicines, medical devices and equipment; and biomedical research. It considers the UK's post-Brexit trade agreements and what they mean for health, and discusses the effects of the COVID-19 pandemic on post-Brexit health law.

To put the legal analysis in context, the book draws on over 400 conversations the authors had with people in the north of England and Northern Ireland, interviews with over 40 health policy stakeholders, details of a film about their research made with ShoutOut UK, the authors' work with parliaments and governments across the UK, and their collaborations with key actors such as the NHS Confederation, the British Medical Association, and Cancer Research UK. The book shows that the language people use to talk about hoped-for legitimate post-Brexit health governance suggests a great deal of faith in law and legal process among 'ordinary people', but the opposite from 'insider elites'.

Not What The Bus Promised puts the authors' knowledge and experiences centre frame, rather than claiming to express 'objective reality'. It will be of interest to any reader who cares about the NHS and wants to understand its present and future.

Hart Studies in Law and Health

Series Editors
Tamara Hervey, City Law School, City University of London
Thérèse Murphy, Queen's University, Belfast

Hart Studies in Law and Health aims to publish the best existing and upcoming voices in scholarship on law and health. Viewing law as a broad church, the series welcomes a range of methodologies from the doctrinal to the critical and including regulation and governance, and law and ethics approaches.

Titles in this series

Compulsory Mental Health Interventions and the CRPD: Minding Equality
Anna Nilsson

The Interplay of Global Standards and EU Pharmaceutical Regulation: The International Council for Harmonisation
Sabrina Roettger-Wirtz

Healthcare, Quality Concerns and Competition Law: A Systematic Approach
Theodosia Stavroulaki

Regulation, Innovation and Competition in Pharmaceutical Markets: A Comparative Study
Margherita Colangelo

Not What The Bus Promised: Health Governance after Brexit
Tamara K Hervey, Ivanka Antova, Mark L Flear and Matthew Wood

Not What The Bus Promised

Health Governance after Brexit

Tamara K Hervey
Ivanka Antova
Mark L Flear
and
Matthew Wood

•HART•
OXFORD • LONDON • NEW YORK • NEW DELHI • SYDNEY

HART PUBLISHING

Bloomsbury Publishing Plc

Kemp House, Chawley Park, Cumnor Hill, Oxford, OX2 9PH, UK

1385 Broadway, New York, NY 10018, USA

29 Earlsfort Terrace, Dublin 2, Ireland

First published in Great Britain 2023

A catalogue record for this book is available from the British Library.

A catalogue record for this book is available from the Library of Congress.

Library of Congress Control Number: 2023938353

ISBN: HB: 978-1-50995-149-9
ePDF: 978-1-50995-151-2
ePub: 978-1-50995-150-5

Typeset by Compuscript Ltd, Shannon

For our families.

Foreword

MAKING SENSE OF Brexit, and the ways it is changing the United Kingdom, is a mammoth task. Coming to terms with these changes means confronting a complexity and variety that is – or at least should be – as daunting for academic researchers as for anyone else. Any hope of meeting the demands of this complexity and variety requires a plurality of academic responses. Working across the different modes they engender can also pose challenges to the infrastructure that makes academic research possible: from departments, disciplines and promotion processes to peer review and the agencies that fund research.

As much they plague any ambition to make sense of Brexit 'as-a-whole', these difficulties also mark research focused on particular subject-areas that make up Brexit processes. The topic tackled in this book – health governance after Brexit – illustrates the complexity of the issues in an important domain of public policy. The path-breaking analysis developed here shows how research virtue can be conjured from these challenges. The multi-disciplinary, multi-modal qualitative study on which the book is based generates significant, original research. The analysis offered in this book provides an enduring point of reference on health governance and on Brexit. It captures multiple aspects of a significant historical moment as it developed. These features would otherwise have been lost to history.

The project team have used the unique analytical and evidential resources they generated in fascinating ways. Recent developments in social history suggest that the project's data may be an important resource for future researchers. Lawrence's (2019) fascinating re-analysis of data generated by classic placed-based community research may have created an appetite for returning to systematically recorded qualitative data.

The authors have not tried to explain why Brexit happened, though their analysis challenges and should inform research that does seek to do so. Moreover, I think that a wide readership would benefit from engaging with this study, including many whose primary interests are not in Brexit *per se*. The potential readership ranges from researchers, research funders, and various non-academic consumers of research, including in the media. Beyond health, health policy and health governance, those interested in socio-legal research, how academic lawyers and political scientists can work together fruitfully, methods for researching stigmatised groups as well as temporality and place in socio-legal/'law and politics' research will all find this study provokes thought and engenders discussion.

The book is the main socio-legal output of an interdisciplinary ESRC-funded project. It picks up classic socio-legal themes around story-telling, place, time and the relation of academic-research to its wider context and builds on them. Two authors (Hervey and Flear) are lawyers who work in law schools, one (Wood) is a political scientist working in a politics department. Antova, who now works outside academia at Northern Ireland's Human Rights Commission, did her PhD in a law school, having previously studied politics and human rights. In keeping with the project's ethnomethodological ethos, the four authors weave personal observations and narratives through the text, offered in a spirit of reflexivity and disclosing the positions with and against which they conducted the research.

For all the interdisciplinarity of health policy research, the project's 'law and politics' mix remains unusual, both in this policy domain and across these disciplines (at least in the UK). Though they research many of the same substantive topics, dialogue between academic law and politics in the UK is strikingly limited. Since they share significant areas of subject matter, the relative absence of interaction between the disciplines could appear odd, or even ironic. Each discipline appears to be heavily invested in its own methods and orientations, so they tend to take different approaches to shared topics. The upshot may be that law and politics are divided because of their shared subject matter, rather than despite it.

The interdisciplinary character of health policy scholarship, and the research community that underpins it, is illustrated by the observations with which the book opens. Hervey reflects on an invitation she received from leading medically-trained public health expert Martin McKee during the Brexit referendum campaign: 'We could do with a lawyer who understands the EU and health – would you join us?' While health policy researchers recognise the need for expertise on law's technicalities, the position of political science in health policy communities (and of health policy in political science) seems different. It is not clear, in other words, that the health policy community takes the same view of politics as it does of law as a scholarly discipline. It is only relatively recently that some political scientists (such as Julia Lynch and Scott Greer) have sought to build bridges between the health enclave in political science and the wider health policy community. This book constructs another such bridge.

As I see it, the motivation for this project was mixed. It came from interests both in post-Brexit health governance and in the politics and practice of expertise. By contributing the legal component to networks of policy experts engaging with Brexit, project members did play something like a participant-observer role in the wider health policy community. So far from making a choice between doctrinal and socio-legal modes, expertise in the legal technicalities ran right through this project: Flear and Hervey were each drawn into a host of commitments as experts in health law and policy research, flowing from their extensive experience in doctrinal scholarship in EU and UK law. A powerful sense of skilled engagement with legal doctrine animates the book.

The project also interrogated expertise, an issue which featured prominently in Brexit politics. Here, the research both built on Wood's long-term academic interests and took an innovative turn. The team embraced an ethnomethodological ethos and stepped well beyond standard empirical methods in political or socio-legal studies. These methodological 'steps' may have been a prerequisite for this all-too-rare example of fruitful interdisciplinary collaboration across political and (socio)legal studies. Even leaving aside their social consequences, if stigmatising narratives come to dominate public discourse they can influence research on stigmatised groups, and hence what we can know about them. These issues amount to a challenge to some forms of 'expert' knowledge – and claims to expertise. The project sought to reconnect and rebalance the valuing of disparate types of knowledges.

Of course, work of this kind eschews generalisability. Quantitative studies, including surveys, provide an essential pillar of social research, in my view, though some surveys are poorly-designed and most can be misused. There is, or should be, scope for rich dialogue among researchers who interrogate what people think about politics and law in a variety of ways, quantitative and qualitative.

The team designed a 'photo elicitation' method to evoke emotional responses from participants. They pursued the research in places typically stigmatised as 'left behind'. (The approach is further elaborated in Wood et al 'What do "Left Behind Communities" Want? A Qualitative Study in the United Kingdom using Photo Elicitation' *American Political Science Review*.) Their findings are striking. The Brexit-bus image evoked complex reactions, which included a widespread sense that it represented a lie, or political bullshit. Though the powerful symbolism of the NHS shines through this research, its connection to the motivation of Brexit appears much more contingent here than in standard accounts of the politics of Brexit. Finally, Boris Johnson, widely lauded for his ability to 'speak to' people beyond traditional bastions of Conservative support, is greeted with scepticism, hostility and even outright hate through this research. (Some reactions to Johnson elicited here are rooted in the politics of Northern Ireland.)

The photo-elicitation results raise questions about how this project relates to other research on public attitudes and Brexit. The project-team's argument that many social research methods struggle to engage with stigmatised groups is compelling. The evidence they gather offers a counterpoint to other forms of social science, including most survey-based research. The book captures evidence about specific places at a particular(ly fraught) time which both enriches and challenges other kinds of knowledge about Brexit processes. Without this study, and some others like it, aspects of these processes would almost certainly have faded, perhaps completely, from the record.

A strong sense of time and place runs through the book. It connects the author's personal narratives and the choice of research locations. Antova's experience as a migrant living and working in the UK – and through her engagement in the Northern Ireland politics – traces an arc through the text. As well as featuring early in the text, Flear's conversations and reflections on growing up 'true-blue' Lincolnshire juxtaposed to his adult life as an academic in Belfast also open the book's concluding chapter. The stories he recounts weave place and time together. Alongside his early research on the relationship between 'expert' and 'non-expert' knowledge in public health, Flear's stories seem to me to prefigure or inform the penultimate section of the book's conclusions on methodology, narrative and socio-legal methods.

In the spirit of the authors' emphasis on positionality and reflexivity, I should note my connection to this research (at a risk of indulging myself). I directed the ESRC programme on Governance after Brexit, the first phase of which funded this project. Contestation over Brexit engendered a hyper-febrile context. The demand for immediate reaction to the numberless twists and turns of the Brexit saga sucked up a huge amount of academic energy and researchers' attention. At times, trying to keep up felt bewildering. It was often exhausting. Through these confusing times, the programme's aim was to anchor its research to basic and enduring academic concerns. This project's impressive combination of innovative primary research and rich public engagement illustrates the enduring value of ambitious social science and shows that these two aspects need not be at odds. Equally, it demonstrates that inventive fundamental social research deserves support (and needs funding) alongside as well as within impact-focused and challenge-oriented work.

The project that underpins this book is one of half-a-dozen or so qualitative projects that developed and deployed broadly ethnomethodological methods to study Brexit processes (several others are cited here). Each making its own significant contributions, these projects also worked off each other in a variety of productive ways. The programme suggests that this suite of methods, which is, of course, more familiar to sociologists and anthropologists, provide the capacity for wider and more profoundly interdisciplinary research. Where they blend work that builds on established disciplinary methods with research that shows nerve to step outside them, cross-disciplinary teams can generate results as valuable as they are original. This project integrated political and (socio)legal studies in novel and productive ways; alongside other projects it has helped capture easily forgotten aspects of unsettled times in UK history.

Again, the methods developed by this project (and those developed by others) in the context of Brexit offer rich opportunities for cross-disciplinary research in a host of other settings. Equally, in my view, disciplines will and should remain a wellspring of social science. Challenge-oriented research funding is here to stay. It would, though, be a pity if the space for the possibilities this book demonstrates was not kept open after the urgency that gave rise to it dissipated.

The project that underpins this book navigated legally and politically febrile times across complex, poorly understood and often neglected terrain. It is no accident that its first reference is to the Ewick and Silbey socio-legal classic, *The Common Place of Law* (1998). The project's innovative methods, empirical and doctrinal, represent a significant development from the Ewick and Silbey research prospectus. Symbols as compelling as the Brexit-bus and NHS logo are not easy to find. Though Brexit-times dramatised stigma, it had, of course, marked people and communities before 2016 and continues to do so. The spirit of photo-elicitation, and the synthesis of its findings with doctrinal expertise, offers something important to socio-legal research in/on seeming 'normal' times. Alongside its specific findings, then, this project should spark debate about cross-disciplinary, conceptually informed and empirically rich research within and beyond socio-legal studies. That the prospects for research of this kind are enticing is, for me, a key lesson of this book.

Professor Dan Wincott
Athro Cyfriath a Chymdeithas Blackwell/
Blackwell Professor of Law and Society;
Prifysgol Caedydd/Cardiff University

Acknowledgements

Many people helped us with this project, and this book.

We would like to thank all the people with whom we talked, and worked, during our research, for giving up their time and energies and for sharing their thoughts – and their stories – with us.

The support of the Economic and Social Research Council (ESRC) ES/S00730X/1 is gratefully acknowledged.

Grateful thanks are also due to Matteo Bergamini and his team at Shout Out UK. We learned a lot from you all. Thank you for being patient with us.

We would like to thank everyone who helped us along the way with the intellectual aspects of the project, especially members of our project steering group. We cannot name everyone here, but we should mention (alphabetically by first name) Adrian Favell, Anastasia Shesterinina, Charlotte O'Brien, Cheryl Misak, Colin Murray, Dan Wincott, Dave Cowan, David Dyzenhaus, David Phinnemore, Francesca Strumia, Holly Jarman, Jack Corbett, James Wilsden, Jean McHale, Jeanette Edwards, Jo Hunt, Jo Shaw, Katherine Fierlbeck, Katy Hayward, Liz Richardson, Mariana Valverde, Mark Dayan, Martha McCarey, Martin McKee, Mary Donnelly, Michaela Benson, Mike Galsworthy, Nick Fahy, Paul James Cardwell, Scott Greer, Simon Rushton and Thomas Schillemans.

We are grateful to the student interns who joined the project (also alphabetically by first name): Annie Cavanagh, Astrid Bloemink, Darcy Foster, Hafsa Yusufi, Hannah Shaw, Jim Murphy, Natalia Miernik, Róisie Connolly and Sarah McCloskey. Thank you also to Katie Pruszinski, Luke Pavoni, Rory Jordan, Sarah Beedham and Susan Burton, who helped enormously with administrative aspects of the project.

We could not ask for a better editorial team than Sinead Moloney and Thérèse Murphy. Thank you for guiding and believing in us.

Finally, thank you to our families. It isn't always easy to understand academic life, and we're grateful to you for bearing with us.

Belfast, London and Sheffield, winter 2022

Contents

List of Authors

Tamara K Hervey is Jean Monnet Professor of EU Law *ad personam* at The City Law School, City, University of London.

Ivanka Antova is the Research Fellow on the Health Governance After Brexit project.

Mark L Flear is a Professor of Law and Socio-legal Studies at Queen's University Belfast.

Matthew Wood is a Senior Lecturer in the Department of Politics at The University of Sheffield.

List of Abbreviations

AIM	Association Internationale de la Mutualité
BME	black and minority ethnic
CAWT	Cooperation And Working Together
CE	Conformité Européenne mark
CENELEC	European Committee for Electrotechnical Standardisation mark
CEO	Chief Executive Officer
CORU	Regulator of health professionals in Ireland (the name CORU originates from an Irish word, 'cóir', meaning fair, just and proper, see https://coru.ie/public-protection/frequently-asked-questions/)
EDQM	European Directorate for the Quality of Medicines and HealthCare
EEA	European Economic Area
EESSI	Electronic Exchange of Social Security Information
EHIC	European Health Insurance Card
EMA	European Medicines Agency
EORI	Economic Operators Registration and Identification number
ERN	European Reference Network
ESIF	European Structural and Investment Funds
ESRC	Economic and Social Research Council
EU	European Union
EU-UK TCA	European Union-United Kingdom Trade and Cooperation Agreement
GDP	gross domestic product
GDPR	General Data Protection Regulation
GHIC	Global Health Insurance Card
GP	General Practitioner
ID	identity documentation
IT	information technology

KCL	King's College London
LOL	laugh out loud (usually ironically)
MHRA	Medicines and Healthcare Products Regulatory Agency
MP	Member of Parliament
NGO	non-governmental organisation
NICE	National Institute for Health and Care Excellence
ONS	Office for National Statistics
PM	Prime Minister
PPE	personal protective equipment
PPERA	Political Parties, Elections and Referendums Act
PRSI	Pay Related Social Insurance
RAND	Research and Development
SOA	Super Output Area
TEU	Treaty on European Union
TFEU	Treaty on the Functioning of the European Union
TTIP	Transatlantic Trade and Investment Partnership
UK	United Kingdom of Great Britain and Northern Ireland
UKICE	UK in a Changing Europe
UKIP	UK Independence Party
USA	United States of America
WA	Withdrawal Agreement
WHO	World Health Organization
WTO	World Trade Organization

Lists of Figures and Tables

Figures

Tables

List of Cases

EU courts (date order)

UK courts (date order)

Treaties (date order)

EU Legislation (date order)

Directives

Regulations

Decisions

Acts of Parliament (UK) (date order)

Bills (UK Parliament) (date order)

Secondary legislation (UK) (date order)

UK Parliamentary Committee Reports (date order)

1

Introduction

SOCIO-LEGAL SCHOLARSHIP HAS a strong narrative tradition, especially in introductions.[1] In keeping with that tradition, we begin with Hervey's story. Here's how she tells it.

My long-time collaborator and friend, Martin McKee, saw it before I did.

"I'm getting a few people together on the health aspects of the EU referendum debate", he explained, in early January 2016.

For Martin, 'a few people' tends to mean, say, members of the House of Lords, or people in the Faculty of Public Health or Royal College of Physicians, or the World Health Organization.

"We could do with a lawyer who understands the EU and health – would you join us?"

This request marked the beginning of my involvement in the EU referendum debates, everything that followed the Leave vote, and what it means for health and the NHS. My contribution is modest, in the grand scheme of things. In the run up to the referendum, I spent an entire weekend reading, re-reading and decoding the negotiating texts of the (now defunct) Transatlantic Trade and Investment Partnership (TTIP). I nervously prepared to speak on Radio 4, appear in a panel for a public event hosted by Sheffield Law School, address a group of interested people at the think-tank Common Vision with Craig Bennett of Friends of the Earth and Lord Andrew Lansley, the former Health Secretary. I learned more about how social media works from Mike Galsworthy of ScientistsForEU. I reluctantly deleted a post on Facebook, because someone in another law school dubbed the post as 'smug' for its claim of expertise.

My then 14-year old daughter searched the internet for a quotation from the late Jo Cox MP, and painstakingly wrote it on our front window, as a small act of solidarity.

[1] See, especially, P Ewick and SS Silbey, *The Common Place of Law: Stories from Everyday Life* (London, University of Chicago Press, 1998), ch 1. For some further examples, see also, J Braithwaite and P Drahos, *Global Business Regulation* (Cambridge, Cambridge University Press, 2000), Dedication; N Creutzfeldt, 'Traditions of Studying the Social and the Legal' in N Creutzfeldt et al, *Routledge Handbook of Socio-Legal Studies* (Abingdon, Routledge, 2020); R Ellickson, *Order Without Law: How Neighbours Settle Disputes* (London, Harvard University Press, 1994), Preface; S Engle Merry, *Getting Justice and Getting Even: Legal Consciousness among Working-Class Americans* (London, University of Chicago Press, 1990), ch 1; LM Friedman, *The Roots of Justice* (Chapel Hill, University of North Carolina Press, 2017), ch 1; A Paterson, *The Law Lords* (London, Palgrave Macmillan, 1982), ch 1; R Kagan, *Regulatory Justice* (New York, Russell Sage Foundation, 1978); M Valverde et al, 'Contested Laws, Contested Societies' in M Valverde et al (eds), *The Routledge Handbook of Law and Society* (Abingdon, Routledge, 2021). S Halliday and P Schmidt's, *Conducting Law and Society Research* (Cambridge, Cambridge University Press, 2009) in effect invites socio-legal scholars to tell the stories of their projects, and the book's Introduction includes the story of how the book came to be written.

> Even by 23 June 2016, there was still a part of me that simply could not believe that the NHS could have been such a central part of the EU referendum debate.

Meanwhile, Antova was engaging with the referendum as a member of People Before Profit, a radical socialist political party which is active on the island of Ireland, on both sides of the border. Here's some of her story.

> As a member of the party but also an EU migrant my feelings before the referendum were complex. Many within the party, as was our official position, supported a left-wing case for leaving the EU, to us a very different approach from the one taken by the likes of Nigel Farage or the pro-Brexit wing of the Tory party. As a socialist I found that both the Leave and the Remain 'camps' were led by people whose politics I have been ardently critical of.
>
> While the EU referendum was essentially about the UK Conservative Party internal disagreements and Westminster politics, and largely ignored the voices in Northern Ireland concerned about a possible re-introduction of a land border between the North and the South of Ireland, once the referendum was called, it was necessary for everyone to deal with the reality, deal with its framing. People Before Profit sides with working class people across the world and at home, and the EU's politics and preoccupation with free trade has not always been supportive of working class people. The most obvious instances of that are the EU's migration policy and the resulting refugee crisis at the periphery of the EU, and the EU's austerity reforms, following the Euro crisis, and how they affected the poorest people in Eurozone countries like Greece, or even my native country, Bulgaria.
>
> While sympathetic with the logic of this position, and mindful of the effects of EU membership on less powerful states, and especially on the people with least power across Europe, I was nonetheless conflicted. I am a Bulgarian citizen, and I owed my residence in Northern Ireland to rights enjoyed in EU law. I had (and have) no desire to 'return home': the island of Ireland *is* my home. I have made my professional career here, and I'm well-known among left-wing activist circles on the island.
>
> A few days prior to the referendum, I found myself in my local pub, *The Errigle*, 'chin wagging' with my friends in the back saloon and about how conflicted I felt:
>
> 'I just don't know how I'm gonna vote'.
>
> My friends stopped, and looked at me. And then I got it. *I wasn't going to have to decide how to vote because I couldn't vote.* This huge constitutional decision, with enormous ramifications for my adoptive country, and for my personal status, including my access to healthcare, was going to be taken *without me having any direct input into the decision.* I was, in short, being made an outsider in my own home. And I was, ironically, torn between the left wing case for leaving the EU and my own very practical concerns, all the while being surrounded by people (politicians) telling me they were looking after me. I was so shocked at my own naivety that I took a picture of my face, expressing that realisation, and posted it on social media.

Campaigning was far from Wood's experience. He was more concerned with informing and educating. Here's how he tells some of his story.

> I don't remember too much, but what I can remember about the run up to the EU referendum is two things. First, that I didn't really get involved in campaigning at all. Everything from my knowledge of British politics suggested there was no need. I thought of the analogies of the Scottish and AV ('Alternative Vote') referendums. Both were set up by the incumbent government, and both went the way of that government. David Cameron had just won a majority, and he was bullish about this referendum. It seemed incomprehensible that a popular vote would go against him. In retrospect, I was probably far too complacent.

> Second, I remember vividly a high-profile public engagement event on *A Better Referendum: the Big EU Debate* that I ran with Matt Flinders at St Mary's Church and Conference Centre, in Sheffield, on 23 May 2016, exactly one month before the referendum. This was before I had done much in the way of outreach work: my research up to then had been about specialist agencies and their decision-making. The University's public engagement team were keen, and helped with the organisation. Around 200 people turned up.
>
> The idea behind the event was to improve the quality of the debate, move beyond soundbites and personalities, and let local people in the audience ask questions and become better informed. I was among the speakers, and we also had Michael Keating from the Constitution Unit in Aberdeen and Simon Bulmer from Sheffield Politics Department – lifelong experts and equipped to answer questions on any aspect of the EU.
>
> But the panel also included Julie Kenny, then Chair and CEO of Pryonix, a Rotherham-based company established in 1986 that makes electronic security systems. When it was Julie's turn to speak, she went on what I can only describe as a massive pro-EU rant in a quite combative, and slightly defensive way. I could see people's faces in the audience starting to turn, and I felt it was my fault, for not briefing her properly in advance. Even though objectively the event was a success, because people said in the feedback that they felt better informed than beforehand, I just remember how badly I felt the event had gone, because we had aimed to make it balanced and with an educational and informative tone, and it really didn't turn out like that. I worried we'd created a backlash by coming over as strident Remainers.

Similar to Wood, Flear is not familiar with campaigning. His story is somewhat different.

> The lead-up to the referendum was quite strange. Here we were about to vote on one – actually, given its implications for the integrity of the UK, it turns out – 'the' most important constitutional issue of our lifetime, and yet the quality of organisation and debate by politicians and those on the different sides seemed miserable. Stranger still, it seemed to me that many of my colleagues, mostly academics, but also other professionals, and the most prominent media commentators, were complacent, over confident and even pretty arrogant.
>
> I was raised in 'true blue' Conservative territory, in the south of Lincolnshire, where many people had strong sympathies with UKIP. So far as I remember, my immediate and wider blood family were all for leaving the EU, and so too were many of the people around them. And having spent around a third of my life at that point living in Belfast, I was also aware of an anti-EU sentiment in Northern Ireland. Why wasn't this simple fact taken more seriously?
>
> Within academia these views were often seen as pretty extreme. It was as though such views were beyond what was acceptable or even thinkable by most of the academics (and other professionals) I know. People holding these views were even held in quite some degree of contempt and scorn. Looked down on. I felt that quite acutely, not simply given that I knew some of these people personally, but also because my own critical views of the EU had, yes, emerged from that earlier part of my life, but also because, being armed with knowledge of the EU, I could sympathise with some anti-EU sentiments, even as I found there was sometimes, but by no means always, no basis for them in fact.
>
> I was annoyed that the views of so many people could be so easily dismissed. At the same time, I was annoyed by how it became very difficult to discuss the referendum with my blood family – it was very different with my family of choice (we were all of the same view – although our reasons were sometimes different and even at odds). The referendum and its result became something that could not be discussed with my blood family until very recently.

> I'm glad that I could discuss the EU with others in the lead up to the referendum. It was quite an experience, particularly as although I could see the benefits of the EU, and tried to correct factual inaccuracies, it was obvious that the EU, as with institutions at the national level of governance, had – and has – its problems. Problems with the Euro, felt acutely in southern Europe, and the plight of refugees and migrants along the southern and eastern edges of the EU were very present in my own mind at the time of the referendum and since. These issues couldn't – and still can't – be set to one side. Yet, in a yes/no vote, it's almost as though they have to be. One has to 'pick a side'.
>
> I've tried to explain to my immediate blood family that, yes, I held and still hold certain views about the EU, UK membership and the referendum. I'm critical of power at whatever level it is being exercised. But my interest at the time, or now, wasn't in telling them how to vote – that would be incredibly arrogant – but instead to inform them from all my years studying and researching the EU. We need to base our decisions on the facts – including how we think of and engage with people about any issue. Returning to facts and learning how to communicate them, and listen to and not just talk down to people, seems to be 'the' big lesson.
>
> A day or so after the referendum result came in, there was an event in one of the big rooms over in the main university building at Queen's. So many of my colleagues were clearly upset and even bewildered. I remember one colleague on the verge of tears. I felt for them. I was quite bewildered too. But I wasn't upset – that came later. It seemed to me that the result wasn't unexpected. This had been brewing for years. But why did so few in privileged positions see this coming?

The frustrations of trying to educate and inform were also part of Hervey's experience. She takes up her story again.

> As I said, even by 23 June 2016, I found it hard to believe that the NHS had become so central to the EU referendum debate. I found this difficult to believe because the way health systems are organised and financed is not an EU competence.[2] The UK retained power to arrange its NHS as it is, along devolved lines, for the entirety of its membership of the EU. The choices made for NHS England to introduce elements of competition within the system were national choices, not required by EU law. I found it difficult to believe because migration from EU countries to the UK is outstripped by migration from elsewhere in the world in most health (and also social care) positions, and in any event represents a small percentage of the healthcare workforce,[3] although of course the localised effects of migration patterns are experienced differently from the big picture.[4] I found it difficult to believe because the numbers of 'health service migrants' receiving care from the NHS when they were not entitled to do so are so few that it is not worth hospitals trying to recover the costs, because recovery schemes involve greater administrative outlay than the sums recovered.[5] I found it difficult to believe because governments have a great deal of discretion on how

[2] Article 168(7) TFEU.

[3] See, eg, B Gershlick and A Charlesworth, *Health and Social Care Workforce: Priorities for the New Government* (London, The Health Foundation, 2019).

[4] See, eg, L Mckenzie, 'The Class Politics of Prejudice: Brexit and the Land of No-Hope and Glory' (2017) 68(S1) *The British Journal of Sociology* S265; C Barnard and A Ludlow, *Unravelling and Reimagining the UK's Relationship with the EU: Public Engagement about Brexit in the East of England* (Cambridge and London, University of Cambridge and UK in a Changing Europe, 2017). For a thoughtful take on the 'migration' aspects of Brexit, see A Favell and R Barbulescu, 'Brexit, "Immigration" and Anti-Discrimination' in P Diamond et al (eds), *The Routledge Handbook of the Politics of Brexit* (Abingdon, Routledge, 2018).

[5] 'Brexit and Health and Social Care – People & Process', *Eighth Report from the Health and Social Care Committee*, HC 640 (2016–17), 37–38.

they implement EU law involving health (even public health standards like food labelling). Much relevant law is in the form of minimum harmonisation directives, which allow EU countries to adopt higher standards if they wish.[6] I found it difficult to believe because EU governments have negotiated health system opt-outs from the EU's external trade agreements.[7]

Yet all of these arguments to the effect that EU membership undermines health and the NHS were made in the referendum debates, and the nuances of the actual legal position became lost, in the way the discussions unfolded.

When you have spent an entire career, as I have, learning about and teaching EU law, and trying, in any small way possible, to use that knowledge to pursue socially progressive agendas, it does feel odd to be arguing *for* the EU. After all, as I have often observed to my students, and as Ivanka recounts, the EU may essentially be understood as an organisation based on the logics of capitalism, seeking to deliver the benefits of free trade, on the basis of opening up markets. Such liberalisation can have unpleasant – and sometimes devastating – effects on those without power.[8]

But the UK referendum on EU membership forced everyone into a yes/no debate. There is no room for the conditional in such a choice. So, at least to begin with, I found myself engaging with people like Ivanka, explaining the *potential* of the EU for change for the better, with illustrations of those things that the EU *has* done (for women, for workers, for impoverished regions, for the environment, to constrain the global tobacco industry, and so on) as evidence of the promise of more.

However, as time went on, I found myself spending a great deal of time simply trying to correct gross factual inaccuracies[9] as they emerged. At that time, I had not appreciated the ways in which the media, in an age of 'instant news', simply reproduce each other's stories, without checking their veracity. This was a disappointment. Along with many others, I also spent a great deal of time trying to use legal arguments to stop misleading uses of the NHS logo,[10] in particular, the infamous image on the Brexit 'battle bus':

'We send the EU £350 million a week. Let's fund our NHS instead. Vote Leave. Take back control'.

But none of these efforts were enough.

On 23 June 2016, the UK voted to leave the European Union.

[6] See, eg, the many examples of national discretion outlined in T Hervey and J McHale, *European Union Health Law: Themes and Implications* (Oxford, Oxford University Press, 2015).

[7] See, eg, the reservations in the EU-Canada Comprehensive Economic and Trade Agreement, Annex II; the EU-Japan Trade Agreement, Annex II. See further, L Pedreschi, *Public Services in EU Trade and Investments Agreements* (Asser Press, The Hague, 2020), 152–53. Though the extent to which such reservations are effective is disputed: see, eg, T Fritz, *CETA and TTIP: Potential Impacts on Health and Health Services* (Brussels, European Public Service Union, 2016).

[8] See, eg, I Ward, *A Critical Introduction to European Union Law* (Cambridge, Cambridge University Press, 2009); but, for a different view, see M Sandu, *The Economics of Belonging: A Radical Plan to Win Back the Left Behind and Achieve Prosperity for All* (Oxford, Princeton University Press, 2020).

[9] See, eg, D Maddox, 'Major Leak from Brussels Reveals NHS Will be "KILLED OFF" if Britain Remains in the EU', *Express*, 3 May 2016 and the response by T Hervey, 'NHS Safer Within EU', 22 June 2016 (ablendedlifeblog.wordpress.com/2016/06/22/nhs-safer-within-eu/).

[10] The NHS Guidelines on the use of the NHS logo suggest that the placing of the logo on the bus meant that the NHS was a 'lead partner' in a collaboration with the Leave campaign (www.england.nhs.uk/nhsidentity/identity-guidelines/partnership-branding/ accessed 16 November 2022). On this, see T Hervey, 'Letter to NHS Identity Helpline', 11 May 2016 (ablendedlifeblog.wordpress.com/2016/06/23/letter-to-nhs-identity-helpline-may-2016/).

2

Aims and Approach I: Stories within a Story, Positionality and Reflexivity

I. INTRODUCTION

THIS BOOK IS an account of the effects of Brexit on health and the NHS in the UK. In particular, the book is about health governance after Brexit. By health governance, we mean the processes of governing health undertaken by government or government-like organisations (such as the EU)[1] over a territory through laws and policies, and the language used in reference to them.[2] For the purposes of this book, our broad temporal frame is from 2016 (the year of the EU referendum) until the end of 2022 (some two years after EU law ceased to apply in Great Britain). Our main period of empirical data-gathering was in 2019. Our spatial focus is on the

[1] See, eg, on the EU as a governance space/entity more generally, G de Búrca and J Scott (eds), *New Governance and Constitutionalism in the EU and the US* (Oxford, Hart Publishing, 2006); M Dawson, *New Governance and the Transformation of European Law: Coordinating EU Social Law and Policy* (Cambridge, Cambridge University Press, 2011); M Dawson and F de Witte, *EU Law and Governance* (Cambridge, Cambridge University Press, 2022); J Scott and DM Trubek, 'Mind the Gap: Law and New Approaches to Governance in the European Union' (2002) 8(1) *European Law Journal* 1. On the EU as a health governance space/entity see, ML Flear, *Governing Public Health: EU Law, Regulation and Biopolitics* (Oxford, Hart Publishing, 2015 hb, 2018 pb (revised)); T Hervey, 'The European Union and the Governance of Health Care' in G de Búrca and J Scott (eds), *New Governance and Constitutionalism in the EU and the US* (Oxford, Hart Publishing, 2006); T Hervey, 'The European Union's Governance of Health Care and the Welfare Modernization Agenda' (2008) 2(1) *Regulation & Governance* 103; T Hervey, '"Adjudicating in the Shadow of the Informal Settlement"?: The Court of Justice of the European Union, "New Governance" and Social Welfare' (2010) 63 *Current Legal Problems* 92; T Hervey and J McHale, *European Union Health Law: Themes and Implications* (Cambridge, Cambridge University Press, 2015); T Hervey and L Trubek, 'Freedom to Provide Health Care Services Within the EU: An Opportunity for Hybrid Governance' (2007) 13(3) *Columbia Journal of European Law* 623; E Mossialos et al (eds), *Health Systems Governance in Europe: The Role of EU Law and Policy* (Cambridge, Cambridge University Press, 2010).

[2] Echoing Bevir, who states 'Governance refers, therefore, to all processes of governing, whether undertaken by a government, market, or network, whether over a family, tribe, formal or informal organization, or territory, and whether through laws, norms, power or language. Governance differs from government in that it focuses less on the state and its institutions and more on social practices and activities', see M Bevir, *Governance: A Very Short Introduction* (Oxford, Oxford University Press, 2012), 1. See also, C Ansell and J Torfing (eds), *Handbook on Theories of Governance Hardcover*, 2nd edn (Cheltenham, Edward Elgar, 2022); RAW Rhodes, *Understanding Governance: Policy Networks, Governance, Reflexivity and Accountability* (Oxford, Oxford University Press, 1997).

changing interactions between the EU, UK and devolved levels of governance for the north of England and Northern Ireland post-Brexit.[3]

More specifically, in this book we look at the likely (or, where data is available, actual) outcomes of these interactions: in what respects have law and policy changed, or are law and policy changing, in health contexts? To assess the significance of those change processes, we seek to uncover public understandings of legitimate health governance post-Brexit, and of who is accountable for those outcomes, and how they should be held to account. We do so in order to show the extent to which these understandings align with the new constitutional settlement for health in the UK, now that it is no longer a Member State of the EU. Our more specific research questions are as follows. What are the meanings of new legal texts ('the law in the books') that determine rights and obligations post-Brexit? What are the implications of these legal texts ('the law in practice')? Through what narratives and metaphorical language are those implications, and the practical effects of legal and policy changes, expressed? What does that story-telling reveal about how key stakeholders understand important aspects of the new constitutional settlement? What are the public understandings of accountability which provide insights into legitimate governance post-Brexit? And finally, how do those understandings of the new constitutional settlement compare ('the law in its political and sociological contexts')?

To achieve our aims, and address our research questions, we rely, in part, on established legal and socio-legal methods. These are, respectively, close doctrinal analysis of pre-existing and novel legal texts and interviews with legal and policy actors, especially in London, Belfast and Dublin. We compare and contrast those outcomes with the aspirations, hopes and dreams of 'ordinary people' for a legitimate post-Brexit future for the NHS, obtained through novel ethnographically-inspired methods. These methods are street conversations in cities and towns in the north of England and Northern Ireland, using photo elicitation, and 'vox pops' from a documentary about the project, filmed in London, the north of England and Northern Ireland, in 2019.

We seek to understand the different world views of our interlocutors through centring language, and especially story-telling and the metaphorical discourses through it, as an important indicator of framings, which themselves elucidate notions of legitimacy of legal and policy outcomes, and of who is and should be held accountable for those outcomes, and how they should be held to account. In doing so, we seek also to reveal and illuminate the nature and scale of epistemological (concerning how people know what they know) and ontological (concerning how people perceive what they perceive to be reality) gaps, seen in terms of legitimacy of post-Brexit health outcomes.

The very nature of this book, as this particular account, means that it is also a narrative: the book tells the story of our involvement in understanding those outcomes through engagement with multiple sources of information, each telling their

[3] Multilevel governance approaches to the study of the EU conceptualise the EU as a regulatory order, nested in and interacting with, a range of other regulatory orders. See, seminally, L Hooghe and G Marks, *Multilevel Governance and European Integration* (Oxford, Rowman & Littlefield, 2001).

particular stories. Stories are central to our overall *methodology*, by which we mean – broadly – the underpinning theoretical framework and rationale for the research, and also to our specific research *methods*, by which we mean the tools chosen, consistent with the methodology, to undertake the research.[4] To underscore the point, we also begin this chapter, the first of two on our methodology, with two stories which also serve to illustrate our overall approach. First, Hervey's:

> It is Saturday 4 June 2016. I am strolling in the sunshine to the concourse outside Sheffield railway station. The concourse is sheltered from a four-lane road by a 'wall of steel' sculpture, fitting for a city with a proud history of steel-building. But the sculpture is also controversial, as the steel used to build this civic monument comes from China, not from Sheffield. I spot a 'Leave UK' campaigner: an earnest and acne-adorned young white man giving out leaflets and engaging passers-by in conversation. The leaflet includes the now infamous picture of the bus: 'We send the EU £350 million a week', it proclaims (falsely). 'Let's fund our NHS instead'.
>
> As I approach, I overhear a middle-aged man interacting with the young Leave campaigner. The middle-aged man is becoming increasingly frustrated and irate. He has worked in the NHS in Sheffield for over 30 years, and now he's a manager in a local hospital. 'I've seen what the Tories have done to it. Do you really think they [in government] would give more money to the NHS? Do you really believe those lies? Those people [in London] don't care what happens to Sheffield or its NHS'. I watch the interaction as I approach, and I think that I can help.
>
> 'He's right', I interject, joining the conversation with the aim of seeking to defuse its increasingly heated nature. After all, everyone present agrees that Sheffield and its NHS are what is important here.
>
> 'Being in the EU isn't harmful to the NHS. In fact, it's beneficial'.
>
> The information that I feel I need for this conversation comes easily to my mind. I've been researching the effects of EU law on health for three decades. These effects are not always as good for health as they could be, but there is no doubt that they help, especially in the context of the UK, which is not in the Eurozone and has not experienced EU- or IMF-imposed austerity. I have just finished a live interview on BBC Radio 4's *Moneybox*. The BBC had finally woken up to some of the health-related aspects of Brexit, and the *Moneybox* production team wanted to know more from a legal expert. Technical legal questions such as 'how does the EHIC card work?, what about UK pensioners who have retired to Spain and access clinics there?' segued into more esoteric interpretative questions such as 'Does being in the EU mean that we cannot renationalise the NHS?'. All of these matters are topics in which I am a technical expert, and I have also been practising making my answers intelligible to a BBC audience.
>
> My knowledge lands with the middle-aged hospital manager.
>
> But it makes no sense at all to the young Leaver. As he struggles to parry our accounts – at least in my case, delivered as calmly and pleasantly as I can muster – a much older 'minder' from the Leave UK campaign comes to his rescue. I do not recall exactly what he said, but I do know that both the middle-aged NHS manager and I retreat almost immediately. I am not sure about the manager's views, but my sense is that there was no point whatsoever in civil engagement with this individual. He seemed quite simply impervious to fact-based or logical argument.

[4] For discussion, see, eg, R Cryer et al, *Research Methodologies in EU and International Law* (Oxford, Hart Publishing, 2011).

Flear's story occurs a little later in time, and indeed between the places where the interlocutors in the conversations were based:

> During the May premiership, from my home in Belfast, Northern Ireland, I had several very halting telephone conversations with my blood family in England. I would call to check in and ask how things were going. There was a definite sense of something, and it was most definitely Brexit, always looming large on the edge of our conversations. Our calls never really went beyond chats about what we had been up to or – that most common topic when others are too tricky or need to be avoided – the weather. That is probably a good thing. At that point, there was so much heat around any discussion of Brexit, so many hurt feelings all around, and not just among family and friends, but also in wider society and across culture, that a conversation always seemed to risk degrading into an unproductive argument where views only become more entrenched.
>
> Conversations were gradually had, during in-person trips, where I explained that I knew and was researching certain things, about the EU and its law, and how they relate to health and the NHS, and the potential impacts of Brexit, and could contribute these to discussion. I was told, more than once, that we are all entitled to our opinions. True, I replied. But we need to distinguish between facts, and opinions based on them, and mere opinions with no basis in facts. I could speak to facts, and keep them separate from my own opinions, shaped through my own perspective, to help develop views and opinions. I think this helped to cool things down a bit. But I could not shake the feeling that no matter how much I tried to speak to facts, they became enveloped in stances about Brexit, my supposed position on it (despite its complexity), and even a sense of identity reduced down to a for/against (I am a mix of both!).
>
> Similar conversations were held during my daily life in Belfast, just out on the streets or in shops going about my normal routines. But they were generally easier conversations, I think because they were usually between strangers, or arose as part of professional interactions. Still, discussing the facts was sometimes quite difficult and took some pauses (both for me and my interlocutors).

These two stories are representations of the threads that fed into our project's research design and agenda, and they illustrate the interlocking phenomena that we have sought – and are still seeking – to understand, underpinned as they are by seemingly quite different epistemologies (ways of knowing what we know) and ontologies (perceptions of the nature of reality). The stories are also examples of the many different conversations we had with various interlocutors across the project, and provide entry points for reflecting on those conversations as integral components of the project summarised in this book.

To be clear, while we broadly sympathise with and often adopt a view that knowledge is socially constructed, we are not claiming all knowledge is constructed through equally valid perspectives. Rather, as legal and political analysts, we are claiming that some of the knowledge on which we report here – specifically 'the law' – is one of a limited number of legally acceptable interpretations of formal legal text as determined by the boundaries and interpretive conventions of the legal system.[5] This is

[5] They are determined in part by epistemic communities. In international law, 'epistemic communities' are understood as 'social groups that perform functions related to the formation of knowledge in the field of international law' see A Bianchi, 'Epistemic Communities' in J d'Aspremont and S Singh, *Concepts for International Law* (Abingdon, Routledge, 2019). See also PB Haas, 'Epistemic Communities' in L Rajamani and J Peel (eds), *The Oxford Handbook of International Environmental Law* (Oxford, Oxford University

more a 'realist' understanding of legal knowledge, in that it assumes the existence of formal legal text the meaning of which is determined (largely though not entirely) independent of (broader extra-legal) processes of social construction.[6] We are, in short, and similar to many socio-legal scholars, neutral in terms of this aspect of social science metatheory.[7]

In the rest of this chapter, we make two introductory methodological points around the sources for this book and the stories it contains. We explain how the stories we tell underline our inherent researcher situated-ness or positionality, as well as that of our research subjects and co-producers. Extending the latter, we interrogate what that means for our obligations as ethical and reflexive researchers, for the claims we are seeking to make and for our research design. The centrality of stories to this book means we are being up-front about that aspect of our methods, positionality and reflexivity, epistemology and ontology, theoretical framework and rationale, and thus – ultimately – methodology. This transparency is relatively unusual in legal (or indeed political science) scholarship, although very common in other fields such as sociology.

We supplement these two points, and extend our transparency, in the next chapter, where we explain further the methods we use to generate our data, specifically the selection of people and (their) locations for our research, going to them or 'into the field', and the types of the data generated from those methods, including the strengths and limitations of such data. In the final chapter of the book, we round out this discussion. We do so by explaining our understanding of how this book adds something new to socio-legal legal studies in two key regards. In particular, we explain how we build on work concerned with the spatial and temporal in law; and on how the book's methods and wider methodology, and its focus on story-telling and the metaphors embedded within narratives, might help us to understand how we might consider the (lack of) legitimacy of legal and policy outcomes, who is accountable for them and what accountability should look like, from disparate positions.

II. SOURCES FOR STORIES ON HEALTH GOVERNANCE AFTER BREXIT

The book draws on information from several sources. The main source is data gathered in a large *Governance after Brexit* grant, funded by the Economic and Social Research Council (ESRC), of which Hervey was Principal Investigator, Wood a Co-Investigator, Flear a Co-Investigator and Antova the Research Fellow. But it also

Press, 2021). For further discussion of epistemic communities and international governance, see the publications collected in PB Haas, *Epistemic Communities, Constructivism, and International Environmental Politics* (Abingdon, Routledge 2015).

[6] See, eg, B Bix, *Law, Language and Legal Determinacy* (Oxford, Oxford University Press, 1995); R Dworkin, 'Law as Interpretation' (1982) 9(1) *Critical Inquiry* 179; J Raz, *Between Authority and Interpretation: On the Theory of Law and Practical Reason* (Oxford, Oxford University Press, 2009), especially chs 9–13; B Tamanaha, *Realistic Socio-Legal Theory: Pragmatism and a Social Theory of Law* (Oxford, Clarendon Press, 1997), especially ch 7.

[7] A Riles, 'A New Agenda for the Cultural Study of Law: Taking on the Technicalities' (2005) 63(4) *Buffalo Law Review* 973; M Valverde, 'Jurisdiction and Scale: Legal "Technicalities" as Resources for Theory' (2009) 18(2) *Social & Legal Studies* 139. See also, D Cowan and D Wincott (eds), *Exploring the 'Legal' in Socio-Legal Studies* (London, Palgrave Macmillan, 2016).

draws on data from a smaller-scale ESRC *Brexit Priority Grant* (led by Jean McHale); Hervey's consultancy work (with Nick Fahy) for the House of Commons and House of Lords; Wood, Hervey, Flear and Antova's collaboration with *UK in a Changing Europe*; Hervey's role as a member of Sheffield Teaching Hospitals NHS Foundation Trust COVID-19 Ethics Committee; and a five-year European Commission-funded Jean Monnet project (led by Katherine Fierlbeck). Wood is drawing on his experience leading a community outreach project for the University of Sheffield Department of Politics in Gleadless Valley, a deprived part of Sheffield that voted Leave in the referendum. More indirectly, Antova is drawing on her experiences for six years as a left-wing political activist and critical scholar in Northern Ireland, and as an EU citizen who has lived in the UK for over a decade. Flear is drawing on his experiences as someone who uses the EU as one site through which to examine the integration of 'expert' and 'non-expert'[8] knowledge and expertise in legal and regulatory decision-making. Hervey is drawing on over 20 years of research in the broad field of European Union (health) law and policy, as well as related fields such as social welfare and equality law, working with colleagues from across Europe and beyond. Although we have tried to document meticulously the sources from which we draw our knowledge, in some instances this was not possible, not because we did not try, but because we cannot now recall where we first came upon a particular idea or analytical insight.

Three of the four authors are *legal* scholars, but as our subtitle (Health *Governance* after Brexit) suggests, we are also inspired by social science and humanities more generally, especially political science and policy studies. Our book presents the results of detailed analyses of the legal and policy texts governing health and the NHS post-Brexit (during transition and afterwards). We analyse both those laws that embody relationship(s) between the UK and the EU, and those which apply internally to the UK. Some of these legal texts have direct implications for health or the NHS. But many of them have only *indirect* effects. Part of our aim is to place those legal texts in their social, political and (to some extent) cultural contexts, so as to uncover what they mean in practice.

One way to achieve this research aim is to ask experts in the health policy community for their views on the unfolding legal and policy landscape. What policy experts say when asked open-ended questions about Brexit and health reveals their experience of how post-Brexit health law is designed and implemented, and highlights key concerns in terms of accountability and transparency. We therefore draw on information from stakeholder consultation workshops and over 40 semi-structured interviews with health policy experts in the four nations/devolved administrations of the UK, and in Brussels, conducted November 2018 to May 2019. Often, these discussions involve story-telling or metaphorical language, which give insights into both the 'big picture' policy challenges of Brexit for health and the NHS, and the human level of its implications.

[8] We have put 'expert' and 'non-expert' in inverted commas here, because part of our message is that the supposed distinction between these types of knowledge is nowhere near as clear-cut as it seems. For a review of the (considerable) literature on 'experts' and forms of expertise, see M Wood, *Hyper-Active Governance: How Governments Manage the Politics of Expertise* (Cambridge, Cambridge University Press, 2019), ch 2. On the integration of 'expert' and 'non-expert' expertise and knowledge, see Flear, *Governing Public Health*, above n 1.

For instance, one interviewee, Bernie McCrory, in Northern Ireland, told us the story of her husband, who, in her words, would probably have died if he had suffered his heart attack at a time before the Good Friday/Belfast Agreement 1998. The cooperation across the Irish border consequent upon that Agreement meant that an ambulance nearest to the patient in a critical condition would now be dispatched, irrespective of jurisdiction. Before that time, she told us, ambulances would stop on the border, and decant the patient from one ambulance to another, sometimes resulting in life-critical delays. For her, Brexit meant a fear of a reversion to pre-1998 arrangements.

These stories, often moving, allow us to unpick the practical effects of Brexit, which either eventuated or, in many instances, were expected at the time of the interview, but subsequently were relieved or compensated for in the settlements (like the Northern Ireland Protocol to the Withdrawal Agreement), which were put in place as the Brexit process moved and is still moving through its various phases.

The book also uses the results of follow-up collaborative legal and policy analysis undertaken with and for a small, select group of those health policy experts, from 2019–21. These legal and policy briefs are where much of the legal detail on which we report was hammered out. The approach we used most often was scenario analysis. We were often able to work with student interns, and we are grateful to Astrid Bloemink, Annie Cavanagh, Darcy Foster, Sarah McCloskey, Natalia Miernik, Jim Murphy, Hannah Shaw and Hafsa Yusufi for their efforts. Our method was to write, collaboratively with the health policy expert, a fictitious scenario or story, which captured real life concerns, drawing on both generalised data and on specific human level stories known to us, or available in the public domain. We then developed a detailed and reasoned legal analysis of the scenario, setting out the legal position under relevant novel legal texts: the Withdrawal Agreement; the European Union (Withdrawal) Act 2018; the European Union (Withdrawal Agreement) Act 2020; other relevant Acts of Parliament; the statutory instruments through which 'retained EU law' is amended; and the EU-UK Trade and Cooperation Agreement. Sometimes we had to reason in the alternative, where the meaning of the legal text was not evident and could be disputed. These legal and policy analyses, of which we completed over a dozen during the life of the project,[9] reveal that Brexit results in diminished rights to cross-border healthcare (see chapters five and six); diminished opportunities for biomedical research (in both the UK and the EU) (see chapter nine); diminished opportunities for the NHS to recruit staff (see chapter seven); and opportunities for changes to regulation in a range of health domains which could offer improvements to human health in the UK, but are far from guaranteed to do so (see chapters eight, nine and 10). The overall picture our analysis paints is that Brexit in all its forms is bad for health and the NHS, though some forms of Brexit would have been worse than others.[10]

[9] Our policy analyses and other project publications are available from 'Health Governance after Brexit: Law, Language and Legitimacy' (www.sheffield.ac.uk/law/news/health-governance-after-brexit-law-language-and-legitimacy accessed 16 February 2023).

[10] N Fahy et al, 'How Will Brexit Affect Health and Health Services in the UK? Evaluating Three Possible Scenarios Against the WHO Health System Building Blocks' (2017) 390(10107) *The Lancet* 2110; N Fahy et al, 'How Will Brexit Affect Health and Health Services in the UK? An Updated Evaluation'

This analytical conclusion is in stark contrast to the idea, implicit in the Brexit bus, circulating in the run-up to the referendum, and featured in Hervey's story at the start of this chapter, that Brexit would be good for the NHS, and consequently for health. That gap between reality and perception, and how to hold politicians to account for it, so as to secure a legitimate post-Brexit health governance settlement, sits at the heart of the book.

To this end, we also reflect on notes of 417 conversations with a total of 489 participants, using photo elicitation, undertaken by Antova and Wood in the street during selected weeks in 2019 in four field sites in Northern Ireland and the north of England. These conversations, and especially the language that people use to describe their feelings about the NHS, Brexit and legitimacy/accountability, give crucial insights into voices that are not readily heard in legal or political discourses.[11] In addition, the book draws on information from social media; and from a film, made as part of the *Governance after Brexit* project, in association with Shout Out UK, using footage of 15 'vox pops' (see Appendix, Table 2.1), which provide similar perspectives.[12]

These sources, while reflecting a distinctly different set of perspectives from those in the discussions with our health policy collaborators, and other experts in the health law and policy domain, are far from reflecting a simple or simplistic understanding of a causal relationship between leaving the EU and improving the NHS. Many of the people with whom we talked, in towns in Northern Ireland and the north of England, revealed that they understood that the implied promise on the 'Brexit bus' was a lie, or 'bullshit' – an untruth that both speaker and listener know to be untrue.[13] While it would be lovely, Steven Shepherd ('Shep'), a pub landlord in Gleadless, Sheffield, told us, if that money would come into the NHS, at the time, he said, everyone knew that this was not to be.

While a common theme in these conversations was a disconnection from politics in general, politicians of all political parties and Brexit in particular (many said they were 'sick of' hearing about Brexit, an interesting metaphor in itself), most people felt a connection with the NHS. Although at no point did we ask people anything about their health, they often told stories of their own NHS experiences, and extrapolated from these into broader truths, or hopes or fears for the future. One man in Rotherham showed us photographs on his phone of his wife, who had, in his perception, been badly treated in a Greek hospital, and subsequently died. Shared membership of the

(2019) 393(10174) *The Lancet* 949; N Fahy et al, 'Assessing the Potential Impact on Health of the UK's Future Relationship Agreement with the EU: Analysis of the Negotiating Positions' (2021) 16(3) *Health Economics, Policy and Law* 290; N Fahy et al, 'Impact on the NHS and Health of the UK's Trade and Cooperation Relationship with the EU, and Beyond' (2022) 17(4) *Health Economics, Policy and Law* 471; UK in a Changing Europe, *No Deal Brexit: Issues, Impacts, Implications* (London, UK in a Changing Europe, 4 September 2019), 25–26; UK in a Changing Europe, *Cost of a No Deal Revisited* (London, UK in a Changing Europe, 3 September 2018).

[11] M Wood et al, 'What Do "Left Behind Communities" Want? A Qualitative Study in the United Kingdom using Photo Elicitation' (2023) *American Political Science Review* (first view doi: 10.1017/S0003055422001186).

[12] Shout Out UK, *Brexit, Health & Me*, 2020.

[13] HG Frankfurt, *On Bullshit* (Oxford, Princeton University Press, 2005); I Antova et al, 'Calling Out "Bullshit" in "Left Behind" Britain', SPERI, 16 September 2019 (http://speri.dept.shef.ac.uk/2019/09/16/calling-out-brexit-bullshit-in-left-behind-britain/).

EU, and the access to emergency care that comes from that, had done nothing to save him from the grief of becoming a widower.

As well as telling a story itself, our book focuses on the stories people told us when we asked them about Brexit, the NHS and health. Language – and especially the metaphors or narratives people use to describe abstract or complex concepts (such as accountability for or legitimacy of post-Brexit governance of health and the NHS) – reveal how people frame, experience and understand the world, its possibilities and impossibilities, likelihoods and improbabilities.

III. OUR POSITION AS RESEARCHERS

This is a book about law, Brexit and health that engages with legal and political scholarship. As we have already noted, it involves detailed technical analysis of legal documents, and situates them within their broader social and political context, analysing how they are received and interpreted by an 'elite' of health policy experts and non-expert actors 'on the ground', in specific times and places. As such, we interact with these people in their particular settings, and do so in order to observe and understand their experiences and perspectives. In other words, our approach is rooted in ethnography, which is a branch of anthropology, the study of humans and their diversity. Hence, as already alluded to above, this book's approach is cross-disciplinary and eclectic.[14] It takes researcher positionality very seriously: much more so than general legal or political science scholarship. Using an ethnographically-inspired method such as ours requires a necessary involvement of the personal identity of the researchers. To put it another way, the researcher ' – a living, breathing, feeling individual – is [understood as] the primary instrument of data collection and interpretation',[15] the key 'instrument of knowing';[16] and knowledge production draws from the people and places, in short, the relational.[17] This means that power and privilege matter. We are not claiming to be neutral observers, constructing a 'real' account of 'what happened' and 'what it means' (although as already noted, we do adopt a more 'realist' understanding of legal knowledge). Rather, as researchers, we are continually asking ourselves (including in relation to legal knowledge): how do we know what we know?

[14] We are in effect adopting a kind of methodological 'bricolage' (drawing on C Lévi-Strauss, *The Savage Mind* (Chicago, Chicago University Press, 1966)): 'cobbling various data and utilising different modes of representation in such a way as they hang together through a sense of narrative coherence – and occasionally through intentional, effective disjuncture', AK Harrison, *Ethnography: Understanding Qualitative Research* (Oxford, Oxford University Press, 2018), 123.

[15] F Stuart, 'Reflexivity: Introspection, Positionality, and the Self as Research Instrument – Toward a Model of Abductive Reflexivity' in C Jerolmack and S Kahn (eds), *Approaches to Ethnography* (Oxford, Oxford University Press, 2018), 211. For a frank account of a socio-legal scholar's journey to such a position, see M Mason, 'On Objectivity and Staying "Native": Researching LGBTQI+ Lawyers as a Queer Lawyer' in N Creutzfeldt et al (eds), *Routledge Handbook of Socio-Legal Theory and Methods* (Abingdon, Routledge, 2020).

[16] S Ortner, 'Resistance and the Problem of Ethnographic Refusal' (1995) 37(1) *Contemporary Studies in Society and History* 173, 173.

[17] D Harper, 'People and Places' in C Jerolmack and S Kahn (eds), *Approaches to Ethnography* (Oxford, Oxford University Press, 2018), 113.

As this observation immediately makes clear, researcher positionality is integral to our research methods and overarching methodology: personal identity and experience matters to how we – the researchers – know what we know. This in turn reflects a broadly social constructivist epistemology (how people know what they know), which is illustrated by the place of the co-authors of this book in the stories threaded throughout. There is a related ontological point here: how people perceive what they perceive to be reality. For the purposes of our research questions about legitimacy and accountability at least, we do not purport to access a reality that exists independently of our ability to perceive, through engagement with research participants, legal texts and the various and many kinds of secondary sources we have consulted to undertake our research and produce various kinds of outputs, including this book. The stories throughout this book provide forms of project data, but they take the form of stylised accounts that are told by us, the researchers, and are also explicit about our positionality and epistemology as researchers. Throughout, we make a distinction between directly reported information (such as verbatim quotes) and knowledge which flows through our logic or inferences we make.

On one level, it is impossible, in any meaningful sense, to understand or know about someone or something that is too 'foreign', removed or remote from what we, as positioned researchers, already know. The information on which this book draws includes some from people whose knowledge and experience is relatively similar to ours: the semi-structured interview data in particular. The 'expert' narratives and experiences of health policy actors across the UK are not dissimilar to ours, as academics. Even so, researcher positionality matters. Our semi-structured interview data was recorded and transcribed, but the interpretations of its meanings and significance in this book are ours, and we do not claim to speak directly for the people whom we interviewed.

But the book also draws on data from people whose stories we are trying to understand who are *geographically* close to home (in the north of England and Northern Ireland), but in terms of respective realities and experiential distance (ours and those of the people with whom with interact) we could be thousands of miles apart. This is the case in particular concerning the distance that is labelled, fuzzily, social class.[18] Consequently, we need to be attentive to the ethics of claiming to understand any 'other'. We cannot ever claim to *really* understand, not from the inside.

This aspect of ethical research means we need to – and do – take the limitations of our position as researchers seriously. So much so that we reflect further on our positionality as researchers, and related matters, in the next section of this chapter: since these form the basis for the claims we are making in this book, and the analysis and stories on which those claims are based. But beforehand, so readers are able to make

[18] We do not attempt to cite general literature on social class here. Our thinking has been influenced by inter alia C Ainsley, *The New Working Class* (Bristol, Policy Press, 2018); C Bush and R Hawley, *Standing at the Sky's Edge* (London, Nick Hern Books, 2022); C Carraway, *Skint Estate* (London, Penguin Random House, 2019); L Handley, *Respectable* (London, Penguin Random House, 2016); D McGarvey, *Poverty Safari* (Edinburgh, Luarth Press, 2017); M Savage et al, *Social Class in the 21st Century* (London, Penguin Random House, 2015); M Valverde, 'Class and Economic Equality' in M Valverde et al (eds), *The Routledge Handbook of Law and Society* (Abingdon, Routledge, 2021).

sense of our claims, we also need to explain some more about us as researchers, our positions and identities.

Hervey is Scottish by education, and has lived in the north of England for 25 years. Although she is the child/grandchild of refugees on both sides of her family, her parents are graduates and had professional careers (in academia and the Anglican church). She enjoyed foreign travel to France and Germany from childhood, and aged 12 lived in Canada for a term with family friends. Hervey is a Professor of EU law and enjoys the associated privileges in terms of material and interpersonal resources. Her partner is a judge, and their children are students/young professionals. She has worked on EU health law for three decades and, although disciplinarily open, she is predominantly drawn to legal scholarly approaches.

Antova is Bulgarian by nationality and has lived in the UK since 2007. Antova is part of the first generation of young Bulgarians who enjoyed the increased freedom to travel, study and work in the EU. Her family has working class roots. Antova's parents are what she would describe as 'poor intelligentsia' (her mother being a doctor and her father being an economist, both chronically underpaid and undervalued as workers) and Antova is the first of her family to defend a PhD. Antova describes herself as an 'awkward early career researcher' torn between disciplines and research interests. At the time of the referendum, Antova was an active political actor on the NI scene not insisting on electoral success but focusing on developing a relationship with working class and migrant communities across the island. She lives in Belfast with her Irish partner and their child.

Wood is English by upbringing and education and has lived in the north of England for 17 years. His grandfather worked as an electrical engineer at a power plant in Sheffield, a career his father also followed in the south of England. His mother grew up in Solihull and has worked in both skilled professional and manual jobs in the area of retail. Wood is a Senior Lecturer in Politics and enjoys the privilege of secure employment in a department regarded as one of the best internationally for his subject. He was the second member of his immediate family to attend university, and the first to pursue postgraduate study, having grown up in affluent suburban Hertfordshire. Wood worked as a summer intern for a local newspaper in Luton during his undergraduate degree. The 'street level' experience he gained reporting on various local policy problems in Luton played a key role in shaping and changing his political and scholarly views about the central importance of diversity, inclusion and participation as social and economic goods in local communities.[19] He has worked in the general field of British and European governance and public policy since obtaining his PhD in 2014.

Flear is English by upbringing and education, although he has always understood himself as British, and then English, and more recently 'of these islands'. That became a reality when he moved to Belfast almost half his life ago to become an academic. Flear was raised in the south of Lincolnshire, with family rooted in the county, although the branch he comes from is descended from his grandfather, who was sent to live with a relative in a small hamlet in the county after the death of his

[19] Wood has elaborated some of these ideas theoretically in M Wood, 'The Political Ideas Underpinning Political Distrust: Analysing Four Types of Anti-Politics' (2022) 2(58) *Representation* 27.

mother and the remarriage of his father in Sheffield, where the family had a business manufacturing carriages. In Lincolnshire, Flear's grandfather led large numbers of people in manufacturing during the Second World War, and then founded a motor and agricultural engineering business. Flear's father and uncle worked there for many years. Flear's wider family are mostly farmers, but farming or engineering were never for him, and as with many of his cousins, he decided to move on from country life and attend university, eventually completing a PhD in Nottingham. University allowed Flear to immerse himself in the world of ideas and to become other than what he was. He is currently a Professor of Law and Socio-Legal Studies. Looking back, it seems strange to him that that happened largely through time living in Belfast, in Northern Ireland, one of the most homophobic parts of the UK. Recently, during a stay at the University of Toronto in autumn 2022, where he was a Visiting Scholar at the Centre for Criminology and Socio-Legal Studies, it became even clearer to Flear how his position as an academic – a privileged one – helps to insulate him from societal homophobia. As Mariana Valverde observed to him over lunch with Audrey Macklin, the Centre's Director, things would be very different if he were a 15-year-old living in the countryside. Still, living in Northern Ireland has provided Flear with (it turns out, much-needed) distance from his English upbringing and an opportunity to look at many things – identity, values, life, work, academia and its pretences and what he is in it for, the 'big island' and 'Europe' – differently.

IV. REFLECTING FURTHER ON POSITIONALITY, REFLEXIVITY AND WHAT IT MEANS FOR OUR RESEARCH DESIGN

Because it focuses on particular positioned stories and information gathered in specific times and places, and yet seeks to explore what general analytical points might be drawn from those stories, this book embodies the tensions encapsulated in Clifford Geertz's observation that 'small facts speak to large issues … because they are made to'.[20] We can never fully resolve those tensions between the dangers of over-claiming from the specific and the dangers of superficiality and irrelevance that come from focusing only on the broader picture.[21] All we can do is recognise them, and be open about our own positionality, as we have just sought to be.[22] Like Steven Lubet,[23] the socio-legal scholars among the authors are able to check the veracity of truth claims made in our datasets, from a legal viewpoint. The tension between the truth-claims from the street conversations and 'vox pops', and the lived experiences they embody, and the legal and policy realities, is a constant theme across the book.

[20] C Geertz, *The Interpretation of Cultures: Selected Essays* (New York, Basic Books, 1973/2017), 26; and see also T Erikson, *Small Places, Large Issues: An Introduction to Social and Cultural Anthropology*, 2nd edn (London, Pluto Press, 2001).

[21] T Pachirat, *Among Wolves: Ethnography and the Immersive Study of Power* (Abingdon, Routledge, 2018), 36–37.

[22] Ortner, 'Resistance and the Problem of Ethnographic Refusal', above n 16; R Berger, 'Now I See It, Now I Don't: Researcher's Position and Reflexivity in Qualitative Research' (2015) 15(2) *Qualitative Research* 219; Harrison, *Ethnography*, above note 14, 29–30, 40–41.

[23] S Lubet, *Interrogating Ethnography: Why Evidence Matters* (Oxford, Oxford University Press, 2018); see also M Duneier, 'How Not to Lie with Ethnography' (2011) 41(1) *Sociological Methodology* 1.

One of the challenges for the project team (and limitations but at the same time promise of the project) was to be constantly reflexive and self-aware about the power dynamics that shaped our conversations, and the distance(s) between ourselves, our lives and knowledges and understandings, and those of our research collaborators. As we said above, the distance was shorter between us and the health policy communities with whom we worked throughout the project. The distance was further when it came to some of the street conversations. This is an aspect of research ethics, broadly understood, and is variously described in the literature(s) as 'ethnographic comportment'.[24] We were conscious that our street conversation data gathering was a privilege, and thus we sought to take care with our interactions in our four field sites. This insight is shown in a passage in Antova's coded field notes (see further chapter three):

> People assume we are trying to sell them something or get something out of them, like money. … Brexit is such a laden and divisive topic, you could be treading on sore toes. Why is a young foreigner, academic, stranger, etc asking me? Why am I being asked at all? … Struggling to find the right formula to get people to stop and chat – Brexit as a topic was so divisive that people didn't want to talk, they felt vulnerable, they might be accused of something. In Newry, a contact told us to ask someone how they voted is to tread on the bigger sectarian picture, because Leave/Remain divided Unionist/Nationalist without even meaning to.

Through reflexivity we sought to ensure that data collection and analysis did not align too closely with our own preconceived assumptions and expectations. Adopting this approach to our research design means that we are taking seriously that the types of knowledge which we seek to understand in this project are always to a greater or lesser extent situational and relational, and thus connected to place and time, rather than independent of the person producing it or objective. This – of course – has drawbacks, in particular in terms of the limitations of generalisability of claims we might make, as well as benefits, such as emerge from detailed situational knowledges and understandings.

In addition to our inner reflexivity, as good social scientists, we also have an inbuilt project reflexivity – as we have explained above, the project team consists of four people with very different backgrounds, at different career stages and different disciplinary preoccupations. The team dialogue through which the project analysis unfolded adds a layer of external accountability to each of us as researchers, as we are constantly interacting within the team, and making explicit the assumptions on which we base our knowledge and understanding. Furthermore, we are interacting with other relevant data, particularly from companion contemporary projects.[25]

[24] Harrison, *Ethnography*, above n 14, 29–30, 40–41.

[25] Especially the work of Jean McHale and Elizabeth Speakman, in the ESRC Brexit Priority Grant, *Health Law Outside the EU: Immediate, Intermediate and Long-Term Implications*, such as J McHale et al, 'Health Law and Policy, Devolution and Brexit' (2021) 55(9) *Regional Studies* 1561; of David Phinnemore, Katy Hayward, Billy Melo Araujo and Lisa Claire Whitten, in the ESRC grant *Governance for 'A Place Between': The Multilevel Dynamics of Implementing the Protocol on Ireland/Northern Ireland*, such as K Hayward, 'Northern Ireland: Demographics and Divisions' in F Fabbrini (ed), *The Law and Politics of Brexit Vol 4* (Oxford, Oxford University Press, 2022); of Aiofe O'Donoghue, S de Mars, C Murray and B Warwick, in the ESRC Governance after Brexit grant *Performing Identities: Post-Brexit Northern Ireland and the Reshaping of 21st-Century Governance*, such as S de Mars et al, *Bordering Two Unions: Northern Ireland and Brexit* (Bristol, Policy Press, 2018); of Chris McCrudden, especially C McCrudden (ed),

In summary, our methodology requires us – as 'aspirational goals'[26] – to detail our methods; represent ourselves as researchers; and to represent the research processes and experiences in the field as honestly and reflexively as feasible.

And so it behoves us to be circumspect with our claims, and explicit about our biases and assumptions – at least, as explicit and self-aware as we can be, as well as constantly seeking to check and question what we perceive we have discovered or understood. Further, we need to attend to the relational in the research: to understand that knowledge 'draws from relationships, interactions, interpretations, and appreciation of the Other'.[27] To do otherwise would be unethical – it would be to lean on our privilege in order to claim a knowledge that is not rightfully ours.

The accounts of our street conversations as project data take the form of a summarised, then reinterpreted and stylised, account that is told by the project team and retold by us as authors of the book from that record. Our records of the street conversations distinguish 'that which is concrete and/or directly observed – for example, verbatim quotes – and that which is inferred, approximated, or logically assumed'.[28] Because we report on the accounts of our conversations, and draw thematic and analytical conclusions from them, we need to mitigate the drawbacks of such an approach.

One way in which the project team did so was to use abductive reflexivity: a process where researchers embrace their otherness, and use both inductive and deductive models of inference.[29] When coding and re-coding the street conversation data, the team strove to be constantly reflexive and self-aware about the power dynamics that shaped our conversations. This is an aspect of research ethics, broadly understood, and is variously described in the literature(s) as 'ethnographic comportment'[30] as noted above, or being aware of and explicit about 'ethical trade-offs' that are inherent in all research.[31] Reflexivity is also a way of countering the problem of interpretative bias, where the data collection and analysis aligns too closely with preconceived assumptions and expectations or hypotheses.

Reflexivity demands a 'process of a continual internal dialogue and critical self-evaluation of [a] researcher's positionality as well as active acknowledgement and explicit recognition that this position may affect the research process and outcome'.[32]

The Law and Practice of the Ireland/Northern Ireland Protocol (Oxford, Oxford University Press, 2022); of Charlotte O'Brien, in the ESRC Governance after Brexit project *The EEA Public Services Research Clinic* and ESRC Future Leaders Project, such as C O'Brien, *Unity in Adversity* (Oxford, Hart Publishing, 2017) and C O'Brien, 'Between the Devil and the Deep Blue Sea: Vulnerable EU Citizens Cast Adrift in the UK Post-Brexit' (2021) 58(2) *Common Market Law Review* 431; of Adrien Favell, Roxana Barbulescu and others, in the ESRC Governance after Brexit grant *Northern Exposure*, such as R Barbulescu et al, *Class, Race and Inequality in Northern Towns*, Runnymede Trust, 2019 (www.runnymedetrust.org/publications/class-race-and-inequality-in-northern-towns); of Catherine Barnard and others, such as C Barnard et al, 'The Changing Status of European Union Nationals in the United Kingdom Following Brexit: The Lived Experience of the European Union Settlement Scheme' (2022) 31(3) *Social & Legal Studies* 365; and Steve Peers, especially on his high quality blogsite *EU Law Analysis* (http://eulawanalysis.blogspot.com/).

[26] Harrison, *Ethnography*, above n 14, 99.

[27] Harper, 'People and Places', above note 17, 113.

[28] Harrison, *Ethnography*, above note 14, 25.

[29] C Jerolmack and S Kahn (eds), *Approaches to Ethnography* (Oxford, Oxford University Press, 2018).

[30] Harrison, *Ethnography*, above note 14, 29–30, 40–41.

[31] Pachirat, *Among Wolves*, above note 21, 101.

[32] Berger, 'Now I See It, Now I Don't', above note 22, 220.

Or, to put it another way, 'the choice of … approach – like the research projects we elect to pursue – is a matter of personal style. … These approaches [to which we are naturally drawn] themselves inform the types of [research] questions we think are interesting or worthwhile'.[33] Adopting this approach to our research design means that we are taking seriously that knowledge is always situational, rather than objective and independent of the person producing it. We return to this point in the next chapter, which elaborates further on the spatial and temporal aspects of our data collection and analysis.

In this way, we pursue what Valverde describes as the 'reflexive dimension' of the Enlightenment project, 'which is the analysis of how we humans create knowledges and devise techniques for managing, classifying, and governing ourselves and our problems'.[34] In seeking to be constantly reflexive and self-aware about the power dynamics that shaped our interactions with research participants, we have also pursued epistemic justice, that is, ensuring justice with our research participants in their status as knowers. In particular, we have tried to ensure we do not discount the credibility of research participants, in particular because of aspects of their social identities, or because their views do not align with what we know of the law. To do otherwise would risk undermining the methodology, and in turn this project's aim of understanding and seeking to bridge legitimacy gaps. We sought throughout to ensure epistemic justice for our research participants. In particular, we tried to attend to both hermeneutical justice and testimonial justice. The former can involve being aware of gaps in the shared tools of social interpretation and trying to correct for them, illustrated in Hervey's story in her attempts to interact with 'the public' – for example through BBC Radio – to explain, before the referendum took place, what the likely effects of Brexit would be for health. To seek to secure the latter, we tried to ensure views are not discounted simply because of social identity, illustrated in Flear's story of keeping lines of communication open with his blood family after the referendum. In these endeavours, we share Miranda Fricker's demand for virtues of reflexive social awareness.[35]

V. CONCLUSION

In summary, the approach of this book requires us to aim to detail our methods, including the centrality of stories; represent ourselves as researchers; and represent the research processes as honestly and reflexively as feasible. We have begun to do so in this initial chapter on our methods and wider methodology, which we will extend in the next chapter. We will also continue to make related points throughout the remainder of the book.

[33] Cryer et al, *Research Methodologies in EU and International Law*, above note 4, 8–9.

[34] M Valverde, *Law's Dream of a Common Knowledge* (Woodstock, Princeton University Press, 2003), 8.

[35] M Fricker, *Epistemic Injustice: Power and the Ethics of Knowing* (Oxford, Oxford University Press, 2007), 170.

3

Aims and Approach II: People, Time and Locations, Conducting Our Research and Analysis

I. INTRODUCTION

IN THIS CHAPTER, we extend the points on methodology made in the previous one. We explain further our selection of people and (their) locations for our research, the temporal frames for our various data gathering and analysis activities, going to our research collaborators/interlocutors or 'into the field', and the types of the data generated from those methods and our analysis, including the strengths and limitations of such data. We do not see a bright-line distinction here between 'data gathering' and 'analysis'. Rather, our analysis of the data overlapped with ongoing data capture, especially as the legal and policy environment was changing fast as we carried out our research.

The chapter is organised as follows. First, we discuss our engagement with 'elite' or 'expert' collaborators/interlocutors. The second half of the chapter discusses our engagement with 'ordinary people'. The distinction between 'experts' and 'ordinary people' is presented as if it were 'bright line' for the purposes of organisation of the material in the chapter, but one of our overall findings in the project is a realisation that it is not so. Those whose expertise means they have a particular engagement with our research agenda on health governance following the EU referendum and Brexit also retain their positionality: we do not engage with those human beings *only* as 'experts'. For example, many of the 'experts' in the health policy community with whom we worked also told us moving individual and personal stories about their feelings about Brexit and health: we have already given an example in the previous chapter. Inversely, some of the 'ordinary people' we talked with in towns in the North of England and Northern Ireland were themselves part of the health policy community, such as medical professionals or hospital managers: Hervey's story in chapter two includes one example. Furthermore, there are some aspects of our data where we find it difficult, and ultimately not necessary, to allocate individuals to one category or another. For example, is Drillminister, the Political Drill Artist, who appears in our film, an 'expert', or an 'ordinary person'?[1]

[1] On the relations between race, education, black music genres, critical legal studies and stories, see BL Love, 'Complex Personhood of Hip Hop & the Sensibilities of the Culture that Fosters Knowledge of Self & Self-Determination' (2016) 49(4) *Equity & Excellence in Education* 414.

II. SELECTING PEOPLE, TIME AND LOCATIONS, GOING 'INTO THE FIELD': THE HEALTH POLICY SECTOR

Our aims are to explore the question of what could be understood as legitimate post-Brexit health law and policy, and the gap between the different world views of our interlocutors, in terms of the legitimacy of legal and policy outcomes, and of who is accountable for those outcomes, and how they should be held to account. To do so we need to understand both the legal and policy landscape for health as it results from the UK leaving the EU, and the UK's future relationships with the EU. That involves doctrinal analysis of legal texts, and interpretations of their effects in practice for health and the NHS. To give just one example, in light of the new legal settlements between the EU and UK, we need to understand the legal position of EU staff working in the NHS, or EU patients involved in a cross-border clinical trial. The relevant legal texts might apply across the whole UK, or in one part of it. The UK encompasses three legal systems (those of England and Wales; Northern Ireland; and Scotland), and four devolved entities with some health competences (England; Northern Ireland; Scotland; and Wales). Our doctrinal legal training means that we are able to decode new legal texts, even if these are very complex, or even deliberately opaque, as some of the relevant legal texts are, the Protocol on Ireland/Northern Ireland being a case in point.

But understanding the meaning of legal texts *in practice* needs more information than that which is written in the legal texts themselves. This aspect of our project is represented in the story at the outset of the previous chapter by Hervey's character, and also that of the middle-aged NHS manager. In our research, we engaged with him, and others like him, because they are people who understand how the NHS works, and are therefore best placed to help us to determine how the new legal settlements apply in practice. This method takes us beyond doctrinal analysis to standard socio-legal data: specifically, we undertook interviews with people with specific relevant knowledge and experience, drawn from our project partners (see Appendix, Table 1) and from the documentary film made as part of our project (see Appendix, Tables 2.1 and 2.2). As our team included Wood and Antova, with political science backgrounds, we were also able to bring an interdisciplinary dimension to our socio-legal approach.

III. INTERVIEWS AND CO-PRODUCTION WITH HEALTH POLICY STAKEHOLDERS

The primary aims of the interviews are twofold. First, we sought to discover the practical realities for our project partners on the ground, and to hear their views and concerns as post-Brexit legal and policy settlements unfolded (and continue to unfold). Second, and in return, we collaborated with them to co-produce analyses of how general legal texts (like the new immigration legislation, or a new UK regulation adjusting the application of the EU's Clinical Trials Regulation)[2] would or will

[2] Regulation (EU) No 536/2014 of the European Parliament and of the Council of 16 April 2014 on clinical trials on medicinal products for human use, and repealing Directive 2001/20/EC [2014] OJ L 158/1.

apply in those practical and sometimes rapidly changing contexts. Here, we bring our doctrinal knowledge, both of the novel legal texts, and of other pre-existing texts that might form models for new UK laws, or for future EU-UK relationships, along with the 'on the ground' experience of our project partners. As we have noted, we thought of these project partners as 'elites' and 'experts', in terms of our original research design. During 2019, we travelled to London, Dublin and Belfast (and also to Leeds, Manchester and Alton, Hampshire) to meet them, and we worked with them into 2022, in their professional roles and capacities, although, as we have already mentioned and will show throughout the book, they often also told us personal stories in our interactions with them.

This brings us to a secondary aim of the interviews. Reflecting back on the interview data, and centering the stories, and metaphorical language, used by our interlocutors, we sought to understand something about not only their understandings of the factual contours of the post-referendum governance landscape they were experiencing. Our analysis also sought to uncover elements of their deeper feelings about its meaning and significance for post-Brexit health governance, and its direction of travel. We use this information throughout the book to illustrate how members of the health policy community experienced (and are experiencing) the post-Brexit health governance settlement, with a view to elaborating how they might feel about its legitimacy, and who should be held to account for its outcomes and effects.

Our selection of project partners was based on two principles: to seek to cover a wide range of facets of health policy, and to build on and deepen existing relationships. Each was critical to the successes of the project. Each also reveals limitations in our project design, and thus our data. We explain how we tried to mitigate those limitations to some extent below, but we acknowledge that they were (and could not be) not fully resolved, within the constraints of the project.

The former principle – seeking to cover a wide range of facets of health policy – resulted in our project partners representing a patient-centred focus; a focus on NHS staffing (people); expertise on regulatory alignment with the EU on medicines, devices, consumables and emerging new health technologies (products and services); and on the effects of trade on health (public health). Although this substantive coverage was wide, we were not able to include every key aspect of the sector. Specifically, we were unable to secure direct collaboration with the medicines or medical devices and consumables industry.

To secure the spatial and jurisdictional dimensions of our project, we included specific expertise on Northern Ireland, and on health policy in the UK Parliament. Again, the project resource limited us to a focus on Westminster and England, and to just one of the UK's devolved entities, Northern Ireland. Our engagement with the specific implications of post-Brexit health governance in Scotland and Wales is consequently limited. Unfortunately, unlike at least one of the other *Governance after Brexit* projects,[3] we were unable to secure any type of direct access to the Westminster government, and only very limited access to the Northern Ireland Executive in Stormont, or the government in Dublin.

[3] See, in particular, *Agri-Environmental Governance post-Brexit: Co-Production of Policy Frameworks* (https://gtr.ukri.org/projects?ref=ES per cent2FS007830 per cent2F1 accessed 16 February 2023), PI Dr Ruth Little. Dr Little left academia in 2022 to work for DEFRA permanently, see Twitter (https://twitter.com/RuthieLittle/status/1575793227382128640).

Several partners covered more than one of these substantive and spatial dimensions of the project. We included both a small and a large health-focused charity (*Kidney Care UK* (Fiona Loud) and *Cancer Research UK* (Mark Heffernan, Zoe Martin, Duncan Sim, Angeliki Yiangou, Oliver Buckley-Mellor, Professor Pamela Kearns)). These partners were not only concerned about the effects on patients of the legal and policy choices made throughout the Brexit process, but also about the effects on clinical research and consequent access to patients of novel medicines or other health technologies. Staffing concerns were differentiated between, on the one hand, the *NHS Confederation/Brexit Health Alliance* (Kate Ling), and the *British Medical Association* (Paul Laffin), each with a broad UK-wide perspective, although with attention to the different parts of the UK, especially Northern Ireland; and, on the other hand, the more specified Northern Ireland focus of *Cooperation and Working Together*, across the border on the island of Ireland (Bernie McCrory), the *Royal College of Midwives* in Belfast (Karen Murray), and *CORU, Health and Social Care Professional Regulators*, in Dublin (Margaret Hynds O'Flannagan). Although the *Royal College of Midwives* and *CORU* focused mainly on staffing, their concerns ranged more widely to other aspects of health governance, while their geographical focus was the island of Ireland. Regulatory alignment for products, and the details of continued product supply, were a key concern for our partners in the House of Commons (Dr Sarah Wollaston, MP; Dr Philippa Whitford, MP), both of whom had been practising health professionals prior to taking up public office. Product supply across the island of Ireland was a critical question for the *Health Information and Quality Authority, Dublin* (Phelim Quinn), given patterns of supply to the Irish NHS. The concerns of *Cooperation and Working Together* covered all aspects of the NHS and health on the whole island. Similarly, the public health aspects of the project, and intersections between trade and health/the NHS, were a key focus for the UK-wide *Faculty of Public Health* (Mark Weiss), but such issues also arose for our partners in Northern Ireland.

The latter principle underpinning our choice of project partners – drawing from our existing relationships – aimed to secure a clear pathway, not only for the dissemination of our research through the usual channels for policy work and practice (websites, social media, policy reports, lobbying, legislative scrutiny), but also for our research to have a practical impact, to be useful in the world outside the academy. Co-production with our partners fostered processes of mutual learning, allowing aspects of the project-in-progress to be configured to best meet stakeholder needs. This aspect of the project was particularly important because we were (and continue to be) studying a volatile legal and policy landscape.

IV. BROADER ENGAGEMENT WITH THE HEALTH POLICY SECTOR

Beyond our close collaborators, we engaged with a wide range of health policy actors. Some of the stories we heard from health policy 'elites' came from the creation of the film of our project. Through *Shout Out UK*, the film maker with whom we collaborated, we met Layla McCay, from the *NHS Confederation*; Priscilla Nkwenti of the charity *Black Health Agency for equality in health and social care*, based in Manchester; Seamus Murphy, from the organisation *Brexitborder* in Newry, Northern Ireland; Raymond Johnson of the *Confederation of Community Groups*, Newry; Femi Oluwole, a prominent Remain campaigner and founder of the pro-EU group *Our Future, Our Choice*; and Paul Blomfield, Labour MP for Sheffield Central and Shadow Minister for Exiting the EU, 2016–19. These more superficial interactions to some extent augmented our deeper interactions with the partners with whom we co-produced socio-legal analysis. However, although we offered to work more closely, on health and Brexit, with both the Department of Health and Social Care, and the Opposition Party (Labour) at the time, these offers were not accepted. The limitations of our data in terms of our lack of direct access to government must therefore be explicitly acknowledged here.

In addition to these formal project partners, we also engaged with a wider range of law and policy actors concerned with Brexit's effects on health and the NHS. As co-investigators on an earlier project led by Jean McHale, at the University of Birmingham, Flear and Hervey participated in five closed, invitation-only, 'Chatham House rules',[4] stakeholder consultation workshops in Birmingham, Brussels (both October 2017), Edinburgh (November 2017); Belfast (December 2017) and Cardiff (January 2018), which involved engaging with around 30 experts in the law and policy field. McHale's project also involved 37 semi-structured interviews conducted by telephone from November 2018 to February 2019. These workshops and interviews were with experts representing a wide range of organisations, including regulatory bodies, professional organisations, relevant sections of ministries of health, special interest groups and cross-border groups. Given the sensitivity of the issues discussed – the effects of Brexit on aspects of the NHS and health at a time where Brexit was particularly politically contentious – interviewees remained anonymous. Outputs from that project form part of our project data. The wider geographical scope of that project, and especially its formal inclusion of Scotland and Wales as equally significant parts of the UK for the purposes of investigating the effects of Brexit on health and the NHS, helped to compensate for our narrower (though deeper) geographical and jurisdictional focus.

V. THE BROADER CONTEXTS FOR THE 'EXPERTS' DATA

Overlapping in time with these UK-focused projects, Hervey participated in a six year European Commission funded project led by Professor Katherine Fierlbeck in Dalhousie, Canada. The project focused on European health law and policy, and involved both research-focused and education-focused outputs, including a website of specialists in health law and policy in universities across Europe and North America, several academic workshops, and policy engagement with relevant Brussels-based

[4] That is, 'When a meeting, or part thereof, is held under the Chatham House Rules, participants are free to use the information received, but neither the identity nor the affiliation of the speaker(s), nor that of any other participant, may be revealed' – 'Chatham House Rule' (www.chathamhouse.org/about-us/chatham-house-rule#:~:text=The per cent20Rule per cent20reads per cent20as per cent20follows,other per cent20participant per cent2C per cent20may per cent20be per cent20revealed accessed 2 February 2023).

actors and entities. Hervey engaged in some of those activities, extending her already-existing European health policy networks, and engaging with entities such as the European Parliament, European Commission, the Council of Europe's European Directorate for the Quality of Medicines and HealthCare (EDQM), the think tank *Observatoire Sociale Européen* and the *Association Internationale de la Mutualité* (AIM), the professional organisation for funding entities for health systems across Europe. Understanding the changing context at EU level was important for our project, especially when it came to matters concerning regulatory alignment.

Through consultancy work, Hervey engaged with the (then) members of the Health and Social Care Committee of the House of Commons, from November 2016 to November 2019; and with the House of Lords EU Home Affairs Sub-Committee through its Inquiry into Brexit and Reciprocal Healthcare, August 2017 to March 2018, and to some extent with those giving evidence before those committees. This was probably the closest the project came to engaging directly with the UK government: for example, Hervey was not only present, but also was offering advice to Committee members, when the then Health Minister, Matt Hancock, gave evidence on Brexit and the NHS/health to Parliament in October 2018. Hervey worked closely with the (then) Chair of the House of Commons Health and Social Care Committee (Wollaston), and with the other specialist advisor, Nick Fahy, who previously worked in the UK civil service in Westminster, the European Commission, and is now Regional Group Director for health and well-being for the research organisation RAND Europe. Fahy's connections to the medicines and devices/consumables/equipment industry were an indirect way in which the project compensated for lack of direct access to those important health policy actors.

Flear was invited to give evidence to the Health and Sport Committee of the Scottish Parliament (2018), and to the UK Department of Health and Social Care (2021) on the compatibility of UK regulatory changes for COVID-19 testing kits with the Ireland/Northern Ireland Protocol and the impact in terms of free movement of goods across the Irish Sea.

Engaging with those giving parliamentary evidence in Westminster is how Hervey met Mark Dayan, of the Nuffield Trust, with whom Flear, Hervey and Wood are currently working on a five-year project observing the effects on health and the NHS of the UK's changing international relationships post-Brexit. Much of this work has focused on Northern Ireland. The Nuffield Trust has strong and long-standing relationships with the health policy sector, including parts of the sector with which we were unable to engage directly.

Both before and after the referendum vote, Hervey and Flear were regularly invited to give talks on EU law and health, including engaging with third sector entities such as the *British Medical Association Patient Liaison Group*, the *Society for Social Medicine*, as well as professional organisations such as the *Royal Society of Medicine, London*. Flear has been involved in DNA governance in Northern Ireland since 2011, as an Independent Member of the *Northern Ireland DNA Governance Board*, which inter alia considered what Brexit might mean for control of DNA and exchange of personal data in Northern Ireland.

Since 2016, Flear has served on the Independent Ethics Advisory Committee of EU-funded projects on respiratory syncytial virus. In 2021, Flear co-founded and co-chaired the *European Commission Health Policy Platform Thematic Network*, leading to a report, through which he has sought to maintain input into discussion at the EU level despite Brexit. Also in 2021, Flear gave his expert view to a *Nuffield Council on Bioethics* horizon scanning event on how Brexit could affect the UK's relationship with European (and not simply EU) and global bioethics institutions. In 2020, Hervey was engaged as a consultant to the COVID-19 Ethics Committee of her local hospitals, the *Sheffield Teaching Hospitals NHS Foundation Trust*. In that context, she engaged, on a confidential basis, with frontline healthcare providers in both hospital and primary care settings, throughout the period from spring 2020 until autumn 2022 when the Committee was disbanded.

Flear has also been widely engaged with questions around the impact of Brexit on health across the island of Ireland through fora for the debate and exchange of ideas that he established: the *Northern/Ireland Health Law and Ethics Network* and the *Health Law and Ethics Seminar Series* at the School of Law, Queen's University Belfast.

Antova is currently working for the *Northern Ireland Human Rights Commission*, an entity with formal obligations to secure oversight over the Ireland/Northern Ireland Protocol.[5] Hervey has contributed to the NI Human Rights Commission's work.[6]

Throughout the project, we engaged with *UK in a Changing Europe (UKICE)*, an organisation which seeks to improve public understanding of social science research, especially in the context of Brexit. For example, Wood published a report for UKICE summarising the project findings.[7] This collaboration brought us into contact with others in the health policy sector, including in March 2018 at an event held in London on Brexit and the NHS, attended by around 80 health policy sector actors. In November 2020, the project team hosted an on-line event with *UK in a Changing Europe*, involving exchanges with some of our existing collaborators, but also Dr Paul Williams MP; Dr Paul Darragh, of the *British Medical Association Board of Science*; and Alison Moore, of the *Health Service Journal*.

Overall, therefore, the project was able to draw on a dense – though incomplete – network of health policy actors, across the UK but especially focused on Northern Ireland and London.

VI. SELECTING PEOPLE, TIME AND LOCATIONS, GOING 'INTO THE FIELD': ACCESSING THE VIEWS OF 'ORDINARY PEOPLE'

Given the focus of our project on what could be understood as legitimate post-Brexit health law and policy, a focus on information from 'experts' in the health policy community is insufficient. To understand the gap between the different world views of our interlocutors in terms of the legitimacy of and accountability for legal and

[5] Sections 69, 78A–78E, Northern Ireland Act 1998, as amended by European Union (Withdrawal Agreement) Act 2020, Schedule 3.

[6] T Hervey, *Brexit, Health and its Potential Impact on Article 2 of the Ireland/Northern Ireland Protocol* (Belfast, Northern Ireland Human Rights Commission, 2022).

[7] M Wood, *Post-Brexit Trade Negotiations and Health Governance* (London, UK in a Changing Europe, 28 July 2020).

policy outcomes, we *also* need to understand the world of the other characters in the stories at the start of the previous chapter. In Hervey's story they comprise the young Leave campaigner and his 'minder'; in Flear's story they comprise his blood family and their friends. Understanding those perspectives is more difficult in that they are not susceptible to the type of data collection that involves formal interviews or even focus groups. To try to reach those perspectives, we instead used a method, inspired by ethnography, involving street conversations. This is a kind of 'hit and run' ethnography,[8] sometimes associated with political science, rather than deep long-term ethnography normally associated with anthropology. Street conversations, and the 'vox pops' gathered for our film about the project,[9] are useful for capturing a diffuse public 'mood' in particular locations identified as important for expectations about post-Brexit health governance. In Hervey's story, these are the 'left behind' places[10] such as the parts of Sheffield and South Yorkshire where the young Leaver and his older minder come from. In Flear's story, these are south Lincolnshire, an area that is predominantly agricultural and also includes 'left behind' places. In the film, they include people in or from Belfast, Derby, London and Sheffield.

VII. THE STREET CONVERSATIONS: CHOOSING PLACES AND TIMES

Our street conversations involved selecting locations, and venues within those locations, and organising week-long fieldwork trips to each of them coinciding with moments during the Brexit process where the public were likely to be more engaged with information about Brexit, because of its presence in mainstream news media. Obviously, our data gathering was limited to the places that we chose to cover, and at the times we were able to be present.

Our choice of fieldwork dates (see Appendix, Table 3) was partially led by practicalities: Wood was committed to a full University teaching load, and other responsibilities flowing from that, in addition to his other research projects. This led to some limitations in the data: for example, if we had been able to carry out the fieldwork in consecutive weeks, this would have secured greater temporal comparability between the sites. Making a virtue out of a necessity, instead we sought to organise the field trips on dates where Brexit would be more likely to be in the minds of the people with whom we engaged. These dates included the run up to the first possible

[8] RAW Rhodes, *Everyday Life in British Government* (Oxford, Oxford University Press, 2011).

[9] Shout Out UK, *Brexit, Health & Me*, 2020.

[10] See, eg, J Goldstone and L Diamond, 'Demography and the Future of Democracy' (2020) 18(3) *Perspectives on Politics* 867; M Goodwin and O Heath, 'The 2016 Referendum, Brexit and the Left Behind: An Aggregate-level Analysis of the Result' (2016) 87(3) *The Political Quarterly* 323; M Goodwin and O Heath, *Brexit Vote Explained* (London, Joseph Rowntree Foundation, 2016); L McKay, 'Left Behind People, or Places? The Role of Local Economies in Perceived Community Representation' (2019) 60(1) *Electoral Studies* 102046; P Norris and R Inglehart, *Cultural Backlash: Trump, Brexit, and Authoritarian Populism* (Cambridge, Cambridge University Press, 2019); Oxford Consultants for Social Inclusion, *Left Behind? Understanding Communities on the Edge* (London, Oxford Consultants for Social Inclusion, 2019); M Watson, 'Brexit, the Left Behind and the Let Down: The Political Abstraction of "the Economy" and the UK's Brexit Referendum' (2018) 13(1) *British Politics* 17; R Wuthnow, *The Left Behind: Decline and Rage in Small-Town America* (Princeton, NJ, Princeton University Press, 2019).

date for formal UK withdrawal from the EU on 29 March 2019 (Newry), following the triggering of the procedure in Article 50 of the Treaty on European Union in March 2017; and the elections to the European Parliament in May 2019 (Rochdale). Admittedly there was some serendipity about this aspect of our data gathering: at the time that we were planning our fieldwork, we did not, for example, know the date of the 2019 Conservative party leadership contest (Rotherham); nor that *The Times* would leak the government's 'No Deal' preparations in August 2019 (Derry/Londonderry). However, the four dates stretched across spring and summer 2019, a time when Brexit was regularly in the UK national news, as well as local news in Northern Ireland and England (and other parts of the UK).

Resourcing for the project meant that we were limited to two broad geographical locations for these interactions: Northern Ireland and the north of England. A focus on two specific geographic areas ensured a deeper, sharper, richer, more textured analysis than would otherwise have been possible with the resource available. The choice of one English region with some competences in health, and a 'devolved' part of the UK, each with a different legal system, also ensured attention to the multi-level elements of the post-Brexit constitutional settlement, as they emerged.

Our approach led us to seek strategic, targeted engagement in four towns in these two regions capturing the 'left behind' demographic, encompassing two places with a strong Leave vote (Rochdale and Rotherham), and two with a strong Remain vote (Newry and Derry/Londonderry). (We also have conversation data from a brief pilot in Sheffield.) Doing so enables us to compare how our approach impacted different kinds of 'left behind' communities, and elicited different (or similar) responses. Our demographic and spatial characteristics include: geographically 'peripheral' towns; low educational attainment; and indicators of Brexit impact. Table 3 (Appendix) summarises each of the locations we chose (Rochdale, Rotherham, Newry and Derry/Londonderry). The choices are justified using prominent datasets measuring multiple deprivation and changing population and employment statistics over time.

First, 'left behind' communities are typically associated with 'overlooked neighbourhoods', typically small to medium-sized towns relatively close to major cities, which tend to be 'overlooked' in terms of employment opportunities, despite growing inward migration. This trend has accelerated since the global financial crisis. As Margaret Bolton et al describe, these communities are close enough to major cities to be considered 'satellite' districts and boroughs, but far enough away to be 'overlooked' in terms of economic investment.[11] Second, and closely related to the first point, 'left behind' communities tend to have low comparative educational prospects, quality of life, health and other key indicators.

All four towns fall within the bounds of a 'small to medium sized' community, ranging from 75,000–300,000 residents.[12] They are satellites to larger cities. Rochdale and Rotherham lie roughly 10 miles from the centre of the large English cities Manchester and Sheffield respectively. Newry and Mourne and Derry and Strabane are located

[11] M Bolton et al, 'England's Overlooked Neighbourhoods: Defining, Understanding and Regenerating "Left Behind" Communities' (2019) 13(2) *Journal of Urban Regeneration and Renewal* 116.

[12] E Cox and S Longlands, *City Systems* (Manchester, Institute for Public Policy Research North, 2016), 6–7.

40 and 60 miles respectively from by far the largest city in Northern Ireland: Belfast. All four can be classed as 'left behind' communities on the basis of the geographical presence of areas with high levels of multiple deprivation. In Newry and Mourne and Derry City and Strabane, a high percentage of locally defined 'Super Output Areas' (SOAs) are listed in Northern Ireland's 100 most deprived areas. 27 per cent per cent of SOAs in Derry and Strabane, and 10 per cent per cent of Newry and Mourne SOAs are listed, making them second and third only to Belfast in the list. Rochdale and Rotherham are more unequal in terms of multiple deprivation index, with both towns also having prosperous suburban areas. Both Metropolitan Boroughs, however, have several wards explicitly classed as 'left behind'.[13] Deprivation is clustered around the centre of the towns of Rochdale and Rotherham.

These towns' 'left behind' status is further justified by changing population and employment statistics in the decade after the global financial crisis. Office for National Statistics (ONS) data shows Rochdale and Rotherham Boroughs saw increases in population of 4.4 per cent and 0.9 per cent respectively between 2009–17. However, they also saw substantial *declines* in full time employment, 12.3 per cent and 10.1 per cent respectively. In Northern Ireland, there is a similar story. Available data on population growth (2001–17) shows a 17 per cent increase in Newry and Mourne District, and a 7.1 per cent increase in Derry City and Strabane. However, between 2009–15 both Districts saw falling full time employment, declining by 1.3 per cent (Newry) and 2.1 per cent (Derry/Londonderry). While this decrease in employment is not as dramatic as in Rochdale and Rotherham, it comes on top of already comparatively poor employment statistics compared to the rest of the UK. These statistics tap into a core element of 'left behind' characteristics: residents are subject to growing populations and simultaneously declining economic opportunities associated with the 'losers' of globalisation.

Lastly, our field sites will be/are being impacted significantly by Brexit, both in general and in the specific area of healthcare. The communities we chose are areas where (projected) negative consequences of Brexit flow from a high reliance on EU funding, in stark contrast to the positive visions of Brexit implied for those communities by the Leave campaign. Most prominently in our research, as we have already noted, these visions include promised access to improved NHS facilities, made via the claim, widely distributed during the referendum on the side of a campaign bus, that 'We send the EU £350 million a week. Let's fund our NHS instead'.

All four areas were highly reliant on EU structural funds (Rotherham and Rochdale), and/or access to an open border with the EU, providing for uniquely close relations with a bordering EU Member State (Ireland) that are salient in the health policy domain (Northern Ireland). In our Northern Ireland locations, there are well-established cross-border health care routes: in Newry, the local hospital has been subject to disinvestment over time, people seek hospital care in Dundalk in Ireland, and in Derry/Londonderry people from both sides of the border access the cancer unit at Altnagelvin Hospital. In addition, the latter sites are in a region with a very specific constitutional position within the UK and uniquely close relations with an EU Member State. As we will show throughout the book, they are also highly exposed

[13] Oxford Consultants for Social Inclusion, *Left Behind?*, above n 10.

to Brexit's impact on healthcare. Given their high levels of multiple deprivation, all four sites have populations highly likely to be heavily reliant on the NHS, and the local hospital with an Accident and Emergency department (see Appendix, Table 4). People in the community are likely to have experienced first-hand contact with the NHS, and therefore to have heightened sensitivity towards the NHS as a political issue raised during the referendum. In reality, they are likely to experience Brexit's effects on healthcare negatively, not least because of the proportion of NHS staff who are EU nationals.[14] However, our central focus for our street conversation data gathering and analysis is on *perceptions* of Brexit effects on the NHS, and hoped-for post-Brexit NHS futures in each of our field sites.

In order to access these perceptions, during our field trips, we strategically chose a specific venue to conduct photo elicitation that would be most likely to allow individuals matching the characteristics identified in Appendix, Table 4 (high levels of multiple deprivation) to participate in our research.

The specific venues we chose were all shopping precincts in town centres, in 'unstructured' public spaces (also like the station concourse in Hervey's story at the outset of the previous chapter), a decision we made to make us more likely to meet members of 'left behind' communities. After the global financial crisis, rising business rates and changing consumer culture led to middle class consumption shifting out from town centres to online retail outlets. By contrast, there has been a growth in town centres of cut-price shops like Poundland, betting outlets like Ladbrokes, and cheap food outlets like Greggs, aimed principally at economically marginalised people. Town centres have also seen significant growth in homelessness and economic precarity since 2010. Learning from the Sheffield pilot (25 people), which took place outdoors on a shopping street with a similar profile of retail outlets, unless the weather was sunny, we strategically positioned ourselves in indoor shopping centres to increase the likelihood of people agreeing to participate because they would remain warm and dry while the conversation took place. For a week, we stayed in locally situated accommodation and recorded handwritten field notes. Using these strategies, overall, we were able to conduct 417 conversations with 489 people (Appendix, Table 5), with some conversations involving more than one participant. There was an even spread of participants across English and Northern Irish sites, with 84 participants in Newry (first field site); 103 participants in Rochdale; 112 in Rotherham; and 165 in Derry/Londonderry (last field site). The lower numbers in Newry compared to Derry/Londonderry are explicable by our improved technique in drawing people into conversations over the course of fieldwork.

VIII. THE STREET CONVERSATIONS: ENGAGING AND INITIALLY RECORDING OUR INTERACTIONS

Our approach to the street conversations was inspired by the benefits of photo elicitation.[15] We asked unobtrusive questions, supported by a photograph of the

[14] N Fahy et al, 'How Will Brexit Affect Health and Health Services in the UK? Evaluating Three Possible Scenarios Against the WHO Health System Building Blocks' (2017) 390(10107) *The Lancet* 2110.

[15] For a more detailed justification, see M Wood et al, 'What Do "Left Behind Communities" Want? A Qualitative Study in the United Kingdom using Photo Elicitation' (2023) *American Political Science Review*

NHS Brexit bus. This type of information gathering aims to capture intuitive conceptions of key ideas, in a context where research participants are more likely to give answers reflecting their intuitive expectations and views in a way that more structured methods like interviews or focus groups do not. Two of us (Antova and Wood) undertook the fieldwork, and set themselves up, as shown in Appendix, Figures 1 and 2, usually in a shopping centre, with our University-branded table and four chairs, between 09:00–16:00 on each fieldwork day, and approached passers-by to ask if they would consent to participating in a research project 'about Brexit and the NHS'. The table was draped in a cloth with University logos to identify both team members as University researchers (Appendix, Figure 1), rather than people selling something, or representing a political party. Both consciously wore casual clothes and adopted a relaxed conversational tone in engaging potential participants.

Our research design involved us being in town centre shopping centres, during the working day. This meant that our demographic was likely to be over-inclusive of some groups, such as retired people, people not in work for various other reasons, such as because of (mental) ill-health, or caring responsibilities for children or adults. These groups meant, for instance, that we were statistically more likely to be in conversation with women (see Appendix, Table 6). We reflect further on the efforts we made to overcome these limitations of our data below.

After agreeing to participate, we offered participants the option to sit down at the table, and showed them a photograph of the Brexit campaign bus, commissioned by Boris Johnson during the referendum campaign, with its implied promise to invest £350 million in the NHS instead of 'sending it to Brussels'. Sitting at a table fostered a sense of a conversation between equals rather than a formal research process involving 'experts' and 'ordinary people', although of course the very different life experiences and material resources between us and our interlocutors means that this cannot be entirely the case. Our initial, extremely open, question was to ask participants what 'comes to mind'. As such, depending on the responses, and the language used, we sought to direct the conversation according to a loose guide or framework aimed at accessing participants' understandings of legitimate post-Brexit health governance.

The framework sought to find out initially whether the person recognised the image, how they felt about it, and whether they perceived that the bus message was true or false, and if false, who should be held to account for the lie? What should the consequences be? From there, we moved to questions about what people perceived as the 'effects of that'; again a very non-specific question allowing for individual responses, led by the person with whom we were talking, rather than a predetermined idea of our research agenda. We might then ask: what did people think happened as a result? Was it a good thing? What were their hopes and expectations for the future?

This framework, already very loose, was adapted in each setting to local circumstances, and was flexed in the context of each individual conversation. Based upon the initial response of the participant – whether they highlighted Brexit, the NHS/health, or did not recognise or understand the image – we asked further open-ended questions seeking to nudge the conversation towards expressing an understanding of legitimacy grounded in who a participant saw as being principally *responsible or accountable* for Brexit, healthcare and the NHS. Focusing on responsibility and accountability provided a way to understand the broader umbrella concept of legitimacy,[16] but we did not posit a pre-established definition of any terms we expected participants to use.

The framework was applied in a flexible manner, because the aim of photo elicitation was to facilitate participants in expressing their emotionally-informed understandings. To ensure participants felt a maximum amount of freedom and safety in articulating their views, we did not record names, ask participants for demographic data, or record their responses on tape. Instead, we kept handwritten 'scratch' notes of all relevant information given by the participant, written immediately after each conversation ended, and noted any relevant demographic data based on our perceptions of the participants and information they volunteered unprompted (Appendix, Table 6). Participants were given a 'business card' as evidence of their participation with a participant ID and email they could contact for further information or to withdraw from the study (none did). We tested the method over two days in a deprived part of Sheffield, which led us to slightly alter how we implemented our working framework, nudging participants more indirectly towards the concepts of responsibility and accountability, and letting the conversations flow more naturally in the direction the participants wished to take them, rather than being led by us.

IX. THE STREET CONVERSATIONS: MAKING SENSE OF OUR DATA

In our conversational data-gathering (the initial 'scratch notes' and the notes written up at the end of each day of fieldwork), and in the subsequent analysis of the fieldwork notes, we paid close attention to the language used in responses. We were especially interested in the metaphors or narratives people use to describe abstract or complex concepts (such as accountability for post-Brexit governance of health and the NHS) – since, consistent with our broader methodology, they reveal how our participants frame, experience and understand the world, its possibilities and impossibilities, likelihoods and improbabilities. These street conversations, following Liz Richardson et al's[17] method, enable researchers to get at the 'snap' views of the

(first view doi: 10.1017/S0003055422001186). See also A Ellard-Gray et al, 'Finding the Hidden Participant: Solutions for Recruiting Hidden, Hard-to-Reach and Vulnerable Populations' (2015) 14(5) *International Journal of Qualitative Methods* 1; D Harper, 'Talking about Pictures: A Case for Photo Elicitation' (2002) 17(1) *Visual Studies* 13; LS Lorenz, 'A Way into Empathy: A "Case" of Photo-Elicitation in Illness Research' (2011) 15(3) *Health* 259.

[16] V Schmidt and M Wood, 'Conceptualizing Throughput Legitimacy: Procedural Mechanisms of Accountability, Transparency, Inclusiveness and Openness in EU Governance' (2019) 97(4) *Public Administration* 727. Also see, eg, M Bovens et al, 'Does Public Accountability Work? An Assessment Tool' (2008) 86(1) *Public Administration* 225; M Bovens et al (eds), *The Real World of EU Accountability* (Oxford, Oxford University Press, 2010); M Bovens et al, 'Public Accountability' in M Bovens et al (eds), *The Oxford Handbook of Public Accountability* (Oxford, Oxford University Press, 2014); C Harlow, *Accountability in the European Union* (Oxford, Oxford University Press, 2002); C Harlow, 'Accountability and Constitutional Law' in M Bovens et al (eds), *The Oxford Handbook of Public Accountability* (Oxford, Oxford University Press, 2014); D Oliver, *Government in the United Kingdom: The Search for Accountability, Effectiveness and Citizenship* (Milton Keynes, Open University Press, 1991); C Scott, 'Accountability in the Regulatory State' (2000) 27(1) *Journal of Law and Society* 38.

[17] L Richardson et al, 'Responsible Citizens and Accountable Service Providers? Renegotiating the Contract Between Citizen and State' (2014) 46(7) *Environment and Planning A* 1716.

public about abstract concepts, in a way they might think about them on a day-to-day basis, through 'fast' thinking.[18]

We recorded conversations in fieldnotes, true to standard ethnographic methods.[19] There are a range of ways of doing this,[20] and the project team felt its way a little in terms of exactly how we did it for this project. Our eventual practice was for each of us to carry a small notebook for any observations at any time during the research that needed an immediate jotting or 'scratch note'.[21] Antova and Wood used these at the end of each conversation.

The intensive fieldwork weeks were written up in a separate notebook specifically dedicated to recording the ethnographic observations. During the conversations, no notes were taken, in order to maintain a personal conversation. But after each conversation, we recorded some scratch notes data on anything disclosed by the person in terms of gender, ethnicity and religion, disability and any other relevant information that we could ascertain (see Appendix, Table 6). In the absence of disclosure, each researcher also noted any perceptions in terms of those categories. From there, Antova and Wood moved from the immediate scratch notes into handwritten and then word-processed fieldnotes.

The word-processed fieldnotes were shared among the four of us and reworked collaboratively from August 2019 until March 2020 into a coded version. Coding involved a process of revisiting the immediate notes, discussing them in the whole project team, in a series of virtual meetings, and thus reconstructing them into thematic narratives and drawing out meanings and significance, as well as evoking a sense of place and time.

We generated an analytic coding framework iteratively and inductively, by hand, consulting the literature, team members and coded data. The coding was done by conversation, not by participant. We identified six themes including: the truth of the claim on the bus; distrust in politicians; (individual) responsibilisation for health; need for frontline NHS resources; NHS and Brexit unrelated; and anti-immigration sentiment. We coded each conversation using colour coding, in collaborative Google Drive documents. The coding of our data relied heavily on our personal interpretations of our own fieldwork notes, and each other's fieldwork notes. To seek to minimise discrepancies arising from such interpretative challenges, we coded a 'control section' of 20 conversations following the same coding template, and arrived at a mutually agreed and consistent coding method. We used the 'comments' function to highlight metaphors and stories. From this reflective analytical process, the team

[18] M Duneier, 'How Not to Lie with Ethnography' (2011) 41(1) *Sociological Methodology* 1; D Kahneman, *Thinking, Fast and Slow* (London, Allen Lane, 2011); G Stoker et al, 'Fast Thinking: Implications for Democratic Politics' (2016) 55(1) *European Journal of Political Research* 3.

[19] See, eg C Jerolmack and S Kahn (eds), *Approaches to Ethnography* (Oxford, Oxford University Press, 2018); S Lubet, *Interrogating Ethnography: Why Evidence Matters* (Oxford, Oxford University Press, 2018); A Kwame Harrison, *Ethnography: Understanding Qualitative Research* (Oxford, Oxford University Press, 2018).

[20] G Walford, 'The Practice of Writing Ethnographic Fieldnotes' (2009) 4(2) *Ethnography and Education* 117.

[21] R Sanjek (ed), *Fieldnotes: The Makings of Anthropology* (London, Cornell University Press, 1990), cited in Kwame Harrison, above n 19, 24.

produced two extended field note documents comprising 30,274 words and 40,772 words respectively.

This process of reflexive evaluation and creation of written 'portraits' from the original scratch notes is consistent with best practice in ethnographic fieldwork. Here we all worked together to create meaningful data by reporting on themes or expressions that occurred repeatedly, so that a certain saturation suggests a reliability in terms of the way that people in the relevant location at the relevant time 'saw' or perceived the matters under discussion. At the same time, we were also looking for unusual, striking or surprising elements in the stories people told in the conversations we recorded. In writing these coded fieldnotes, we paid particular attention to the narratives used by those whom we brought into conversation: any metaphorical language they used and stories that they told. The fieldnotes from the conversations provided an insight into political, legal and social interpretations of accountability, and hence of the extent of the socially perceived legitimacy of post-Brexit health governance. The writing of the fieldnotes in itself was thus also a form of analysis.[22]

We acknowledge that the way that we told the stories at the beginning, in the uncoded fieldnotes, is an example of how notes taken at the time might subsequently be worked into a narrative with significance for the project, and we note the limitations of this method. We also acknowledge that our own feelings and experiences at the time of coding will have influenced the ways in which we approached the coding, and how we interpreted the metaphors and stories contained in the fieldwork notes. For example, at one point in the coded notes, we have recorded that the coding took place on 13 December 2019, the date of the announcement of the results of the General Election in which Johnson's Conservative Party won a landslide victory. Wood was feeling 'very shaken' because, for the first time, he had volunteered to help in a local 'get out the vote' exercise, and had been subjected to a 'large burly guy', ex Armed Forces, launching into an anti-Corbyn tirade: 'How can you support those traitors, we need to get Brexit done, "will of the people, mate"; you're a risk to national security'. Wood noted that he felt that, on that day, he was seeing the street conversation data differently to the way he previously saw it. As we have already explained, we have sought to compensate for those limitations through being explicit (to ourselves and to the reader) about our positionalities, and through 'ethical comportment'.

X. COMPLEMENTING AND SUPPLEMENTING THE STREET CONVERSATIONS: BROADER ENGAGEMENT WITH 'ORDINARY PEOPLE'

We complemented the dense data gathered in the street conversations with three further sources of information: community representatives in our field sites; engagement with members of the public through 'vox pops' recorded for our film; and information in the wider public domain, especially traditional and social media.

First, during our fieldwork weeks, we undertook activities seeking more immersive engagement in the field sites, seeking out community representatives with whom we

[22] L Richardson and EA St Pierre, 'Writing: A Method of Inquiry' in N Denzin and Y Lincoln (eds), *The Sage Handbook of Qualitative Research*, 5th edn (London, Sage, 2018).

engaged to enrich our understandings of the communities we studied and the effect of Brexit on health and the NHS in those communities. To some extent this strategy drew on our existing networks, especially Antova's relationships flowing from her engagement as a political activist in Northern Ireland (see chapters one and two).

Engagement with community representatives allowed us to mitigate to some extent the temporal and spatial limitations of the street conversations: we went to these community representatives at a time and place that worked for them, during the fieldwork week. Given the small amount of time spent in the field, we cannot claim to have become fully 'embedded' in an anthropological ethnographic sense. Instead, we claim 'intensive immersion', visiting communities and organisations for short intensive periods: what Rod Rhodes calls 'hit and run' ethnography.[23] Where feasible, these were people with some insights into health or the NHS, but they did not necessarily need to be. We reached community representatives in part through snowballing techniques, where local networks lead from one person to another: 'oh, you're interested in Brexit and the NHS. You should talk to X, in Y organisation'. Our activities included talking to people in community organisations and religious groups, or other figures connected with the community. On one occasion, a former local Member of Parliament took us on a two-hour guided tour of the constituency (Rochdale). On another occasion a community organiser we met through Antova's local contact volunteered to speak with us at length to provide context about the local situation around the Irish border (Newry). These opportunities gave us a type of immersive understanding of the communities, summarised in our reflexive post-fieldwork notes.

Our approach to the film as part of our research data was inspired by the benefits of 'vox pops'.[24] Like the responses to the photograph of the Brexit bus, we saw the film footage involving impromptu interviews in the street, as well as in selected venues such as a pub in Gleadless, a deprived part of Sheffield, as constituting a way to access snap thoughts and feelings about complex ideas. The film team asked unobtrusive questions about what Brexit might mean for aspects of health to the person being interviewed, and filmed their responses. We had access to all the film footage, not only that which is included in the final film, but for transparency purposes, in this book we only rely on footage that is available in the public domain.

Throughout, we were also mindful of the need to meet people who are not in the demographics represented predominantly in the street conversations. So, for instance, in Newry which is a predominantly Irish nationalist community, we were mindful of the need to reach Unionist as well as Muslim and Polish communities present there. Everywhere we went through the project, we were attentive to the need to enter into conversations with Leave and Remain voters, and people from the 'left' and 'right' of the political spectrum (if that remains a meaningful categorisation in contemporary UK politics). Everywhere we seek, to the extent we are able, to compensate for polarisations. The combination of the street conversations and the conversations

[23] Rhodes, *Everyday Life in British Government*, above n 8.

[24] L Richardson, 'Engaging the Public in Policy Research: Are Community Researchers the Answer?' (2014) 2(1) *Politics and Governance* 32.

with community representatives, including through the film, is a compromise between various possible sampling strategies, which all have inherent limitations.[25]

Finally, we rely on information in the public domain. Obviously, we have included references to relevant academic literature. We also followed traditional news sources, especially print media, such as broadsheets, and the BBC, and online media sources, especially Twitter and Facebook, throughout the project.

Even more broadly, we drew on our previous and contemporaneous experiences. We already mentioned Wood's experience leading a community outreach project in Gleadless Valley, in a deprived part of Sheffield that voted Leave in the referendum. This community engagement led to the choice of filming site in Sheffield. We also already mentioned Antova's experiences as a political activist and critical scholar.

XI. CONCLUSION

To conclude this chapter, and indeed this opening part of the book: our research design involved an interplay between engagement with 'experts' in the health policy community and 'ordinary people' in selected places. The temporal frame for the project is – at its broadest – 2016–22, but the core data gathering and co-creation time frame is the year from late February 2019 to March 2020. The different facets of the research met and interacted in us, as embodied researchers making sense of an unfolding legal and policy position, of high political, social, and cultural contention. This book is our attempt to make sense of the project in all its messy complexities.

Our overall research ambitions are twofold. First, we offer insights on the significance of changes to health governance pursuant upon Brexit. Outside the EU, the UK is reshaping the laws and policies that affect its NHS and health provision in England, Northern Ireland, Scotland and Wales. The UK has renegotiated its agreements with the EU, and is negotiating with the rest of the world. The details of these agreements, and how they are interpreted and applied, (will) affect the NHS and public health, mainly indirectly through their effects on the economy, on migration, and on trade, and in some respects directly. Across the following chapters five to 10, we explain the unfolding changes to law and policy concerning health and the NHS, and explore its likely (or, where data is available, actual) effects.

Second, we contrast those effects with the aspirations, hopes and dreams of 'ordinary people' for a legitimate post-Brexit future for the NHS. We consider who is or should be accountable for the effects of those changes. Although this aspect of our analysis is threaded throughout the book, we develop this part of our agenda more fully in chapter 11.

Our focus of attention was always health and the NHS, but we also understood our research within larger Brexit legal and political debates. To that end, the next chapter (four) explains the apparent puzzle that UK membership of the EU essentially concerns trade and geopolitical security, and yet that health and the NHS became profoundly implicated in the referendum, Brexit and the UK's changing relationship with the EU.

[25] For discussion, see Kwame Harrison, *Ethnography*, above n 19, 47.

4

Scope: The Effects of EU Law on Health and the NHS

I. INTRODUCTION

IN MARCH 2019, just days away from the first possible date on which the UK might have left the EU under the terms of Article 50 TEU, Hervey and Wood interviewed Dr Sarah Wollaston MP. Dr Wollaston is a Devon-based GP, who was elected to parliament as a Conservative MP in 2009. In June 2014, she became Chair of the House of Commons Health and Social Care Select Committee. Under Dr Wollaston's leadership, the Committee conducted two formal Inquiries into the effects of Brexit on health and the NHS.[1] Dr Wollaston took the view that the members of the Committee, including herself, probably did not know enough about the EU and how it affects health and the NHS. She therefore secured expert advice to support those Inquiries. Hervey was one of the appointed advisers.

Dr Wollaston was one of a small number of MPs who publicly switched sides from Leave to Remain during the referendum campaign. At that time, she spoke of her discomfort with the 'untruth' of the claim that leaving the EU would mean more money for the NHS.[2] When we interviewed her, she had just left the Conservative Party, on the basis that she could not support PM Theresa May's approach that ran the serious risk of the UK leaving the EU without having negotiated a Withdrawal Agreement. The idea of a 'No Deal Brexit' was widely described in terms of falling off a cliff edge, with all the associated disaster, and Dr Wollaston shared that understanding. She spoke of the 'extraordinary turmoil' and deep uncertainty of those times, and of the profound consequences of leaving the EU on those terms for health, for social care, and for biomedical research. Yet she perceived that health had been side-lined in the parliamentary discussions, which seemed to be about remote matters for the electorate, like 'WTO terms', in stark contradistinction to the idea that Brexit would help the NHS: 'the greatest non-fact that anyone remembered from the referendum', as Dr Wollaston put it.

This chapter untangles those apparently contradictory ideas. How is it that health and the NHS are so profoundly implicated in the UK's changing relationship with

[1] 'Brexit and Health and Social Care – People & Process', *Eighth Report from the Health and Social Care Committee*, HC 640 (2016–17); 'Brexit: Medicines, Medical Devices and Substances of Human Origin', *Fourth Report from the Health and Social Care Committee*, HC 392 (2017–2019).

[2] 'EU Referendum: MP Sarah Wollaston Swaps Sides Over "Untrue" Leave Claims', BBC, 9 June 2016.

the EU, when EU membership is essentially about trade and geopolitical security? We start with the political and media narratives, and then discuss the legal and policy position. At the same time, we outline the scope of the rest of the book, and give a broad overview of the details that are coming in later chapters.

II. THE 'NHS BREXIT BUS' CAMPAIGN

> Would we have won without £350m/NHS? All our research and the close result strongly suggests No.[3]

Vote Leave's 'NHS Brexit bus' stated: 'We send the EU £350 million a week. Let's fund our NHS instead. Vote Leave. Take back control'. The bus began its tour of Britain in early May 2016. The bus did not, in fact, tour in Northern Ireland, although some of the people we talked with in Derry/Londonderry and Newry felt that it had: an example of its effectiveness. Pictures of the bus were widely circulated through traditional and social media. The image became an enduring symbol of the Brexit campaign. Although the veracity of its claim was almost immediately discredited,[4] there is little doubt that the idea that voting Leave was a 'pro-NHS' position had a crucial effect on the referendum vote, although of course it was far from the only relevant factor.[5]

[3] D Cummings, 'On the Referendum #21: Branching Histories of the 2016 Referendum and "the Frogs Before the Storm"', 9 January 2017 (https://dominiccummings.com/2017/01/09/on-the-referendum-21-branching-histories-of-the-2016-referendum-and-the-frogs-before-the-storm-2/).

[4] 'The Economic and Financial Costs and Benefits of the UK's EU Membership', *First Report from the Treasury Committee*, HC 122 (2016–17), paras 32–37; '£350 million EU Claim "A Clear Misuse of Official Statistics"', Full Fact, 19 September 2017 (https://fullfact.org/europe/350-million-week-boris-johnson-statistics-authority-misuse).

[5] See, eg, M Barnier, *My Secret Brexit Diary: A Glorious Illusion* (Cambridge, Polity Press, 2021); S Becker et al, 'Who Voted for Brexit? A Comprehensive District-Level Analysis' (2017) 32(92) *Economic Policy* 601; C Browning, 'Brexit Populism and Fantasies of Fulfilment' (2019) 32(3) *Cambridge Review of International Affairs* 222; M Carreras et al, 'Long-Term Economic Distress, Cultural Backlash, and Support for Brexit' (2019) 52(9) *Comparative Political Studies* 1396; H Clarke et al, *Brexit: Why Britain Voted to Leave the European Union* (Cambridge, Cambridge University Press, 2017); S Douglas Scott, 'Brexit, Boundaries and the Power of Images' (2019) 13(1) *Pólemos* 63, 74–76; M Goodwin and O Heath, 'The 2016 Referendum, Brexit and the Left Behind: An Aggregate-Level Analysis of the Result' (2016) 87(3) *The Political Quarterly* 323; M Goodwin and O Heath, *Brexit Vote Explained* (London, Joseph Rowntree Foundation, 2016); M Goodwin and C Milazzo, 'Taking Back Control? Investigating the Role of Immigration in the Vote for Brexit' (2017) 19(3) *The British Journal of Politics and International Relations* 450; M Goodwin et al, 'For and Against Brexit: A Survey Experiment of the Impact of Campaign Effects on Public Attitudes Toward EU Membership' (2018) 50(2) *British Journal of Political Science* 481; C Grey, *Brexit Unfolded: How No One Got What They Wanted (and Why They Were Never Going to)* (London, Biteback Publishing, 2021); S Kettell and P Kerr, 'The Brexit Religion and the Holy Grail of the NHS' (2021) 20(2) *Social Policy and Society* 282; L Mckenzie, 'The Class Politics of Prejudice: Brexit and the Land of No-Hope and Glory' (2017) 68(S1) *The British Journal of Sociology* S265; L Mckenzie, '"It's Not Ideal": Reconsidering "Anger" and "Apathy" in the Brexit Vote Among an Invisible Working Class' (2018) 21(3) *Competition & Change* 199; P Norris and R Inglehart, *Cultural Backlash: Trump, Brexit, and Authoritarian Populism* (Cambridge, Cambridge University Press, 2019); T Shipman, *All Out War* (London, William Collins, 2016); M Sobolewska and R Ford, *Brexitland: Identity, Diversity and the Reshaping of British Politics* (Cambridge, Cambridge University Press, 2020); M Sorace and S Hobolt, 'A Tale of Two Peoples: Motivated Reasoning in the Aftermath of the Brexit Vote' (2021) 9(4) *Political Science Research and Methods* 675; K Swales, *Understanding the Vote to Leave* (London, National Centre for Social Research, 2016); M Watson, 'Brexit, the Left Behind and the Let Down: The Political Abstraction of "the Economy" and the UK's Brexit Referendum' (2018) 13(1) *British Politics* 17.

A KCL Policy Institute study found that a significant proportion of people who had heard the claim still believed it in 2018.[6]

The message on the bus resonated with a perception that the EU was exploiting the UK through the budgetary contributions made as a requirement of EU membership. The bus message also suggested that EU membership had led to a deterioration in access to NHS care, especially primary care, because of the presence of 'non-Brits' in 'our' GP surgeries. This latter perception turned out to be inaccurate at a national level. In fact, if a national of one of the other EU countries was present in an NHS setting, it was probably more likely they were *providing* healthcare than receiving it, given the proportions of healthcare professionals from other EU countries,[7] and the age and health status of EU nationals in the UK.[8] Nonetheless, the idea was an accurate depiction of the experience of some people, especially because of the effects of austerity policies on the NHS across the UK.[9] For example, the experience was felt in places like the North East of England, Nottinghamshire or Lincolnshire, where central and Eastern European families had settled because of opportunities to provide labour in the farming sector.[10]

However, the claim on the bus was far from universally believed. We can infer this view from the way that bus image was co-opted to create many memes[11] which express the understanding that its message represented a false promise. This understanding resonates with our street conversations. Many of the people we talked with understood that the bus message was untrue. They called it 'the bus of lies', 'a complete hoax', 'a load of old crap', 'a joke and a lie'.[12] People in places associated with strong patterns of Leave voting, and people who (voluntarily) told us that they had voted to Leave, said that they knew the claim on the bus was untrue.

[6] The Policy Institute, IPSOS Mori and UK in a Changing Europe, *The Public's Brexit Misperceptions*, October 2018 (www.kcl.ac.uk/policy-institute/assets/brexit-misperceptions.pdf accessed 16 November 2022).

[7] See, N Fahy et al, 'How Will Brexit Affect Health and Health Services in the UK? Evaluating Three Possible Scenarios Against the WHO Health System Building Blocks' (2017) 390(10107) *The Lancet* 2110, 2110–13; N Fahy et al, 'How Will Brexit Affect Health and Health Services in the UK? An Updated Evaluation' (2019) 393(10174) *The Lancet* 949, 950.

[8] M Dayan, 'The Facts: EU Immigration and Pressure on the NHS', Nuffield Trust and Full Fact, 15 June 2016 (https://www.nuffieldtrust.org.uk/resource/the-facts-eu-immigration-and-pressure-on-the-nhs); M Fernández-Reino, 'The Health of Migrants in the UK', The Migration Observatory, 21 August 2020 (https://migrationobservatory.ox.ac.uk/resources/briefings/the-health-of-migrants-in-the-uk/).

[9] B Anderson et al, 'Modes of Uncertainty and Futures in an Impasse' (2020) 45(2) *Transactions of the Institute of British Geography* 256, 262; M Greenfields et al, *The Impact of Migration in the Fenland Area: A Scoping Report*, Rosmini Centre, Wisbech, UK, 31 October 2019 (https://arro.anglia.ac.uk/id/eprint/704980/); L Mckenzie, 'The Class Politics of Prejudice: Brexit and the Land of No-Hope and Glory' (2017) 68(S1) *The British Journal of Sociology* S265–S280; L Mckenzie, '"It's Not Ideal": Reconsidering "Anger" and "Apathy" in the Brexit Vote Among an Invisible Working Class' (2017) 21(2) *Competition & Change* 199.

[10] C Cook, 'How Immigration Changed Boston, Lincolnshire', BBC, 10 May 2016; J Harris, 'They Say After Brexit There'll Be Food Rotting in the Fields. It's Already Started', The Guardian, 5 August 2017.

[11] It is easy to do this through 'meme generators' such as imgflip (https://imgflip.com/memegenerator/248632192/Brexit-Bus-Blank accessed 15 February 2023).

[12] Derry 201A; Newry 36A; Newry 38A; Newry 26B. See also Sheffield 2B, 9B, 10B; Newry 38A, 51A, 55A, 19B, 38B; Rochdale 75A, 91A, 100A, 101A, 41B, 50B, 57B, 59B, 63B, 66B, 70B, 74B, 76B, 78B; Rotherham 123A, 140A, 149A, 94B, 105B, 120B; Derry 161A, 165A, 172A, 176AA, 177A, 180A, 194A, 200A, 203A, 211A, 214A, 215A, 224A, 129B, 137B, 142B, 145B, 148B, 152B, 154B, 155B, 158B, 159B, 164B, 165B, 166B, 172B, 173B, 175B, 178B, 179B, 182B.

Ten of our 103 conversations in Rochdale, a north western English town with a high Leave vote of 60.1 per cent, began this way: 'lies', 'pack of lies', 'it's all lies', 'lies and deceit'. Some people, with greater nuance, saw the bus message as 'manipulation' or 'bullshit'. Bullshit is a particular kind of untruth, where both the speaker and the listener are complicit in an understanding that what is being said is untrue.[13]

It seems to us, reflecting on those conversations, that the reality is more complex than people believing or not believing the message on the bus.[14] At one and the same time, people are both drawn to the idea implicit in the image, while knowing on another level that it is false. This shifting and contradictory sense of 'knowledge' is illustrated in a conversation[15] where the person we talked with used the term 'bullshit', but did not dispute the figure. Yet he *also* felt that the money would never be put in the NHS, while *at the same time* feeling that there would be a greater chance that the NHS would be more generously funded if the UK were to leave the EU. Our analysis suggests that the claim on the bus works to manipulate the hopes of people who would like to see a better-funded NHS, by offering an implicit promise that the benefits associated would emerge from the process of leaving the EU, but without ever explaining how that process would lead to the desired outcome. Rather than being based on an explanation of the UK's relationships with the EU and what they mean for the NHS, the promise plays on 'common sense' or 'folk theories':[16] it 'stands to reason' that if money does not 'go' to the EU, it can 'stay' in 'our' NHS.

One of the things we noticed as our research progressed is the longevity of the Brexit bus image: versions of it were still circulating into 2022.[17] For instance, the journalist Tim Walker used a bus meme to highlight the links between the UK leaving the EU and the shortage of fuel experienced across the UK in September 2021.[18] A Facebook post by an 'artist' named 'Dayvid' from 31 January 2022 involves a meme of the bus commenting critically on the just-announced increase in National Insurance.[19] It follows that the image still resonates, and – at the least – suggests that many people still understand a complex connection between their support for the NHS and their support for the UK leaving the EU. From our point of view though, especially Hervey

[13] HG Frankfurt, *On Bullshit* (Oxford, Princeton University Press, 2005). See also A Green, 'Speaking Bullshit to Power: Populism and the Rhetoric of Bullshit' (2019) *SSRN*; J Hopkin and B Rosamond, 'Post-Truth Politics, Bullshit and Bad Ideas: "Deficit Fetishism" in the UK' (2018) 23(6) *New Political Economy* 641; M O'Dwyer, 'The Intersectional Politics of Bullshit' (2018) 1(3) *European Journal of Politics and Gender* 405.

[14] I Antova et al, 'Calling out "Bullshit" in "Left Behind" Britain', SPERI, 16 September 2019 (http://speri.dept.shef.ac.uk/2019/09/16/calling-out-brexit-bullshit-in-left-behind-britain).

[15] Newry 25A.

[16] N Clarke et al, *The Good Politician: Folk Theories, Political Interaction, and the Rise of Anti-Politics* (Cambridge, Cambridge University Press, 2018).

[17] One example online includes (and this is a quotation from the source): 'The start of the Brexit riots. A tale of two buses. 2016: Brexit lies. 2021: Brexit reality' (juxtaposing the bus with a burning bus in Belfast during the summer of 2021 when there were protests (allegedly) against the Ireland/Northern Ireland Protocol) (www.reddit.com/r/brexit/comments/mmwr3g/the_start_of_the_brexit_riots/ accessed 15 November 2022).

[18] Commenting, 'I'd laugh if life under @BorisJohnson weren't so bloody tragic' above an image of the bus with the line 'We have no fuel for this bus [sic] But that's ok [sic] because we have no driver either', 26 September 2021 (https://twitter.com/ThatTimWalker/status/1442022244729987073).

[19] Commenting, 'Instead of giving the NHS £350 million a week why dont [sic] we just put up national insurance and let the plebs pay for it. Brexit was never about you it was just a career move' (www.facebook.com/photo/?fbid=469121381440792&set=a.182793620073571 accessed 16 November 2022).

and Flear's as scholars of EU law, it was rather puzzling that membership of the EU should be associated with detriment to the NHS, because the EU's formal legal competence to affect national health systems is significantly constrained.

III. THE EU'S LACK OF COMPETENCE OVER NATIONAL HEALTH SYSTEMS

To explain our initial puzzlement, we need to outline briefly our understanding of how the EU is legally constituted as an organisation.[20] The EU is not a state. Legally speaking, the EU is an entity created through several international agreements

[20] There is significant literature on this, including different views on the legal nature of the EU as an entity. See, eg, NW Barber, 'Legal Pluralism and the European Union' (2006) 12(3) *European Law Journal* 306; T Beukers et al (eds), *Constitutional Change through Euro-Crisis Law* (Cambridge, Cambridge University Press 2017); AM Burley and W Mattli, 'Europe Before the Court: A Political Theory of Legal Integration' (1993) 47(1) *International Organization* 41; P Craig, 'Constitutions, Constitutionalism and the European Union' (2001) 7(2) *European Law Journal* 125; M Dawson and F de Witte, 'Constitutional Balance in the EU After the Euro-Crisis' (2013) 76(5) *The Modern Law Review* 817; M Dawson and F de Witte, 'Self-Determination in the Constitutional Future of the EU' (2015) 21(3) *European Law Journal* 371; G de Búrca and JHH Weiler (eds), *The Worlds of European Constitutionalism* (Cambridge, Cambridge University Press, 2011); B de Witte, 'Direct Effect, Primacy and the Nature of the Legal Order' in P Craig and G de Búrca (eds), *The Evolution of EU Law*, 3rd edn (Oxford, Oxford University Press, 2022); B de Witte, 'The European Union as an International Legal Experiment' in G de Búrca and JHH Weiler (eds), *The Worlds of European Constitutionalism* (Cambridge, Cambridge University Press, 2012); B de Witte, 'Structure and Evolution of Union law' in PJ Kuijper et al (eds), *The Law of the European Union*, 5th edn (Alphen aan der Rijn, Wolters Kluwer, 2018); B de Witte, 'Guest Editorial: EU Emergency Law and Its Impact on the EU Legal Order' (2022) 59(1) *Common Market Law Review* 3; M Fichera and O Pollicino, 'The Dialectics Between Constitutional Identity and Common Constitutional Traditions: Which Language for Cooperative Constitutionalism in Europe?' (2019) 20(8) *German Law Journal* 1097; S Garben et al (eds), *Critical Reflections on Constitutional Democracy in the European Union* (Oxford, Hart Publishing, 2019); S Griller and J Ziller (eds), *The Lisbon Treaty: EU Constitutionalism Without a Constitutional Treaty?* (Berlin, Springer, 2008); D Grimm, 'Does Europe Need a Constitution?' (1995) 1(3) *European Law Journal* 282; J Klabbers, 'Volkerrechtsfreundlich? International Law and the Union Legal Order' in P Koutrakos (ed), *European Foreign Policy: Legal and Political Perspectives* (Cheltenham, Edward Elgar, 2011); N MacCormick, 'Democracy, Subsidiarity, and Citizenship in the "European Commonwealth"' (1997) 16(4) *Law and Philosophy* 331; N MacCormick, *Questioning Sovereignty* (Oxford, Oxford University Press, 1999); M Maduro, 'Contrapunctual Law' in N Walker (ed), *Sovereignty in Transition* (Oxford, Hart Publishing, 2003); M Maduro and L Azoulai (eds), *The Past and Future of EU Law: The Classics of EU Law Revisited on the 50th Anniversary of the Rome Treaty* (Oxford, Hart Publishing, 2010); F Mancini, ''The Making of a Constitution for Europe' (1989) 26(4) *Common Market Law Review* 595; AJ Menéndez, 'A European Union in Constitutional Mutation' (2014) 20(2) *European Law Journal* 127; J-C Piris, 'Does the European Union Have a Constitution? Does It Need One?' (1999) 24(6) *European Law Review* 557; A Rosas and L Armati, *EU Constitutional Law* (Oxford, Hart Publishing, 2012); M Ruffert and P Leino-Sandberg, 'Next Generation EU and Its Constitutional Ramifications: A Critical Assessment' (2022) 59(2) *Common Market Law Review* 433; SA Scheingold, *The Rule of Law in European Integration* (New Haven CT, Yale University Press 1965); F Schorkopf, 'The European Union as an Association of Sovereign States: Karlsruhe's Ruling on the Treaty of Lisbon' (2009) 10(8) *German Law Journal* 1219; J Snell, '"European Constitutional Settlement", and Ever-Closer Union, and the Treaty of Lisbon: Democracy or Relevance?' (2008) 33(5) *European Law Review* 619; K Tuori and S Sankari (eds), *The Many Constitutions of Europe* (Abingdon, Routledge, 2016); F Timmermans, 'The Constitutionalization of the European Union' (2002) 21(1) *Yearbook of European Law* 1; N Walker, 'The Idea of Constitutional Pluralism' (2002) 65(3) *The Modern Law Review* 317; N Walker, *Sovereignty in Transition* (Oxford, Hart Publishing, 2003); N Walker, 'Beyond Boundary Disputes and Basic Grids: Mapping the Global Disorder of Normative Orders' (2008) 6(3–4) *International Journal of Constitutional Law* 373; N Walker et al (eds), *Europe's Constitutional Mosaic* (Oxford, Hart Publishing, 2011); JHH Weiler, 'The Transformation of Europe' (1991) 100(8) *Yale Law Journal* 2403.

between EU Member States, which bind themselves in international law to comply with specified legal obligations.[21] In the language of law and international relations scholarship, the EU countries are 'Masters of the Treaties':[22] nothing is imposed on them except that to which they agree. In that sense, every EU country continues to be a 'sovereign' state.

However, at least according to the Court of Justice of the EU, the nature and qualities of EU law are different to those of ordinary international law. This much was already established about the (then EEC, now) EU when the UK joined in the early 1970s.[23] EU Member States agree to the EU's systems and structures, which include possibilities for Member States to be under obligations to which they have not explicitly and specifically agreed. The EU Treaties establish a shared institutional process – involving 'qualified majority voting' in Council[24] – whereby the EU's legislature (the European Commission, Parliament and Council) adopts law that binds its Member States, without specific agreement of every national government. Governments of Member States of the EU do not have veto powers over EU legislation. Furthermore, interpretation of the wording of the legal obligations imposed on Member States in EU law changes over time. The Court of Justice of the EU (whose decisions bind Member States, again, by agreement)[25] and national courts interpret very broad and general legal rules in surprising ways.[26] Member States may be obliged by their EU membership to make legal and policy choices that they might not have made outside the EU. But the national health service is not, in general, a place in which those obligations arise.

This is the case because one of the important features of the EU is that it is an organisation with constrained powers. The EU institutions only enjoy the formal competence that is *conferred* on them by the Treaty on European Union and the Treaty on the Functioning of the European Union. Any competence that is not conferred on

[21] The key agreements are the Treaty on European Union and the Treaty on the Functioning of the European Union, see Consolidated versions of the Treaty on European Union and the Treaty on the Functioning of the European Union [2016] OJ C 202/1.

[22] On the nature of the legal relationship between the Member States and the EU, see the literature cited above n 20, and see A von Bogdandy et al, 'Guest Editorial: A Potential Constitutional Moment for the European Rule of Law – The Importance of Red Lines' (2018) 55(1) *Common Market Law Review* 983; M Cremona, 'The Treaties that Created Europe' in G Amato et al (eds), *The History of the European Union: Constructing Utopia* (London, Hart Publishing, 2019); A Grzelak, 'Are the EU Member States Still Masters of the Treaties? The European Rule of Law Concept as a Means of Limiting National Authorities' in T Drinóczi and A Bień-Kacała (eds), *Rule of Law, Common Values, and Illiberal Constitutionalism: Poland and Hungary Within the European Union* (Abingdon, Routledge, 2020).

[23] Case 6/64 *Costa v ENEL* ECLI:EU:C:1964:66; Case 26/62 *Van Gend en Loos v Nederlands Administratie de Belastingen* ECLI:EU:C:1963:1.

[24] Article 294 TFEU.

[25] Article 258 TFEU; Article 267 TFEU.

[26] There is a significant literature on this topic. See, eg, K Alter, 'The European Court's Political Power' (1996) 19(3) *West European Politics* 452; R Chicowski, *The European Court and Civil Society: Litigation, Mobilization and Governance* (Cambridge, Cambridge University Press, 2009); G de Búrca and JHH Weiler (eds), *The European Court of Justice* (Oxford, University Press, 2002); Burley and Mattli, 'Europe Before the Court', above n 20; T Pavone and RD Kelemen, 'The Evolving Judicial Politics of European Integration: The European Court of Justice and National Courts Revisited' (2019) 25(4) *European Law Journal* 352; E Stein, 'Lawyers, Judges, and the Making of a Transnational Constitution' (1981) 75(1) *American Journal of International Law* 1; Weiler, 'The Transformation of Europe', above n 20; JHH Weiler, 'A Quiet Revolution' (1994) 26(4) *Comparative Political Studies* 510.

the EU remains with Member States, unlike in a federal state where power remains with the centre unless it is devolved to sub-national or regional units.

The Treaty on the Functioning of the EU explicitly states that competence to define health policy and to organise and deliver national health services lies with Member States.[27] EU membership thus has no direct effect whatsoever on the ability of an EU Member State to resource and structure its health service, or to provide healthcare to its population. In that context, the claim made on the Brexit bus seems almost laughable. The figure of how much the UK supposedly gave to the EU was false, and in any event did not include the significant economic benefits the UK enjoyed as a EU Member State. Funding given from Member States to the EU is not simply a resource 'lost', but a resource shared to the benefit of all Member States. To EU Member States, the EU is 'us', not 'them'. It follows that the UK could choose to fund the NHS better, whether it remained in the EU or not. Nothing about EU membership constrained the UK in funding the NHS: these decisions were *domestic* policy choices.

IV. HOW EU LAW AND POLICY *DOES* AFFECT THE NHS

Nonetheless, EU law and policy *does* have important *indirect* effects on national healthcare systems in EU Member States. Many EU health law and policy scholars describe the EU as having a transversal[28] health law and policy, which cuts across many areas of EU law and policy. This is the sense in which Dr Wollaston was seeking to deepen the House of Commons Health Select Committee's understanding of EU law, so as to grasp the effects of leaving the EU on the NHS, and on health, across the UK. In this chapter, we set out a map of the ways in which health is affected by the UK's post-Brexit trade and other international relationships – both with the EU and with other countries across the world. The rest of the book explores these implications of Brexit for health and the NHS in more detail.

Health as a transversal EU policy field is not well-represented in political institutions either in the EU, because of its constrained competence in health, or in the UK, because in general health is perceived as quite separate from trade and international relations. Consequently, EU health law and policy is relatively difficult to conceptualise or communicate clearly.[29] To say that EU law and policy affects every aspect of the NHS might be superficially true, but it is misleading, as effects are stronger and more significant in some aspects of healthcare provision across the UK than in others. In the run up to the referendum, many policy effects on the NHS or health were more

[27] Article 168(7) TFEU.

[28] T Hervey, 'EU Health Law' in C Barnard and S Peers (eds), *European Union Law* (Oxford, Oxford University Press, 2023), 662; T Hervey and J McHale, *European Union Health Law: Themes and Implications* (Cambridge, Cambridge University Press, 2015). Also see, eg, A de Ruijter, *EU Health Law & Policy: The Expansion of EU Power in Public Health and Health Care* (Oxford, Oxford University Press, 2019); ML Flear et al, *European Law and New Health Technologies* (Oxford, Oxford University Press, 2012); ML Flear, *Governing Public Health: EU Law, Regulation and Biopolitics* (Oxford, Hart Publishing, 2015 hb, 2018 pb (revised)); S Greer et al, *Everything You Always Wanted to Know About European Union Health Policies but Were Afraid to Ask*, 2nd edn (revised) (Copenhagen, European Observatory on Health Systems and Policies, 2019).

[29] This is implicit, eg, in the title of Greer et al, ibid.

or less completely hidden, and only came to light later on. But certain highly specific topics rose to the attention of the media.

V. VISIBLE HEALTH TOPICS IN THE REFERENDUM DEBATES

One of the topics that excited media attention before June 2016 was the entitlement, in EU law, to cross-border healthcare. We analyse cross-border healthcare further in chapters five and six. In itself quite complex, and based on three totally different sources of EU law,[30] this entitlement had been the subject of some controversy in 2002, when Yvonne Watts, the mother of journalist Julie Harding, had forced Bedford Primary Care Trust to allow her to go to France for a hip replacement, thereby 'jumping the queue' for treatment at home. Whether this was appropriate use of spare capacity in France, by under-resourced English NHS Trusts, or an opportunity for relatively healthy and wealthy British patients, comfortable with foreign travel, to hasten their access to non-urgent operations,[31] it certainly demonstrated one way in which 'our' NHS was in fact closely linked with national health systems in other EU Member States.[32]

A second specific topic that received media attention both in the run up to the EU referendum, and thereafter, was the 'EHIC card'. This card demonstrates that visitors from other EU Member States are entitled to access necessary healthcare, on the same terms as residents of the country they are visiting. These reciprocal healthcare arrangements are linked to the EU's single market. Because the UK did not seek a relationship with the EU that would mean continued access to that single market, for most of the period 2016–21, we – along with others – understood the continuity of these beneficial arrangements to be in jeopardy.[33] One of the messages we sought to

[30] They are Article 56 TFEU; Directive 2011/24/EU of the European Parliament and of the Council of 9 March 2011 on the application of patients' rights in cross-border healthcare [2011] OJ L 88/45; Regulation (EC) No 883/2004 of the European Parliament and of the Council of 29 April 2004 on the coordination of social security systems [2004] OJ L 166/1.

[31] Hervey, 'EU Health Law' above n 28, 647–48; Hervey and McHale, *European Union Health Law*, above n 28. Also see, eg, ML Flear, 'Developing Euro-Biocitizens Through Migration for Healthcare Services' (2007) 14(3) *Maastricht Journal of European and Comparative* Law 239; ML Flear, '"Together for Health"? How EU Governance of Health Undermines Active Biological Citizenship' (2008) 26(3) *Wisconsin International Law Journal* 868; V Hatzopoulos, '*Killing* National Health and Insurance Systems but *Healing* Patients? The European Market for Health Care Services After the Judgments of the ECJ in *Vanbraekel* and *Peerbooms*' (2002) 39(4) *Common Market Law Review* 683; C Newdick, *Who Should We Treat? Rights, Rationing and Resources in the NHS*, 2nd edn (Oxford, Oxford University Press, 2004); C Newdick, 'Citizenship, Free Movement and Health Care: Cementing Individual Rights by Corroding Social Solidarity' (2006) 43(6) *Common Market Law Review* 1645.

[32] M Ferrara, *The Boundaries of Welfare. European Integration and the New Spatial Politics of Social Protection* (Oxford, Oxford University Press, 2005); S Leibfried and P Pierson, *European Social Policy: Between Fragmentation and Integration* (Washington DC, Brookings Institute Press, 1995).

[33] Fahy et al, 'How Will Brexit Affect Health and Health Services in the UK?', above n 7; Fahy et al, 'How Will Brexit Affect Health and Health Services in the UK? An Updated Evaluation', above n 7; N Fahy et al, 'Assessing the Potential Impact on Health of the UK's Future Relationship Agreement with the EU: Analysis of the Negotiating Positions' (2021) 16(3) *Health Economics, Policy and Law* 290; N Fahy et al, 'Impact on the NHS and Health of the UK's Trade and Cooperation Relationship with the EU, and Beyond' (2022) 17(4) *Health Economics, Policy and Law* 471.

communicate during that time was a warning that this aspect of healthcare would no longer be available once the UK left the EU.

The potential loss of cross-border healthcare was particularly poignant for specific groups of patients. Fiona Loud, spokesperson for the charity *Kidney Care UK*, explained the effects of these arrangements on the equality and dignity of the patients she represents. Over the years of UK membership of the EU, these patients had built up relations with kidney dialysis clinics in France, Spain or Greece. The EHIC meant kidney dialysis patients could receive the treatment they needed while visiting their EU-based extended families, or enjoying a holiday abroad, like other people.[34] People whose health profiles meant travel insurance would be prohibitively expensive, or simply unavailable,[35] were similarly affected: Hervey had a direct family experience of this, as her 90-year-old mother-in-law with a grandchild in Denmark is one such person.

We were mistaken in our assumption that these arrangements would not continue post-Brexit. Despite the EU's formal position that a non-EU Member State could not enjoy the benefits of single market access, the UK negotiated continued access to necessary healthcare through bespoke arrangements, both in the Withdrawal Agreement, and in the EU-UK Trade and Cooperation Agreement.[36] The wording of the relevant provisions of the Trade and Cooperation Agreement is almost identical to the equivalent provisions of EU law. However, vital medical treatment that is only available through a specialised medical unit (which includes kidney dialysis) now needs prior authorisation from the host Member State (or the UK). A new 'GHIC' (Global Health Insurance Card) provides evidence of visitors' continued entitlement to receive necessary healthcare in the EU, on the same basis as residents in the relevant country. The UK accepts EHICs from EU Member States when visitors from the EU need to access healthcare in the UK. The Specialised Committee on Social Security Coordination (a new institution set up under the Trade and Cooperation Agreement) agreed in July 2021[37] that the practicalities of continued access would be managed through the EU's Electronic Exchange of Social Security Information. The openness of the UK's NHS to those of EU Member States, and vice versa, in terms of visitors accessing necessary healthcare, continues in the post-Brexit era.

A third topic that was discussed in the run up to the referendum is much less well understood in England, but was obvious in Northern Ireland. Since the implementation of the Belfast/Good Friday Agreement of 1998, the NHS in Northern Ireland,[38] especially the Western and Southern Health and Social Care Trusts, became more and more closely entwined with the Irish NHS.[39] The geography and scale of the island

[34] See further ch 5.

[35] D McKee and M McKee, 'What Might Brexit Mean for British Tourists Travelling to the Rest of Europe?' (2018) 48(2) *Journal of the Royal College of Physicians of Edinburgh* 134.

[36] T Hervey, 'Analysis 1 of the Brexit Deal: Healthcare Entitlements in the EU-UK Trade and Cooperation Agreement', 29 December 2020 (http://eulawanalysis.blogspot.com/2020/12/analysis-1-of-brexit-deal-healthcare.html).

[37] Specialised Committee on Social Security Coordination, *First Meeting of the Specialised Committee on Social Security Coordination: Minutes*, 6 July 2021.

[38] The formal title of the NHS in Northern Ireland is 'Health and Social Care Northern Ireland'. However, people in Northern Ireland call it 'the NHS' in Northern Ireland, and we wanted to reflect this in our book.

[39] We use the state's formal name, 'Ireland', where we mean the geopolitical entity. Where we mean the geographical space, we use 'the island of Ireland'.

of Ireland are such that it makes sense to share some specialist health facilities, and to provide certain types of healthcare collaboratively, especially across the border in the north west of the island where Ireland's County Donegal hugs Northern Ireland's Fermanagh, Tyrone and Londonderry to their west. Since 1992, the Health Service Executive in Ireland has been collaborating with the Western and Southern Health and Social Care Trusts, the Health and Social Care Board and the Public Health Agency in Northern Ireland.

This partnership is known as 'Cooperation and Working Together' (CAWT) for health gain and social wellbeing in border areas. CAWT seeks to 'add value' to cooperation between the health systems, and to access EU funding to support these activities. We heard from Bernie McCrory, the former Chief Officer of CAWT, of the very advanced level of integration of the two health systems, with over 30 service-level agreements between the relevant NHS authorities in Northern Ireland and Ireland. This depth of interaction, and enmeshment of the two health systems, was confirmed in the conversations we had with people in Newry and Derry/Londonderry, both border towns. We heard many stories of people in Northern Ireland accessing healthcare across the border, especially in the children's heart unit at Our Lady Children's Hospital in Dublin, which serves the whole island, and in the cancer unit at Altnagelvin Hospital in Derry/Londonderry. People we talked with in Newry and Derry/Londonderry expressed concern about continued access to healthcare, with several people worrying especially about children and young people, for example whether they could continue to access mental health support across the border.[40]

This sharing and openness of one part of the UK's NHS to the healthcare system in another EU Member State is not only about the efficiency of making good use of available resources. It is also about creating common public structures and organisations, as one part of the bedrock of continued peace on the island of Ireland.[41] Although not directly based on EU law or policy, the shared healthcare arrangements on the island of Ireland were legally supported by common membership of the EU. The qualifications of healthcare professionals working across the border were mutually recognised under EU law. Common regulatory standards for medicines, medical devices and equipment, and substances of human origin (blood, human tissue or cells) apply in all EU countries. Possible implications of Brexit, therefore, included a concern reflected in our interviews[42] that a patient, say, resident in Donegal, would be discharged from a hospital in Northern Ireland with a supply of prescribed medicines. If the regulatory standards for medicines in Northern Ireland were to diverge

[40] Newry 14A, 36A; Derry 185A, 213A.

[41] O Doyle et al (ed), *The Brexit Challenge for Ireland and the United Kingdom: Constitutions Under Pressure* (Cambridge, Cambridge University Press, 2021); S de Mars and C Murray, 'With or Without EU? The Common Travel Area After Brexit' (2020) 21(5) *German Law Journal* 815; S de Mars et al, *Bordering Two Unions: Northern Ireland and Brexit* (Bristol, Policy Press, 2018); K Hayward, 'Northern Ireland: Demographics and Divisions' in F Fabbrini (ed), *The Law & Politics of Brexit: Volume IV. The Protocol on Ireland/Northern Ireland* (Oxford, Oxford University Press, 2022); C McCrudden (ed), *The Law and Practice of the Ireland-Northern Ireland Protocol* (Cambridge, Cambridge University Press, 2022); D Phinnemore and K Hayward, *UK Withdrawal ('Brexit') and the Good Friday Agreement* (Brussels, European Parliament Policy Department for Citizens' Rights and Constitutional Affairs, 2017); D Phinnemore, 'Northern Ireland – A "Place Between" in UK-EU Relations?' (2020) 25(4) *European Foreign Affairs Review* 631.

[42] Interview with Bernie McCrory, April 2019.

from those in the EU, the medicines dispensed could potentially be illegal in Ireland. As it has turned out, the alignment of Northern Ireland with EU standards and rules for medicines so far is intended to be secured through the Ireland/Northern Ireland Protocol, agreed between the EU and UK as part of the Withdrawal Agreement in 2020. Ongoing uncertainty about the UK government's compliance with that Protocol continues as we write (in winter 2022), including an April 2022 EU law effectively postponing full application of the Protocol to medicines regulation in Northern Ireland for three years from 1 January 2022,[43] and a UK government suggestion to 'remove medicines from the Protocol' altogether.[44]

Furthermore, the EU had also financially supported many of CAWT's projects, through its 'cohesion funds', which are supposed to provide extra investment to less developed regions in the EU.[45] Some of the relevant projects also involved the west of Scotland. Membership of the EU in this context opened up possibilities for increased funding for NHS infrastructure and services: the polar opposite of the implied message on the bus. When we talked with people in Belfast, Derry/Londonderry and Newry in 2019, we formed a clear impression that 'our NHS' in Northern Ireland was understood as very much open to and interacting with the NHS in Ireland. Our professional knowledge, and the interviews we undertook with health sector stakeholders on the island of Ireland, told us that EU membership was a key to underpinning that openness.

So these kinds of specific examples of how EU law and policy affects health and the NHS – and especially the NHS in Northern Ireland – already attracted some attention before the referendum vote. But in order to understand the full range of points of contact, where EU law or policy intersects with national health law or policy, we need to take a broader view.

VI. A BROADER VIEW OF TRANSVERSAL EU HEALTH LAW AND POLICY

Here, we are drawing on work that we undertook with several colleagues, led by Nick Fahy, of RAND Europe and the University of Oxford, and Martin McKee of

[43] Council of the EU, 'EU-UK relations: The Council Adopts Legislation to Ensure Continued Supply of Medicines', Press Release, 12 April 2022. See Directive (EU) 2022/642 of the European Parliament and of the Council of 12 April 2022 amending Directives 2001/20/EC and 2001/83/EC as regards derogations from certain obligations concerning certain medicinal products for human use made available in the United Kingdom in respect of Northern Ireland and in Cyprus, Ireland and Malta [2022] OJ L 118/4; Regulation (EU) 2022/641 of the European Parliament and of the Council of 12 April 2022 amending Regulation (EU) No 536/2014 as regards a derogation from certain obligations concerning investigational medicinal products made available in the United Kingdom in respect of Northern Ireland and in Cyprus, Ireland and Malta [2022] OJ L 118/1.

[44] Cabinet Office and Lord Frost, 'Lord Frost's Statement on the Protocol on Ireland/Northern Ireland', 17 December 2021.

[45] See Regulation (EU) 2021/1060 of the European Parliament and of the Council of 24 June 2021 laying down common provisions on the European Regional Development Fund, the European Social Fund Plus, the Cohesion Fund, the Just Transition Fund and the European Maritime, Fisheries and Aquaculture Fund and financial rules for those and for the Asylum, Migration and Integration Fund, the Internal Security Fund and the Instrument for Financial Support for Border Management and Visa Policy [2021] OJ L 231/159.

the London School of Hygiene and Tropical Medicine, whom we already mentioned in chapter one. Fahy was also a specialist advisor to the House of Commons Health Select Committee when Dr Sarah Wollaston was its Chair. Our work was developed in part to help the Committee to conceptualise the breadth of evidence that would be necessary to scrutinise government decisions about Brexit for their effects on the NHS and health.

In order to get a sense of the scope of effects of Brexit on health and the NHS – and hence also of the scope of this book – it is necessary to consider every aspect of a health system. The World Health Organization (WHO)'s 2007 model for conceptualising national health systems[46] is the inspiration for our model for understanding the effects of Brexit on the NHS. We took the WHO's 'health system building blocks', and arranged them into the order in which our initial analysis suggested the most to the least serious effects from Brexit. The 'building blocks' are: health workforce; financing; medical products, vaccines and technology; information; service delivery; and leadership and governance.

Our 2017 analysis[47] showed that every form of Brexit would be bad for health and the NHS, but some forms would be worse than others – especially if the UK were to leave the EU without an agreement on the terms of withdrawal (a 'No Deal Brexit'). As the negotiations between the EU and UK continued, we were able to offer a series of updated analyses, published in 2019,[48] 2020[49] and 2022,[50] showing where the detrimental (and some potentially beneficial) outcomes for health and the NHS would arise, in the context of each of the 'building blocks' of the NHS. We explain the details later in the book, but here we summarise each of the key areas where Brexit has an effect on health and the NHS.

VII. HEALTH WORKFORCE

Writing in 2017, Fahy and co-authors observed that the UK cannot conceivably be self-sufficient in its health (or social care) workforce any time in the foreseeable future. At the time, some 58 000 people from the rest of the EU worked in the NHS across the UK, and a further 90 000 in adult social care.[51] One in 10 doctors working

[46] World Health Organization, *Everybody's Business: Strengthening Health Systems to Improve Outcomes* (Geneva, World Health Organization, 2007), 3.

[47] Fahy et al, 'How Will Brexit Affect Health and Health Services in the UK?', above n 7.

[48] Fahy et al, 'How Will Brexit Affect Health and Health Services in the UK? An Updated Evaluation', above n 7.

[49] Fahy et al, 'Assessing the Potential Impact on Health of the UK's Future Relationship Agreement with the EU', above n 33.

[50] Fahy et al, 'Impact on the NHS and Health of the UK's Trade and Cooperation Relationship with the EU, and Beyond', above n 33. See also, M Dayan et al, 'Medicines' in UK in a Changing Europe, *UK Regulation After Brexit Revisited* (London, UK in a Changing Europe, 19 October 2022); M Dayan and T Hervey, 'Breaking the Northern Ireland Protocol Would Create Problems for Health and Care' (2022) 378 *British Medical Journal* o1673; M Dayan et al, 'Boosterism Blinds Us to the Possible Benefits of Brexit', Nuffield Trust, 3 March 2022 (www.nuffieldtrust.org.uk/news-item/boosterism-blinds-us-to-the-possible-benefits-of-brexit); M Dayan et al, 'Protocol Politics Mean Hard Times Ahead for Health in Northern Ireland', Nuffield Trust, 6 July 2022 (www.nuffieldtrust.org.uk/news-item/protocol-politics-mean-hard-times-ahead-for-health-in-northern-ireland).

[51] 'Brexit and Health and Social Care', above n 1, 13.

in the NHS was from the EU or Norway, Iceland and Liechtenstein (the 'European Economic Area').[52] These general figures hid specific concentrations: we heard about one hospital in the Highlands of Scotland where 11 of the 12 surgeons were non-UK EU nationals.[53] NHS institutions in London and the South East of England were (and still are) particularly reliant on nationals of other EU countries. And, as we have already explained, the NHS workforce in Northern Ireland was (and remains) in many respects shared with the NHS workforce in Ireland.

At that time, the people from other EU Member States working in the NHS were relying on a dense web of rights based on EU law. These EU law rights include the automatic recognition of medical qualifications and training undertaken in other EU Member States;[54] the right to move; reside in a host Member State; take up offers of work; receive social security entitlements, including pensions, healthcare and family benefits; residence rights for many members of a migrant EU citizen's family (irrespective of their nationality); a right for children of migrant EU citizens to access state education, including university education; all on the same basis as if the migrant EU citizen were a national of the host Member State.[55] EU law also supports the way people live their lives across EU borders: it includes a right to essential healthcare (including when giving birth) when visiting anywhere in the EU; and the right to retire, and receive a pension, and healthcare, anywhere in the EU.[56] Before the end of 2020, in the UK, these EU law rights applied without the need for specific documentation evidencing entitlement: all that was necessary was to show citizenship of an EU Member State. To all intents and purposes, before the EU referendum, these people working in the NHS were treated as if they were UK nationals. Formally, their legal status continued until the end of 2020, after which a new 'settled status' took effect in UK law. In practice, many EU nationals working for the NHS felt differently about being in the UK after 23 June 2016. We explore NHS staffing in more detail in chapter seven.

VIII. HEALTH FINANCING

We touched already on the main area where Brexit impacts directly on health financing. Individuals who move around the EU, for work, to visit family, to travel, can rely on reciprocal arrangements allowing access to necessary healthcare, based on EU law. These rights are based on reciprocal arrangements, which are replicated to a significant degree in the Withdrawal Agreement and Trade and Cooperation Agreement.[57]

[52] Ibid.

[53] Interview with Dr Philippa Whitford MP, February 2019.

[54] Directive 2005/36/EC of the European Parliament and of the Council of 7 September 2005 on the recognition of professional qualifications [2005] OJ L 255/22.

[55] Directive 2004/38/EC of the European Parliament and of the Council of 29 April 2004 on the right of citizens of the Union and their family members to move and reside freely within the territory of the Member States amending Regulation (EEC) No 1612/68 and repealing Directives 64/221/EEC, 68/360/EEC, 72/194/EEC, 73/148/EEC, 75/34/EEC, 75/35/EEC, 90/364/EEC, 90/365/EEC and 93/96/EEC [2004] OJ L 158/77; Regulation (EC) No 883/2004 of the European Parliament and of the Council of 29 April 2004 on the coordination of social security systems [2004] OJ L 166/1.

[56] Directive 2011/24, above n 30; Regulation 883/2004, above n 30.

[57] H Verschueren, 'The Complex Social Security Provisions of the Brexit Withdrawal Agreement, to be Implemented for Decades' (2021) 23(1) *European Journal of Social Security* 7.

The cost to the NHS in England, Scotland and Wales of people from EU countries accessing necessary healthcare while visiting the UK remains unchanged. This is also true for the Northern Irish NHS, where the Common Travel Area rules provide continuity.[58]

In addition, EU membership provided opportunities for capital financing for the NHS. The UK was not a major recipient of resources from the EU's structural funds, which are used to enhance infrastructure and improve economic performance in the less well-developed parts of the EU. However, as we discovered, the UK did receive some of this funding for health projects, such as local projects on mental health in deprived areas such as Sheffield, Leeds and the Humber.[59] Furthermore, the European Investment Bank was an important source of funding for public-private partnerships to fund new hospitals across the UK. The Royal Hospital for Sick Children, Edinburgh is one example.

There is insufficient empirical research available at present (winter 2022) to determine whether the new funding streams from the UK government, such as the Johnson government's 'levelling up funds', will involve equivalent levels of support.[60] Paul Copeland and Patrick Diamond have shown significant limitations in the UK's deployment of EU regional funding while a Member State, which continue into the post-Brexit era.[61] The Sunak government expressed continued commitment to this funding in late October 2022.[62] In principle, UK regional/cohesion funding is available to support health infrastructure and projects, although the White Paper on *Levelling Up the United Kingdom*, with its 'levelling up capitals framework', does not include health centrally in its approach. The White Paper's focus is on employment, private investment, infrastructure and civic pride. Notwithstanding, poor health is mentioned as an outcome of vicious circles of under-investment, is related to well-being, and the White Paper's 'mission 7' is to narrow the gap in healthy life expectancy across the UK.[63] Several hospital 'upgrade' investments are planned, and a 'Community Diagnostic Centre' in Barnsley and 'Centre for Child Health Technology' in Sheffield, both near where we undertook our fieldwork in Rotherham.[64] A White

[58] N Fahy et al, 'Impact on the NHS and Health of the UK's Trade and Cooperation Relationship with the EU, and Beyond', above n 33.

[59] Ibid, citing Ministry of Housing, Communities and Local Government, Department for Work and Pensions, Department for Environment, Food and Rural Affairs and Rural Payments Agency, 'European Structural and Investment Funds (ESIF)' (www.gov.uk/european-structural-investment-funds accessed 30 November 2022).

[60] A 2021 report cited lack of transparency as impeding research on the Levelling Up Funds, see Centre for Inequality and Levelling Up, *Funding Levelling Up: The Story So Far* (London, University of Westminster, 2021).

[61] P Copeland and P Diamond, 'From EU Structural Funds to Levelling Up: Empty Signifiers, Ungrounded Statism and English Regional Policy' (2022) 37(1–2) *Local Economy* 34.

[62] B Edgar, 'Rishi Sunak Commits to Levelling Up in First PMQs', The Northern Echo, 26 October 2022; P Madeley, 'Rishi Sunak Pressed Over Commitment to Levelling Up in the West Midlands', Express & Star, 27 October 2022.

[63] Department for Levelling Up, Housing and Communities and HM Government, *White Paper: Levelling Up the United Kingdom*, CP 604, 2 February 2022, 200–06; Department for Levelling Up, Housing and Communities and HM Government, *Levelling Up the United Kingdom: Missions and Metrics Technical Annex*, CP 604, 2 February 2022, 11, 29–31 and 32.

[64] *White Paper: Levelling Up the United Kingdom*, ibid, 206, 294; Department for Levelling Up, Housing and Communities, HM Government, *Levelling Up – Delivering for All Parts of the UK*, 2 February 2022, 46.

Paper on *Health Disparities* had been promised for later in 2022, but appears to have been shelved.[65] As things currently stand, therefore, it is difficult to discern whether it will become less easy, or easier, to secure resources for health projects in relatively deprived parts of the UK than it was before Brexit.[66]

Indirectly, the UK's overall position in terms of public finances impacts on the NHS as the largest discretionary part of UK public expenditure. Anything that affects the wider UK economy will obviously affect the ability to raise funding for the NHS and other public services. Although the Leave campaign originally claimed there would be no economic detriment due to Brexit, this claim was quietly dropped when it became clear that it was unsustainable on any reputable economic modelling. It is now difficult to disentangle the effects of the COVID-19 pandemic on the UK's economy, but an independent study from June 2022 suggested the UK economy was 5.2 per cent smaller than it would have been without the referendum vote,[67] and the Office for Budget Responsibility's March 2022 (latest as at winter 2022) analysis shows a 4 per cent long-run reduction in productivity, compared to staying in the EU.[68]

IX. MEDICAL PRODUCTS, VACCINES AND TECHNOLOGY

Supplies of medicines, including vaccines, medical devices and equipment reach NHS hospitals and clinics, GP surgeries and pharmacies through a complex trade network. Before 2020, there was very little awareness of the ways in which, for example, the production and distribution of a commonly used medicine, or tubing for a hospital machine, might involve the product crossing several internal EU borders before it reached a pharmacy or hospital in the UK. In 2017, the House of Commons Health Committee sought to ask the government for detailed information about supply routes for medicines used in the NHS, so as to understand what the implications would be for trading with the EU 'on WTO terms' (without any trade agreement in place).[69] The information was not forthcoming. The later global pandemic, with the

[65] H Clarke-Ezzidio, 'A Message to the New Health Secretary: Don't Scrap the Health Inequalities Review', The New Statesman, 28 October 2022; B Smith, 'MPs Demand Answers on "Scrapped" Health Inequalities paper', Civil Service World, 19 October 2022; E Thornton, 'Withholding of Health-Inequalities White Paper "Tough to Swallow" says Bishop of London', Church Times, 12 October 2022.

[66] See also G Iacobucci, '"Levelling Up" Plan Needs More Funding and a Focus on Health Inequalities, Say Experts' (2002) 376 *British Medical Journal* o303 on the limitations of effects of the levelling up funds on health inequalities.

[67] J Springford, 'What Can We Know About the Cost of Brexit So Far?', Centre for European Reform, 9 June 2022 (www.cer.eu/publications/archive/policy-brief/2022/cost-brexit-so-far).

[68] Office for Budget Responsibility, 'Brexit Analysis', 26 May 2022 (https://obr.uk/forecasts-in-depth/the-economy-forecast/brexit-analysis/#assumptions); Office for Budget Responsibility, *Economic and Fiscal Outlook*, CP 648, March 2022, 62–63; Office for Budget Responsibility, *Fiscal Risks and Sustainability*, CP702, July 2022, 63; HM Government, *EU Exit: Long-Term Economic Analysis*, CM 9742, November 2018; A Hantzsche et al, *The Economic Effects of the Government's Proposed Brexit Deal*, National Institute of Economic and Social Research, London, 2018; T Sampson and S Dhingra, 'The Economic Consequences of the Brexit Deal', 29 November 2018 (https://blogs.lse.ac.uk/businessreview/2018/11/29/the-economic-consequences-of-the-brexit-deal-the-case-of-trade/). Of course, Brexit economic effects are difficult to disentangle from COVID-19 pandemic effects, but some analyses, including that of the Office for Budget Responsibility, seek to do so.

[69] 'Brexit: Medicines, Medical Devices and Substances of Human Origin', above n 1.

associated difficulties of securing supply, increased understanding of how reliant the NHS is on smooth global trade patterns. 'Just in time' supply chains are 'efficient', in that they do not require significant investment in warehouses or storerooms to keep stocks. But the pandemic also revealed the fragility of 'just in time' supply models, in a way that can be literally deadly, for instance, if it means that essential personal protective equipment is not available for frontline NHS staff.

The EU's common customs union laws mean that products reaching the EU from the rest of the world do so through a standard set of customs formalities and charges. The EU's internal market laws mean that products can circulate freely within the EU once they are inside. Leaving the EU means the imposition of new administrative formalities when products move from the EU to the UK (and vice versa), because products crossing that border are in the formal legal categories of 'imports' and 'exports'. Even in a free trade agreement, where customs duties do not apply, or even if a particular product is 'zero rated', which is the case for medicines, products cannot lawfully simply cross a border: an associated administrative cost always applies.

There are also costs arising from regulatory formalities. The EU protects consumers and others within its internal market by ensuring that products circulating in that market meet certain regulatory standards. The EU has developed a dense web of law covering medicines, including vaccines;[70] medical devices and equipment;[71] and substances of human origin (blood, cells, human tissue).[72] This EU legislation protects patients, and also seeks to promote the European health industry. Products may only be marketed in the EU in accordance with EU regulatory standards – including being sold to a national health system within the EU. But a medicine that meets the EU's standards and has a marketing authorisation may lawfully be sold anywhere in the EU – allowing manufacturers to take advantage of economies of scale. There are essentially three such large markets for medicines globally: the USA, China and the EU. New medicines typically reach these larger markets sooner than smaller ones. Although there are significant differences between the ways countries choose to regulate medicines,[73]

[70] See, eg, Directive 2001/83/EC of the European Parliament and of the Council of 6 November 2001 on the Community code relating to medicinal products for human use [2001] OJ L 311/67; Directive 2011/62/EU of the European Parliament and of the Council of 8 June 2011 amending Directive 2001/83/EC on the Community code relating to medicinal products for human use, as regards the prevention of the entry into the legal supply chain of falsified medicinal products [2011] OJ L 174/74; Regulation (EC) No 1394/2007 of the European Parliament and of the Council of 13 November 2007 on advanced therapy medicinal products and amending Directive 2001/83/EC and Regulation (EC) No 726/2004 [2007] OJ L 324/121; Regulation (EU) No 536/2014 of the European Parliament and of the Council of 16 April 2014 on clinical trials on medicinal products for human use, and repealing Directive 2001/20/EC [2014] OJ L 158/1.

[71] See, eg, Regulation (EU) 2017/745 of the European Parliament and of the Council of 5 April 2017 on medical devices, amending Directive 2001/83/EC, Regulation (EC) No 178/2002 and Regulation (EC) No 1223/2009 and repealing Council Directives 90/385/EEC and 93/42/EEC [2017] OJ L 117/1; Regulation (EU) 2017/746 of the European Parliament and of the Council of 5 April 2017 on in vitro diagnostic medical devices and repealing Directive 98/79/EC and Commission Decision 2010/227/EU [2017] OJ L 117/176.

[72] See, eg, Directive 2002/98/EC of the European Parliament and of the Council of 27 January 2003 setting standards of quality and safety for the collection, testing, processing, storage and distribution of human blood and blood components and amending Directive 2001/83/EC [2003] OJ L 33/30; Directive 2004/23/EC of the European Parliament and of the Council of 31 March 2004 on setting standards of quality and safety for the donation, procurement, testing, processing, preservation, storage and distribution of human tissues and cells [2004] OJ L 102/48.

[73] A Pezzola and CM Sweet, 'Global Pharmaceutical Regulation: The Challenge of Integration for Developing States' (2016) 12 *Global Health* 85.

some countries map their regulatory standards to one of these larger markets, so as to reap the benefit of being part of a larger market.[74] Until it left the EU, the UK already enjoyed that benefit. The EU accounts for 22 per cent of global healthcare spending; the UK just 3 per cent.[75]

The EU-UK Trade and Cooperation Agreement envisages that Great Britain will be able to choose different regulatory standards to those of the EU. The main divergence so far in the health field has been in the context of the EU's falsified medicines regulatory system.[76] A falsified medicine is defined as a medicine with inferior quality ingredients, or ingredients in an incorrect dosage, or a medicine that has been fraudulently labelled wrongly to conceal its true source. The EU system involves affixing a 'unique identifier', in the form of a barcode, and an anti-tamper device to each pack of medicines, and uploading information to a central EU online system. The information is checked at various points along the supply chain, especially at the end by a pharmacy or hospital, to make sure that the package has not been tampered with before it is used. The UK does not require the same processes for medicines to be sold in Great Britain,[77] although in theory the rules continue to apply in Northern Ireland.[78] We discuss this further in chapter eight.

The UK also diverged in practice from the EU's standards for medical devices, when the EU brought in new, more stringent provisions in 2021.[79] The UK government ran a consultation on a new regulatory regime for medical devices in autumn 2021,[80] and new legislation has been promised for 2023.[81] As the UK in a Changing Europe 'Divergence Tracker'[82] points out, it is not at all clear whether the UK will have regulatory capacity to diverge significantly from EU standards, especially as the Medicines

[74] P-L Lezotre, *International Cooperation, Convergence and Harmonization of Pharmaceutical Regulations* (London, Academic Press, 2014).

[75] P Foster, 'Medical Devices Industry Tests UK plans for Post-Brexit Divergence', Financial Times 18 July 2021.

[76] See Directive 2011/62/EU of the European Parliament and of the Council of 8 June 2011 amending Directive 2001/83/EC on the Community code relating to medicinal products for human use, as regards the prevention of the entry into the legal supply chain of falsified medicinal products [2011] OJ L 174/74; Commission Delegated Regulation (EU) 2016/161 of 2 October 2015 supplementing Directive 2001/83/EC of the European Parliament and of the Council by laying down detailed rules for the safety features appearing on the packaging of medicinal products for human use [2015] OJ L 32/1.

[77] Regulation 2016/161, ibid, was repealed by Human Medicines (Amendment etc.) (EU Exit) Regulations 2019, Schedule 9.

[78] G Peretz and X Borrás, 'A Case of Unforeseen Adverse Side-Effects? The Ireland/Northern Ireland Protocol and Medicines Regulation' (2021) 5(4) *European Pharmaceutical Law Review* 175.

[79] Regulation (EU) 2017/745 of the European Parliament and of the Council of 5 April 2017 on medical devices, amending Directive 2001/83/EC, Regulation (EC) No 178/2002 and Regulation (EC) No 1223/2009 and repealing Council Directives 90/385/EEC and 93/42/EEC [2017] OJ L 117/1; Regulation (EU) 2017/746 of the European Parliament and of the Council of 5 April 2017 on in vitro diagnostic medical devices and repealing Directive 98/79/EC and Commission Decision 2010/227/EU [2017] OJ L 117/176 (which is being introduced in stages over the next five years).

[80] Medicine and Healthcare Products Regulatory Agency and S Javid MP (Secretary of State for Health and Social Care), *Consultation on the Future Regulation of Medical Devices in the United Kingdom*, 16 September 2021.

[81] Ibid, 'Executive Summary'.

[82] UK in a Changing Europe, 'UK-EU Divergence Tracker', October 2021; UK in a Changing Europe, 'UK-EU Divergence Tracker' 2nd edn, December 2021.

and Healthcare Products Regulatory Agency (MHRA) has been downsized in 2021,[83] to the concern of many in the sector.[84] The government's 'Brexit Benefits' paper is very light on specifics in the area of health policy.[85] This is all the more disappointing as the independent Cumberlege report, published in July 2020, made specific recommendations for tighter medical device regulation and more effective adverse effects reporting, so as to protect patients and their dignity.[86]

At present (winter 2022), there has been little other divergence between the EU and the UK in the context of health-related products.[87] So the question of whether medicines, medical devices and equipment will become more expensive for the NHS in England, Scotland and Wales, as a result of being a smaller market, is an open one. It is also possible that new medicines will reach that market later: the time lag is typically six to 12 months.[88] The prospect that a new medicine might be available in England, but not in Northern Ireland is particularly problematic for the UK government: this has apparently already taken place for Ropinirole, a generic version of a medicine for Parkinson's disease produced by Sciecure Pharma.[89] The EU offered a partial solution in its legislation applicable for three years from January 2022,[90] which gives the UK's Medicines and Healthcare Products Regulatory Agency a period of up to six months for its marketing authorisations to be valid for Northern Ireland, while the EU's European Medicines Agency 'catches up' with its assessment of quality and safety. We explore post-Brexit regulation of medicines, medical devices and equipment further in chapter eight.

X. INFORMATION (DATA STANDARDS)

Understanding how EU law affects health law and policy also involves considering EU law and policy on information gathering, and the use of that information by public

[83] C Smith, 'Key Covid Medicine Agency Cuts Drug Assessor Staff by a Third', The Times, 25 October 2021.

[84] V Zainzinger, 'Budget Cuts at UK Medicines Regulator Raise Eyebrows', Chemistry World, 25 August 2021; 'Staffing Reductions at the Medicines and Healthcare products Regulatory Agency' (Early Day Motion), EDM 479 (2020–2021), 22 September 2021.

[85] HM Government, *The Benefits of Brexit: How the UK is Taking Advantage of Leaving the EU*, January 2022.

[86] Independent Medicines and Medical Devices Safety Review, *First Do No Harm*, July 2020. On the deficiencies of the UK's post-Brexit approach, see, eg L Downey et al, 'The Changing Face of Medical Devices Regulation? A Consultation & Expected New Regulations', 11 April 2022 (blog.bham.ac.uk/everydaycyborgs/2022/04/11/the-changing-face-of-medical-devices-regulation-a-consultation/); M Quigley and L Downey, 'Integrating the Biological and the Technological: Time to Move Beyond Law's Boundaries' in E Dove and N Nic Shuibne (eds), *Law and Legacy in Medical Jurisprudence: Essays in Honour of Graeme Laurie* (Cambridge, Cambridge University Press, 2021).

[87] Dayan et al, 'Medicines', above n 50; M Dayan et al, 'Parallel, Divergent or Drifting? Regulating Healthcare Products in a Post-Brexit UK' (2023) *Journal of European Public Policy* https://doi.10.1080/13501763.2023.2213721.

[88] 'Brexit: Medicines, Medical Devices and Substances of Human Origin', above n 1, 25; interview with Phillipa Whitford, February 2019.

[89] Nuffield Trust and Health and International Relations Monitor, 'Written Evidence (NIP0037)' submitted to House of Lords Sub-Committee on the Protocol on Ireland/Northern Ireland (https://committees.parliament.uk/writtenevidence/113370/html/ accessed 30 November 2022).

[90] See legislation above n 43.

bodies or private entities. We explain some consequences of this aspect of leaving the EU for biomedical research in chapter nine. When tackling communicable diseases, such as COVID-19, or in the case of clinical trials that have recruited patients from across several countries, the EU is in a strong position to collect and share personal data that can be used to improve health and reduce burdens on national health systems. Over the decades since the first 'Europe against Cancer' programme,[91] the EU has made a significant contribution to healthcare improvement by gathering and collating comparable data.[92] This is no mean feat. Using data to improve health across the EU involves technical complexity; detailed negotiations about the way in which national datasets are gathered; and harmonised legal provisions.

Personal data may not be gathered or used in the EU unless the process complies with the 'General Data Protection Regulation' (GDPR).[93] Data may not be transferred from the EU to a third state outside the EU, unless the EU formally recognises that state's data protection laws as 'adequate'. The EU-UK Trade and Cooperation Agreement allowed for a 'grace period' of recognition. During that time, the EU took the necessary formal decision that the UK's data protection law is counted as 'adequate' for GDPR purposes.[94] This decision means that data, for instance from clinical trials, can still be shared between the EU and the UK. The UK amended its data protection law in effect to recognise the EU's data protection regulation as consistent with UK law.[95] As things currently stand, health data can therefore flow in both directions.

This is not necessarily a permanent settlement. The UK is exploring the possibilities of a different approach to data regulation. It is entitled to do so under the EU-UK Trade and Cooperation Agreement, which includes a clause allowing either the EU or the UK to regulate digital trade.[96] If the UK rules diverge too far in the future, the EU may no longer recognise the UK as providing adequate protection for personal data. That would mean that for data to be shared in biomedical or other health-related research projects with UK and EU partners, the projects would need to bear the costs of alternative measures.[97] If that happened, there would likely be a disincentive to include UK patients, or research entities, in such projects.

[91] See Council Decision 90/238/Euratom, ECSC, EEC and the representatives of the Member States meeting within the Council on 17 May 1990 adopting a 1990–1994 action plan in the context of the 'Europe against cancer' programme [1990] OJ L 137/31.

[92] L Trubek et al, 'The Construction of Healthier Europe: Lessons from the Fight Against Cancer' (2008) 26(2) *Wisconsin International Law Journal* 868.

[93] Regulation (EU) 2016/679 of the European Parliament and of the Council of 27 April 2016 on the protection of natural persons with regard to the processing of personal data and on the free movement of such data, and repealing Directive 95/46/EC (General Data Protection Regulation) [2016] OJ L 119/1 ('GDPR').

[94] Commission Implementing Decision (EU) 2021/1772 of 28 June 2021 pursuant to Regulation (EU) 2016/679 of the European Parliament and of the Council on the adequate protection of personal data by the United Kingdom [2021] OJ L 360/1.

[95] Data Protection, Privacy and Electronic Communication (Amendments etc) (EU Exit) Regulations 2019.

[96] Article 198 EU-UK TCA. The EU-UK TCA only entered into force provisionally to begin with. A final 'legally scrubbed' text, confirmed by the EU's and the UK's legislatures, formally entered into force on 1 May 2021. References throughout are to that text.

[97] A Phillips and T Hervey, 'Brexit and Biobanking: GDPR Perspectives' in S Slokenberga et al (eds), *GDPR and Biobanking. Individual Rights, Public Interest and Research Regulation Across Europe* (Charn, Switzerland, Springer, 2021).

XI. SERVICE DELIVERY

The actual delivery of health services within a national health system is the area where EU law and policy has the least effect. The TFEU explicitly states that the organisation and delivery of health services is a matter of national competence.[98] That said, we identify a few areas where EU law and policy makes a difference to such aspects of the NHS. One is the way in which EU employment law – especially rules on working time – applies to doctors in training. This topic was highlighted by David Cameron in 2013 when he began the process which eventually led to the EU referendum.[99] There is no consensus in the health policy sector or NHS concerning how best to manage this question, even now that the UK is outside the EU. Some want to relax EU rules, to improve flexibility in terms of availability of junior doctors. The junior doctors themselves, however, negotiated that the relevant EU rules be embedded in their new national employment contract in 2017.[100] The COVID-19 pandemic, with its extraordinary pressures on all NHS staff, overtook this conversation. Working hours ('work/life balance') are just one aspect of the complex question of how to ensure trainee medical professionals across the UK choose to stay in the profession.[101]

A second area is service delivery for patients with rare diseases. Around four million people in the UK have been diagnosed with a rare disease. When we wrote in 2017, hospitals in the UK were participating in nearly all of the 24 EU-funded networks for rare diseases, and UK researchers/clinicians were leading a quarter of them. These networks bring together specialists and enable patients to be diagnosed and treated with the state-of-the art of medical knowledge about their rare condition. By 2022, clinicians based in hospitals in the UK were no longer able to lead or be members of such networks.[102]

The third important facet of health service delivery where EU law affects national law and policy in the UK is in Northern Ireland. We have already touched on the many ways in which health service delivery is integrated on the island of Ireland. We explore those further in chapters six, seven and eight. Leaving the EU removed one of the legal foundations on which that integrated service delivery is built. It continues on a different basis, especially the law and administrative practice that creates what is known as the 'common travel area'. It also continues in a series of contractual relationships, and in the provisions in the Ireland/Northern Ireland Protocol, especially its Article 2 which provides that there should be 'no diminution' of human rights protection in Northern Ireland as a result of Brexit.

[98] Article 168(7) TFEU.

[99] D Cameron, 'EU Speech at Bloomberg', 23 January 2013, cited in N Fahy et al, 'How Will Brexit Affect Health and Health Services in the UK?', above n 7.

[100] 'Brexit and Health and Social Care – People & Process', above n 1.

[101] See, eg, FK Lock and D Carrieri, 'Factors Affecting the UK Junior Doctor Workforce Retention Crisis: An Integrative Review' (2022) 12 *British Medical Journal Open* e059397.

[102] The list of European Reference Networks and their members is available online (https://ec.europa.eu/health/european-reference-networks/networks_en accessed 15 November 2022). For discussion of the impact see M Tischkowitz et al, 'A No-Deal Brexit will be Detrimental to People with Rare Diseases' (2021) 397(10268) *The Lancet* 20.

XII. LEADERSHIP AND GOVERNANCE

The sixth and final 'building block' of a health system on which we based our 2017 and subsequent analyses is leadership and governance. This covers the broader context within which a national health system operates, especially regulation for public health matters, such as clean air and water, food, alcohol and tobacco, and communicable disease control. The regulatory choices a state makes about public health matters affect the overall health of its population, and hence the call on its national health system for healthcare and treatment for a range of preventable illnesses.

The regulatory choices a state is able to make in these areas are *also* dependent on the obligations in international law to which that state has committed in its trade agreements. The UK's post-Brexit trade position, and what it means for health, is the subject of chapter 10. When it was an EU Member State, the UK was required to align with EU public health law. A great deal of UK environmental law was determined at EU level. There is also a considerable body of EU law on food regulation, including alcohol, and on tobacco, especially its labelling and advertising within the EU. Outside of the EU, there is an opportunity for the UK to choose higher standards, which are more protective of public health, but these choices will make economic sense only if the UK's trade agreements do not in effect mean that less healthy products made elsewhere in the world can be easily traded on the UK's market.

This was a major concern for the Faculty of Public Health, with whom we worked from 2016 onwards. We were particularly collaborating with Mark Weiss, their then European policy officer. Hervey recalls a phone call with him, on a hot August day in 2016, when they first discussed the idea that Brexit should 'do no harm' to public health. It is too soon to tell whether the decisions that the UK makes outside of the EU will improve or harm human health in this more general sense. But we believe that it is important to track those regulatory decisions, and measure their effects.[103]

Another aspect of health governance that is affected by the EU's trade relationships is the rules that apply to NHS purchasing of services and products, as well as investing in its infrastructure. EU law imposes strict procedural rules on such public procurement, to seek to open markets for firms in any EU Member State to compete for public contracts. The EU's rules can seem inefficient, and many in the NHS were keen to be free of the shackles of EU law in this respect, especially as one way to comply with the letter of the EU rules is to split up NHS contracts into smaller ones, which fall below the thresholds at which the EU rules apply.

The interactions between biomedical research and the NHS are also part of this health system 'building block'. Funding for research from the EU is an obvious part of this aspect of the indirect effects of EU law on the NHS. There are also benefits from being within a broader set of EU networks; from common legal frameworks and standards for clinical trials, and data protection; from being part of a regional bloc in terms of having a voice in global science policy; and from the free movement of people within the EU. When we wrote in 2017, the UK had a reputation for being an excellent place to build a career as a biomedical researcher, because of the relative openness of its academic institutions, their long-standing collaborations with research-intensive

[103] This is the subject of the project we are currently undertaking with the Nuffield Trust, funded by the Health Foundation.

hospitals, developing and trialling cutting-edge treatments. In 2014/15, about 16 per cent of the academic workforce in the UK was from the rest of the EU.[104]

Finally, a robust national health system's governance is characterised by strong engagement with all health policy stakeholders, and by the quality of scrutiny of its laws and policies. Here, the structure of the EU, and in particular the 'transversal' nature of health policy in EU institutional contexts, are problematic. We have been critical of the EU in this respect, especially for the ways that EU law and policy interprets health as almost an inconvenient exception to the 'rule' of market competition. The 2020 'Manifesto for a European Health Union',[105] in which Hervey and Flear are collaborators, is in part a response to this critique.

The ways in which decisions were taken by the UK government from 2016–22 left a great deal to be desired in terms of stakeholder engagement and scrutiny. We will explain this further throughout the rest of the book, and especially in chapter 11, but we will give just one example for now. Dr Wollaston described the UK government's approach to the health impacts of Brexit as 'nothing to see here'. At every stage, in her experience, the House of Commons needed to force greater transparency. A particularly egregious example was the first UK government Brexit planning documents. These were initially kept secret, but subsequently were made available in a reading room in the Treasury for MPs only. Dr Wollaston was expecting to have to set aside time for a month to take in all the detail about health – because, as we have shown in this chapter – there are significant details to be considered. There is, in fact, 'a lot to see here', and every stakeholder was pointing this out: medical professionals, researchers, patient groups, the voluntary sector, MPs including the Health and Social Care Select Committee, the Science and Technology Committee and the Public Accounts Committee.[106] Whereas in fact, it took Dr Wollaston less than an hour to read the relevant documents: they were, in her words, an 'almost childlike summary' of the issues.

Leaving the EU provides an opportunity, at least in theory, to put human health front-and-centre in law and policy making across the UK. It means a chance to take decisions necessary to make the NHS in England, Northern Ireland, Scotland and Wales more closely match the hopes and aspirations for healthcare that we heard about in the conversations we had in Sheffield, Rotherham, Rochdale, Newry and Derry/Londonderry during our research in 2019.

XIII. CONCLUSION

Dr Wollaston was not returned by her constituency in the December 2019 election. In January 2020, Jeremy Hunt MP took over as Chair of the Health and Social

[104] The Royal Society, *UK Research and the European Union: The EU Role in International Research Collaboration and Researcher Mobility* (London, The Royal Society, 2016).

[105] European Health Union Initiative and Manifesto, 'European Health Union Initiative and Manifesto', European Health Forum Gastein (www.ehfg.org/projects-events/europeanhealthunion accessed 21 November 2022).

[106] See, eg, 'Brexit, Science and Innovation', *Second Report from the Science and Technology Committee*, HC 705 (2017–19); 'Brexit and the UK Border', *Seventh Report from the Committee of Public Accounts*, HC 558 (2017–19).

Care Select Committee. Hunt's staff had one telephone meeting with Dr Wollaston's specialist Brexit advisers in March 2020, just as the COVID-19 pandemic emerged in Europe. The Committee did not contact us again. The effects of Brexit on health were no longer an explicit focus for parliamentary scrutiny. But, as we have shown in this chapter, those effects are wide-ranging, and this continues to be reflected in the work of the Committee.

For example, in November 2021, the Committee opened an Inquiry into NHS and social care staffing,[107] which included questions about the balance between national and international recruitment of health and social care staff in the short, medium and long term, asking about how the UK government could make it easier to recruit appropriately qualified staff from other countries. The word 'Brexit' had disappeared, but the consequences continue.

[107] House of Commons Health and Social Care Committee, 'Workforce: Recruitment, Training and Retention in Health and Social Care Inquiry' (https://committees.parliament.uk/work/1647/ accessed 30 November 2022).

5

Cross-Border Healthcare in Great Britain

I. INTRODUCTION

NICOLA HAWKINS HAD problems with her kidneys from childhood. Nonetheless, she lived a full life, working as a fund-raiser until ill-health prevented her from continuing in employment. Sadly, Nicola died in 2020,[1] shortly after the transplant she had waited for many years to receive. In 2018, Nicola wrote poignantly of her life on regular dialysis, and the contrast with travelling to Italy with her daughter, Nadine:

> The thing is, if you always do the same thing and if that same thing happens to be sitting tethered to a haemodialysis machine for hours at a time, well, life can get a bit flat, predictable and sometimes a little depressing. I reckon it does everyone the world of good to feel their eyes turn into saucers every so often, to be surprised by the unusual, to have your pulse racing and your whole system on alert! The challenge of language, map reading, bus timetables and an exciting destination, all while bathed in warm sunshine and no work pressures, is a liberating one. And it feels normal. By that I mean I can actually forget that I have any health issues, I'm just being me.[2]

Nicola described the mental health benefits that flow from travel, not only from the actual travel itself, but also from the planning and anticipation of a trip. She implied that a chance to travel meant she enjoyed greater equality with those who do not need regular dialysis, and that being able to travel was an aspect of her human dignity. When travelling, Nicola felt free from being defined by her illness and disability.

Nicola was one of many people with kidney disease who are supported by the small charity Kidney Care UK. Around 30,000 people across the UK are on dialysis.[3] We learned about Nicola's story through our work with the charity, collaborating on its interventions in the political domain over Brexit,[4] and helping the charity to provide

[1] 'In Memory of Nicola Jane Hawkins' (www.justgiving.com/fundraising/Larry-Lawes accessed 1 July 2022, link no longer live).

[2] N Hawkins, 'Please Don't Take Away My EHIC Card', 31 August 2018 (www.kidneycareuk.org/news-and-campaigns/news/please-dont-take-away-my-ehic-card/).

[3] Interview with Fiona Loud, February 2019.

[4] Evidence from Fiona Loud to the House of Commons Health Committee Inquiry on 'Brexit: Medicines, Medical Devices and Substances of Human Origin', HC 392, 5 December 2017 (http://data.parliament.uk/writtenevidence/committeeevidence.svc/evidencedocument/health-and-social-care-committee/brexit-the-regulation-of-medicines-medical-devices-and-substances-of-human-origin/oral/75419.html).

clear information about the legal position at various points in time from 2018–21. Over time, as its Policy Director Fiona Loud explained to us, Kidney Care UK built up information about a network of dialysis units across Italy, France, Spain and the Greek islands. The charity acts as a conduit for sharing information among its clients. Some of them, like Nicola, go abroad for a holiday, but often the travel is to visit family members who are themselves unable to leave home. The peer advice, and small amounts of financial support from Kidney Care UK, meant that, according to the charity's estimates,[5] 3000–5000 people on dialysis were able to go abroad each year, having carefully planned and pre-booked their dialysis, taken out insurance for unexpected eventualities, relying on the rights evidenced by the European Health Insurance (EHIC) card. Nicola's blog explained that, without the EHIC, she calculated that she would be able to travel only once every five years, rather than once every three. The joy and dignity of each of these trips were underpinned by entitlements in EU law.

The EHIC kidney dialysis example is just one of many instances of cross-border healthcare entitlements that are covered by EU membership. In this chapter, we explain how these entitlements were jeopardised by Brexit, how they were significantly mitigated by the Withdrawal Agreement, and we outline the current legal settlement between the UK and the EU. This chapter covers the position of patients resident in Great Britain. The next chapter looks at the position on the island of Ireland. Throughout, as we have in this introduction, we reflect on the extent to which the legal position reflects the views of the people we encountered during our research, in terms of what they hoped for in a post-Brexit NHS.

II. HOW DOES CROSS-BORDER HEALTHCARE WORK IN THE EU?

As we mentioned in chapter four, cross-border healthcare in the EU is covered by at least three different sources of EU law. These are a Regulation on coordination of social security benefits (the EHIC and S2 funding routes);[6] a Directive on 'patients' rights to cross-border healthcare' (the EU Directive route);[7] and part of the Treaty on the Functioning of the EU on freedom to receive cross-border services in the internal market.[8] These sources of EU law are based on the EU's internal market: an area within which, among other factors of production, people and services are legally entitled to move freely, without unjustified discrimination against non-nationals. A fourth source of EU law, which we do not cover here, but touch on in chapter nine, is the enrolment of patients in cross-border clinical trials, particularly in the case of 'European Reference Networks' for rare diseases.

[5] Interview with Fiona Loud, February 2019.

[6] Regulation (EC) No 883/2004 of the European Parliament and of the Council of 29 April 2004 on the coordination of social security systems [2004] OJ L 166/1.

[7] Directive 2011/24/EU of the European Parliament and of the Council of 9 March 2011 on the application of patients' rights in cross-border healthcare [2011] OJ L 88/45.

[8] Article 56 TFEU.

III. MEDICAL CARE THAT BECOMES NECESSARY DURING A VISIT

EU law entitles patients to medical treatment that becomes necessary during their stay in the territory of another EU country.[9] The relevant Regulation takes legal effect without action from a Member State's national parliament or government.[10] The Regulation also applies in preference to any contradictory domestic law.[11]

Effectively, under EU law, anyone who is covered by the national healthcare system of any EU Member State, or Iceland, Liechtenstein and Norway (EEA Member States), who needs to access medical treatment in another EU/EEA Member State during a visit to that EU/EEA Member State, is treated in the same way as local residents. The underlying aim of this legislation is that there should be no detriment to people who move around the EU/EEA during their lives.[12] The costs of any healthcare received are offset by a system of reimbursement between EU/EEA Member States. The system is supported by the Electronic Exchange of Social Security Information[13] (EESSI), an IT system enabling the exchange of personal data across national social security institutions.[14] The right to access cross-border healthcare under this system is administered in the form of the EHIC, granting access to free or reduced cost healthcare within the EU/EEA.[15] The free EHIC extends cross-border healthcare to include access to a range of non-emergency but necessary medical treatment, including kidney dialysis.[16]

Many people in the UK valued access to EHIC healthcare: continued access was one of the questions raised in the national debate in the run up to the referendum.[17] In response to our picture of the Brexit bus, a Spanish man in Sheffield showed us his EHIC card. He felt there had not been enough attention to the loss of cross-border

[9] Article 19, Regulation 883/2004, above n 6. Article 1(va)(i), Regulation 883/2004, 'for the purposes of Title III, Chapter 1 (sickness, maternity and equivalent paternity benefits), benefits in kind provided for under the legislation of a Member State which are intended to supply, make available, pay directly or reimburse the cost of medical care and products and services ancillary to that care. This includes long-term care benefits in kind'.

[10] Article 288 TFEU.

[11] According to the principle of supremacy of EU law see Case 26/62 *Van Gend en Loos v Nederlands Administratie de Belastingen* ECLI:EU:C:1963:1.

[12] Recital 5, Regulation 883/2004, above n 6, 'it is necessary, within the framework of such coordination, to guarantee within the community equality of treatment under the different national legislation for persons covered'; Recital 13, 'The coordination rules must guarantee that persons moving within the Community and their dependents and survivors retain the rights and the advantages acquired and in the course of being acquired'.

[13] Provided for in Article 78, Regulation 883/2004, above n 6.

[14] Employment, Social Affairs and Inclusion, European Commission, 'Electronic Exchange Of Social Security Information (EESSI)' (https://ec.europa.eu/social/main.jsp?catId=869 accessed 21 November 2022). Implemented by Regulation (EC) No 987/2009 of the European Parliament and of the Council of 16 September 2009 laying down the procedure for implementing Regulation (EC) No 883/2004 on the coordination of social security systems [2009] OJ L 284/1, Article 3(3). Data exchange that is compliant with EU law is provided for in Recital 40, Regulation 883/2004, above n 6.

[15] T Powell, *Healthcare (International Arrangements) Bill 2017–2019*, Briefing Paper Number 08435, House of Commons Library, 17 January 2019.

[16] Regulation 883/2004, above n 6 and the European Commission, 'Explanatory Note on Necessary Care', January 2011 (https://ec.europa.eu/social/main.jsp?catId=559 accessed 6 February 2023).

[17] 'Would My EHIC Card be Valid Post-Brexit?', BBC, 8 June 2016; 'Reality Check: What Would Brexit Mean for Health Costs?', BBC, 6 April 2016.

healthcare for a diabetic like him.[18] A man we spoke with in Rochdale described his experience in a Belgian hospital as 'A class',[19] a sentiment implicitly echoed by a self-reporting Leave voter in the same town who asserted that the Belgian health system is much better than England's.[20] But access to healthcare in other EU Member States was not always associated with positive expectations. In chapter two, we already mentioned the man in Rotherham,[21] who told us that his wife had died following poor medical care in a Greek hospital. He felt that EU membership was supposed to secure *equally good* healthcare across the whole EU (an assumption which is inaccurate), and in his case, EU membership had failed him. Although his wife had access to emergency care flowing from the EHIC, this had done nothing to save him from his grief. In fact, only a handful of our street conversations in England raised the issue of cross-border healthcare as a positive aspect of EU membership. By contrast, as we discuss in the next chapter, cross-border healthcare on the island of Ireland is seen quite differently.

IV. BEFORE THE WITHDRAWAL AGREEMENT

In the run-up to the UK and EU agreeing the Withdrawal Agreement, one health-related concern associated with a 'No Deal' Brexit was the effect on cross-border healthcare, for patients covered by the NHS across the UK when visiting EU Member States, and vice versa. A 'No Deal' Brexit would have meant no reciprocal healthcare agreements would operate between the UK and the EU-27 as a bloc. UK patients would have immediately lost their EU law rights to access treatment in EU/EEA Member States. Several people, including Nick Fahy and others, writing with us; Jean McHale; and Sarah Wollaston in her interview with us, were concerned that a patient could have been left in legal limbo, as their legal rights would have been 'turned off' from one moment to the next.[22] Many patients with pre-existing conditions were unable to access private health insurance cover for travel. Either they could not afford it,[23] or the insurance products simply were not available. Fiona Loud told us that Kidney Care UK talked with the insurance industry in early 2019, but the reply was 'that's a good idea, we'll think about it'. This left people who had booked travel in a position of extreme uncertainty.

[18] Sheffield 10B.

[19] Rochdale 41B.

[20] Rochdale 60B.

[21] Rotherham 133A.

[22] Interview with Dr Sarah Wollaston MP, March 2019; evidence from Professor Jean McHale to the Select Committee on the European Union, Home Affairs Sub-Committee Inquiry, 'Brexit: Reciprocal Healthcare', 11 October 2017 (https://data.parliament.uk/writtenevidence/committeeevidence.svc/evidencedocument/eu-home-affairs-subcommittee/brexit-reciprocal-healthcare/oral/71279.html); N Fahy et al, 'How Will Brexit Affect Health and Health Services in the UK? Evaluating Three Possible Scenarios Against the WHO Health System Building Blocks' (2017) 390(10107) *The Lancet* 2110.

[23] D McKee and M McKee, 'What Might Brexit Mean for British Tourists Travelling to the Rest of Europe?' (2018) 48(2) *Journal of the Royal College of Physicians of Edinburgh* 134; 'Brexit: Reciprocal Healthcare', *Thirteenth Report from the European Union Committee*, HL 107 (2017–2019).

But there would have been alternative possibilities for patients to access treatment. One possibility would have been for the UK to secure bilateral agreements with each EU Member State, or with the EU as a whole, and to implement these through domestic law. The Healthcare (European Economic Area and Switzerland Arrangements) Act 2019 established the legal basis for implementing reciprocal healthcare arrangements after the UK left the EU. The UK government proposed that, even in the event of a 'No Deal' scenario, reciprocal healthcare would continue until the end of December 2020. However, this proposal was not accepted by the EU, and our analysis, and that of others like the NHS Confederation,[24] suggested that it is difficult to see how it could have been. As the EU lead negotiator Michel Barnier himself, and commentators like Chris Grey have explained, the European Commission's negotiating mandate insisted on the idea that the internal market is not divisible.[25] This interpretation of the internal market meant that, because the UK was not seeking to agree to free movement for people, no aspect of internal market law could be included in the eventual EU-UK settlement. As we will see, however, *in the context of cross-border healthcare for visitors*, this is not how matters eventually turned out.

A second possibility would have been for patients to rely on the national law in the country they were visiting. By July 2019, many EU countries, such as Ireland, Spain, Italy, France and Greece, had already adopted domestic legislation that would have come into effect in the case of a 'No Deal' Brexit.[26] The practical aspects of its implementation for cross-border healthcare would have been highly complex, however, because in the event of a 'No Deal' Brexit, the EU would have immediately treated the UK as potentially non-compliant with EU data protection law.[27] Without what is known as an 'adequacy decision',[28] or 'appropriate safeguards',[29] EU Member States

[24] NHS Confederation, 'Reciprocal Healthcare Arrangements in a No Deal Brexit Scenario: Overview of the Reciprocal Healthcare Arrangements within the Context of the UK Exiting the EU' (www.nhsconfed.org/regions-and-eu/nhs-european-office/brexit-and-the-nhs/brexit-implications-for-health-and-care/reciprocal-healthcare accessed 16 November 2022). Also see 'Healthcare (European Economic Area and Switzerland Arrangements) Bill', Hansard, HL Vol 796, cols 1372–75 (19 March 2019).

[25] European Council, *Guidelines following the United Kingdom's notification under Article 50 TEU* EUCO XT 20004/17, 29 April 2017; M Barnier, *My Secret Brexit Diary: A Glorious Illusion* (Cambridge, Polity Press, 2021). The notion of the 'indivisibility' of the internal market has been challenged, see, eg, C Barnard and S Butlin, 'Free Movement vs Fair Movement: Brexit and Managed Migration' (2018) 55 (Special Issue) *Common Market Law Review* 203; S Bulmer and L Quaglia, 'The Politics and Economics of Brexit' (2018) 25(8) *Journal of European Public Policy* 1089; Editorial, 'Is the Indivisibility of the Four Freedoms a Principle of EU Law?' (2019) 56 *Common Market Law Review* 1; C Grey, *Brexit Unfolded: How No One Got What They Wanted (and Why They Were Never Going to)* (London, Biteback Publishing, 2021).

[26] D Foster and T Hervey, *Kidney Dialysis Patients Seeking Care in Selected EU Member States Following Brexit: The Expected Legal Position Under the Withdrawal Agreement and 'No Deal'*, Kidney Care UK Briefing Note, 2019 (www.sheffield.ac.uk/media/9187/download).

[27] Regulation (EU) 2016/679 of the European Parliament and of the Council of 27 April 2016 on the protection of natural persons with regard to the processing of personal data and on the free movement of such data, and repealing Directive 95/46/EC (General Data Protection Regulation) [2016] OJ L 119/1 ('GDPR').

[28] Article 45, GDPR, ibid.

[29] Article 57, GDPR, above n 27. One such appropriate safeguard is the use of standard contractual clauses. The Information Commissioner's Office produced guidance on what organisations need to include in contracts for data transfer: Information Commissioner's Office, 'What Needs to be Included in the Contract?' (https://ico.org.uk/for-organisations/guide-to-data-protection/guide-to-the-general-data-protection-regulation-gdpr/contracts-and-liabilities-between-controllers-and-processors-multi/what-needs-to-be-included-in-the-contract/ accessed 16 November 2022). The Health Research Authority's

would have been forbidden from sharing patient data with NHS entities in the UK, making follow-up care extremely difficult once a visiting patient returned home.

Furthermore, as the *legal framework* which governs the transfers of personal data from EU institutions to the UK would have had to change immediately in the event of a 'No Deal' Brexit, so would the *procedures* which administered the transfer of patient data. A new system for transferring payments for emergency treatments would also have been needed, as the EESSI would have no longer been available. Such a new system would have had to be created and implemented in a 'No Deal' scenario. No planning for such a new system had taken place at all. In short, there would have been a great deal of legal, administrative, and practical complexity, which would have arisen overnight, with no opportunity to plan for the ensuing chaos, and potentially life-threatening outcomes for UK patients visiting EU Member States. Fortunately, this did not take place.

V. THE WITHDRAWAL AGREEMENT

The EU and UK agreed the terms of the UK's withdrawal from the EU in a Withdrawal Agreement, which came into effect on 1 February 2020.

The Withdrawal Agreement continued the application of EU law during the transition period,[30] which ran from 1 February until 31 December 2020, even though the UK was no longer an EU Member State during that time. 'EU law' includes the EU measures on cross-border healthcare, and everything that flows from those, which includes EHIC, and the EESSI, as well as planned cross-border healthcare.

The Withdrawal Agreement meant that the EU legal provisions upholding UK patients' rights to access cross-border healthcare could still be relied on by patients seeking cross-border healthcare (like the dialysis patients supported by Kidney Care UK) until 31 December 2020.[31] The Withdrawal Agreement also explicitly covered the situation where a patient was abroad visiting an EU Member State on 31 December 2020. Those patients were able to continue to rely on their rights under the Withdrawal Agreement until they left that Member State.[32] Neither the maximum duration of stay, nor the reason for the stay, was determined by law. Therefore, for instance, a holiday period with 31 December 2020 falling within it was covered.

In addition, on the administrative side, the Withdrawal Agreement explicitly provided that the UK would continue to be in the EESSI during the transition period, and that the UK would continue to pay its share of the costs.[33] Under the Withdrawal Agreement, EU rules from the General Data Protection Regulation (GDPR) continued

guidance confirmed the lawfulness of such data transfers, see MJ Taylor et al, 'United Kingdom: Transfers of Genomic Data to Third Countries' (2018) 137(8) *Human Genetics* 637, 639, citing Health Research Authority NHS, 'Legal Basis for Processing Data' (www.hra.nhs.uk/planning-and-improving-research/policies-standards-legislation/data-protection-and-information-governance/gdpr-detailed-guidance/legal-basis-processing-data/ accessed 16 November 2022).

[30] Article 126 WA.

[31] Article 127 WA.

[32] Article 32(1)(c) WA.

[33] Article 34(2) WA. Payment of costs is provided for in Regulation 987/2009/EU, above n 14.

to apply to the UK during transition.[34] This continuity was important because practically, for cross-border healthcare to operate successfully, personal data concerning the patient must be transferred between the relevant countries, and because the EESSI is the process through which reciprocal payments are made under the scheme of the relevant EU law.

The Withdrawal Agreement thus avoided all the chaotic uncertainty about cross-border healthcare that would have been associated with a 'No Deal' Brexit. But what happened next? The EU's position in terms of access to the benefits of the EU's single market,[35] and the UK's determination to end free movement of people into the UK[36] seemed to mean that it would be impossible to continue cross-border healthcare entitlements in an EU-UK Agreement applying after the end of the transition period.

VI. THE EU-UK TRADE AND COOPERATION AGREEMENT

Amazingly, to us, the Trade and Cooperation Agreement between the EU and the UK (EU-UK TCA), agreed on 24 December 2020, which entered into force on 1 January 2021,[37] includes a short chapter on coordination of social security provisions.[38] This means the EU-UK TCA covers an equivalent source of rights to that contained in one of the sources of EU law on cross-border healthcare. Why was this aspect of EU internal market law regarded as severable from the non-negotiable aspects associated with the EU's position to the effect that the UK could not 'have its cake and eat it'? Certainly, the relevant EU legislation[39] is based (in part) on the EU's powers to create a single European market within which people can move. If the EU was insisting that the UK could not secure access to some aspects of the EU's internal market without submitting to the disciplines of the EU's internal market rules across all factors of production (people, as well as goods, services and capital), why was coordination of social security different? Nothing in our research data, or in the published literature we have read,[40] explains why, although it is possible that the repeated attention to the 'loss of EHIC rights' in the public narratives in both the EU

[34] Article 126 WA.

[35] European Council, *Directives for the Negotiation of a New Partnership with the United Kingdom of Great Britain and Northern Ireland*, 5870/20 ADD 1 REV 3, 25 February 2020.

[36] See, eg, D Ferguson et al, *Will Free Movement end from 31 October 2019?* (London, House of Commons Library, 2019); HM Government Home Office, *Media Factsheet: EU Citizens and Freedom of Movement* (https://homeofficemedia.blog.gov.uk/2019/08/19/media-factsheet-eu-citizens-and-freedom-of-movement/ accessed 6 February 2023).

[37] The EU-UK TCA only entered into force provisionally to begin with. A final 'legally scrubbed' text, confirmed by the EU's and the UK's legislatures, formally entered into force on 1 May 2021. References throughout are to that text.

[38] Articles 488–491 EU-UK TCA. The scope of these provisions includes healthcare, see Article SSC.3, Protocol on Social Security Cooperation, EU-UK TCA.

[39] Regulation 883/2004, above n 6, the legal basis of which is Article 48 TFEU, within the title on free movement of persons, services and capital *and* Article 352 TFEU, which gives the EU competence to attain an objective where there is no other explicit power to do so in the Treaties.

[40] See, eg, Barnier, *My Secret Brexit Diary*, above n 25, which is rather exhaustive on the EU's negotiating position, and its rationales, does not explain why – in fact Barnier only mentions this part of the TCA on 4 out of 450 pages. Grey, *Brexit Unfolded*, above n 25, which is mainly focused on the UK's position, does not mention EHIC at all.

and the UK played some role.[41] To our knowledge, neither the EU negotiating team nor European Council ever explicitly engaged in a public or transparent way with this question.

A possible legal argument supporting the eventual agreement to include cross-border healthcare between the EU and UK is that the relevant part of EU internal market law involves mere *coordination* of very separate national social security systems (including national healthcare systems), not the removal of barriers to movement by creation of harmonised EU-level rules. The EU's Court of Justice has implicitly confirmed the distinction, by holding that the EU's EHIC rules 'help to facilitate' free movement of people,[42] but not that those rules directly create the internal market.

One possible political explanation relates more to the ideological position propagated by the UK government during the negotiations, and the Commission's response to that position. The UK was in a position of weakness, but nonetheless adopted a 'hard bargaining' position. This bargaining choice may have been, as Gabriel Siles-Brügge shows, because the UK framed the negotiations as an 'opportunity' to institute a new ideological approach to trade. That approach was based on an 'alternative' type of economic modelling that advocated aligning trade relationships based on emotional attachments to English-speaking economies with a similar (albeit vaguely defined) set of liberal 'values'.[43] In this 'emotional' mode, when negotiating with states that do not belong in that group, the UK government adopts an aggressive trade negotiation strategy. Alternatively, Benjamin Martill and Uta Stager suggest that the British approach of 'hard bargaining' from a point of weakness was a largely cultural facet of British policy making.[44] Either way, the EU had to respond to the UK's 'hard bargaining' position. By recognising it, and making some delimited concessions, the Commission could make the UK negotiating team feel like they were 'winning' something from a weak position, despite overall failing to achieve what they set out to achieve. The concessions about cross-border healthcare also benefit nationals of EU Member States who need healthcare when travelling to the UK. The lack of public discussion of the UK 'win' was necessary for the EU, because of its insistence on the unity of the internal market.

The EU-UK TCA entitles someone who is covered by the national healthcare system in either the UK or an EU Member State to receive 'healthcare which becomes necessary on medical grounds' during a visit to either an EU Member State or the UK, on a reciprocal basis.[45] What counts as 'necessary' is determined in practice

[41] See, eg, 'Brexit: Reciprocal Healthcare', *Thirteenth Report from the European Union Committee*, HL 107 (2017–2019); 'Brexit and Health and Social Care – People & Process', *Eighth Report from the Health and Social Care Committee*, HC 640 (2016–17); BBC, above n 17.

[42] For example Case C-56/01 *Inizan v Caisse primaire d'assurance maladie des Hauts-de-Seine* ECLI:EU:C:2003:578, para 21; Case C-368/98 *Vanbraekel and Others v Alliance nationale des mutualités chrétiennes* ECLI:EU:C:2001:400, para 32.

[43] G Siles-Brügge, 'Bound by Gravity or Living in a "Post Geography Trading World"? Expert Knowledge and Affective Spatial Imaginaries in the Construction of the UK's Post-Brexit Trade Policy' (2019) 24(3) *New Political Economy* 422.

[44] B Martill and U Staiger, 'Negotiating Brexit: The Cultural Sources of British Hard Bargaining' (2021) 59(2) *Journal of Common Market Studies* 261.

[45] Article SSC.5 (equality of treatment); Articles SSC.17 (1) and SSC.25 (pensioners), Protocol on Social Security Cooperation, EU-UK TCA.

by medical professionals in the country that the patient is visiting, using the same approach that is used for national patients, according to the nature of the medical need, and how long the patient is staying in the country. Someone who travelled with the purpose of accessing medical treatment is not covered.[46] We heard opposition to such 'health tourism' in our street conversations.[47] So in this respect, the post-Brexit arrangements reflect what some people hoped for in terms of access to the NHS.

The relevant necessary healthcare is provided on the same basis as it would be to a domestically-based patient. In those EU Member States where patients are required to pay up-front for their healthcare, but are reimbursed by a national social insurance system, the EU-UK TCA provides that the country where the patient is resident (which is normally responsible for their healthcare) must fully reimburse any payments made.[48] These TCA provisions are almost identical to the equivalent provisions in EU law, that apply to people moving from one EU Member State to another for a visit.[49]

The obligations under the EU-UK TCA were implemented in the UK by the introduction of the 'GHIC' – the 'Global Health Insurance Card'. To date, despite apparent UK government intentions,[50] there is nothing particularly 'global' about this card: in fact, it secures access to necessary healthcare in fewer countries than the EHIC, because Iceland, Liechtenstein and Norway are not included, although Switzerland has been included since November 2021.

Patients covered by the NHS in England, Scotland and Wales are entitled to a free GHIC on application. Patients covered by the NHS in Northern Ireland, who are also entitled to a free GHIC, are in a more complex position, which we discuss in the next chapter.

In EU law, EHIC access to necessary healthcare during a visit to another EU Member State covers all necessary healthcare. There is no need to secure authorisation for the healthcare in advance of the visit. By contrast, under the EU-UK TCA, some treatments do need a prior authorisation from the home country, which is usually responsible for the patient's healthcare.[51] These treatments are those that are 'only available through a specialised medical unit', a category which includes, but is not limited to, kidney dialysis; oxygen therapy (sometimes called supplemental oxygen); special asthma treatment; echocardiography to track cardio-vascular strain in the case of chronic autoimmune diseases, for example rheumatoid arthritis; and chemotherapy. For patients like Nicola Hawkins, therefore, a GHIC would not be enough to secure access to kidney dialysis necessary to go on holiday. Permission in advance from the NHS in the UK is now needed too.[52]

[46] Although a passenger or someone working on a ship or aircraft who became ill during the voyage or flight is covered.

[47] Newry 45A; Rochdale 60A.

[48] Article SSC.30, Protocol on Social Security Cooperation, EU-UK TCA.

[49] Articles 19, 20, 27, Regulation 883/2004, above n 6.

[50] HM Government Department of Health and Social Care, 'UK Launches Global Health Insurance Card', Press Release, 11 January 2021 (www.gov.uk/government/news/uk-launches-global-health-insurance-card).

[51] Appendix SSCI-2 referring to the entitlements under Article SSC.17 (2), Protocol on Social Security Coordination, EU-UK TCA.

[52] NHS, 'Treatment Abroad Checklist' (www.nhs.uk/using-the-nhs/healthcare-abroad/going-abroad-for-treatment/treatment-abroad-checklist/ accessed 16 November 2022).

In February 2021, in our written evidence to the House of Lords,[53] we pointed out that patients in the UK needed to know the details of the rules applicable for prior authorisations under the EU-UK TCA. Would the UK require prior authorisation for other treatments than those (non-exhaustively) listed in the TCA? Would different authorisation entitlements apply in England, Scotland and Wales? What would the basis be for successful applications for authorisation? Would it be possible to challenge a refusal to grant prior authorisation, and on what grounds? What procedure, and what forms, should be used? Neither how to apply for such permission, nor the criteria on which it will be granted, are obvious from the NHS website(s).[54] Procedurally, it seems that it has been subsumed into the arrangements for *planned* cross-border medical care, which we outline below. A single unit – the European Cross Border Healthcare Team – seems to deal with England, Scotland and Wales. The problem with the approach of combining GHIC rights for which authorisation is needed with the planned care arrangements is that one of the criteria for accessing planned cross-border medical care (under either the 'S2 funding route' or the 'EU Directive route') is that the treatment not be available at home without undue delay, a criterion that could never be met by someone who is going to the EU for a visit, but needs to access dialysis or oxygen therapy, and so on, while they are there.

The EU-UK TCA explicitly obliges the UK (and EU) to ensure that the Protocol on Social Security Coordination annexed to the TCA has the force of law in the UK (and EU).[55] But this is not the same as in EU law, which, if it applied to the Protocol, would mean that it had the force of law without any action on the part of the UK parliament or government, and would be directly effective, that is, enforceable by individuals in a domestic court or tribunal. Consequently, there is no obvious legal route to enforcing the rights that the EU-UK TCA gives in this context, unless they are effectively implemented in practice by the UK.

VII. PLANNED CROSS-BORDER MEDICAL CARE

EU law also entitles people covered by a national healthcare system in an EU Member State to access *planned* cross-border medical care. Because of the different sources of EU law we mentioned above, there are two bases for this, known as the 'S2 funding route' and the 'EU Directive route'.[56] The main differences are that patients have

[53] House of Lords EU Environment Sub-Committee, 'Future UK-EU Relations: Energy, Environment and Health. Inquiry' (https://committees.parliament.uk/work/944/future-ukeu-relations-energy-environment-and-health/ accessed 16 November 2022). Our evidence is available under 'Written Evidence EEH0007, 4 February 2021' (https://committees.parliament.uk/writtenevidence/22314/html/).

[54] NHS, 'Going Abroad for Treatment' (www.nhs.uk/using-the-nhs/healthcare-abroad/going-abroad-for-treatment/ accessed 21 November 2022). Comprehensive information for Scotland and Wales does not appear to be available, at least not on a centralised basis, except for NHS 111 Wales, 'Travel Health' (https://111.wales.nhs.uk/travelhealth/ accessed 21 November 2022), but for Northern Ireland see: Health and Social Care Board (Northern Ireland), 'Patients Travelling Outside Northern Ireland for Treatment' (https://online.hscni.net/travelfortreatment/ accessed 21 November 2022).

[55] Article SSC.67, Protocol on Social Security Coordination, EU-UK TCA.

[56] In practice, the 'EU Directive route', under Directive 2011/24, above n 7, has subsumed the TFEU entitlement.

to pay up-front for medical treatment under the EU Directive route, and that the S2 funding route cannot be used to access private medical treatment. Under either route, the treatment must be available in principle to a patient with that medical need in the national healthcare system in the home country, covered by the national healthcare system in the country where the patient wants to go, medically necessary according to a qualified health professional, and not accessible in the home country without undue delay, assessed on medical grounds.

Only the S2 funding route remains available to people covered by the NHS across the UK, under the terms of the EU-UK Trade and Cooperation Agreement.[57] The EU Directive route remained available under the terms of the Withdrawal Agreement for medical treatment in the EU that began, or was approved by a NHS in the UK, before 1 January 2021, the end of the transition period. The S2 funding route is managed for the whole of the UK by the NHS Business Services Authority.[58] The relevant NHS website, however, refers (incorrectly) to the need to be ordinarily resident in England to access cross-border medical treatment.[59] In fact, ordinary residence in Scotland or Wales[60] also entitles patients to access planned cross-border healthcare under the EU-UK TCA. The position in Northern Ireland is more complex, but the S2 funding route is included.

Apart from the Anglo-centric website, the eligibility criteria for the S2 funding route are transparent. The processes for review and appeal are also outlined. In this respect, the UK has complied with the obligations in the Protocol on Social Security Coordination, and there is continuity with the pre-Brexit situation, for a patient covered by a NHS in the UK to have authorised, planned medical treatment in an EU Member State, where they cannot access that treatment in the UK without undue delay.

VIII. CONCLUSIONS

For patients who are covered by the NHS in England, Scotland or Wales, there is much more continuity with the pre-Brexit situation in terms of access to cross-border

[57] Article SSC.5 (equality of treatment); Articles SSC.18, Protocol on Social Security Cooperation, EU-UK TCA.

[58] NHS Inform (NHS Scotland), 'Travelling to Europe for Planned Healthcare – the S2 Scheme' (www.nhsinform.scot/care-support-and-rights/health-rights/european-cross-border-healthcare/travelling-to-europe-for-planned-healthcare-the-s2-scheme accessed 21 November 2022); Health and Social Care Board (Northern Ireland), 'Treatment Under S2 Arrangements (E112)' (https://hscboard.hscni.net/travelfortreatment/s2/), more comprehensively see Health and Social Care Board (Northern Ireland), 'Patients Travelling Outside Northern Ireland for Treatment', above n 54; information for the NHS in Wales is less clearly available on a centralised basis, see Meddygfa Borth Surgery (NHS Wales), 'Travelling to Europe for Planned Healthcare – the S2 Scheme' (www.borthsurgery.wales.nhs.uk/health-resources/15887-travelling-to-europe-for-planned-healthcare-the-s2-scheme accessed 21 November 2022).

[59] NHS, 'The S2 Funding Route' (www.nhs.uk/using-the-nhs/healthcare-abroad/going-abroad-for-treatment/what-is-the-s2-route/) NHS accessed 21 November 2022).

[60] NHS Inform (NHS Scotland), 'Travelling to Europe for Planned Healthcare', above n 58; Health and Social Care Board (Northern Ireland), 'Treatment Under S2 Arrangements (E112)' and Health and Social Care Board (Northern Ireland), 'Patients Travelling Outside Northern Ireland for Treatment', above n 54; Meddygfa Borth Surgery (NHS Wales), 'Travelling to Europe for Planned Healthcare', above n 58.

healthcare than we had originally feared. For many patients, the GHIC gives continued access to healthcare that becomes necessary when in an EU Member State, for example, if someone falls ill or has an accident while on holiday, travelling with work, or visiting family. Equally, people resident in the EU who are visiting England, Scotland and Wales can access the NHS there for necessary healthcare.

Those people who felt that 'our' NHS was offering treatment to too many 'Europeans' are likely to be disappointed with this outcome.

But there are some discontinuities. The UK government could point to these as a legitimate response to a national narrative about 'others' in 'our' healthcare settings, even just on a visiting basis, which is one part of a much broader narrative about human migration and a desire to 'control' inward flows of people. We will say more about this theme in the chapter on healthcare professionals. For some patients – including patients like Nicola Hawkins – there are extra procedural steps that need to be taken before accessing cross-border healthcare in the way they were able to do before the UK left the EU. There is insufficient transparency on exactly what is the basis for decisions to authorise treatments under the EU-UK TCA, with the processes being collapsed into the planned healthcare entitlements, rather than being seen as part of GHIC entitlements for visitors. There are no longer any individually enforceable *rights* to access cross-border healthcare that have been agreed in the EU-UK TCA, although there is a process for raising reviews, appeals, concerns and complaints.[61]

The website which contains the relevant information is written in terms of *English* residents, whereas actually people who are normally covered by the NHS in Scotland or Wales are also covered. This aspect of health governance after Brexit is consistent with a general national discourse which constantly downplays the different legal and policy arrangements in the devolved nations or jurisdictions of Scotland and Wales. The next chapter turns to Northern Ireland, where the position on cross-border healthcare is quite different.

[61] NHS, 'The EU Directive Route' (www.nhs.uk/using-the-nhs/healthcare-abroad/going-abroad-for-treatment/what-is-the-s2-route/#criteria accessed 21 November 2022).

6

Cross-Border Healthcare in Northern Ireland

I. INTRODUCTION

PROVISION OF HEALTHCARE in Northern Ireland is distinctive, and has been so since the foundation of the national health system in 1948.[1] One important difference from England, and indeed Scotland and Wales, is that in Northern Ireland healthcare and social care have been part of an integrated system since 1973. Another difference is that in many respects, especially in the geographical north of the island, Northern Ireland and Ireland have a shared set of health services.

The position of Northern Ireland was understood as a matter of significant concern from very early on in the Brexit process.[2] We cannot do justice here to the breadth and depth of just how challenging Brexit is for the settlement overall on the island of Ireland.[3] In particular, the idea of a reintroduction of a land border on the island of Ireland, with the checks on people and products associated with the EU's external border, instilled nothing short of fear among large sections of the population that all of the progress made towards peace on the island over the last decades would be lost. Flear recounts some of how this felt for him:

> I'm an 'outsider insider' in Northern Ireland: I'm not 'from' in the sense that I wasn't born and raised there, and don't have the lived experience of the Troubles or its immediate aftermath. So, I can't quite grasp the full depth and breadth of feeling of many in Northern Ireland about what Brexit might mean for the hard won peace. But I am a longtime resident, and Northern Irish in that sense, and have a sense of the feeling around Brexit and its implications for my home.

[1] In Northern Ireland, integration of health and social care occurred under the Local Government (Northern Ireland) Act 1972 and Health and Personal Social Services (Northern Ireland) Order 1972 (Northern Ireland Orders in Council, 1972 No 1265 (NI 14)), with changes under both being implemented in 1973. The former divested local government of its responsibilities in respect of many policy areas, including health and personal social services, which were transferred to statutory boards under the latter. The Health and Social Care (Reform) Act (Northern Ireland) 2009 reduced the number of organisations involved in delivering health and social care, and established the Health and Social Care Board, five Health and Social Care Trusts and five local commissioning groups working alongside them.

[2] J McCormack, 'Brexit: How the Irish Border Issue Was Viewed During Campaigning', BBC, 12 October 2019.

[3] See, eg, S de Mars and C Murray, 'With or Without EU? The Common Travel Area After Brexit' (2020) 21(5) *German Law Journal* 815; S de Mars et al, *Bordering Two Unions: Northern Ireland and Brexit* (Bristol, Policy Press, 2018); M Dougan, *The UK's Withdrawal from the EU: A Legal Analysis* (Oxford,

> There's been a long running feeling among many people I know, who are 'from' Northern Ireland, that Brexit could really undermine peace. I know people who seem to worry most about the possibility of a hard border with the rest of the island. I know other people who seem most concerned about the prospect of Northern Ireland losing its standing in the United Kingdom.
>
> All around, people have been and are concerned, but views differ sharply on how, and sometimes whether it is even possible and desirable, to resolve tensions around preventing a hard border on the island, while also delivering Brexit, and ensuring there is no diminution of Northern Ireland's position in the United Kingdom. There is fear, yes absolutely. There's also despondency. I've also picked up on a feeling that Brexit could deliver benefits for the Northern Irish economy: we can have the 'best of both worlds'. Seeming to cut across many of these views is a feeling that Brexit is something happening that is beyond the control of most people. So: why worry too much?

Our focus in this book is on the implications for health and the NHS. The legal position is complex, still unfolding and difficult to determine. In this chapter, we seek to explain the position concerning access to cross-border healthcare for people on the island of Ireland. In later chapters, we will explain questions of NHS staffing and of supply of medicines, equipment and the other products needed to treat patients in Northern Ireland. As ever, our overarching question is the extent to which the post-Brexit position reflects hoped-for post-Brexit futures for health and the NHS, in the views of the people ('experts' and 'people on the street') with whom we interacted during our research.

II. BEFORE BREXIT

Before 1 January 2021, the arrangements for cross-border healthcare on the island of Ireland were underpinned by EU law, but in many respects, EU membership was not the legal basis of collaboration between the NHS in Northern Ireland and Ireland's National Health Service, or receipt of cross-border healthcare services by patients on the island of Ireland. Instead, to understand both the pre-Brexit and the current situation, we need to consider two different sources of law: the Common Travel Area and the Belfast/Good Friday Agreement 1998.

The description 'Common Travel Area' makes these arrangements seem like an international agreement, but actually the arrangements only comprise parallel national rules, policies and practices – between Ireland and the UK as well as the

Oxford University Press, 2021), ch 8; M Dougan, 'The "Brexit" Threat to the Northern Irish Border: Clarifying the Constitutional Framework' in M Dougan (ed), *The UK After Brexit* (Cambridge, Intersentia, 2017); O Doyle et al (ed), *The Brexit Challenge for Ireland and the United Kingdom: Constitutions Under Pressure* (Cambridge, Cambridge University Press, 2021); K Hayward, 'Northern Ireland: Demographics and Divisions' in F Fabbrini (ed), *The Law & Politics of Brexit: Volume IV. The Protocol on Ireland/Northern Ireland* (Oxford, Oxford University Press, 2022); C McCrudden (ed), *The Law and Practice of the Ireland-Northern Ireland Protocol* (Cambridge, Cambridge University Press, 2022); D Phinnemore and K Hayward, *UK Withdrawal ('Brexit') and the Good Friday Agreement* (Brussels, European Parliament Policy Department for Citizens' Rights and Constitutional Affairs, 2017); D Phinnemore, 'Northern Ireland – A "Place Between" in UK-EU Relations?' (2020) 25(4) *European Foreign Affairs Review* 631.

Crown Dependencies of the Isle of Man and Jersey and Guernsey. These national measures in effect treat citizens of each of the jurisdictions concerned as if they were domestic citizens, for certain purposes.[4] Chief among these purposes is crossing a border in the area ('travel'), but the Common Travel Area arrangements also include access to national healthcare services.

The 1998 Agreement is formally speaking two agreements. One is the result of multi-party talks and was agreed by most political parties in Northern Ireland.[5] The other is between the UK and Irish governments. The 1998 Agreement thus is a kind of blend of (domestic) constitutional and international law. It is constitutional law in that it sets out how Northern Ireland's law and policies are determined and the relationship between Northern Ireland and the UK government in Westminster. It is international law because it is an agreement between two countries: Ireland and the UK. The Agreement, implemented in the UK by the Northern Ireland Act 1998, sets up the Northern Ireland Assembly and Executive, as the centrepiece of a new constitutional arrangement for Northern Ireland. This arrangement involves devolved powers over a range of policy areas, including healthcare.[6] Matters such as foreign affairs and immigration however remain 'reserved' to the UK government in Westminster. Alongside these arrangements, which seek to build relationships within Northern Ireland, the 1998 Agreement also seeks to build 'North-South' relations (between Northern Ireland and Ireland)[7] and 'East-West' relations (between Great Britain and Ireland). The practical working out of these relationships incorporates a pre-existing partnership between the healthcare and social care services providers in the border areas on the island of Ireland, called Co-operation and Working Together (CAWT).

Bilateral cooperation between the UK and Ireland under the Common Travel Area and the 1998 Agreement covers a wide range of cross-border healthcare services. These include Accident and Emergency healthcare; mental health provision; children's health services; cancer care; and primary care from GPs. Many of these initiatives were and continue to be supported by CAWT. In 2018, Damien McCallion, then Director-General at CAWT, estimated that as many people were using these mechanisms to access cross-border healthcare on the island of Ireland as using EHIC, S2 and the other EU law mechanisms discussed in the previous chapter.[8]

Loss of the cross-border healthcare arrangements on the island of Ireland was one of the concerns strongly associated with a 'No Deal' Brexit. Cross-border healthcare is widely acknowledged to be one of the success stories of the 1998 Agreement.[9] An immediate rupture in continuity of legal relations between the EU and the UK

[4] See B Ryan, 'The Common Travel Area between Britain and Ireland' (2003) 64 *The Modern Law Review* 855.

[5] The political parties who signed the Agreement included the Ulster Unionist Party, the Social Democratic and Labour Party, Sinn Féin, the Alliance Party and the Progressive Unionist Party. The Democratic Unionist Party (DUP), which later became the largest unionist party, did not support the Agreement.

[6] Section 4, Schedules 2 and 3, Northern Ireland Act 1998.

[7] The Annex to Strand 2 of the Agreement, on the North South Ministerial Council, Point 11 covers 'Health – Accident and Emergency Services and Other Related Areas'.

[8] 'Brexit: Reciprocal Healthcare', *Thirteenth Report from the European Union Committee*, HL 107 (2017–2019), para 100.

[9] 'Brexit: UK-Irish Relations', *Sixth Report from the European Union Committee*, HL 76 (2016–17).

would have raised significant questions for continued cross-border healthcare provision. In particular, a reintroduction of a land border, the logical consequence of a 'No Deal' Brexit, would have stopped the people, goods and services associated with health service provision from moving freely, and also stopped patients from moving to receive health services on either side of the border.[10] These concerns were extremely well understood by those with the relevant expertise, and were among the matters that needed to be addressed in the Agreement between the EU and the UK on the terms of the UK's withdrawal from the EU, which included the Protocol on Ireland/Northern Ireland. As we will see over this chapter and those which follow, this Protocol was highly contentious, and continues to be so, including in ways which are important for health and the NHS on the island of Ireland.

Giving evidence to the House of Lords, Bernie McCrory, then Chief Officer at CAWT, expressed the view that patients themselves would not accept changes to cross-border healthcare services on the island of Ireland.[11] She elaborated these views when we interviewed her in 2019, stressing that having to stop at a border in an acute medical situation would literally be the difference between life and death for someone. She talked of an increasingly ageing population, dispersed across a very rural and already disadvantaged area. In this situation, it is essential to deploy scarce healthcare resources as effectively as possible, and that means allowing people to cross the border quickly when they need urgent care. For Bernie McCrory, it was simply unacceptable to contemplate going back to pre-1998 Agreement days:

> So, you can imagine … and I remember the border very well, Mark, if you had a child who was very sick and it was taking you half an hour to get through a checkpoint, you're not going to try and do it that way. No matter if it's 25 miles back, you will move towards Letterkenny hospital and [you're] not going to have to be stopped at the border and explain. … So, that for me, it would be that the patients who so routinely take, don't even think about it now, come across and get whatever their requirements met here, that we provide here and vice versa. …
>
> When you have a child who needs urgent cardiac surgery, a very much life-saving thing, then you know we would blue light them at the minute. But if you can't get through that border crossing, if you lose time, if they've had taken a cardiac arrest in the streets of Donegal town, by the time they were in [a hospital] they were dead.

Like many of the people we spoke with, both 'experts' and 'ordinary people', Bernie McCrory went on to relate her broader perceptions of the life-endangering risks of 'No Deal' Brexit to a personal story:

> … And my husband was one of those. He took a cardiac arrest last July and he was within 55 minutes from our farms in Donegal, and he was transported immediately to Altnagelvin where he was stented, and his life was saved. And that has happened to maybe

[10] 'Brexit and Health and Social Care – People & Process', *Eighth Report from the Health and Social Care Committee*, HC 640 (2016–17); 'Brexit: Reciprocal Healthcare', above n 8; N Fahy et al, 'How Will Brexit Affect Health and Health Services in the UK? Evaluating Three Possible Scenarios Against the WHO Health System Building Blocks' (2017) 390(10107) *The Lancet* 2110; N Fahy et al, 'How Will Brexit Affect Health and Health Services in the UK? An Updated Evaluation' (2019) 393(10174) *The Lancet* 949; M Tischkowitz et al, 'A No-Deal Brexit will be Detrimental to People with Rare Diseases' (2021) 397(10268) *The Lancet* 20.

[11] 'Brexit: Reciprocal Healthcare', above n 8, para 112.

> a hundred odd patients … So, you couldn't possibly impede an emergency vehicle. For me that's the single biggest challenge we need to resist, we need to make sure, we cannot allow to go back to when the emergency vehicles can't get through.

These sentiments were echoed by people with whom we talked on the street in Newry and Derry/Londonderry. Destroying cross-border health initiatives, we heard, would be 'a disaster'.[12] For the mother who described cross-border healthcare this way, the continuity of shared healthcare on the island of Ireland meant the difference between life and death for her child. Some people also felt that the benefits of EU membership for health, so critical for Northern Ireland, were invisible to the majority of the British public.[13]

We heard about emergency or EHIC care, like from the woman from Donegal who had been in France in 2018 with a friend who had a heart attack, and 'didn't pay a penny'.[14] But we also heard of the benefits, particularly to vulnerable people, of the economies of scale associated with shared healthcare facilities on the island for planned medical treatments. Some of these were also known in the public domain, especially the radiotherapy centre in the Western Trust at Altnagelvin Hospital, which opened in 2016 after being planned and co-funded by Northern Ireland and Ireland;[15] the children's Ear Nose and Throat service in the Southern Trust in Northern Ireland,[16] and, above all, Our Lady's Children's Hospital, Crumlin, Dublin, which serves the whole island.[17] We also heard about the 'health corridors' on the island, within which patients moved to find the quickest access to specialist medical treatments and the cheapest medicines.[18] Unlike in England, no one with whom we spoke felt that these arrangements meant that 'others' were 'taking up space' in 'their' NHS.

III. THE WITHDRAWAL AGREEMENT'S ARRANGEMENTS FOR CROSS-BORDER HEALTHCARE IN NORTHERN IRELAND

The worst outcomes in terms of cross-border healthcare on the island of Ireland were avoided by the Withdrawal Agreement. For Irish and UK nationals, the Common Travel Area arrangements secure continuity of many rights, irrespective of EU law. But that is not the case for the tens of thousands of citizens of the other 26 EU countries estimated to be resident in Northern Ireland, and the hundreds of thousands of non-Irish EU nationals estimated to be resident in Ireland.[19] The Withdrawal

[12] Derry 216A.

[13] Derry 159B.

[14] Derry 159B.

[15] 'Brexit: Reciprocal Healthcare', above n 8, para 103. Derry 185A.

[16] 'Brexit: Reciprocal Healthcare', above n 8, para 104.

[17] Interview with Bernie McCrory, April 2019; Newry 14A, 36A; Derry 185A, 213A.

[18] Newry 35A; Newry 41A; Derry 167A, 179A, 128B, 146B.

[19] See, eg, Border People, 'Brexit: The Complex New Boundaries Between Different Groups of Citizens in Northern Ireland', 14 January 2019 (https://borderpeople.info/media_news/brexit-the-complex-new-boundaries-between-different-groups-of-citizens-in-northern-ireland); Central Statistics Office, 'Population and Migration Estimates' (released on 20 August 2020)' (www.cso.ie/en/releasesandpublications/er/pme/populationandmigrationestimatesapril2020/ accessed 21 November 2022), cited in T Lock, 'A Common Travel Area? Brexit and the New (Northern) Irish' in C McCrudden (ed), *The Law and Practice of the Protocol on Ireland/Northern Ireland* (Cambridge, Cambridge University Press, 2022).

Agreement secured continuity, rather than immediate legal rupture, in two respects: first, during the transitional period until the end of 2020, and second, in its provisions on citizens' rights. These cover both EU/UK citizens and certain members of their family irrespective of citizenship. The rights include residence rights, and rights not to be discriminated against in work contexts, as well as coordination of social security, essentially the same as the EHIC and S2 provisions we explained in chapter five. This is how the Withdrawal Agreement links to cross-border healthcare on the island of Ireland.

The Withdrawal Agreement included permission for the UK and EU Member States to establish a 'constitutive system' of rights.[20] Under such a system, an individual is required to *formally apply* for a specific status, such as 'permanent resident in France', in order to enjoy rights under the Agreement.[21] Thirteen EU Member States, plus the UK, have chosen to establish a constitutive system under the Withdrawal Agreement. The remaining EU Member States, including Ireland,[22] operate a 'declaratory system', under which individuals who fall within the rights given by the Withdrawal Agreement automatically benefit from its rights. The combination of the UK's choice of a constitutive system and Ireland's choice of a declaratory system introduces an imbalance in terms of how individuals are required to behave so as to secure and enforce their rights under the Agreement. For instance, let us envisage two families of non-Irish EU citizens who are resident on either side of the border on the island of Ireland, perhaps a Polish family in Northern Ireland, and a Bulgarian family in Ireland. These families could live just a few hundred metres apart. In practice, as we have explained, they access healthcare on both sides of the border, depending on their particular healthcare needs. But their legal position is different: the Polish family must formally apply to secure their rights under the Withdrawal Agreement, the Bulgarian family need not do so. This does not matter in practice if the UK complies with the Withdrawal Agreement's obligations, but it does matter if the UK fails to do so (because UK recognition of rights under the Agreement is not automatic).

The UK's implementation of the Withdrawal Agreement included the 'settled status scheme', under which EU citizens and their families who have lived in the UK for five years or more are entitled to apply for 'settled status' which is a permission to remain indefinitely in the UK under UK immigration law. For eligible people who have not yet lived in the UK for five years, a 'pre-settled status' gives temporary permission to remain for five years, at which point an application for 'settled status' must be made.

In terms of individuals' entitlements to cross-border healthcare on the island of Ireland, EU nationals who were resident in Northern Ireland were thus entitled to

[20] Article 18 WA.

[21] See, eg S Fella et al, *UK-EU Withdrawal Agreement: Implementation of Citizens' Rights* Briefing Paper Number 9657, House of Commons Library, 2 November 2022; A Neville et al, *Implementation of the Withdrawal Agreement: Financial Provisions, Citizens Rights and the Northern Ireland Protocol* (Brussels, European Parliament Research Service, January 2022).

[22] European Commission, 'Residence Rights of UK Nationals and Their Family Members Under the Citizens' Rights Part of the Withdrawal Agreement – Overview of Implementation' (https://ec.europa.eu/info/sites/default/files/overview_ms_residence_rights.pdf accessed 21 November 2022).

apply for 'settled or pre-settled status', to secure their continued right to reside. By March 2021, over 79 000 people resident in Northern Ireland had applied, including significant numbers of Polish, Lithuanian and Romanian nationals.[23] Access to the NHS in Northern Ireland is residence-based, so for the majority of EU citizens within Northern Ireland, and their family members irrespective of nationality, continued access to cross-border healthcare flows from their continued access to healthcare provided by the NHS in Northern Ireland, as residents with settled status. Residents of Northern Ireland with Irish nationality, and residents of Ireland with British nationality, enjoy a right to reside under the Common Travel Area rules, and continue to have access to cross-border healthcare, via either the NHS in Northern Ireland, or the Irish NHS, on the basis of their residence. So in the majority of situations, the current legal position is one of practical continuity from pre-Brexit entitlements, even if the legal basis of entitlements is different.

But the arrangements under the Withdrawal Agreement, in their intersections with the Common Travel Area and the 1998 Agreement, create a complex array of categories of people living on the island of Ireland. We cannot be exhaustive here, and others like Colin Murray, Sylvie de Mars, Ben Warwick and Aoife O'Donoghue, Anthony Soares and Jeremy Bierbach have outlined in much greater detail the various permutations and practical consequences in healthcare and other contexts.[24] From the point of view of access to cross-border healthcare, though, a significant group of people are 'frontier workers' and their families. When we talked with people in Newry and Derry/Londonderry, we often heard about frontier working as a normal way of life, with the border being largely invisible.[25]

Frontier workers also enjoy rights under the Withdrawal Agreement. Frontier workers are defined in EU law as 'any person pursuing an activity as an employed or self-employed person in an EU country and who resides in another EU country to which he returns as a rule daily or at least once a week'.[26] That definition also applies under the Withdrawal Agreement,[27] and in the UK domestic law implementing it.[28] So EU nationals (whether Irish or nationals of another EU Member State)

[23] 'Over 79,000 EU Citizens in Northern Ireland Have Applied for UK's EU Settlement Scheme', Schengen Visa News, 16 March 2021 (www.schengenvisainfo.com/news/over-79000-eu-citizens-in-northern-ireland-have-applied-for-uks-eu-settlement-scheme/). A report from 2018 suggested a significant reduction in the numbers of EU-26 workers in Northern Ireland since 2016, see 'NI Sees 26% Drop in EU Workers Since Brexit Vote', BBC, 28 June 2018 (www.bbc.co.uk/news/uk-northern-ireland-44642297).

[24] See, eg, JB Bierbach, 'The "Person of Northern Ireland": A Vestigial Form of EU Citizenship?' (2021) 17(2) *European Constitutional Law Review* 232; Border People, 'Brexit', above n 19; S de Mars et al, *Continuing EU Citizenship 'Rights, Opportunities and Benefits' in Northern Ireland after Brexit* (Dublin and Belfast, Irish Human Rights and Equality Commission and Northern Ireland Human Rights and Equality Commission, March 2020); S de Mars and C Murray, 'With or Without EU?', above n 3, 819; G McKeever, 'Brexit, the Irish Border and Social Security Rights' (2018) 25(1) *Journal of Social Security Law* 34; A Schymyck, 'How Does Brexit Affect Irish Citizens in the UK?' (https://freemovement.org.uk/how-will-brexit-affect-irish-citizens/ accessed 21 November 2022).

[25] Newry 14A, 35A, 37A, 41A, 49A, 14B, 30B, 34B, 35B; Derry 161A, 167A, 173A 174A, 179A, 204A, 207A, 216A, 222A, 128B, 131B, 146B, 149B, 151B, 159B, 167B, 182B.

[26] Article 1(f), Directive 2004/38/EC of the European Parliament and of the Council of 29 April 2004 on the right of citizens of the Union and their family members to move and reside freely within the territory of the Member States [2004] OJ L 158/77.

[27] Article 9(b) WA.

[28] Regulation 3, Citizens' Rights (Frontier Workers) (EU Exit) Regulations 2020.

who were living in Ireland, but working or self-employed in Northern Ireland before the end of December 2020, are covered by the Withdrawal Agreement as frontier workers, for as long as they continue to do so.[29] Continuity of residence is defined by reference to EU law, and allows for absences of up to six months a year, and longer for important reasons such as giving birth.[30] Their family members are also covered, irrespective of their nationality.

Frontier workers have rights in EU law to access healthcare either where they work or where they live,[31] but in the case of some EU Member States (including Ireland, and formerly the UK), these rights do not extend to family members, except where the healthcare is necessary at a time when the family member is present in the EU Member State in which the frontier worker is working.[32] These rights are carried over under the Withdrawal Agreement.[33] The Withdrawal Agreement permits the UK to have a constitutive system for frontier workers' rights too, and the UK has introduced a frontier worker permit scheme. Irish citizens are permitted to apply, though they need not do so. The scheme not only covers the right to work in the UK (here Northern Ireland) or EU (here Ireland), but also, for a frontier worker resident in Ireland, to access to healthcare provided by the NHS in Northern Ireland; or for a frontier worker resident in Northern Ireland, to access healthcare provided by the Irish NHS.

IV. ARRANGEMENTS AFTER 1 JANUARY 2021

To add to the complexity, the EU-UK Trade and Cooperation Agreement's provisions on cross-border healthcare, discussed in the previous chapter, also need to be factored into the analysis. As we already explained, the EU-UK TCA meant that the UK was obliged to introduce a 'Global Health Insurance Card' (GHIC) which entitles patients to access necessary healthcare when they are in one of the 27 EU Member States (or Switzerland), so long as they have the necessary permission if the medical treatment is one of those listed. So this is another possible legal foundation for cross-border healthcare to take place on the island of Ireland.

BorderPeople,[34] a charity active in improving North-South relations on the island of Ireland, offered this summary of entitlements to cross-border healthcare for frontier workers in early December 2021. We have reproduced it in full, to give a sense of how complex, and therefore opaque, the rules are.

> *Healthcare for frontier workers – EU rights (Withdrawal Agreement)*
>
> If you are an Irish, British or EU citizen and you moved across the border or started a cross-border job by 31st December 2020 then the Withdrawal Agreement applies to you and EU social security rules will continue to apply to you.

[29] Article 10(1)(c) WA.

[30] Article 16(3), Directive 2004/38, above n 26.

[31] Articles 17 and 18, Regulation (EC) No 883/2004 of the European Parliament and of the Council of 29 April 2004 on the coordination of social security systems [2004] OJ L 166/1.

[32] Articles 17, 18, 19 and Annex III, ibid.

[33] Articles 30(1), (2) and (3), 31(1) WA.

[34] Border People, 'Healthcare for Frontier Workers – EU Rights (Withdrawal Agreement)', 7 December 2021 (https://borderpeople.info/a-z/healthcare-for-frontier-workers-eu-rights-withdrawal-agreement.html).

Under the EU rules frontier workers are entitled to healthcare both where they live and where they work.

Frontier workers living North, working South

- Are entitled to health care in NI, as they are legally resident in NI
- Are entitled to apply for an Irish Medical Card, subject to a means test

Frontier workers living South, working North

- Are entitled to a NI medical card, however, their spouse and children are not eligible
- Are eligible for free GP services
- Are eligible to register with a dentist
- Are eligible for maternity services from a GP, a midwife and an obstetrician in a hospital if necessary

If you belong to one of the following groups, you are also eligible for an Irish Medical Card under EU Regulations (without a means-test):

- You are living in Ireland and receiving a social security pension from another European Union /European Economic Area (EU/EEA) country or Switzerland and you are not getting an Irish social welfare payment (apart from Child Benefit or Early Childcare Supplement). You must not be liable to contribute to the Irish Social Welfare System, (i.e. PRSI)
- You are living in Ireland and working in another EU/EEA country or Switzerland and are liable to pay Social Insurance Contributions in that country
- You are living in Ireland and you are the dependent spouse or child of someone employed in another EU/EEA country and Switzerland. You must not be getting an Irish Social Welfare Payment apart from Child Benefit or Early Childcare Supplement and you must not be liable to contribute to the Irish social welfare system (PRSI).

For further information please visit the HSE website (opens in new tab)

Retired Cross-Border Workers

Retired cross border workers may be entitled to NHS healthcare for continued treatment of an existing condition.

Retired cross-border workers are no longer entitled to NI healthcare when they cease working in Northern Ireland. However, there is one important exemption to note: Under Article 28 of EU regulation 883/2004 cross-border workers who retire due to "old age or invalidity" are entitled to access continuing treatment for a condition for which they are already receiving services in Northern Ireland. Continuation of treatment is defined as "the continued investigation, diagnosis and treatment of an illness". However, retired cross border workers must access all other health services in the Republic of Ireland, it is only the continued treatment of a condition which can be provided for free in Northern Ireland. It is very important to clarify your situation with your GP and local Health Trust prior to retiring or moving across the border.

For further information please visit EU Coordination of social security systems – Regulation (EC) No 883/2004 – Search the document for Article 28.

The *BorderPeople* advice *only* covers entitlements under the Withdrawal Agreement and EU-UK Trade and Cooperation Agreement, and it *only* covers frontier workers. Notice that the gap in protection for family members of frontier workers is not filled by the EU-UK TCA.

But there is yet more complexity to understand. The entitlements to cross-border healthcare in the Withdrawal Agreement and EU-UK TCA are explicitly stated to be 'without prejudice to any arrangements made between the United Kingdom and Ireland concerning the Common Travel Area'.[35] So in order to understand the full picture for cross-border healthcare, we also need to factor in any entitlements that flow from the Common Travel Area arrangements.

The UK government Guidance on the frontier workers scheme, from April 2021, was much simpler, but, as we will see, rather incomplete, and also confusing in terms of its relationship with the Common Travel Area:[36]

> Irish citizens enjoy a right to work and reside in the UK which is not reliant on the UK's membership of the EU. This means Irish citizens do not need to apply for a frontier worker permit and do not need to hold one in order to enter the UK to work. Nonetheless, Irish citizens can make an application under the frontier worker permit scheme, should they wish to do so.[37]

The 'right to work and reside in the UK' mentioned here is a right under the Common Travel Area arrangements.[38] Rights to access healthcare flow from residence rights. When it comes to access to cross-border healthcare for non-residents in Northern Ireland, some of these are covered in Northern Irish law.[39] Equivalent provisions apply to access to the Irish NHS for non-residents, including entitlement to the Irish medical card.[40]

British patients resident in Ireland needing to access the shared healthcare facilities in Northern Ireland, and Irish patients resident in Northern Ireland who need to access shared healthcare facilities in Ireland, are thus protected by the Common Travel Area arrangements. This means that people resident on the island of Ireland who are not frontier workers continue to be able to access infrastructure such as the cancer service in Altnagelvin Hospital, or the children's autism centre; or the paediatric heart services in Our Lady's Children's Hospital, Dublin. This was confirmed in our policy engagements in autumn 2021: we heard, for example, that an Irish health professional, resident in Ireland, working in Ireland, had recently been referred by his GP for a scan in Northern Ireland, and the scan had taken place without him needing to show any entitlements under the Withdrawal Agreement or EU-UK TCA.

But there are some problems with this position. First is that access to cross-border healthcare flows from residence. The Common Travel Area arrangements only give residence rights to British and Irish nationals, not to nationals of other EU countries. So EU-26 nationals are obliged to comply with the UK's settled status scheme in order to secure their residence in Northern Ireland. Anyone vulnerable to not having secured settled status is therefore also vulnerable to loss of healthcare rights – for example, as Charlotte O'Brien has comprehensively shown, children, women, people

[35] Article SSC.4(2), Protocol on Social Security Cooperation, EU-UK TCA.

[36] See de Mars et al, *Continuing EU Citizenship*, above n 24, 65–67.

[37] Home Office, *Frontier Worker Permit Scheme Guidance. Version 2.0*, 1 April 2021, 9.

[38] See Immigration Act 1971, as amended by Immigration and Social Security Co-ordination (EU Withdrawal) Act 2020, Section 2 (2).

[39] Regulation 6, Provision of Health Services to Persons Not Ordinarily Resident Regulations (Northern Ireland) 2015.

[40] Department of Health and Social Care, Foreign and Commonwealth Office, and Foreign, Commonwealth and Development Office, 'Healthcare for UK Nationals Living in Ireland' (www.gov.uk/guidance/healthcare-in-ireland accessed 21 November 2022).

who are not IT literate, who do not read or write English, or who are vulnerable in other ways.[41] And as Sylvia de Mars and her collaborators have pointed out, frontier workers on the island of Ireland come from all socioeconomic classes.[42]

Second, the problem with 'rights' under the Common Travel Area arrangements is – to be brief – that not all aspects of the Common Travel Area can be understood as 'rights'. Some are administrative arrangements, policies or practices. Even by early 2022, we found that some of the arrangements for cross-border healthcare were not set out in formal law, but were simply taking place through administrative agreement.[43] One important example is the Northern Ireland Planned Healthcare Scheme and its companion the Republic of Ireland (ROI) Reimbursement Scheme. These schemes were set up in July 2021[44] to try to combat some of the backlog of planned surgeries which had arisen following the onset of the COVID-19 pandemic in early 2020. This kind of arrangement, where healthcare entitlements are not embodied in law, is obviously acceptable as long as everything works as it should at a practical or bureaucratic level. It becomes problematic when a patient is refused access to cross-border healthcare to which they are entitled. In that situation, a legal right that can be enforced is necessary.

Hervey's work for the Northern Ireland Human Rights Commission in 2021[45] threw up just one such example that had already taken place: but one where the lack of access to cross-border healthcare is concerning, and potentially a matter of life and death:

> A non-English speaking, BME, national of an EU-26 country gave birth to a premature baby in a hospital in Northern Ireland. The baby was critically ill, and was therefore transferred to the all-island children's heart unit in Dublin. It was unclear whether the mother would be able to go with the baby (in terms of her immigration status), or access the healthcare that she needed if she did go. The hospitals concerned adopted a very cautious position: initially suggesting the mother would need to pay for non-emergency aspects of her healthcare. The situation was resolved by the intervention of an NGO, which was able to send staff to both the Belfast and Dublin hospitals to advocate for the mother and her child.

But there are other examples where loss of rights to healthcare has the potential to leave vulnerable people worse off than before Brexit. Child victims of human

[41] See, for instance, C O'Brien, 'Between the Devil and the Deep Blue Sea: Vulnerable EU Citizens Cast Adrift in the UK Post-Brexit' (2021) 58(2) *Common Market Law Review* 431.

[42] de Mars et al, *Continuing EU Citizenship*, above n 24, 66.

[43] See M O'Connor et al, Assistant Secretary General, R&D and Health Analytics Division, Department of Health, 'Opening Statement to Seanad Special Select Committee on the Withdrawal of the UK from the EU', 30 September 2021 (https://data.oireachtas.ie/ie/oireachtas/committee/dail/33/seanad_special_committee_on_the_withdrawal_of_the_united_kingdom_from_the_european_union/submissions/2021/2021-10-19_opening-statement-muiris-o-connor-et-al-assistant-secretary-general-r-d-and-health-analytics-division-department-of-health_en.pdf). On the general legal status and 'significant shortcomings' of common travel area 'rights', see de Mars and Murray, 'With or Without EU?' above n 3, 819; McKeever, above n 24.

[44] Health and Social Care (Northern Ireland), 'The Health Services Republic of Ireland Reimbursement Scheme – Latest Guidance and Application Form' (https://online.hscni.net/travelfortreatment/roi-reimbursement/ accessed 21 November 2022).

[45] T Hervey, *Brexit, Health and Its Potential Impact on Article 2 of the Ireland/Northern Ireland Protocol* (Belfast, Northern Ireland Human Rights Commission, 2022).

trafficking in Northern Ireland are a case in point. Under EU law,[46] trafficked children have a right to access necessary medical care, including mental healthcare for psychological disorders, and healthcare arising from a possible pregnancy, while criminal proceedings are underway.[47] The UK government took the view that no changes to national law were necessary to secure compliance with the new EU law on child trafficking; the European Commission disagreed. This disagreement remained unresolved at the end of the transition period, during which the then current rules continued to apply. Thereafter, the matter is covered by domestic law, including rights under the Withdrawal Agreement, including the Ireland/Northern Ireland Protocol, annexed to that Agreement. The law in Northern Ireland does give rights to free emergency healthcare and family planning services, for anyone present in Northern Ireland.[48] But no specific law applicable in Northern Ireland gives trafficked children rights to access non-emergency treatment for psychological trauma, or maternity care or abortion services. Before the UK left the EU, a trafficked child seeking to access that type of healthcare would have been able to rely on a right in EU law.

The European Union (Withdrawal) Act, section 4, retains 'rights … which, immediately before [31 December 2020 – the end of the transition period] are recognised and available in domestic law by virtue of section 2(1) of the European Communities Act 1972, and are enforced, allowed and followed accordingly'.[49] But what is the legal position of rights like those in the EU law on human trafficking where there was a dispute between the European Commission and the UK government about whether the rights were already part of UK law or not? Are they covered by section 4? This is unclear.[50]

To summarise, the arrangements for cross-border healthcare on the island of Ireland are legally opaque: at least as matters stand in winter 2022. The Withdrawal Agreement and EU-UK TCA do not completely continue the previous arrangements under EU law. It is not clear whether the Common Travel Area fills the gaps, at least for British and Irish people. It certainly does not do so for people from the other 26 EU Member States. Even if the Common Travel Area fills the gaps, Common Travel Area arrangements are not in the form of *rights* to access cross-border healthcare. In the past, EU law had offered cross-border healthcare as *rights*.

[46] Article 11, Directive 2011/36/EU of the European Parliament and of the Council of 5 April 2011 on preventing and combating trafficking in human beings and protecting its victims, and replacing Council Framework Decision 2002/629/JHA [2011] OJ L 101/1.

[47] Article 11(5) and (7), ibid.

[48] Regulation 4(1), Provision of Services to Persons Not Ordinarily Resident Regulations (Northern Ireland) 2015.

[49] Section 4, European Union (Withdrawal) Act 2018, as amended by European Union (Withdrawal Agreement) Act 2020 and the Nationality and Borders Act 2022.

[50] The lack of clarity ('there is confusion which requires remedy', para 3.3) has been noted in Northern Ireland Human Rights Commission and Equality Commission for Northern Ireland, *Joint NIHRC / ECNI Briefing Paper on the Modern Slavery and Human Trafficking and Electronic Travel Authorisation provisions in the Nationality and Borders Bill*, 27 January 2022. Section 68, Nationality and Borders Act 2022 (not yet in force) explicitly disapplies retained EU law deriving from the EU Trafficking Directive 2011/36/EU, above n 46.

V. THE 'NO DIMINUTION OF HUMAN RIGHTS' RULE IN THE PROTOCOL

The complexity of the legal position here, and the fact that there are – or at least seem to be from the publicly available records – gaps in access to healthcare on the island of Ireland that had arisen from the Brexit settlement under the Withdrawal Agreement led us to consider whether these gaps might be protected by a different part of the Withdrawal Agreement: the Protocol on Ireland/Northern Ireland.

The Protocol is annexed to the Withdrawal Agreement and has the same legal status as the Agreement itself. As we will see in chapter eight, the settlement for movement of products between Great Britain and Northern Ireland, and between Northern Ireland and Ireland/the EU, reached in the Protocol by the Johnson government, has continued to be a source of political tension into late 2022, as we write. These tensions have ramifications for supply of the medicines and other products that the NHS in Northern Ireland needs to provide care for its patients. But the Protocol also at least potentially has ramifications for the cross-border healthcare provisions in place on the island of Ireland, especially those aspects relating to the shared healthcare infrastructure. To understand this potential, we need to begin with analysis of the Belfast/Good Friday Agreement 1998.

As we explained, the 1998 Agreement supports, among several areas for cooperation between entities in Northern Ireland and Ireland, 'Cooperation and Working Together' (CAWT) in healthcare. Most of CAWT's activities take place in border areas on the island of Ireland, but there are also EU-funded collaborations with the NHS in Scotland. CAWT is widely regarded as one of the success stories of the 1998 Agreement. The 1998 Agreement also has a section entitled 'Rights, Safeguards and Equality of Opportunity'. In this section, the parties to the Agreement affirm their commitment to the human rights of 'everyone in the community'.

The preamble to the Ireland/Northern Ireland Protocol states that the Protocol protects the 1998 Agreement 'in its entirety'. The preamble is not a source of binding obligations, but it does assist in interpreting the binding rules in the Protocol. Article 2 of the Protocol *is* legally binding. Its legal text is quite complex, and opaque in several respects:

> Article 2(1) The United Kingdom shall ensure that no diminution of rights, safeguards and equality of opportunity as set out in that part of the 1998 Agreement entitled Rights, Safeguards and Equality of Opportunity results from its withdrawal from the Union, including in the area of protection against discrimination as enshrined in the provisions of Union law listed in Annex 1 to this Protocol, and shall implement this paragraph through dedicated mechanisms.

The 'dedicated mechanisms' part of Article 2 has been brought into effect by obliging the Northern Ireland Human Rights Commission[51] and the Equality Commission for Northern Ireland to monitor implementation of Article 2 of the

[51] Sections 69(1) and 78A, Northern Ireland Act 1998, as amended by European Union (Withdrawal Agreement) Act 2020, Schedule 3.

Protocol. But what does 'no diminution of rights' mean? How should the part of the 1998 Agreement entitled 'Rights, Safeguards and Equality of Opportunity' be interpreted? Who is in 'the community' which it protects? And what does it mean to say no diminution of rights 'results from' the UK leaving the EU? As Northern Ireland specialists like Katy Hayward, Colin Harvey and Chris McCrudden[52] have pointed out, none of these questions is legally (or politically) settled. We cannot elaborate the considerable academic and policy debate on these questions in general – but we do explain our views on what they might mean for cross-border healthcare.

We wonder whether the Protocol's Article 2 might be the basis of continued rights to cross-border healthcare on the island of Ireland. One possible view is that the right to healthcare on the island of Ireland includes the right to avail oneself of an integrated all-island health system. That right was previously underpinned by EU law – this is no longer the case. If it is accepted that the right to health is covered by the relevant part of the 1998 Agreement, any change in entitlements consequent on Brexit constitutes a diminution of rights under the Protocol. We have outlined several changes above, and Hervey outlined others in her work for the Northern Ireland Human Rights Commission. This view of what the Protocol might mean for cross-border healthcare on the island of Ireland is obviously untested.

Thinking more broadly, the mismatch between the messaging from the UK government about the Protocol and the changes on the ground on the island of Ireland is troubling. The narratives from the UK government are to the effect that the integrated healthcare system on the island of Ireland is not changed, or challenged, by Brexit, and that there is nothing problematic or controversial about the effects of the Protocol on healthcare services. (The narratives about problems are all about supply of *goods* – including medicines – we will discuss those issues in chapter eight.) In the larger political debates on Brexit, especially, but not only, in Northern Ireland, health is merely incidental.

Our research – and that of many others – suggests otherwise. Healthcare is not incidental to the Brexit process: it is a matter of central concern. Especially in Northern Ireland, specific measures would have been necessary to ensure that healthcare did not suffer as a result of the UK leaving the EU. Plenty of evidence and analysis, from 2016 onwards, outlined what would be necessary to provide legal, political and administrative continuity and clarity. But the UK government did not follow through on that advice. Across all of our data – whether it is from health policy experts, conversations in the street in Northern Ireland, or 'vox pops' from Belfast for our project film – as one might expect, health is a central and core priority. It is particularly so for the border communities with whom we talked in Newry and Derry/Londonderry. But because health was seen as incidental in the broader politics of Brexit, it could be – and was – sacrificed to larger political aims.

[52] McCrudden (ed), *The Law and Practice of the Protocol on Ireland/Northern Ireland*, above n 3.

VI. CONCLUSION

The overall message of this chapter is that, even by winter 2022, the legal position in Northern Ireland on cross-border healthcare is complex, opaque and therefore very difficult to understand. At the same time, though, there is little evidence that major changes have taken place in practice: what seems to be happening is a kind of continuity that is operating at a practical level outside of or despite the legal position. We, along with Liz Speakman,[53] have called this situation one of 'alegality'. What we mean by 'alegality' is related to, but different from, the well-known gap between 'law in the books' and 'law in action', as described over 100 years ago by the legal scholar Roscoe Pound,[54] and built on by 'law and society' or socio-legal scholars ever since. What we mean is that there are situations where there appears to be no agreed or accepted applicable law, but ongoing practice in that legal vacuum as if there were. As we have already noted, this may be acceptable so long as everything continues to function smoothly, but it becomes unacceptable when someone is refused access to healthcare to which they are actually entitled.

The main changes in cross-border healthcare in Northern Ireland are a movement away from the legal solidity of EU law and the enforceable rights it offers, along with the administrative and other legal structures that support it. Instead, we see a movement toward a patchwork of less legally secure arrangements. These include the service level administrative agreements that underpin the Northern Ireland Planned Healthcare Scheme; the Common Travel Area rules; and, possibly, Article 2 of the Ireland/Northern Ireland Protocol. Each of these offers something less than EU law. Service level administrative agreements are time-bound and not enforceable as individual rights. The Common Travel Area rules do not apply to everyone covered by the NHS in Northern Ireland, are revisable national law, and indeed there is no conclusive and easily discoverable list of what the provisions are. The Protocol is unusually opaque as a legal text, making it almost impossible to know what it means for patients seeking cross-border healthcare, and is yet to come fully into effect and may never do so, given the political contentions that surround it.

The contemporary legal precariousness of cross-border healthcare in the island of Ireland is at odds with our data on what people want for post-Brexit health governance. Both the 'experts' and 'ordinary' people whom we discussed health and the NHS post-Brexit in Northern Ireland shared a complex understanding of the island of Ireland as a fragile, but functioning, debordered space. There was no sense that people from Ireland receiving healthcare in Northern Ireland were perceived as somehow 'other', as EU citizens, and therefore should be excluded from access to healthcare. Instead, there was a strong sense of shared healthcare infrastructure, and of 'health corridors' through which people access the healthcare they need on either side of the border, depending on convenience and cost. The vast majority of people

[53] T Hervey and EM Speakman, 'The Immediate Futures of EU Health Law in the UK after Brexit: Law, "Alegality" and Uncertainty' (2018) 18(2–3) *Medical Law International* 65.

[54] R Pound, 'Law in Books and Law in Action' (1910) 44(1) *American Law Review* 12.

we talked with expressed concern, or even fear, that this precious and precarious way of life would be lost as the UK's relationships with the EU unfolded. Cross-border healthcare provision was just one aspect of the fragility of cross-border lifestyles that are fundamentally changed by Brexit.

As we write in winter 2022, the position in Northern Ireland is also fragile for another reason. Disputes over the Ireland/Northern Ireland Protocol mean that there is currently no functioning Executive or Assembly in Stormont. The practical effects of that are a paralysis in terms of decision-making in a range of areas where Northern Ireland has devolved powers: health and social care is one of those.

7

NHS Staffing

I. INTRODUCTION

ON 25 JUNE 2016, the day after the EU referendum result, Nottingham University Hospitals NHS Trust wrote to every one of its EU national staff, reassuring them that they are still valued, and hoping that they would remain. Dr Charlotte Goedvolk, a Consultant Paediatrician, recalled in a Channel 4 report which aired in September 2016:[1]

> I actually felt really really upset and hurt. Because for me Brexit has changed something. Life is going on as normal, and I'm still doing my job. But actually maybe I'm not wanted here.

Dr Goedvolk qualified in medicine in the Netherlands, in 2003, and came to the UK in 2005. She has worked in several English hospitals, including in Birmingham, Cambridge, Huntington, Manchester and Warrington. She is one of around 15 per cent per cent of NHS staff in England who are (or were in 2016) not UK citizens.[2] She spoke not only for highly-qualified and well-paid people working within the English NHS:

> It shouldn't be just because I'm a consultant in critical care I can stay. Other people from Europe bring just as much contribution. A lot of our cleaners and support staff are from Europe and I can't do my job without them.

So far, we have considered the position of people who relied on EU law to *receive* healthcare. The focus of this chapter is on the people who *provide* healthcare. Because of the close connections between healthcare and social care, and because health and social care are an integrated system in Northern Ireland, we discuss both the NHS and the social care workforce, though our main focus is the NHS. What do the law and policy changes that flow from Brexit mean for people like Dr Goedvolk, for the people she spoke for, and more broadly, for staffing in the NHS and in social care across the UK? As we will explain, answering this question is made more complicated by the COVID-19 pandemic, the effects of which are extremely difficult to disentangle from those of Brexit.

[1] 'What Does the Future Hold for EU NHS staff?', Channel 4 News, 11 September 2016 (www.facebook.com/watch/?v=10154046588376939).

[2] C Baker, *NHS Staff from Overseas: Statistics*, Commons Library Research Briefing 7783, House of Commons Library, 20 September 2021.

II. BEFORE THE WITHDRAWAL AGREEMENT

The potential effect on NHS and social care staffing was one of the early concerns that emerged in the aftermath of the EU referendum vote. A significant amount of expert evidence[3] showed that any changes to law or policy that resulted in EU national NHS staff, or social care staff, *leaving* the UK would have huge, and potentially seriously detrimental, consequences for the care that the NHS is able to offer. When we asked an NHS employee who preferred to remain anonymous, in our film, how it would affect her as a nurse, if we were to lose European nationals who are nurses from the NHS, her immediate response was 'We can't afford to lose anyone else. We really can't.'[4] We heard this concern in some of our conversations in the street too, for example with a woman from Newry who worked in the NHS.[5] Furthermore, any law or policy that made it more difficult to recruit *new* NHS or social care staff from the EU would also be detrimental to the NHS. Kate Ling, from the NHS Confederation, confirmed that the most concerning aspect, even by March 2019, was the uncertainty:[6]

> I don't think I would be inclined to get a job in the UK, not knowing what the future is going to hold. So uncertainty, I think, is worse than knowing. … So, for example, people who come from America or Australia or whatever, they know what they have to do, they know they have to get visas and this, that and the other. So long as you know, that's not necessarily a deterrent, but actually not knowing what's going to happen one way or the other, and how it's going to affect, for example, your dependents, your family. … That's number one [worrying aspect of Brexit].

Uncertainty was also the biggest concern for Margaret Hynds O'Flanaghan, of CORU, the health and social care professionals regulator in Dublin, when we spoke with her in May 2019.

In 2016, in England, around 10 per cent of NHS hospital doctors, around 7.5 per cent of nurses and health visitors, nearly 5 per cent of scientific, therapeutic and technical staff and around 1.5 per cent of ambulance staff, were from EU countries.[7]

[3] 'Brexit and Health and Social Care – People & Process', *Eighth Report from the Health and Social Care Committee*, HC 640 (2016–17). See also, J Beech et al, *Closing the Gap. Key Areas for Action on the Health and Care Workforce*, The Health Foundation, The King's Fund, Nuffield Trust, March 2019; M Dayan et al, *Understanding the Impact of Brexit on Health in the UK*, Nuffield Trust, December 2020; N Fahy et al, 'How Will Brexit Affect Health and Health Services in the UK? Evaluating Three Possible Scenarios Against the WHO Health System Building Blocks' (2017) 390(10107) *The Lancet* 2110; N Fahy et al, 'How Will Brexit Affect Health and Health Services in the UK? An Updated Evaluation' (2019) 393(10174) *The Lancet* 949; Nuffield Trust, 'Brexit and Health and Social Care' submitted to the Health Select Committee Inquiry, November 2016 (www.nuffieldtrust.org.uk/files/2017-05/brexit-submission-to-health-select-committee-formatted-final.pdf); UK in a Changing Europe, *No Deal Brexit: Issues, Impacts, Implications* (London, UK in a Changing Europe, 4 September 2019), 25–26; UK in a Changing Europe, *Cost of a No Deal Revisited* (London, UK in a Changing Europe, 3 September 2018).

[4] Shout Out UK, *Brexit, Health & Me*, 2020.

[5] Newry 36A.

[6] Also confirmed in a 2018 British Medical Association survey of EEA doctors in the UK, discussed in Paul Laffin Interview, May 2019: '… asked them what Brexit means to them. Uncertainty, and uncertainty translates into over a third of them considering leaving the UK'. See British Medical Association, *Brexit Briefing: The Medical Workforce and Future Immigration Policy*, London, 2018.

[7] Baker, *NHS Staff from Overseas*, above n 2.

Figures for Northern Ireland, Scotland, Wales were less widely reported, but in its submission to the 2017 Parliamentary Inquiry on *Brexit and Health and Care: People & Process*,[8] the Nuffield Trust[9] reported some relevant information from outside England. General Medical Council data showed 11 per cent of doctors across the UK had qualified in an EU/EEA country – a number greater than all the doctors in Scotland and Wales put together. Around 7 per cent of the nursing workforce across the UK as a whole were born in the EU. In 2016, the trends in NHS staffing – and especially in nursing – were to increase reliance on people from EU countries. Over 30 per cent of new nursing recruits in 2015 were from EU countries, a figure which had been going up since 2008.[10]

These general figures hide significant variations across the UK. London and the South East of England had – and still have – higher proportions of EU nationals than other parts of England. Parts of Scotland were also particularly vulnerable to loss of EU national staff. When we interviewed Dr Philippa Whitford, MP for Central Ayrshire, who is also a breast surgeon, in 2019, she was concerned about the Scottish Highlands and Islands. One quarter of GPs in the Shetland Islands were EU nationals, she told us; perhaps as many as 10 per cent of social care staff in remote rural places in Scotland;[11] and she had been told that, in the Western Isles Hospital, in Stornoway in the Outer Hebrides, 11 of the 12 consultants were EU nationals. We sought to check that specific figure, but did not receive a reply to our query. Nonetheless, the point stands that parts of the UK were more vulnerable than others in terms of EU nationals among NHS and social care staff. And of course, as we discussed in the last chapter, the health and social care systems on the island of Ireland are highly integrated, with an unknown number, but many, staff working across the border as if it were not there.[12]

Karen Murray, from the Royal College of Midwives, whom we interviewed in Belfast in May 2019, spoke of the benefits to the healthcare workforce in Northern Ireland of the border settlement following the Belfast/Good Friday Agreement 1998, and the underpinning of EU law to the open border on the island of Ireland:

> We would have community midwives working in and around Newry, who in the course of a day may cross the border half a dozen times … never once do they think, 'I need to think about car insurance, I need to think about a driving licence, I need to consider having ID with me, passport or anything else'. … Since the Good Friday Agreement, those checkpoints are gone, and it's just a road. … [Previously], some of those roads that I'm now saying healthcare workers will drive up and down because they need to access various places, were either blocked because they were purposely blown up and there was a crater in them so you couldn't drive down them, or you had great big concrete water pipes filled with concrete blocking the road.

[8] 'Brexit and Health and Social Care – People & Process', above n 3.

[9] Nuffield Trust, 'Brexit and Health and Social Care', above n 3.

[10] Ibid, 4.

[11] Scottish Government, *The Contribution of Non-UK EU Workers in the Social Care Workforce in Scotland*, June 2018.

[12] Interview with Bernie McCrory, April 2019; Interview with Margaret Hynds O'Flanagan, May 2019; Interview with Paul Laffin, May 2019.

Before the Withdrawal Agreement, there was also significant uncertainty about how information about whether health professionals working across the border on the island of Ireland are fit to practise would be able to be shared, if the UK were not recognised by the EU as 'adequate' under its data protection law, the General Data Protection Regulation (GDPR). Margaret Hynds O'Flanaghan explained how EU Member States share information on professional qualifications through the Internal Market Information System, and that she was worried that, without access to that system, it would be significantly more difficult to make checks on health professionals working across the border, potentially jeopardising health outcomes for patients because of delays in recruiting staff.

Overall, the UK has had an exceptionally high reliance on doctors from other countries, compared to other countries of a similar level of development.[13] Those non-national staff on whom the NHS relies are not only from EU Member States: they are also from countries like India, the Philippines or Nigeria. Some of the reasons for this trend, other than domestic law and policy choices, include that the UK is an English-speaking country, and English is the language of international medicine; and also the UK's strong research record in life sciences more generally, making the UK an attractive place to make a biomedical career in research and clinical roles. We discuss the position of the UK in that regard in chapter nine.

The potential changes in the UK's relationship with the EU that would affect NHS and social care staffing were not only the ability of health and care staff to come to the UK and reside there, with their families. Ending free movement of workers and freedom of establishment would mean that everyone – including NHS and social care staff – would be required to comply with whatever new immigration regime the UK brought in. Removing EU law rights meant removing rights not to be discriminated against on nationality grounds. This would be the case both for EU nationals who were already in the UK, and when entering the UK, except, as we saw in the last chapter, Irish nationals, who could rely on the Common Travel Area rules. EU law not only gives equal access to enter and reside in another EU Member State with home nationals. It also gives a raft of rights including access to employment; the right to have EU qualifications recognised (subject to language competency); housing and other benefits; education for a migrant's children (including university education); access to healthcare; the ability to build up a pension and draw on it wherever a migrant chooses to retire in the EU; and some voting rights, such as in local elections. These rights in EU law amount to the detail of *EU citizenship*, a legal but also symbolic category of inclusion, which was removed from all UK nationals on Brexit, and is no longer recognised in UK law. To us, when Dr Goedvolk says that perhaps after all she 'isn't wanted' in England any more, she is evoking more than the loss of rights, she is evoking the loss of a status of belonging. Some of our EU national academic colleagues also said as much to us, about how they were feeling at the time.[14]

[13] J Buchan et al, *Health Professional Mobility in a Changing Europe*, Observatory Study Series 32 (Copenhagen, European Observatory on Health Systems and Policies, 2014).

[14] K Nicolaïdis, *Exodus, Reckoning, Sacrifice: Three Meanings of Brexit* (London, The Unbound Press, 2019).

By May 2017, in the run up to the General Election, the independent King's Fund reported that the referendum vote was already having an impact on NHS and social care staffing, even though the UK had not yet left the EU.[15] These effects were particularly stark in nursing: the number of EU nationals registering as nurses in the UK fell by 96 per cent compared to in 2016.[16] There was also a fall in EU nationals as new recruits in the social care sector. Whether these figures were attributable to Brexit was disputed: for example it seems likely that changes in the rules for nursing bursaries also played a role.[17]

III. THE WITHDRAWAL AGREEMENT, EU-UK TCA AND SETTLED STATUS SCHEME

As we explained in chapters five and six, the Withdrawal Agreement provided the legal basis for the UK to implement a new migration policy. For EU-26 nationals already resident in the UK (Irish nationals could rely on the Common Travel Area), the relevant new law is the 'settled status scheme'.[18] EU citizens and their families who have lived in the UK for five years or more are entitled to apply for 'settled status'. This status, or its precursor, 'pre-settled status', became available for people like Dr Goedvolk, and the hundreds of thousands of NHS and social care staff across the UK who are EU nationals, and their families. Legally speaking, settled and pre-settled status give permission to remain indefinitely in the UK under UK immigration law.

As an alternative, some EU nationals were able to successfully apply for UK citizenship. This is available to non-nationals who have been continuously resident in the UK for five years, and have a form of 'indefinite leave to remain', either because of settled status, or another form of such permission. A UK citizenship application costs around £1400 for an adult, and just over £1000 for a child. This is a significant proportion (18 per cent) of net family income for a family of four on an average nurse's salary of around £34,000 a year.[19] We do not have figures on how many NHS or social care staff have become UK citizens since the EU referendum, but we imagine that this is a route that only more highly paid people working in the sector have taken.

The settlement between the UK and the EU embodied in the Withdrawal Agreement gave the possibility for NHS and social care staff, and their families, to experience continuity in residence rights, and in the many rights that flow from residence. These include access to education, social benefits, housing and so on. But there are still some gaps left. One concerns professional qualifications. The other concerns employment rights.

[15] The Kings Fund, 'Big Election Questions: the Brexit Workforce', May 2017, no longer accessible; see also C Ham, 'The General Election, the NHS, and Social Care' (2017) 357 *British Medical Journal* j2840.

[16] S Lintern, 'Exclusive: "Crash" in EU Nurses Working in UK Since Brexit Referendum', Health Service Journal, 12 June 2017.

[17] Department of Health and Social Care, *NHS Bursary Reform*, Policy Paper, 27 January 2017.

[18] Section 1, Immigration Act 1971; Section 7, European Union (Withdrawal Agreement) Act 2020, and the Immigration Rules, Appendix EU.

[19] Nurses, 'The UK Nursing Salary and Pay Scale Guide – 2022' (www.nurses.co.uk/careers-hub/nursing-pay-guide/ accessed 21 November 2022); Net Salary Calculator, 'Net Salary Calculator UK 2022' (www.netsalarycalculator.co.uk/34000-after-tax/ accessed 21 November 2022).

First, in terms of professional qualifications, EU law[20] provides for automatic recognition across the EU, the EEA and Switzerland of the qualifications for certain regulated professions. These include doctors, general care (not specialist) nurses, midwives, pharmacists and dentists. Other professions are covered by a system of recognition that is not automatic, but legally requires recognition of regulated professions, or where the differences between professions in the two countries are significant, allows for recognition after a period of adaptation or an aptitude test. The measures make it much easier for healthcare professionals to move around the EU/EEA/Switzerland, making those countries a more appealing place to make a career, and easing recruitment processes. These rules applied to recognition of EU qualifications by the UK until 31 December 2020. After that, the EU-UK Trade and Cooperation Agreement (EU-UK TCA) makes no provision for continuity.[21] There is an option in the EU-UK TCA for possible future collaboration, and mutual recognition agreements between the UK and individual EU Member States, using an institution set up by the EU-UK TCA called the Partnership Council.[22] This is obviously significantly less convenient than EU law, and has not yet been used.

For continuity, the UK government unilaterally decided to continue to recognise EU/EEA medical qualifications. Those professionals who were already registered were not required to take any action. Professionals coming to the UK to work in the NHS after 31 December 2020 could have their EEA qualifications recognised by 'similar' processes to EU law.[23] Obviously these policies only provide temporary certainty: they take the form of Guidance and can be removed or changed at any time, following only a ministerial decision. In our interviews, we heard concerns about drift in common health training standards, eventually meaning that student and trainee health professionals would choose somewhere other than the UK, because they felt their experience would be less valued than equivalent experience in a hospital in the EU.[24] In addition, for the island of Ireland, the relevant professional organisations have exchanged memoranda of understanding, to the effect that they will continue to recognise each other's training and qualifications.[25] Neither of these legal positions have the same certainty, or enforceability, as EU law, but they do provide practical continuity. Furthermore, the UK is no longer part of the EU Internal Market Information system through which information about medical malpractice is shared between countries[26] – a system which became crucial when various countries, especially

[20] Directive 2005/36/EC of the European Parliament and of the Council of 7 September 2005 on the recognition of professional qualifications [2005] OJ L 255/22.

[21] Article 158 EU-UK TCA.

[22] Article 158 EU-UK TCA.

[23] Department of Health and Social Care, 'EEA-Qualified and Swiss Healthcare Professionals Practising in the UK', 31 December 2020 (www.gov.uk/guidance/eea-qualified-and-swiss-healthcare-professionals-practising-in-the-uk).

[24] Interview with Bernie McCrory, April 2019; Interview with Karen Murray, May 2019.

[25] See, eg, S Ford, 'Unions Sign Unique Deal Designed to "Brexit proof midwives"', The Nursing Times, 22 January 2018.

[26] Part of the Internal Market Information System, see Regulation (EU) No 1024/2012 of the European Parliament and of the Council of 25 October 2012 on administrative cooperation through the Internal Market Information System and repealing Commission Decision 2008/49/EC ('the IMI Regulation') [2012] OJ L 316/1.

England, used NHS staff from other countries on a temporary basis. The UK ceased registering healthcare professionals qualified in EU/EEA countries for temporary and occasional services at the end of December 2020.[27] The exclusion of the UK from that system is also problematic in Ireland, given the numbers of UK-qualified health professionals working in Ireland, and indeed providing healthcare in Northern Ireland.[28]

Second, in terms of employment rights, a great deal of UK employment law comes from the EU. Across the sector, but especially in nursing and social care, health and safety at work laws provide employees with important rights, for instance to protection from musculoskeletal conditions arising from manual handling. Some EU laws are specific to the healthcare sector, like the law on protection from medical 'sharps' – instruments like needles which can cut, prick or cause injury or infection.[29] The Working Time Directive offers significant protections from long hours at work: junior doctors in England negotiated the terms of EU law as part of their contracts in 2016.[30] Several healthcare professional organisations, such as the Royal College of Nursing,[31] have pointed out that these EU laws not only protect NHS and social care staff – they also make an important contribution to patient safety.

Many of these EU employment laws take the form of Directives. Member States are formally obliged by Directives to achieve a legal outcome, but the Directive itself does not specify how that outcome should be achieved. When it was an EU Member State, much of the UK's employment law flowed from EU Directives. The law could be relied on by individual employees in a court or tribunal, as well as being enforced by the Health and Safety Executive. Any parts of EU law which were not already part of UK law in that way automatically became part of UK law on 31 December 2020, under the European Union (Withdrawal) Act 2018.[32]

The extent to which UK law that was required when the UK was an EU country – called 'retained EU law' – can and will be changed in the future has been much debated. Kenneth Armstrong[33] explains that the time dimension to the Brexit process is important here: an initial unilateral alignment by the UK does not necessarily mean longer term alignment with the EU. But the EU has a track record of influencing

[27] Department of Health and Social Care, 'EEA-Qualified and Swiss Healthcare Professionals Practising in the UK', above n 23. Paul Laffin of the British Medical Association told us of a Romanian surgeon, with 30 years' experience, who worked between Romania and London: 'If free movement stops, if mutual recognition stops, if life becomes too difficult for him … he'll choose one of those jurisdictions'. Interview with Paul Laffin, May 2019.

[28] Interview with Margaret Hynds O'Flannaghan, May 2019; interview with Paul Laffin, May 2019.

[29] Council Directive 2010/32/EU of 10 May 2010 implementing the Framework Agreement on prevention from sharp injuries in the hospital and healthcare sector concluded by HOSPEEM and EPSU [2010] OJ L 134/66.

[30] Directive 2003/88/EC of the European Parliament and of the Council of 4 November 2003 concerning certain aspects of the organisation of working time [2003] OJ L 299/9; Section 10, NHS Terms and Conditions of Service Handbook.

[31] Royal College of Nursing, Briefing for 'Exiting the EU and Workers' Rights', Hansard, HC Vol 616, cols 1302-64 (7 December 2016).

[32] Sections 3 and 4, EU (Withdrawal) Act 2018. Provisions in EU Directives, which is the form taken by much of this law, were already implemented in UK law, as required.

[33] KA Armstrong, 'Regulatory Alignment and Divergence After Brexit' (2018) 25(8) *Journal of European Public Policy* 1099.

regulatory decisions in countries that are not in the EU,[34] so we might expect at least some influences to continue. This is the case especially because of the position in Northern Ireland. Hussein Kassim and colleagues[35] have pointed out that 'regulatory divergence' does not get much public attention, but is hugely important, because the details of these sorts of legal provisions affect how people across the UK live their lives, across a very wide range of areas, not only employment rights. What Kassim and his collaborators observe is significant changes in the systems, structures and processes of regulation in Great Britain, but much less change in the actual substance of regulation: the formal rules and standards that apply. They also explain that the vast majority of people affected, across a range of business and public-sector areas, are not keen on change or regulatory uncertainty. That said, 'regulatory divergence' also links to much higher profile Brexit narratives about 'freedom' and 'taking back control'.

We will discuss regulatory divergence and control further in chapters eight and nine, where we consider continued supply of products to the NHS and regulating the research that leads to creation of new NHS products. For now, in terms of the rights of NHS staff, we note that the Johnson government suggested in January 2021[36] that there would be an 'axing' of labour rights, but no changes were made at that time.[37] As we write in 2022, there has been no major divergence in UK law from the 2020 EU rules. It remains unclear whether the Retained EU Law (Revocation and Reform) Bill will be adopted by parliament under the Sunak government, but if it is in its current form, the EU law – including employment law – that was 'rolled over' at the end of transition will cease to apply at the end of 2023, unless specific legislation is adopted to retain it. The Welsh NHS Confederation has expressed significant concern about capacity to take the necessary action within the time frame.[38]

But of course, irrespective of the UK's action, the EU continues to develop its law and guidelines.[39] In that way, as a minimum, there will be some divergence over time

[34] A Bradford, *The Brussels Effect: How the European Union Rules the World* (Oxford, Oxford University Press, 2020).

[35] UK in a Changing Europe, *UK Regulation After Brexit Revisited* (London, UK in a Changing Europe, 19 October 2022).

[36] P Foster et al, 'UK Workers' Rights at Risk in Plans to Rip Up EU Labour Market Rules', Financial Times, 14 January 2021.

[37] M Morries, *What Does the UK-EU Deal Mean for Workers' Rights?* (London, Institute for Public Policy Research, January 2022).

[38] M Phillips, Welsh NHS Confederation response to the Legislation, Justice and Constitution Committee on the Retained EU Law (Revocation and Reform) Bill, 17 November 2022 (www.nhsconfed.org/publications/wnhsc-response-retained-eu-law-revocation-and-reform-bill).

[39] Writing in winter 2022, we found no new EU law in the health and safety field since 31 December 2020, and new guidelines published in 2022 and 2021 either do not apply to the health and social care sector (eg 'European Framework Agreement on the Protection of Occupational Health and Safety in the Hairdressing Sector' (https://osha.europa.eu/en/legislation/guidelines/european-framework-agreement-protection-occupational-health-and-safety-hairdressing-sector accessed 21 November 2022) and 'Non-Binding Guidelines for the Hairdressing Sector' (https://osha.europa.eu/en/legislation/guidelines/non-binding-guidelines-hairdressing-sector accessed 21 November 2022), or were adopted in 2020, even if published in 2021 (eg, 'Non-Binding Guidelines Regarding Directive 92/58/EEC' (https://op.europa.eu/en/publication-detail/-/publication/5079cf93-7811-11ec-9136-01aa75ed71a1/language-en/format-PDF/source-250782696 accessed 21 November 2022)). The only new guidelines that do apply in the health and social care sector are those concerning safety signs at work (https://osha.europa.eu/en/legislation/guidelines/non-binding-guidelines-regarding-directive-9258eec-safety-and-health-signs-work

between the employment standards, including health and safety at work, that apply in the UK and the EU. These may have an effect on decisions that migrant NHS and social care staff make, and whether they decide to come to the UK.

Legally speaking, there are now significantly fewer limitations on what successive UK governments may change in the future. The EU-UK TCA provides for what is known as a 'level playing field' between the EU and the UK. As two large and geographically proximate economies, each is concerned that the other might in effect undercut the other, by lowering standards, including in employment law. To counter this threat, the EU and UK have agreed not to 'weaken or reduce' these standards below the law as at 31 December 2020 in a way that would affect trade or investment between the EU and UK.[40] These clauses in the EU-UK TCA are standard trade agreement clauses, enforceable only between the EU and UK,[41] and not by individual employees, by contrast with EU law. It is unlikely that, for example, changes to working time applicable only, say, to doctors would be enough to have an effect on trade and investment. This is because a sector has to be exposed to the wider market for a link to be made between 'level playing field rules' and trade and investment. So even in England, where the NHS is organised in terms of a (partial) market, the EU-UK TCA is very unlikely to be a legal barrier to any future changes to worsen employment law rights. In Northern Ireland, Scotland or Wales, the NHS is not organised in a way that means NHS staff are covered by the EU-UK TCA. In theory, those jurisdictions could legally worsen employment law rights too. In practice, though, neither Northern Ireland, Scotland nor Wales could take advantage of the different structure of their market to reduce employment protection for NHS staff, because these aspects of employment law are not a devolved matter. Any changes to employment rights in Northern Ireland, Scotland or Wales would also have to apply to workers in England.[42] In any event, any major divergence from EU standards would exacerbate existing difficulties in staff recruitment, and so is likely to be politically very difficult. In summary, therefore, although divergence from EU employment law standards is now legally feasible, it has not yet taken place and remains relatively unlikely in the context of the NHS, given staff recruitment needs.

IV. IMMIGRATION LAW AND NHS STAFFING

The context in which the NHS recruits new staff is affected by the changing UK immigration law following the end of the transition period on 1 January 2021. That new law and policy is consistent with a widely-recognised desired outcome from the EU

accessed 6 February 2023), which provide examples of signboards, but which permit deviations from those so long as the same meaning is conveyed.

[40] Article 387 EU-UK TCA.

[41] Article 388 and 408–10 EU-UK TCA.

[42] As we explained in our evidence 'Written Evidence EEH0007, 4 February 2021' (https://committees.parliament.uk/writtenevidence/22314/html/), submitted to House of Lords EU Environment Sub-Committee, 'Future UK-EU Relations: Energy, Environment and Health. Inquiry' (https://committees.parliament.uk/work/944/future-ukeu-relations-energy-environment-and-health/ accessed 16 November 2022).

referendum. Many Leave voters were convinced that EU membership was detrimental to the UK because of the implications of EU membership for human migration.[43] Several studies have shown that immigration – along with 'sovereignty' – is a key reason for Leave voting. One poll on 23 June 2016, of over 12,000 voters, suggested that a third of Leave voters felt that controlling immigration was the main reason for their vote.[44]

This is consistent with many of the conversations we had in the street, especially, but not only, with people in Rochdale, Rotherham and Sheffield, in the north of England.[45] At least one person felt that post-Brexit there would be more inward migration to the English NHS from countries like India, a view which, as we will see, was quite prescient at the time.[46] In some conversations, people explicitly said they would prefer the UK to have a 'points based' immigration system, like the system in Australia.[47] These conversations ranged from open racism ('Africa would be heaven if it wasn't for the blacks'; 'the problem is all the blacks here who take social security and give nothing') to apparently more nuanced views, encapsulated in the phrase 'no offence to you, love', aimed at Antova as an obvious foreigner carrying out the fieldwork. This particular phrase became the subject of dark humour among the four of us on the project, as it is obviously extremely offensive. Some of the conversations were distinctly disturbing to us, from our perspectives and experiences, and taking into account our knowledge of how the NHS and social care is actually staffed across the UK. We discussed Wood and Antova's experiences of carrying out the fieldwork when the team worked together on coding the data. Having read the literature and followed press reporting, of course we expected this kind of reaction from some people, but that does not make it any more comfortable to be on the receiving end of an overtly racist conversation. Wood recalled having to have a 15 minute break after one such conversation in Newry.[48] Sometimes the people with whom we talked, like this Liverpudlian mother of three,[49] felt that their views were likely to be out of kilter with ours – presumably because we presented as part of the privileged middle class, associated with equality and economic openness to non-Brits:

> Sees the bus [picture] and looks around. Says she doesn't want to express her views. I encourage her to do so and say I will not record her name. She states, 'honestly, stick

[43] See, eg, C Browning, 'Brexit Populism and Fantasies of Fulfilment' (2019) 32(3) *Cambridge Review of International Affairs* 222; H Clarke et al, *Brexit: Why Britain Voted to Leave the European Union* (Cambridge, Cambridge University Press, 2017); D Goodhart, *The Road to Somewhere: The Populist Revolt and the Future of Politics* (Oxford, Oxford University Press, 2017); M Goodwin and C Milazzo, 'Taking Back Control? Investigating the Role of Immigration in the Vote for Brexit' (2017) 19(3) *The British Journal of Politics and International Relations* 450; M Goodwin and O Heath, *Brexit Vote Explained* (London, Joseph Rowntree Foundation, 2016); G Magni, 'Economic Inequality, Immigrants and Selective Solidarity: From Perceived Lack of Opportunity to In-Group Favouritism' (2021) 51(4) *British Journal of Political Science* 1357.

[44] Lord Ashcroft, 'How the United Kingdom Voted on Thursday … and Why', 24 June 2016 (https://lordashcroftpolls.com/2016/06/how-the-united-kingdom-voted-and-why/).

[45] Sheffield 1A, 11B; Newry 43, 44A, 45A, 24B; Rochdale 61A, 70A, 84A, 94A, 41B, 60B, 62B; Rotherham 112A, 114A, 131A, 88B, 92B, 95B, 99B, 107B, 108B, 121B, 122B; Derry 176AA, 174B.

[46] Rotherham 137A.

[47] Sheffield 10A; Rotherham 131A.

[48] Newry 32B.

[49] Newry 32B.

> them on a banana boat. Send them home'. I enquire as to what she means. She says, 'You wouldn't like my views, you'll get me arrested'. … I ask her what her experience is with the NHS. She says, 'we don't want so many people here using it – you wouldn't like my views'. Her tone is hushed. I have to assure her again it is anonymous.

This particular conversation captures a significant epistemological dissonance between the person speaking and our own positions. Her understanding seems to be that she is in a position of disadvantage because of the difference between her views and ours, which might even be dangerous to divulge. She seems to believe that we have the power of the (criminal) law on our side, and we would use it to prevent articulation of her views ('you'll get me arrested'). From our point of view, we have no such power, and, in fact, it is the power of Leave voters like her who have led the UK to the position in which it currently finds itself, with all the consequences for health and the NHS (including its staff) on which we report in this book.

Overall in our street conversations, there was very little awareness of the significant proportion of NHS roles occupied by non-British EU citizens, although one person in the north of England suggested there are 'too many immigrants [in the NHS]: we should be training our own'.[50] Furthermore, there was no understanding of the legal contexts that supported the relevant economic migration behaviours, or that British immigration law was only partially affected by EU membership. When we spoke with people in a pub in the deprived Gleadless area of Sheffield in 2018, as part of the documentary film about our project, the idea of a self-sufficient NHS, staffed by a British workforce, was appealing. Steven Shepherd ('Shep'), the pub landlord, spoke of aspirations for his own children and grandchildren to train as nurses or other care workers. He hoped that Brexit would mean that the government would provide bursaries for that training, pointing to the disincentive of student loans in place at that time and still in place now.[51]

But our research suggests that it was not as simple as 'ordinary people' in 'left behind' places wanting to stop migration to the UK.[52] Some people we spoke with in our street conversations understood the link between migration and positive benefits for the NHS. This was especially the case in Northern Ireland,[53] but also in a few instances in the north of England.[54] For example, one woman in Sheffield was very keen to express her gratitude to the 'foreign doctor' who saved her life from cancer.[55] A man in Rochdale was worried about the problems that would follow from NHS staff from the EU leaving the UK.[56]

The public and governmental narratives on migration and NHS staffing were quite ambivalent during this time (and continue to be so). For NHS and social care

[50] Sheffield 3B.

[51] Shout Out UK, *Brexit, Health & Me*, above n 4.

[52] Others have also pointed out the deficiencies of this simplistic narrative see, eg, GK Bhambra, 'Brexit, Trump, and "Methodological Whiteness": On the Misrecognition of Race and Class' (2017) 68(1) *British Journal of Sociology* S214.

[53] Newry 16A, 36A, 38A 47A; Derry 171A, 189A, 219A.

[54] Sheffield 3A, 10A; Rochdale 72A; Rotherham 131A.

[55] Sheffield 10A.

[56] Rochdale 72A.

staff already in the UK, there were attempts to remove the requirement to apply for settled or pre-settled status altogether. In November 2019, Liberal Democrat MP Christine Jardine sponsored a Private Members Bill,[57] which would have given all non-UK citizen NHS workers indefinite leave to remain in the UK. The Bill attracted support from a range of health policy sector actors, but never became law. To attract new NHS and social care staff, at one point in early 2019, the Johnson government announced a planned 'NHS visa',[58] suggesting governmental awareness of the need to continue to recruit from outside the UK to many roles in the NHS and social care system. This announcement was not consistent with broader narratives on migration control and on securing domestic supply of NHS and social care workers. The new 'Health and Care Worker Visa'[59] first came into effect on 21 October 2020, and is now part of the post-transition arrangements for migration into the UK which we discuss below.

Overall, the Withdrawal Agreement and EU-UK TCA provided the necessary certainty, and avoided the undesirable effects of a 'No Deal' Brexit. For EU nationals already in the UK and those arriving in the UK to work in the NHS and social care, at least there was certainty. If people had arrived in the UK before 31 December 2020, they would be protected by EU law, and all EU nationals in the NHS and social care across the UK were covered by the new pre-settled and settled status rules. These rules did not provide the same security as EU law. As we explained in the previous chapter, they are a 'constitutive', not 'declaratory' system, which means that NHS staff can – and do – fall through the gaps if they do not take action to secure their status, or if they do not have the necessary evidence to show continuous residence in the UK for the relevant time. The provisions could always be reversed by a UK government and parliament, although to do that would be to breach the Withdrawal Agreement. But at least the new provisions provided clarity. Although some of the protections offered to NHS and social care staff by EU law were removed, in practice there was a great deal of continuity, and migration arrangements affecting NHS and social care staffing were not a chaotic disaster.

V. COVID-19, THE TRANSITION PERIOD AND ITS AFTERMATH

In March 2020, just a few weeks after the UK formally left the EU, but while EU law still applied across the UK during the transition period, human migration to the UK more or less ceased, but for a totally different reason. The COVID-19 pandemic resulted in restrictions on movement and border closures across the world.[60] Travel into England

[57] The Immigration (Health and Social Care Staff) Bill 2019–21.

[58] A Gates-Lincoln, 'Granting Indefinite Leave to Remain to Migrant NHS Workers', Federal Trust, 12 March 2021 (https://fedtrust.co.uk/granting-indefinite-leave-to-remain-to-migrant-nhs-workers/).

[59] UK Visas and Immigration, 'Health and Care Visa: Guidance for Applicants', 21 October 2020 (www.gov.uk/government/publications/health-and-care-visa-guidance-for-applicants).

[60] 'Coronavirus: Travel Restrictions, Border Shutdowns by Country', Al Jazeera, 3 June 2020 (www.aljazeera.com/news/2020/6/3/coronavirus-travel-restrictions-border-shutdowns-by-country); C Flood et al (eds), *Borders and Pandemics* (Abingdon, Routledge, 2023).

was not formally legally constrained until June 2020,[61] an approach which has been criticised by the House of Commons Home Affairs Committee.[62] Travel between Northern Ireland and Ireland was also exempted from the relevant rules.[63] But other countries prevented people from leaving their borders.[64] Recruitment of staff to the NHS and social care across the UK from other countries was hugely disrupted, as the world confronted the effects of the new coronavirus on a population with no natural immunity. Accurate figures are not available, because surveys of passengers arriving in UK ports and airports were suspended in March 2020, with consequent disruption for other measures of inward and outward migration.[65] But even where human movement is measurable, the effects of Brexit on migration and NHS staffing become very difficult to disentangle from the effects of COVID-19 from this point onwards.

The UK, like every country in the world, became more reliant on NHS workers than ever before. Lack of personal protective equipment (PPE), like gloves, gowns and masks, for frontline health and social care workers had the effect of requiring NHS staff to undertake extraordinary service. NHS workers were applauded as 'heroes' during the start of the COVID-19 pandemic in spring and summer 2020. The Prime Minister himself offered public praise to Luis Pitarma, a Portuguese nurse on the team looking after Johnston when he was hospitalised with COVID-19. But an online petition of over 48,000 signatures; a recommendation from the House of Commons Home Affairs Committee;[66] and letters in the press,[67] were insufficient for a change in national law to automatically grant non-UK national NHS workers UK citizenship, or even indefinite permission to remain in the UK. In April 2020, the Home Office announced a temporary pause in the requirement for non-national migrants working in some NHS roles to apply regularly for permission to stay in the UK: this amnesty lasted initially until October 2020, and was extended until March 2021, temporarily removing the time and money costs associated with the need to reapply to continue to legally reside and work in the UK.[68] By autumn 2020, a cross-party coalition of MPs were supporting the Parliamentary Bill to automatically offer NHS workers indefinite

[61] Health Protection (Coronavirus, International Travel) (England) Regulations 2020.

[62] 'Home Office Preparedness for COVID-19 (Coronavirus): Management of the Borders', *Fifth Report from the Committee on Home Affairs*, HC 563 (2019–2021).

[63] For rules on travel from Northern Ireland into Ireland see the Health Act 1947 (Section 31A – Temporary Requirements) (Covid-19 Passenger Locator Form) Regulations 2020 were introduced in May 2020 and required persons other than children arriving at a port or airport to complete a Covid-19 Passenger Locator Form. Various categories of persons were exempted from this requirement, including persons arriving from Northern Ireland. Also see, E Carolan and A O'Neill, 'Ireland: Legal Response to Covid-19' in J King and O LM Ferraz et al (eds), *The Oxford Compendium of National Legal Responses to Covid-19* (Oxford, Oxford University Press, 2021).

[64] For detailed information on dozens of countries, see the country reports in the open access *Lex Atlas Covid-19*, published by Oxford University Press (https://lexatlas-c19.org/ accessed 21 November 2022).

[65] G Parker et al, 'How Two Decades of EU Migration Went into Reverse', Financial Times, 1 April 2021.

[66] C Hymas, 'All Foreign NHS Staff Should Be Offered Chance of UK Citizenship After Serving on Frontline in Covid-19 Pandemic, Say MPs', The Telegraph, 14 June 2020; 'Immigration (Health and Social Care Staff)', Hansard, HC Vol 679, cols 62–64 (1 September 2020).

[67] 'Letters: NHS Workers Should Be Given UK Citizenship as Well as Protection', The Guardian, 8 April 2020.

[68] 'Home Office Backtracks on NHS Visa Extensions', Bindmans Blog, 20 April 2020 (www.bindmans.com/insight/covid/home-office-backtracks-on-nhs-visa-extensions); Gates-Lincoln, 'Granting Indefinite Leave to Remain to Migrant NHS Workers', above n 58.

leave to remain[69] – but even that limited gesture, which would have offered peace of mind, and freed many NHS and especially social care staff from having to apply repeatedly for permission to stay in the UK, was not successful. For EU nationals already in the UK, the settled and pre-settled status scheme procedures were mandatory, even if at the same time those self-same EU nationals were 'our NHS heroes'. We found the inconsistencies in this policy position uncomfortable.

For new arrivals to the UK, the Immigration and Social Security Co-ordination (EU Withdrawal) Act 2020 removed all traces of EU law migration rights from UK immigration law from 1 January 2021. This was a key legal plank of 'getting Brexit done' that had featured so strongly in the Conservative election campaigns of 2017 and especially Johnson's campaign in 2019.[70] Recruitment of all non-UK and non-Irish nationals, from anywhere in the world, to the NHS in England, Northern Ireland, Scotland and Wales is now governed by the same rules: there is no separate treatment of nationals of the 26 EU countries other than Ireland, or the EEA countries and Switzerland.

The UK's immigration policy has been described Maya Goodfellow and many others[71] as creating an increasingly 'hostile environment' for non-nationals. The public narratives, and the implementation of complex and almost-constantly changing policy detail so as to be seen to be 'tough on immigration', are at odds with economic and social realities. As a matter of law, encapsulated in the notion of national 'sovereignty' over borders, in theory, a UK government could, with sufficient parliamentary support, adopt almost any migration policy as law. The only legal limitations at present are the need to comply with international obligations such as embodied in the Human Rights Act 1998 and Northern Ireland Act 1998, and even these could also, at least in theory, be removed by legislation. But it is 'pure fantasy', in Sheona York's words, to think that any government could simply expect long term residents, who are contributing to the UK's economy and society, and their families, to 'go home'.[72]

Instead, as Adrian Favell and Roxana Barbulescu point out, UK immigration law and policy means foreign workers are discriminated against or excluded from the UK labour market, however much they may be objectively 'needed'.[73] In the context of the

[69] Immigration (Health and Social Care Staff) Bill 2019-21 – see, C Jardine, ' The Government Must Take on My Bill to Give NHS Heroes the Right to Live in the UK', Liberal Democrats, 14 January 2021 (www.libdems.org.uk/nhs-heroes-at-risk).

[70] L Cooper and C Cooper, '"Get Brexit Done': The New Political Divides of England and Wales at the 2019 Election' (2020) 91(4) *The Political Quarterly* 751.

[71] M Goodfellow, *Hostile Environment: How Immigrants Became Scapegoats* (London, Verso, 2019); C Briddick, 'Fortress Europe: Cause or Consequence of Europe's "Migrant Crisis"', The London School of Economics and Political Science, 28 August 2015 (http://blogs.lse.ac.uk/eurocrisispress/2015/08/28/fortress-europe-cause-or-consequence-of-europes-migrant-crisis/), cited in A Favell and R Barbulescu, 'Brexit, "Immigration" and Anti-Discrimination' in P Diamond et al, *The Routledge Handbook of the Politics of Brexit* (Abingdon, Routledge, 2018); N Shukla (ed), *The Good Immigrant: 21 Writers Reflect on Race in Contemporary Britain* (London, The Unbound Press, 2017); M Ruhs and B Anderson (eds), *Who Needs Migrant Workers? Labour Shortages, Immigration and Public Policy* (Oxford, Oxford University Press, 2010).

[72] S York, *The Impact of UK Immigration Law: Declining Standards of Public Administration, Legal Probity and Democratic Accountability* (London, Palgrave Macmillan, 2022), 10.

[73] Favell and Barbulescu, 'Brexit, "Immigration" and Anti-Discrimination', above n 71; H Jones, 'UK Immigration Policy in a Hostile Environment' in B Jones et al (eds), *Politics UK*, 10th edn (Abingdon, Routledge, 2022).

NHS, one of the most ironic aspects of this discriminatory treatment was the 'NHS immigration surcharge': a fee introduced in April 2015[74] and now required as part of a visa application process, to entitle non-nationals to access the NHS. Whether the surcharge could be applied also to some EU nationals (in effect, those who were not contributing to the economy) was a matter of unresolved legal debate.[75]

The idea that outsiders from the EU or elsewhere were 'taking advantage' of the NHS, and should be excluded from accessing healthcare in the UK, was evident in our conversations too. In Newry, we heard concerns about 'foreigners queuing up on the hill' [where the local hospital is situated], meaning it takes 'too long' to get an appointment.[76] In Rotherham, one man told us 'I don't want to be racist but we need to stop these 'auslanders' coming here and using [the NHS] for free and not contributing'.[77] Another conversation in Rotherham suggested that the UK government should stop 'foreigners' taking up space in hospitals:

> I had a drip hanging from a light in a hospital. People in the waiting room were asleep in chairs. Never seen anything like it. … They're taking all – houses, hospitals, and schools.[78]

We found these conversations difficult, especially in light of our knowledge that, statistically speaking, an EU-national in a hospital or GP surgery was more likely to be *giving* medical treatment than *taking* it.

Legalised discrimination against non-nationals now applies to all foreign NHS and social care staff, who have to comply with the requirements of the UK's immigration laws, despite widespread labour shortages across the entire sector.[79] The independent Nuffield Trust's NHS staffing tracker[80] shows available data in the sector for NHS England. In February 2021, the Nuffield Trust reported that the NHS simply does not have enough staff to meet demand, with one in 16 posts in England unfilled, and higher vacancy rates in London.[81] Available data from Northern Ireland,[82] Scotland[83]

[74] Immigration (Health Charge) Order 2015; Foreign and Commonwealth Office, 'UK Introduces Health Surcharge' (www.gov.uk/government/news/uk-introduces-health-surcharge accessed 21 November 2022).

[75] Now see C-247/20 *VI v Commissioners for Her Majesty's Revenue and Customs* ECLI:EU:C:2022:177. See also, S de Mars, 'Economically Inactive EU Migrants and the NHS: Unreasonable Burdens Without Real Links?' (2014) 39(6) *European Law Review* 770; E Frantziou and C Murray, 'C-247/20 *VI v The Commissioners for Her Majesty's Revenue & Customs* and the Implications of Preliminary References During the Transitional Period: A Case Study in Legal Complexity', 17 March 2022 (https://europeanlawblog.eu/author/colinmurray/).

[76] Newry 10B.

[77] Rotherham 108B.

[78] Rotherham 121B.

[79] The NHS Support Federation, an independent entity, gathered data on NHS and social care staff shortages from numerous independent reports in 2022- see 'Fund Our NHS' (https://nhsfunding.info/symptoms/10-effects-of-underfunding/staff-shortages/ accessed 21 November 2022).

[80] Nuffield Trust, 'NHS Staffing Tracker' (www.nuffieldtrust.org.uk/nhs-staffing-tracker accessed 21 November 2022).

[81] Nuffield Trust, 'The NHS Workforce in Numbers (www.nuffieldtrust.org.uk/resource/the-nhs-workforce-in-numbers accessed 21 November 2022).

[82] 'Nursing and Midwifery Workforce Gaps', Agenda NI, January 2021; G Hargen, 'Concern Over "Dangerous Staffing Levels" in NI Health System with Thousands of Nursing and Social Work Vacancies', Belfast Telegraph, 11 August 2021; H Moorhead and M Fitzsimons, 'Securing the Health and Wellbeing of Our Population 2022–2027: Informing the Public Debate Ahead of the May 2022 Northern Ireland Assembly Elections', NHS Confederation, 22 April 2022.

[83] B Christie, 'Scotland's New Staffing Plan is Criticised for Failing to Tackle Retention Problems' (2022) 376 *British Medical Journal* o674; C Loudon, 'NHS at "Crisis Point" as Funding on Temporary Staff

and Wales[84] suggests similar and possibly worse problems with NHS staffing gaps. So although foreign NHS staff are discriminated against, in that they are required to meet immigration requirements that domestic staff are not required to meet, foreign NHS staff are not excluded from the UK. Far from it. In fact, as we shall see, the health and social care sector across the UK has become more reliant on non-nationals from *outside of* the EU than ever before.

For non-UK and non-Irish nationals who come to the UK to work, a visa is necessary for entry and continued lawful residence. Permission to reside in the UK can last for up to five years, but once it lapses, it is necessary to reapply, which is obviously both time consuming and costly, a potential chill-factor in the recruitment and retention of NHS and social care staff.

The Health and Care Worker Visa, which is in effect a part of the Skilled Worker Visa (formerly called the 'Tier 2 visa'), applies to a wide range of jobs in the NHS, NHS suppliers (in England) and adult social care,[85] including hospital doctors and GPs; nurses, including student nurses and midwives; pharmacists; opticians; dentists; radiographers; paramedics; and many mental health practitioner roles. To be eligible for this type of visa, someone's salary must meet a specific threshold. The threshold salary for those jobs is lower than for the Skilled Worker Visa more generally: in 2022, it was £20,480 in general, but higher where the 'going rate' for the job, in terms of negotiated NHS salaries, is higher.[86] Different threshold salary figures apply in England, Northern Ireland, Scotland and Wales, reflecting the devolved NHS pay settlements in each NHS. From April 2021, a list of 'shortage occupations' applies. If a job falls in a 'shortage occupation' in the relevant part of the UK, the visa application fee is reduced. In practice, almost every medical role that falls within the Health and Care Worker Visa list is a shortage occupation, and so are nursing auxiliaries and assistants,[87] care workers and senior care workers, along with management roles in the health and social care sector.[88] Following political pressure, especially during the

Reaches £423m', STV News, 12 June 2022; Royal College of Nursing, *Nursing Workforce in Scotland Report*, 29 March 2022.

[84] Royal College of Nursing, 'RCN Wales Publishes Nursing in Numbers 2021 Report Revealing Current Workforce Statistics', 23 November 2021 (www.rcn.org.uk/news-and-events/news/w-rcn-wales-publishes-nursing-in-numbers-2021-report-revealing-current-workforce-statistics-231121); Royal College of Physicians, 'A Lack of NHS Staff Will Continue to Limit COVID-19 Recovery Plans', 22 April 2022 (www.rcplondon.ac.uk/news/lack-nhs-staff-will-continue-limit-covid-19-recovery-plans). Also see, C David, 'Nurse Says She "Dreads" Coming into Work Due to Staff Shortages Which Are Putting Patients at Risk', Cymru Online, 8 June 2022 (www.walesonline.co.uk/news/wales-news/nurse-says-dreads-coming-work-24158222).

[85] UK Visas and Immigration, 'Skilled Worker Visa: Eligible Healthcare and Education Jobs' (www.gov.uk/government/publications/skilled-worker-visa-eligible-healthcare-and-education-jobs/skilled-worker-visa-eligible-healthcare-and-education-jobs accessed 21 November 2022).

[86] UK Visas and Immigration, 'National Pay Scales for Eligible Healthcare Occupation Codes' (www.gov.uk/government/publications/national-pay-scales-for-eligible-healthcare-jobs/national-pay-scales-for-eligible-healthcare-occupation-codes accessed 21 November 2022).

[87] UK Visas and Immigration, 'Skilled Worker Visa: Shortage Occupations for Healthcare and Education' (www.gov.uk/government/publications/skilled-worker-visa-shortage-occupations-for-health-and-education/skilled-worker-visa-shortage-occupations-for-healthcare-and-education accessed 21 November 2022).

[88] UK Visas and Immigration, 'Skilled Worker Visa: Shortage Occupations' (www.gov.uk/government/publications/skilled-worker-visa-shortage-occupations/skilled-worker-visa-shortage-occupations accessed 21 November 2022).

COVID-19 pandemic, people who are eligible for the Health and Care Worker Visa no longer have to pay the NHS immigration surcharge.[89]

More accurately, therefore, whatever may be the case in terms of public narratives or lived experience, the *legal* environment is hostile only against some people: in practice, there are categories of 'desirable migrants'. Virtually every role within the NHS and social care in the UK is legally categorised as one where it would be desirable to have the role filled by someone who is not a UK or Irish national – or at least more desirable than leaving the role unfilled. The problems with this migration policy are twofold. First, it may be difficult to sustain democratically, given the populist narratives associated with control of migration, by both the Conservatives and Labour.[90] Second, it is inconsistent with the political, social and cultural treatment of such migrants as 'undesirable' solely on account of their nationality and/or race or ethnicity. Musa Okwonga writes powerfully of his fury and then exhaustion at this type of endemic and structural discrimination and racism, despite his parents' significant contribution to the UK as medical professionals:[91]

> I could not change some of my peers' perceptions of black people merely by being as hardworking and as agreeable as possible; I became the exception that proved their rule. I realised this when having a pub meal with a friend. Out of nowhere, he launched into an astonishing rant against migrants, and when I pointed out that my parents and I were no different from those he was denigrating, he told me that 'I don't see you as a migrant, Musa. I see you as a friend.'

Musa Okwonga was one of the many people who decided to leave the UK following the referendum vote.

Overall, it seems from available data that the UK's *general* reliance on inward migration has changed fundamentally as a result of Brexit and COVID-19.[92] But this pattern has not been replicated in the health and social care sector. Instead, what we see is a turn to non-EU/EEA nationals to attempt to fill the workforce gaps. This is particularly stark in nursing, where in England the proportions of EU (9 per cent) and non-EU (91 per cent) non-nationals joining the workforce in 2020/21 are more or less the polar opposite of those proportions in 2014/15.[93] The UK's new 'Anglosphere'-focused immigration policy[94] has resulted in some international

[89] UK Visas and Immigration, 'Pay for UK Healthcare as Part of Your Immigration Application' (www.gov.uk/healthcare-immigration-application/who-needs-pay accessed 21 November 2022). Also see, M Gower, *The Immigration Health Surcharge*, Number CBP 7274, House of Commons Library, 18 June 2020; K Proctor et al, 'Tory MPs Call for End to "Immoral" Surcharge for Migrant Health Workers', The Guardian, 21 May 2020.

[90] See, eg, Favell and Barbulescu, 'Brexit, "Immigration" and Anti-Discrimination', above n 71.

[91] M Okwonga, 'The Ungrateful Country' in N Shukla (ed), *The Good Immigrant: 21 Writers Reflect on Race in Contemporary Britain* (London, The Unbound Press, 2017).

[92] Parker et al, 'How Two Decades of EU Migration Went into Reverse', above n 65. For independent data and analysis on UK migration, see Compas (www.compas.ox.ac.uk/ accessed 6 February 2023) and Migration Observatory (www.migrationobservatory.ox.ac.uk accessed 6 February 2023).

[93] Nuffield Trust, 'Number of EU and Non-EU Nurse Registrations, UK, 1990/91 to 2020/21' (www.nuffieldtrust.org.uk/chart/number-of-eu-and-non-eu-nurse-registrations-uk-1990-91-to-2017-18 accessed 21 November 2022).

[94] A Gamble, 'The Brexit Negotiations and the Anglosphere' (2021) 92(1) *The Political Quarterly* 108.

agreements to try to plug the NHS staffing gaps, such as the UK-India NHS workforce framework agreement from July 2022.[95]

How does this health governance outcome stack up with what people in the UK might regard as a legitimate post-Brexit settlement for NHS staffing? In 2017, Simon Hix, Eric Kaufmann and Thomas Leeper showed that people who voted Leave are even less keen on migrants from the rest of the world than they are on migrants from the EU.[96] Our data from our street conversations suggests this is also true for NHS staffing.

Furthermore, as Daisuke Wakisaka and Paul James Cardwell explain, the model adopted by the UK means that 'highly skilled' migration may be politically acceptable, but the details of the policy administration mean it is actually more difficult than the public narratives suggest to successfully recruit highly skilled migrants.[97] Sheona York has argued that the administrative arrangements of the UK's migration law and policy are fundamentally deficient. The frequent changes to the detail of UK immigration law makes it confusing to follow, and lead to the types of uncertainty which, as we outlined at the start of this chapter, Kate Ling suggested to us may make the UK a less desirable place than others to forge a career in the NHS or social care, or even just to come to the UK for a short time to work in the sector.

VI. CONCLUSIONS

The general settlement in the Withdrawal Agreement, and the UK's independent migration policy, has had to be modified to navigate a national discourse of exclusion of 'others' with a reality of a health and social care system that was never designed to be staffed only by 'insiders'. Although the effects of the COVID-19 pandemic are extremely difficult to disentangle from those of Brexit, it is unlikely that the UK's NHS staffing situation would be as it currently is in 2022 if it were not for Brexit.

The post-Brexit governance of NHS staffing is characterised by a major change in the legal position of EU-26 nationals who work, or who might come to the UK to work, in the NHS and social care. Legally speaking, the biggest change is from a form of law (rights in EU law) that are inclusive and require non-discrimination on nationality grounds, are difficult to change, and can be enforced in national courts if an EU Member State does not comply with them. The relevant new laws have much less permanence, and can be changed by the UK government, with parliamentary support, relatively easily. But, in practice, the change was achieved in a way that has

[95] Department for International Trade, 'Framework Agreement Between the Government of India and the Government of the United Kingdom of Great Britain and Northern Ireland for Collaboration on Health Care Workforce', 21 July 2022 (www.gov.uk/government/publications/uk-and-india-collaboration-on-healthcare-workforce-framework-agreement/framework-agreement-between-the-government-of-india-and-the-government-of-the-united-kingdom-of-great-britain-and-northern-ireland-for-collaboration-o).

[96] S Hix et al, 'UK Voters, Including Leavers, Care More about Reducing Non-EU Than EU Migration', The London School of Economics and Political Science, 30 June 2017 (https://blogs.lse.ac.uk/europpblog/2017/05/30/uk-voters-including-leavers-care-more-about-reducing-non-eu-than-eu-migration/).

[97] D Wakisaka and PJ Cardwell, 'Exploring the Trajectories of Highly Skilled Migration Law and Policy in Japan and the UK' (2021) 9(1) *Comparative Migration Studies* 43.

resulted in a great deal of continuity, not the chaos that would have been associated with a 'No Deal' Brexit. The national position concerning NHS and social care staffing is at least in part attributable to COVID-19, rather than Brexit, although the combination of effects has exacerbated existing challenges.

The discussion in this chapter confounds the perception that a disconnection between 'experts' and 'ordinary' people characterises the post-Brexit UK. When we talked with people in the street in towns in Northern Ireland and the north of England, we did often hear blatant racism, sometimes expressed quasi-apologetically ('no offence to you, love'). People implicitly expressed the view that the UK, and especially England, took a wrong turn in its labour supply policies (including to the NHS) not only through EU membership but also through openness to Britain's former colonies. But we also heard more complex understandings about migration of labour, especially where people had experienced care in the NHS from people they perceived to be 'not British'. On the island of Ireland, 'not British' NHS and social care staff include Irish nationals, whom we heard are very much considered to be 'insiders'.

'Experts' and 'ordinary people' share a concern about NHS and social care staffing. The current staffing levels are worrying in terms of patient care,[98] and also staff retention, as over-stretched staff burn out and leave after working more hours or harder to cover the gaps. The COVID-19 pandemic has exacerbated matters.[99] Recruitment to and retention of staff in the NHS remains the most worrying topic for the health policy experts with whom we talked from 2019–22. Staffing levels are beginning to have measurable effects on patients' views on the care they receive. For example, in July 2022, in a sharp change from previous years, nearly half of the 720,000 people polled in England reported themselves as 'dissatisfied' rather than 'satisfied' with access to their GP.[100] Many of our street conversations revealed a hope for more staff, especially frontline staff and particularly nurses.[101] Some people felt that NHS staff should be paid more.[102] Independent policy organisations, such as the Health Foundation in January 2021, have called for a greater investment in nursing training.[103]

[98] B Palmer, 'Failure to Adequately Plan for Workforce Putting Patient Care at Risk', Nuffield Trust, 25 July 2022 (www.nuffieldtrust.org.uk/news-item/failure-to-adequately-plan-for-workforce-putting-patient-care-at-risk); A Homer, 'Growth in NHS Recruits from Abroad Prompts Concern About Over-Reliance', BBC, 5 August 2022 (www.bbc.co.uk/news/uk-61230287).

[99] 'Workforce Burnout and Resilience in the NHS and Social Care', *Second Report from the Health and Social Care Committee*, HC 22 (2021–22).

[100] NHS England, 'GP Patient Survey 2022' (www.england.nhs.uk/statistics/2022/07/14/gp-patient-survey-2022/ accessed 22 November 2022); J Wise, 'Patient Satisfaction in GP Services Falls Sharply in Latest Survey' (2022) 378 *British Medical Journal* o1764; N Edwards, 'The GP Crisis We Have Long Feared is Arriving', Nuffield Trust, 14 July 2022 (www.nuffieldtrust.org.uk/news-item/the-gp-crisis-we-have-long-feared-is-arriving).

[101] Sheffield 3A, 5A, 7B; Newry 13A, 39A, 43A, 47A, 12B, 13B, 15B, 19B, 29B, 31B, 33B, 35B, 36B, 37B, 38B; Rochdale 61A, 63A, 68A, 90A, 92A, 98A, 109A, 48B, 49B, 54B, 57B, 70B, 73B, 82B; Rotherham 114A, 127A, 83B, 84B, 87B, 88B, 89B, 93B, 95B, 99B, 104B, 105B, 108B, 110B, 113B, 115B; Derry 162A, 165A, 214A, 125B, 132B, 139B, 142B, 144B, 145B, 151B, 153B, 162B, 184B, 188B.

[102] Sheffield 3A; Rochdale 63A, 90A; Rotherham 87B, 88B, 93B, 104B, 113B; Derry 214A, 132B.

[103] A Charlesworth, 'Staff Shortages Left the NHS Vulnerable to the COVID-19 Storm', The Health Foundation, 21 January 2021 (www.health.org.uk/news-and-comment/blogs/staff-shortages-left-the-nhs-vulnerable-to-the-covid-19-storm?gclid=Cj0KCQjwz96WBhC8ARIsAATR250x15tuNYQqejXo6Zr7emv2tZX9JC7ZDeCkpb7GKsAVwQbFqJPG98YaAtdfEALw_wcB).

Yet these shared views between the 'ordinary people' and the 'experts' do not translate into law, or even policy. Freed from the obligation to treat EU national students and staff in the same way, the UK could invest in its domestically-educated health and social care workforce. In Scotland, higher education fees are covered by the government, and for medical professionals such as nursing, bursaries to help with the cost of living are also available.[104] The Welsh health minister confirmed in April 2022 that the NHS bursary scheme, which covers fees and some living expenses, will continue at least until 2024.[105] In Northern Ireland, fees for health professional courses such as nursing and midwifery are fully funded, and a modest bursary for living expenses is provided.[106] Doctors and dentists receive bursaries for the fifth (and any later) years of study.[107] But despite the UK leaving the EU, and the gaps in the NHS workforce, in England, full bursaries that cover both fees and living expenses are available only for medicine and dentistry students, and only in the final year of their courses. Students must be in one of several residence-based categories at the start of the relevant year of their course.[108] Student nurses, midwives and allied health professionals are eligible for different, and less generous, extra funding.[109] Pay increments for NHS and social care staff, particularly those at the lower end of the pay scale, might fill staffing gaps and encourage greater staff retention. Instead, the Johnson government made a public pay settlement of just 3 per cent in 2021, and 4.5 per cent for doctors and dentists, and up to 9.3 per cent for others in the NHS in 2022.[110] This was in the context of inflation then running at around 6 per cent according to Bank of England estimates.[111] In winter 2022, as we write, the Sunak government is grappling with inflation at a rate of around 10 per cent.[112]

Overall, we have shown that *general* narratives about how, in the UK, Brexit means that the 'othering' that comes from immigration law now applies to EU

[104] Nursing and Midwifery Student Allowances (Scotland) Regulations 2007.

[105] Welsh Government, 'NHS Bursary Extended in Wales', 19 April 2022 (https://gov.wales/nhs-bursary-extended-wales).

[106] Article 44, Health and Personal Social Services (Northern Ireland) Order 1972 and see 'Health Professional Courses' (www.nidirect.gov.uk/articles/health-professional-courses accessed 6 February 2023).

[107] Ibid.

[108] Section 63, Health Services and Public Health Act 1968; Education (Student Fees, Awards and Support) (Amendment) Regulations 2021.

[109] S Rogers, 'NHS Bursary', Complete University Guide, 16 November 2022 (www.thecompleteuniversityguide.co.uk/student-advice/finance/nhs-bursary#NHSbursaryandfundingfornursingandalliedhealthprofessionsinEngland).

[110] Department of Health and Social Care and Steve Barclay MP, 'NHS Staff to Receive Pay Rise', 19 July 2022 (www.gov.uk/government/news/nhs-staff-to-receive-pay-rise). But this news does not apply across the UK – see, eg, L Smyth, 'Pay Rise for Northern Ireland Healthcare Staff Looks Set to be Delayed', Belfast Telegraph, 20 July 2022.

[111] R Joyce et al, 'The Cost of Living Crunch', Institute for Fiscal Studies, 12 January 2022 (https://ifs.org.uk/publications/15905?gclid=Cj0KCQjwxIOXBhCrARIsAL1QFCZhPYRswNKkwkA011T54QS-ViNCKg1bfEb7qyKRoIJVH2bguTjm0RUaAq5_EALw_wcB); Bank of England, 'Monetary Policy Summary and Minutes of the Monetary Policy Committee Meeting Ending on 15 December 2021', 16 December 2021 (www.bankofengland.co.uk/-/media/boe/files/monetary-policy-summary-and-minutes/2021/december-2021.pdf).

[112] Office for National Statistics, 'Consumer Price Inflation, UK: September 2022' (www.ons.gov.uk/economy/inflationandpriceindices/bulletins/consumerpriceinflation/september2022 accessed 22 November 2022); Office for National Statistics, 'Inflation and Price Indices' (www.ons.gov.uk/economy/inflationandpriceindices accessed 22 November 2022).

nationals too,[113] need some extra nuance when it comes to the NHS and social care staff. In practice, 'our' NHS de facto includes many 'others', and these are recognised as in a special category in some public discourses. But the changes to the form of law applicable to staffing also have a symbolic implication. Overnight, as Robert Gonzales and Nando Sigona put it, EU nationals changed from being 'citizens' to being 'immigrants'.[114] As Marijke van Eerd, a senior staff nurse and colleague of Dr Goedvolk's, who also features in the Channel 4 report, says:

> When I asked [my colleague], 'what was the main reason you voted Leave?', they said, 'oh well, the immigrants'. And I said, 'well, I am an immigrant'. And she went, 'no, I don't mean you'.

[113] N Yuval-Davis et al, 'Everyday Bordering, Belonging and the Reorientation of British Immigration Legislation' (2018) 52(2) *Sociology* 228.

[114] R Gonzales and N Sigona, 'Mapping the Soft Borders of Citizenship' in R Gonzales and N Sigona (eds), *Within and Beyond Citizenship* (Abingdon, Routledge, 2017), 2–3.

8

Medicines, Medical Devices and Equipment

I. INTRODUCTION

> How do you explain to people ... where is the real threat [of Brexit] for health? Okay well, [imagine] your mother [is a cancer patient] ... and needs treatment with medical isotopes, some of which have a half-life of only a few hours; cannot be stockpiled. So, if we are leaving without a deal, there will be no ... treatment of cancer patients ... like your mother the day after we leave with no deal.[1]

IN THIS CHAPTER, we show how the supply of medicines, medical devices and equipment to the NHS across the UK was jeopardised by the possibility of a 'No Deal' Brexit, how matters were significantly mitigated by the Withdrawal Agreement, and we outline the current legal settlement between the UK and the EU, and its implications for supply of the products that the NHS needs to provide good healthcare to its patients. We place the position in Northern Ireland front and centre. We elaborate how Northern Ireland is in effect on the way to becoming a tiny regulatory jurisdiction for medicines, medical devices and equipment, and we contrast the position there with the position in Great Britain and in the EU.

II. GLOBAL MARKETS

The products that any healthcare system needs to care for its patients – medicines, medical devices and equipment – are supplied through global markets, involving complex and still little-understood supply chains. Our work with the House of Commons Health and Social Care Committee in 2018 found that a product used in the English NHS might cross the EU-UK border several times in the process from manufacture to patient bedside.[2] The COVID-19 pandemic showed how deeply dependent national health systems like those in the UK are, when it comes to supply of the products needed to safely provide effective patient care. The UK is certainly not self-sufficient in such products, and indeed no European country even aspires to be so.

[1] Interview with Paul Laffin, May 2019. See also interview with Philippa Whitford, February 2019.

[2] 'Brexit: Medicines, Medical Devices and Substances of Human Origin', *Fourth Report from the Health and Social Care Committee*, HC 392 (2017–2019).

But each jurisdiction regulates each element of what we might think of as the 'regulatory life cycle' of medicines, medical devices and equipment.[3] Countries regulate the research that leads to creation of new products to be used to treat or diagnose patients; the clinical trials that test their safety and efficacy; the lawful placing of a product on the market in that country ('marketing licence/authorisation'); the quality of manufacture, including, for medicines, the safety of batches of a particular product; the packaging and labels for the product; and whether a product may be bought by a national health system. These regulatory standards vary from country to country, because of the particular political decisions that each country takes, balancing the risks and benefits of medical treatments. Different countries also have different processes by which a producer or importer may show that a particular product complies with relevant national laws – the (electronic) paperwork needed to show that these essential quality standards are met, so as to ensure patient safety and confidence in the healthcare system as a whole.

In international trade law, these kinds of regulatory requirements are known as 'non-tariff barriers' to trade. They are barriers to trade for the following reasons. The need to comply with more than one set of regulatory processes and standards, and to show that a product meets the requirements for the market in which it is to be supplied, creates a 'double regulatory burden'. Having to show regulatory compliance makes it more costly for companies established outside a particular market to supply that market than for companies established inside the market, who are already showing compliance for their home market. The 'double burden' applies both to what the regulatory standards *are* (the acceptable levels of the electromagnetic field generated by a heart pacemaker, for example), and how they are *evidenced* (a certification of quality, for example, or a marketing licence).

International trade is, of course, also characterised by tariff barriers. Tariffs are taxes that are charged when a product crosses a border. In terms of the discussion in this chapter, these barriers pose less of an inhibition on trade, as products like medicines are 'zero rated' globally, meaning that there is relief from tariffs payable when these products cross a border.[4] Relief means that, provided the importer can show the appropriate information, either no duty is payable or the duties paid will be repaid by the customs authorities. Nonetheless, even for a zero rated product, the (electronic) paperwork associated with the tariff aspects of a product crossing a border also add extra expense compared to the costs faced by a domestic producer.

Within the EU, both tariff and non-tariff barriers to trade in products like medicines, medical devices and equipment have been largely removed. Tariffs are prohibited

[3] N Fahy et al, 'How Will Brexit Affect Health and Health Services in the UK? Evaluating Three Possible Scenarios Against the WHO Health System Building Blocks' (2017) 390(10107) *The Lancet* 2110; N Fahy et al, 'How Will Brexit Affect Health and Health Services in the UK? An Updated Evaluation' (2019) 393(10174) *The Lancet* 949; N Fahy et al, 'Assessing the Potential Impact on Health of the UK's Future Relationship Agreement with the EU: Analysis of the Negotiating Positions' (2021) 16(3) *Health Economics, Policy and Law* 290; N Fahy et al, 'Impact on the NHS and Health of the UK's Trade and Cooperation Relationship with the EU, and Beyond' (2022) 17(4) *Health Economics, Policy and Law* 471.

[4] HM Revenue and Customs, 'Explanatory Notes' (www.gov.uk/government/publications/uk-trade-tariff-customs-duty-relief-on-pharmaceutical-products/explanatory-notes accessed 22 November 2022).

when products cross borders within the EU's internal market: free movement of products is a cornerstone of EU law. When products move within the EU, they are not 'imports' or 'exports', with all the associated (electronic) paperwork. When it comes to non-tariff barriers, EU law harmonises many (but not all) elements of the 'regulatory pipeline' for medicines, medical devices and equipment. 'Harmonises' in this sense either means making the regulations the same for every country, or making the *aims* or *outcomes* of the regulations the same, but leaving it up to each EU Member State the means by which that is achieved. Therefore it can be the case that differences remain between EU Member States in the governance of medicines, medical devices and equipment.

The EU regulates many – though not all – aspects of clinical trials,[5] as well as some aspects of biomedical research, for example the protection of personal data.[6] For the vast majority of new and innovative medicines, a licence must be secured from the European Medicines Agency before a product is marketed in the EU for the first time. This licence is called a 'centralised marketing authorisation' and grants permission to market anywhere in the EU. A centralised marketing authorisation is necessary, for example, for new treatments for viral diseases (like COVID-19), cancers, diabetes, neuro-degenerative diseases (like Alzheimer's disease, Parkinson's disease or multiple sclerosis), for biotechnological medicines, and for medicines for rare diseases. Other medicines, like generics, are authorised by national bodies, and EU Member States are also legally obliged to mutually recognise such 'decentralised' marketing licences granted by other Member States.

Medical devices and equipment must comply with minimum safety standards determined at EU level. Manufacturers are required to show evidence of compliance (CE[7] or CENELEC[8] marking) by certification from a standards body (a 'Notified Body') established in an EU Member State. The latest version of these EU measures, introduced in response to an incident in which sub-standard breast implants were released onto the EU market, entered into force in May 2021 and May 2022.[9]

Medicines must be manufactured in accordance with EU requirements on 'good manufacturing practice'. Batches of medicines must be tested, and each batch certified by an EU-based entity. The EU imposes labelling rules, including a system

[5] Regulation (EU) No 536/2014 of the European Parliament and of the Council of 16 April 2014 on clinical trials on medicinal products for human use, and repealing Directive 2001/20/EC [2014] OJ L 158/1.

[6] Regulation (EU) 2016/679 of the European Parliament and of the Council of 27 April 2016 on the protection of natural persons with regard to the processing of personal data and on the free movement of such data, and repealing Directive 95/46/EC (General Data Protection Regulation) [2016] OJ L 119/1 ('GDPR').

[7] The European standard, recognised by the system overseen by CEN (European Committee for Standardisation), a non-profit body responsible for coordinating European safety standards for products, see https://www.cencenelec.eu/about-cen/ (accessed 22 November 2022).

[8] The European Committee for Electrotechnical Standardisation, a non-profit body responsible for European standards in electrotechnical products, see www.cencenelec.eu/about-cenelec/ (accessed 22 November 2022).

[9] Regulation (EU) 2017/745 of the European Parliament and of the Council of 5 April 2017 on medical devices, amending Directive 2001/83/EC, Regulation (EC) No 178/2002 and Regulation (EC) No 1223/2009 and repealing Council Directives 90/385/EEC and 93/42/EEC [2017] OJ L 117/1; Regulation (EU) 2017/746 of the European Parliament and of the Council of 5 April 2017 on in vitro diagnostic medical devices and repealing Directive 98/79/EC and Commission Decision 2010/227/EU [2017] OJ L 117/176.

designed to prevent falsified medicines from circulating on the EU market: a bar code must be scanned and registered with a central EU authority (the European Medicines Verification System, which is essentially an electronic hub that connects national health systems) at various stages along the production and distribution line, and checked before the medicine is given to a patient.

Decisions about whether a product is authorised for purchase by a national health system remain a national competence, and therefore vary between different EU Member States, posing some barriers to free trade. That said, there have been moves to share information about such 'health technology assessments' between EU Member States for a couple of decades, and a Regulation on health technology assessment was adopted in late 2021.[10]

The EU's regulatory approach applies to all products (including medicines, medical devices and equipment) to be supplied anywhere in the EU, irrespective of where they are produced. This phenomenon is known as 'the Brussels effect',[11] meaning the way that the EU's institutions, based in Brussels, in effect impose their standards on companies elsewhere in the world. When a product crosses the border into the EU, it is subject to the rules established by the EU's 'common customs code'. These include payment of any tariffs due, and specified procedural and documentary requirements, which are the same whichever EU Member State the products enter. Companies are required to use a single code – the 'Economic Operators Registration and Identification number' (EORI) for all communications about customs and tariffs, and must meet the various documentary requirements to bring products into the EU, even temporarily. The EU's customs rules and formalities also apply to exports. As well as complying with these rules related to tariffs, it is also necessary to show compliance with the EU's safety and quality regulations, before a product is cleared for access to the EU's market. The need for compliance adds costs to the supply of medicines, medical devices and equipment from outside the EU, but the size of the EU's market, at 22 per cent of global health spending, can make it worthwhile meeting these costs, especially as a single set of rules applies to the whole market.

Overall, the effects of EU law are to establish a relatively high regulatory barrier at the outside border of the EU, which must be met if products are to be sold in the EU. At the same time, EU law removes many non-tariff barriers to trade in medicines, medical devices and equipment *within* the EU, creating a single large market for which global providers of medicines, medical devices and equipment need to meet – and evidence – just one set of regulatory requirements in order to access the whole market. As well as allowing manufacturers located in the EU to take advantage of the economies of scale of a large market, this approach makes the EU an attractive place to market new medicines and other novel health technologies, as well as to supply with established, tried-and-tested, products. Global medicines companies and other companies in the global bioscience sector have established themselves in EU Member States, so as to take advantage of that large market.

[10] Regulation (EU) 2021/2282 of the European Parliament and of the Council of 15 December 2021 on health technology assessment and amending Directive 2011/24/EU [2021] OJ L 458/1.

[11] A Bradford, *The Brussels Effect: How the European Union Rules the World* (Oxford, Oxford University Press, 2020).

As we will see, all of this legal detail about supply of medicines, medical devices and equipment is important, because the post-Brexit legal position leaves most of the UK – Great Britain (England, Scotland and Wales) – outside of the customs union and single market for products, but one part of the UK – Northern Ireland – still *inside* it.

III. THE RUN-UP TO THE WITHDRAWAL AGREEMENT

Before the EU and UK negotiated the Withdrawal Agreement, therefore, the spectre of 'No Deal' Brexit would have meant that trade in many medicines, medical devices and equipment (all those sourced from the EU, and those where the supply process involved crossing the EU's external border, even when the product is made in the UK) would have immediately been subject to tariff and non-tariff barriers, arising from the 'Brussels effect'. For tariffs, many relevant products are 'zero rated' under WTO law, but as we have explained above, this does not mean free movement of a product across the EU's external border without cost, as there are administrative formalities associated with imports to and exports from the EU. 'No Deal' Brexit would have immediately made it unlawful to move products into the EU without complying with all the procedural and documentary requirements – and, without any planning or infrastructure in place, that would have been impossible in practice. Moving a product into the EU without complying with those impossible requirements would have become illegal overnight.

The UK government sought to reassure the public that a 'No Deal' Brexit would not be a problem for supply of the NHS, because the UK would immediately 'open its borders' to products produced in the EU which complied with EU rules. After all, reasoned the government, the relevant rules would be the same in the UK, as the UK planned to 'roll over' all existing EU law on Brexit Day, so that existing EU law became part of UK law as 'retained EU law'.[12] But this would have been only a partial solution, because the administrative formalities (and costs) associated with *exports* from the EU, and with any crossing of the border from the UK into the EU along the way to eventual use in the NHS, would have applied *as a matter of EU law* irrespective of the UK's governance response. From the point of view of the EU, there is a 'hard' regulatory border at the edge of the EU, which protects patients and consumers within the EU. A single product might cross into the EU several times on its way to patients in the UK, for example, being brought from India eventually to the UK, but packaged in the EU; being held in a distribution centre in the Netherlands or Belgium before shipping to its final destination. That means that the UK did not – and does not – have practical control over product supply in the way that the government tried to imply in its assurances made during the period between June 2016 and 1 January 2021. When we read or heard these assurances, given our knowledge of EU law, we found them unconvincing, and frustrating.

[12] Sections 2–7, European Union (Withdrawal) Act 2018.

As we heard in our interviews,[13] the NHS across the UK works on a 'just in time' supply model. Products are usually only supplied a few weeks before they are needed. Distributors typically keep 10 days' worth of stock, and even manufacturers usually only stock up to four months' supply.[14] There are good reasons for this: medicines usually have short shelf lives, and the costs of storage, and ensuring optimal stock rotation, are not necessarily appropriate for a publicly funded entity like a national health system to bear. In an attempt to reassure the public, in the run up to the various possible Brexit dates in 2019, the UK government asked suppliers to increase their normal supplies so as to build up a buffer of six weeks of supply of prescription-only and pharmacy-only medicines. The industry was able to do this,[15] but of course at some cost. We sought to discover, and so did the Health and Social Care Committee of the House of Commons, where the costs of this stockpiling fell, but we were unable to do so. This lack of transparency was also something we found frustrating.

The government also altered the rules about when pharmacists may substitute one medicine, or type of medicine, for another, when there are serious shortages, to make substitution easier.[16] This caused concern in some patient groups, such as epilepsy sufferers, because some patients cannot tolerate different medicines or delivery mechanisms, and need oversight from a doctor if a substitution is to be made. Epilepsy medicine was eventually exempted from the new rules.[17] Some patients (understandably) privately stockpiled too,[18] thus in effect introducing further inefficiencies into the system.

More worryingly, some products cannot be stockpiled. Medical radioisotopes, used in the diagnosis and treatment of many cancers, are an effective type of medical intervention because they 'decay' – in other words cease to emit radiation after a certain period of time. Some 700,000 patients a year across the UK benefit from these technologies.[19] The most commonly used medical radioisotope – technetium Tc-99 – lasts only a few hours. Radioisotopes can only be produced in a nuclear reactor, and the UK does not have its own supply. Radioisotopes used in the NHS mainly come from two European suppliers, using reactors situated in six EU Member States.[20] When we talked with Dr Whitford, MP in late February 2019, just weeks from the first possible 'No Deal Brexit' date of 29 March 2019, she expressed her frustration in trying to secure governmental attention for the immediate disruption to thousands of

[13] Interview with Bernie McCrory, April 2019; interview with Philippa Whitford, February 2019; interview with Sarah Wollaston, March 2019. See also 'Brexit: Medicines, Medical Devices and Substances of Human Origin', above n 2.

[14] 'Brexit: Medicines, Medical Devices and Substances of Human Origin', above n 2, 49.

[15] M Dayan, 'How Will Brexit Affect the Supply of Drugs to UK Patients? A Q&A', Nuffield Trust, 16 November 2020 (www.nuffieldtrust.org.uk/news-item/how-will-brexit-affect-the-supply-of-drugs-to-uk-patients).

[16] The National Health Service (Amendments Relating to Serious Shortage Protocols) Regulations 2019.

[17] Epilepsy Society, 'Brexit Contingency Plans for Epilepsy Medication' (https://epilepsysociety.org.uk/contingency-plans-epilepsy-medications-case-no-deal-brexit accessed 22 November 2022).

[18] S Marsh and F Ryan, 'Revealed: UK Patients Stockpile Drugs in Fear of No-Deal Brexit', The Guardian, 18 January 2019.

[19] 'Brexit: Medicines, Medical Devices and Substances of Human Origin', above n 2, 50.

[20] World Nuclear Association, 'Radioisotopes in Medicine' (https://world-nuclear.org/information-library/non-power-nuclear-applications/radioisotopes-research/radioisotopes-in-medicine.aspx accessed 22 November 2022).

diagnoses and treatments, in the event of a No Deal Brexit, because plans for continued supply were, frankly, not credible:

> In a general sense, there is not a good understanding of the impact of Brexit on health. I think it has grown just recently, just because of talk about the stockpiling of drugs and things like this, and the fact that I've raised that you can't stockpile things like radioisotopes. It's taken a very long time; I must have had to ask that question half a dozen times to even get it on people's brains that this is an issue you have to look at. So I think there is a very poor understanding … they think it is all about trade … I think a lot of this [contingency planning] is back of a fag packet … I would say that until probably almost the last five or six weeks, when I would raise questions, they would just be dismissed, or patronised, or ignored. I asked about radioisotopes … and I was asked to google what the French government was doing … just utterly dismissing it, instead of responding to it. Now more recently, … there's, 'well, we're going to fly isotopes in'. OK, when are they coming in? When are they going to arrive? Is it an airport that's used to handling isotopes? How are you going to get them out to all the hospitals? … I lived through shortages from 2008–2010 … world shortage of radioisotopes. I had to sit in clinics and work out who I was going to do the bone scan on, who had the greatest need. … [T]hey would say, 'you can do one patient this week, pick who you're going to do'. … I've been trying to raise that issue for almost two years, and initially it was all, 'that's nonsense, that's nothing, that's not a problem'.

All of the policy work associated with preparing for a No Deal Brexit, in terms of NHS supply, and the associated legal changes, was characterised by a lack of transparency, and a lack of specific detail on the government's plans. It was extremely difficult to learn what was happening, which added to the levels of public concern, especially among the health policy community. Here is Dr Wollaston on the subject:

> [T]here's just so many aspects of this where I would say, you hear Ministers sort of minimise it. A kind of 'nothing to see here' approach, I would say. Where in fact there is a lot to see here, and it's been a steady drum beat, from clinicians, from researchers, from the voluntary sector, from parliamentarians, certainly within the Health and Social Care Select Committee, and others, to be fair, the Science and Technology Committee and the Public Accounts Committee pointing this out. Whereas the government should be the responsible body for informing the public about the risk. It's had to be dragged out of them at every stage. So if you look at the contingency planning papers, you've had to have these sort of motions within the House [of Commons] that are forcing the government to publish, so none of it has been voluntary. And in some cases, if you look at some of the original documentation around Brexit planning … the bit that I found most shocking about it was just how completely basic it was, an almost childlike summary of the issues.

There was also concern among ordinary patients. Even where information was available, it was insufficiently detailed to be reassuring, as these examples of responses from suppliers on The Epilepsy Society website[21] demonstrate: 'Until there is formal agreement, we will continue to implement our contingency plans for all scenarios, including no deal'; 'We do not anticipate any supply issues with [name of medicine] with either outcome of Brexit'; or, even more simply, and unconvincingly, 'We do not anticipate any problem with the supplies'.

[21] Epilepsy Society, 'Brexit Contingency Plans for Epilepsy Medication', above n 17.

Even though this topic was far from the prompt for our conversations in the street, we occasionally heard about these types of concerns in that context too, for example from a woman who works in the NHS, with whom we spoke in Newry. She said that, as an insider, she already saw problems for the NHS, for example medicines expiring in trucks being stuck at the border.[22] We heard worries about medicines supply from our friends and families too, especially people who take medicines on a daily basis to keep healthy.

Fortunately, the Withdrawal Agreement, and the EU-UK Trade and Cooperation Agreement (EU-UK TCA), meant that there was no abrupt break in arrangements for trade in medicines, medical devices and equipment between the EU and the UK. But the settlement reached in the Withdrawal Agreement created a different type of problem, which continues as we write in 2022.

IV. THE PROTOCOL ON IRELAND/NORTHERN IRELAND

The Withdrawal Agreement established that the hard regulatory border at the edge of the EU would apply once the transitional period ended, and EU law was no longer applicable in the UK as a matter of EU law. The EU and UK subsequently entered into a trade and cooperation agreement, which confirms that the UK (or rather, Great Britain) is outside of the EU's customs union and single market. The EU-UK TCA is not significantly different from many of the EU's other trade agreements in this respect. Apart from the EEA countries, and in some complex ways, Switzerland, no other country anywhere in the world has agreed a trade deal with the EU that gives their traders access to the EU's internal market in the same way as companies set up in EU countries. This was, as we explained in chapter five, and will touch on again in chapter nine, the logical consequence of the EU negotiating position, and the UK's insistence that it did not want to agree access to the customs union or single market in a similar model to Norway's relationship with the EU.

Whether the UK unilaterally chose to continue to apply the same standards as the EU's standards was not relevant to the EU in these negotiations. Part of what protects the EU's internal market, and people and traders within it, is the way in which the EU institutions, including its Court of Justice, provide oversight of compliance with the rules. Unilateral voluntary application of the EU's rules does not, consequently, translate into access to the EU's market. Furthermore, of course, even if the UK's rules were exactly the same as the EU's on 1 January 2021, now that the UK is no longer an EU Member State, the UK is no longer obliged to continue to change its rules as the EU's rules change over time. This kind of 'dynamic alignment' was not acceptable to the UK government, at least not for Great Britain, because it became associated in political conversations with lack of 'control' over regulation. The external border that arose on 1 January 2021 between the EU and Great Britain means that products moving into the EU from Great Britain are treated the same as products coming from any other non-EU state. They count as 'imports', and are subject to the same

[22] Newry 36A.

administrative and regulatory burdens as goods produced in, say, India, the USA, or China. Products moving from the EU to Great Britain count as 'exports' from the EU, again with the associated administrative requirements.

However, neither the EU nor the UK wanted a hard regulatory border on the island of Ireland. For people, as we have seen in chapters six and seven, existing arrangements under the 'Common Travel Area' meant that people moving between Ireland and Northern Ireland would not be checked. But what about products? To impose the kinds of border structures associated with imports and exports on the island of Ireland was regarded as both impossible in practice and politically highly undesirable. It is impossible in practice because the border on the island of Ireland stretches for 310 miles (499 kilometres) across open countryside, including many minor roads which are border crossings. We show one of these 208 border crossings[23] in our film[24] – there is no border infrastructure present at all. It is politically undesirable because any border controls on the island ran the risk of attracting unlawful opposition, and the consequent need to assert legal controls, for example through border policing. Such a police presence would jeopardise the peace settlement on the island embodied in the 1998 Belfast/Good Friday Agreement, which marked an end to decades of violence in Northern Ireland.

The EU and UK therefore negotiated a withdrawal from the EU that maintained a porous ('soft') border between Northern Ireland and Ireland, not only for people, but also for products. The settlement reached under the Johnson administration involved a Protocol on Ireland/Northern Ireland, annexed to the Withdrawal Agreement, and legally binding on both the EU and the UK.

The Protocol's wording includes respect for the United Kingdom as a territorial whole. But, as Stephen Weatherill,[25] among others,[26] forcefully pointed out at the time, the Protocol does not do what it says it does. In order to protect the EU's internal market, the Protocol in effect places a regulatory border between Great Britain and Northern Ireland. This is highly problematic for supply of medicines to the NHS in Northern Ireland, as over 90 per cent of such supply is from, or transiting through, Great Britain.

V. THE POST-JANUARY 2021 POSITION IN NORTHERN IRELAND

What happened in practice was that both the EU and the UK delayed full implementation of the Protocol's provisions. As we write (winter 2022), the Protocol is

[23] 'Revealed: Number of border crossings between Northern Ireland and Republic', Belfast Telegraph, 27 April 2018.

[24] Shout Out UK, *Brexit, Health and Me* 2020.

[25] S Weatherill, 'Interpreting the Protocol' in C McCrudden (ed), *The Law and Practice of the Ireland/Northern Ireland Protocol* (Cambridge, Cambridge University Press, 2022); S Weatherill, 'The Protocol on Ireland/Northern Ireland: Protecting the EU's Internal Market at the Expense of the UK's' (2020) 45(2) *European Law Review* 222; S Weatherill, ' The Protocol on Ireland/ Northern Ireland: What It Says Is Not What It Does', 17 March 2020 (http://eulawanalysis.blogspot.com/2020/03/the-protocol-on-ireland-northern.html).

[26] See, eg, S de Mars and C Murray, 'With or Without EU? The Common Travel Area After Brexit' (2020) 21(5) *German Law Journal* 815; S de Mars et al, *Bordering Two Unions: Northern Ireland and Brexit*

still not fully implemented. According to the Withdrawal Agreement, the legal intention is that the Protocol is supposed to be managed through a Joint Committee and a Specialised Committee on Northern Ireland.[27] In fact, although this collaborative institutional structure has been used to some extent,[28] what has taken place mainly in the context of medicines supply is unilateral actions from both sides. This approach has created a position of legal complexity and uncertainty, and to some extent of confrontation, which, we heard in our interactions with the health policy community in spring and summer 2022, is unhelpful in terms of securing product supply to the NHS in Northern Ireland. Flear outlines his personal concerns about being able to continue accessing medicines in this regulatory environment:

> I'm currently on a long course of medication. The medication appears to be working well. But I've been concerned about whether Brexit will jeopardise supply and the success of this course of treatment. Like the vast majority of medicines supplied to the NHS in Northern Ireland, the medicine enters the United Kingdom through Great Britain, and from there transits into Northern Ireland. What will the Protocol and its delayed application mean for my access to these medicines?
>
> Friends in Northern Ireland have been asking similar questions about their access to medicines post-Brexit. One friend has Type 2 diabetes and has repeatedly expressed their concerns about continued access to insulin post-Brexit: 'All my insulin [sic] are made in Denmark. I've got to admit it [Brexit] does worry me. And it makes me miss Theresa May LOL'.

An initial 'grace period' formally delaying the application of the rules for medicines from the EU point of view was due to run out on 31 December 2021.[29] It became obvious that a longer period of time would be needed to secure supply to Northern Ireland, but also to Ireland, Cyprus and Malta, countries which historically have been reliant on Great Britain for medicines supply. The European Commission therefore put in place a further temporary 'grace period',[30] which stayed in place until the

(Bristol, Policy Press, 2018); O Doyle et al (ed), *The Brexit Challenge for Ireland and the United Kingdom: Constitutions Under Pressure* (Cambridge, Cambridge University Press, 2021); K Hayward, 'Northern Ireland: Demographics and Divisions' in F Fabbrini (ed), *The Law & Politics of Brexit: Volume IV. The Protocol on Ireland/Northern Ireland* (Oxford, Oxford University Press, 2022); C McCrudden (ed), *The Law and Practice of the Ireland-Northern Ireland Protocol* (Cambridge, Cambridge University Press, 2022); D Phinnemore, 'Northern Ireland – A "Place Between" in UK-EU Relations?' (2020) 25(4) *European Foreign Affairs Review* 631; D Phinnemore and K Hayward, *UK Withdrawal ('Brexit') and the Good Friday Agreement* (Brussels, European Parliament Policy Department for Citizens' Rights and Constitutional Affairs, 2017).

[27] Article 164 WA.

[28] European Commission, 'Meetings of the EU-UK Joint and Specialised Committees Under the Withdrawal Agreement' (https://ec.europa.eu/info/strategy/relations-non-eu-countries/relations-united-kingdom/eu-uk-withdrawal-agreement/meetings-eu-uk-joint-and-specialised-committees-under-withdrawal-agreement_en#meetingsofthespecialisedcommittees accessed 22 November 2022).

[29] Commission Notice – Application of the Union's pharmaceutical acquis in markets historically dependent on medicines supply from or through Great Britain after the end of the transition period 2021/C 27/08 [2021] OJ C 27/11. The Commission Notice implements the EU's unilateral declaration on medicinal products made in the Joint Committee meeting of 17 December 2020.

[30] Communication to the Commission, Approval of the content of a draft Commission Notice on the application of the Union's pharmaceutical acquis in markets historically dependent on medicines supply from or through parts of the United Kingdom other than Northern Ireland, Brussels, 17 December 2021, C(2021) 9668 final.

European Parliament and Council could adopt more legislation. This legislation was adopted in April 2022 and lasts until 31 December 2024. It takes the form of multiple time-limited amendments to the general measures that regulate medicines supply in the EU.[31]

Meanwhile, the UK was also responding to the challenges of supply of products to Northern Ireland consequent upon the Protocol. The general public debate focused mainly on food supply, with a series of 'grace periods' arising unpredictably and sometimes at the last minute.[32] But specific new rules were also put into place for medicines.[33] For example, prescription-only medicines authorised in Great Britain may, 'exceptionally', be supplied to the NHS in Northern Ireland, without a marketing authorisation for Northern Ireland.[34] Overall, the Johnson government, in effect, refused to comply with its duties under the Protocol. It is not terribly clear, as we write (winter 2022) what the Sunak government will do in the future. The Northern Ireland Protocol Bill 2022–23 (which as we write has been adopted by the House of Commons and is currently at the report stage in the House of Lords) in effect permits the UK government to renege on certain of its obligations under the Protocol. Those obligations concern movement of products between Great Britain and Northern Ireland – the measures which have the effect of applying EU law to products in Northern Ireland. The UK government justifies this breach of international law by reference to the 1998 Agreement, and the need to ensure parity between people in Northern Ireland and people in Great Britain.[35]

The political disagreement over the Protocol means that there is at present (winter 2022) no functioning Executive in Stormont. In June 2022, the EU recommenced legal action in retaliation under the terms of the Withdrawal Agreement.[36] The implications of this impasse – and of the post-Brexit governance settlement more generally – for supply of medicines, medical devices and equipment to the NHS in Northern Ireland are therefore still unsettled and unfolding.

[31] Directive (EU) 2022/642 of the European Parliament and of the Council of 12 April 2022 amending Directives 2001/20/EC and 2001/83/EC as regards derogations from certain obligations concerning certain medicinal products for human use made available in the United Kingdom in respect of Northern Ireland and in Cyprus, Ireland and Malta [2022] OJ L 118/4.

[32] P Foster, 'UK Extends Northern Ireland "Grace Periods" for Third Time', Financial Times, 6 September 2021. See also, the references above n 25.

[33] Medicines and Healthcare Products Regulatory Agency, 'The Northern Ireland MHRA Authorised Route (NIMAR)' (www.gov.uk/government/publications/the-northern-ireland-mhra-authorised-route-nimar/the-northern-ireland-mhra-authorised-route-nimar accessed 22 November 2022); Medicines and Healthcare Products Regulatory Agency, 'Supplying Authorised Medicines to Northern Ireland' (www.gov.uk/guidance/supplying-authorised-medicines-to-northern-ireland accessed 22 November 2022).

[34] Ibid.

[35] 'We are taking this action to uphold the Belfast/Good Friday agreement, which has brought peace and political stability to Northern Ireland. The Northern Ireland protocol is undermining the function of the agreement and of power sharing. It has created fractures between east and west, diverted trade and meant that people in Northern Ireland are treated differently from people in Great Britain. It has weakened their economic rights. That has created a sense that parity of esteem between different parts of the community, an essential part of the agreement, has been damaged', Elizabeth Truss MP, in 'Northern Ireland Protocol Bill', Hansard, HC Vol 717, cols 38–39 (27 June 2022).

[36] European Commission, 'Commission Launches Infringement Proceedings Against the UK for Breaking International Law and Provides Further Details on Possible Solutions to Facilitate the Movement of Goods Between Great Britain and Northern Ireland' (https://ec.europa.eu/commission/presscorner/detail/en/IP_22_3676 accessed 22 November 2022).

The NHS serves 1.9 million people in Northern Ireland. Hospitals alone in Northern Ireland treat around 600,000 patients a year.[37] There are shared healthcare facilities with the Irish population, of around 4.9 million. This is a large number of patients to be in a position of such uncertainty.

As Hafsa Yusufi and co-authors[38] explain, the relationships between the Department of Health and Social Care in the UK government in Westminster, the Northern Ireland Executive in Stormont, the NHS in Northern Ireland, the English NHS and the NHS in Ireland were already complex. They became more so on 1 January 2021. In Northern Ireland, the NHS not only relies on product supply from Great Britain. It also relies on marketing authorisation decisions of the European Medicines Agency (in practice required for all new and innovative medicines), and of the UK's Medicines and Healthcare products Regulatory Authority (MHRA) for all other medicines. Medicines may not be marketed in Northern Ireland without an authorisation from one of those entities. The European Medicines Agency used to be based in London, and worked very closely with the MHRA. The MHRA drew much of its resourcing from the work it carried out for and with the European Medicines Agency, and the MHRA's work was very highly regarded by the health policy sector across the European Union.[39] The European Medicines Agency relocated to Amsterdam in March 2019, taking a significant proportion of its staff with it. Operating with reduced capacity, the MHRA is now responsible for decentralised marketing authorisation decisions for Northern Ireland, as well as both decisions for 'centralised' (innovative) and 'decentralised' (other, for example generic medicines and over-the-counter medicines) medicines for all of Great Britain.

If the Protocol is ever fully implemented, medicines that need a 'centralised' marketing authorisation decision will have to be authorised by the European Medicines Agency if they are to be marketed in Northern Ireland. It may arise that there is a delay between the MHRA authorisation for a product to be marketed in Great Britain and the European Medicines Agency authorisation for Northern Ireland. Patients in Northern Ireland would therefore potentially have delayed access to a new medicine, in comparison with patients in Great Britain. It may arise that some medicines would be authorised for marketing in Great Britain, but not in Northern Ireland. This is a normal outcome of the regulatory divergence associated with the UK's position that it would not seek access to the EU's single market, with the 'dynamic alignment' that would have been necessary for that access. People in the health policy sector with whom we spoke with in Northern Ireland in 2022 described a situation where patients in Northern Ireland did not have the same access to medicines as patients in Great Britain as 'unacceptable'.

[37] See Department of Health (Northern Ireland), 'Release of Northern Ireland Inpatient, Day Case and Outpatient Hospital Statistics for 2019/20', 6 August 2020 (www.health-ni.gov.uk/news/release-northern-ireland-inpatient-day-case-and-outpatient-hospital-statistics-201920). Figures for 2020 onwards will of course be significantly affected by the COVID-19 pandemic.

[38] H Yusufi et al, 'The NHS in Northern Ireland Post-Brexit: The Legal Position on Product Supply' 2021 29(2) *European Journal of Health Law* 165.

[39] Interview with Paul Laffin, May 2019.

Detailed research by the Nuffield Trust in summer 2022 discovered that there were in fact *already* some discrepancies between some new medicines authorised for Great Britain and those authorised for Northern Ireland.[40] For example, in May 2022, an ADHD treatment called atomoxetine was authorised in a 4mg/ml oral solution for Great Britain, but not for Northern Ireland. This is a medicine that is not subject to the 'centralised' procedure, so it is not explicable by a slower or different process at the European Medicines Agency. It would be explicable by the supplier not having applied for a marketing authorisation for Northern Ireland for that particular medicine in that particular form, or by the MHRA being slower to take decisions for Northern Ireland than for Great Britain. Another example is a generic version of a medicine called Ropinirole, produced by the company Sciecure Pharma Ltd. This has a licensing authorisation for Great Britain, but not for Northern Ireland.[41] The discrepancies in available medicines are – so far – only a particular company's version of a medicine. The product in general is still available in Northern Ireland, but of course a smaller number of suppliers could mean increased costs for the NHS in Northern Ireland.

Other regulations applicable to medicines may also diverge between the UK and EU, leaving supply of the Northern Ireland market less appealing than the Great Britain or EU markets because of the need to comply with two different sets of rules. For *just one* of the relevant stages of governance – securing safe manufacture of medicines – the EU and UK agreed in the EU-UK Trade and Cooperation Agreement (TCA)[42] that they would recognise each other's decisions that medicines have been made in accordance with 'good manufacturing practice'. Recognition of good manufacturing practice involves regulators inspecting medicines manufacturing sites, to ensure that the production is safe, consistent, and in line with what has been approved for sale in a marketing authorisation. The EU and UK agreed to accept the results of each other's inspections, and the certificates that verify these results, and to share information with each other when asked. By not requiring two sets of inspections, or two sets of documents, this agreement removes *just one* of the many non-tariff barriers to trade in medicines. All the others – such as testing batches of medicines to make sure they are consistent; packaging and labelling rules; and tracing of medicines to prevent falsified medicines from entering the market – remain. If the Protocol comes fully into force, and if a medicine is to be used in the NHS in Northern Ireland, that medicine will need to comply with the EU rules on all these matters. At the same time, though, some things about medicines supply in Northern Ireland remain a question of national competence, and not covered by EU measures. EU regulation does not cover many aspects of clinical and biomedical research; decisions on which medicines to pay for within the NHS, which are taken by the National Institute for Clinical Excellence, in England, for patients in Northern Ireland; and details of matters such

[40] M McCarey et al, *Health and Brexit Six Years On* (London, The Nuffield Trust, 2022).

[41] Nuffield Trust and Health and International Relations Monitor, 'Written Evidence (NIP0037)' submitted to House of Lords Sub-Committee on the Protocol on Ireland/Northern Ireland (https://committees.parliament.uk/writtenevidence/113370/html/ accessed 30 November 2022).

[42] EU-UK TCA, Annex 12, 'Medicinal Products'.

as the roll-out of a vaccine programme. Caught between these two regulatory spaces, if the Protocol is ever fully enforced, the net effect will be to make Northern Ireland into a tiny market for medicines. Companies may then decide that it is not worth supplying such a small market.

Even in the shorter term, the position involves risks for the NHS in Northern Ireland in terms of medicines supply. Companies may also decide not to supply a market if a regulatory position is too uncertain, or likely to change quickly. Since January 2019, by law, a company which is supplying a medicine to the NHS must give six months' notice if it intends to cease supplying that medicine.[43] A letter to Lord Jay of Ewelme, the Chair of the UK parliamentary committee that investigated the situation under the Protocol, from Lord Frost, of the Cabinet Office, in July 2021, warned that over 280 medicines had been notified for discontinuation to Northern Ireland.[44] When we spoke with health policy stakeholders in Belfast in spring 2022, they said that there had indeed been a huge increase in such notifications during 2021, but that supply had in fact continued once the new EU legislative 'grace period', which runs until end December 2024, had come into effect.[45] Overall, the position for medicines supply in Northern Ireland seems to be relatively secure until that time, but very uncertain thereafter. June 2024 will be a critical moment, as this is the latest that a notification for discontinuation of supply can be given within the new six-month rules.

The position for medical devices and equipment is different, at least in the short term. The UK unilaterally decided to continue to accept *general* 'CE' marks as evidence that a product is safe and has met the relevant quality standards until 31 December 2024.[46] This ongoing recognition of EU standards applies to medical equipment for the whole of the UK.

The UK's unilateral acceptance of CE marks for medical devices continues until 23 June 2023. New EU laws on medical devices, and in vitro diagnostic medical devices, delayed because of the COVID-19 pandemic, came into force in May 2021 and May 2022 respectively. For now, companies can reach the whole EU market, plus the UK, including Northern Ireland, by complying with these new rules, and using a 'Notified Body' in the EU to show compliance. In effect, this is an example of 'dynamic alignment' between the UK and the EU, because the UK has essentially followed the EU's rules as they changed, after 1 January 2021.[47] Supply of medical devices and equipment to Northern Ireland is mainly from the EU, and so this continued removal

[43] Health Service Products (Provision and Disclosure of Information) Regulations 2018, Regulation 29.

[44] Letter from Lord Frost to Lord Jay of Ewelme, Chair of the Protocol on Ireland/Northern Ireland Sub-Committee, House of Lords, 28 July 2021 (https://committees.parliament.uk/publications/7011/documents/72907/default/).

[45] M Dayan et al, 'Protocol Politics Mean Hard Times Ahead for Health in Northern Ireland', Nuffield Trust, 6 July 2022 (www.nuffieldtrust.org.uk/news-item/protocol-politics-mean-hard-times-ahead-for-health-in-northern-ireland).

[46] Department for Business, Energy and Industrial Strategy, 'Guidance: Using the UKCA Marking', 31 December 2020, updated 14 November 2022.

[47] Note that UK in a Changing Europe disagrees with our categorisation here. They categorise Medical Devices Regulation as 'passive divergence', with a view to becoming 'active divergence', see UK in a Changing Europe, 'UK-EU Divergence Tracker' (London, UK in a Changing Europe, October 2021), 28–29.

of non-tariff barriers to trade between the EU and Northern Ireland is helping to secure continued supplies. This is borne out through second-hand knowledge passed to Flear by several users of medical devices in Northern Ireland:

> Several of my friends use medical devices manufactured in the EU and certified for use by a Notified Body based there. For instance, one friend, mentioned already, has Type 2 diabetes and uses a glucose monitor, which attaches to their arm, and is linked up to an app on their phone. There is some concern about what Brexit may mean for continued access to the monitor, including updates. I got chatting to my friend about their concerns a few times, most recently in autumn 2022. My friend told me: 'The company that makes them [the monitoring devices] is based in the US, but they're manufactured in various places including Ireland – which I've got to hope means we're OK supply wise in Northern Ireland'. Glucose monitoring has not been interrupted by Brexit, for the time being at least. Thankfully for my friend and others in a similar situation.

Northern Ireland seems to be better served than Great Britain by continued alignment with EU standards, and a realignment with a divergent Great Britain would likely result in a net loss overall.[48]

However, such a realignment is currently on the cards. When the UK ceases to recognise the EU's 'CE' marks, which it is set to do on 31 December 2024 in general,[49] but on 30 June 2023 for medical devices,[50] medical devices and equipment for the market in England, Scotland and Wales will need to be certified by the new UK Conformity Assessment (UKCA) process. This includes having a UK-based person (or company) responsible for the various regulatory compliance tasks, such as registering a medical device with the MHRA. It includes using a 'UK Approved Body' to show compliance.[51] The EU's system obviously will not recognise the UKCA process, so two processes will be needed if a product is being supplied to both Great Britain and the EU. To deal with the position for products in Northern Ireland, which otherwise would *always* need both EU and UK approvals, the Withdrawal Agreement made special provision for products intended only for the Northern Ireland market. They can have a 'UKNI' mark, certified by a designated 'UK Notified Body', recognised by the EU. At present (winter 2022), though, no such bodies exist.[52]

The UK Guidance for medical devices currently (winter 2022) says:

> The Government has introduced new legislation [hyperlink to the Northern Ireland Protocol Bill] to make changes to how the Northern Ireland Protocol will apply. You should continue to use the guidance below for now. It will be updated in due course, giving you time to prepare for any new requirements.

[48] Dayan et al, 'Protocol Politics Mean Hard Times Ahead for Health in Northern Ireland', above n 45.

[49] Department for Business, Energy and Industrial Strategy, 'Placing Manufactured Products on the Market in Great Britain' (www.gov.uk/guidance/placing-manufactured-goods-on-the-market-in-great-britain accessed 22 November 2022).

[50] Medicines and Healthcare Products Regulatory Agency, 'Regulating Medical Devices in the UK' (www.gov.uk/guidance/regulating-medical-devices-in-the-uk accessed 22 November 2022).

[51] Medicines and Healthcare Products Regulatory Agency, 'Approved Bodies for Medical Devices' (www.gov.uk/government/publications/approved-bodies-for-medical-devices accessed 22 November 2022).

[52] Medicines and Healthcare Products Regulatory Agency, 'Regulating Medical Devices in the UK', above n 50.

This example adds to the ongoing uncertainty that characterises the regulatory environment that applies to supply of the products that the NHS needs in Northern Ireland.

VI. THE POST-2021 POSITION IN GREAT BRITAIN

While Northern Ireland is in a uniquely precarious position in terms of supply of medicines from the EU, and in a relatively good position only in the short term in terms of supply of medical devices and equipment, it is not the case that the rest of the UK is in a particularly good position post-Brexit. The UK makes up just 3 per cent of the global market in the global life sciences industries: medicines, medical devices and equipment. The House Commons Health and Social Care Committee, reviewing all the evidence available in 2018, reflected the widely-held view that the UK's share of the industry is too small for the UK to 'go it alone' in terms of regulation.[53] This view was also endorsed by the UK Life Science Industrial Strategy,[54] and virtually every type of stakeholder in the sector. Smaller markets are less appealing to the global industry: for example, new treatments typically reach smaller markets six to 18 months later than the 'big three' of the USA, EU and China.[55]

Overall, then, and putting this in simple terms, the UK faces a regulatory choice in terms of securing supply of existing and new medicines, medical devices and equipment for the NHS.[56] The UK can choose one of three positions. Either it can align with another large market, so as to continue to be an attractive place for the global industry to supply, without having the ability to influence the regulatory decisions taken for that market. Or it can seek to attract supply, and indeed inward investment, by deregulating the sector substantially, lowering or removing standards, potentially placing patients at risk. Or it can develop a completely new framework, which risks making the UK unattractive for companies because of the extra costs associated with a double regulatory burden (that is, where companies are required to comply with two sets of regulations, those in the place of production and sale).

In the short term, for Great Britain, in practice the UK government adopted the first position. For example, it unilaterally accepted all existing EU medicines marketing authorisations as at 31 December 2020 (a process sometimes called 'grandfathering');[57] and all subsequent EU regulatory processes, for new medicines marketing authorisations until the end of December 2023.[58] The UK gave companies

[53] 'Brexit: Medicines, Medical Devices and Substances of Human Origin', above n 2, paras 28–30.

[54] Ibid, 14, fn 36.

[55] 'Brexit: Medicines, Medical Devices and Substances of Human Origin', above n 2, 10; interview with Philippa Whitford, February 2019.

[56] Fahy et al, 'How Will Brexit Affect Health and Health Services in the UK?', above n 3.

[57] Medicines and Healthcare Products Regulatory Agency, 'Great Britain Marketing Authorisations (MAs) for Centrally Authorised Products (CAPs)' (www.gov.uk/government/publications/great-britain-marketing-authorisations-mas-for-centrally-authorised-products-caps accessed 22 November 2022).

[58] Medicines and Healthcare Products Regulatory Agency, 'European Commission (EC) Decision Reliance Procedure' (www.gov.uk/guidance/european-commission-ec-decision-reliance-procedure accessed 22 November 2022).

until 31 December 2024 to make packaging changes to reflect the new marketing authorisation holder or UK-based representative.[59] CE marking for medical devices is recognised in the UK until 30 June 2023.[60]

At the same time, though, despite this *reality*, the UK government articulated a *narrative* of regulatory divergence from the EU. This was most evident in the marketing authorisations for the Oxford/AstraZeneca (Vaxzevria) and Pfizer/BioNTech COVID-19 vaccines (Comirnaty) in December 2020.[61] One example of this is found in the government's report *The Benefits of Brexit*, from January 2022, which refers to the 'significant benefits' arising from 'properly' regulated cutting-edge medical technology, 'allowing rapid and safe deployment – such as with COVID-19 vaccines'.[62] The narrative in this report suggests a divergence from the EU's more cautious approach to patient and consumer protection:

> Our regulatory system will recognise that not every potential harm of an emerging technology turns into an actual harm of an established technology, while continuing to place the protection of consumers at the forefront of decision-making.

A narrative concerning the benefits of regulatory divergence in the health sector was also evident in the introduction of a new 'fast track' approval process, the 'Innovative Licensing and Access Pathway', which opened on 1 January 2021.[63] Belzutifan, a new medicine used to treat a rare cancer, was the first medicine to use this pathway, at the end of February 2021.[64]

However, it seems to us that there may be more wishful thinking than reality over the UK government's claims that faster track approvals will work to entice the global biosciences industry to supply the UK ahead of other larger global markets. The COVID-19 vaccines were approved using an exceptional procedure[65] consistent with EU law, that any EU Member State could have used. In fact, the European Medicines Agency lagged behind the MHRA by only a few weeks, giving its marketing authorisation for Comirnaty on 21 December 2020,[66] and Vaxzevria on 29 January 2021. As for Belzutifan, although it is not yet (as at November 2022) authorised for EU

[59] Medicines and Healthcare Products Regulatory Agency, 'Great Britain Marketing Authorisations (MAs) for Centrally Authorised Products (CAPs)', above n 57.

[60] Medicines and Healthcare Products Regulatory Agency, 'Regulating Medical Devices in the UK', above n 50.

[61] Medicines and Healthcare Products Regulatory Agency, 'Regulatory approval of Pfizer/BioNTech vaccine for COVID-19' (www.gov.uk/government/publications/regulatory-approval-of-pfizer-biontech-vaccine-for-covid-19# accessed 22 November 2022); Medicines and Healthcare Products Regulatory Agency, 'Oxford University/AstraZeneca COVID-19 Vaccine Approved' (www.gov.uk/government/news/oxford-universityastrazeneca-covid-19-vaccine-approved accessed 22 November 2022).

[62] HM Government, *The Benefits of Brexit: How the UK is Taking Advantage of Leaving the EU*, January 2022, 26.

[63] Medicines and Healthcare Products Regulatory Agency, 'The MHRA Innovative Licensing and Access Pathway is Open for Business' (www.gov.uk/government/news/the-mhra-innovative-licensing-and-access-pathway-is-open-for-business accessed 22 November 2022).

[64] S Neville, 'Cancer Drug is First to Begin Fast-Track UK Approval Process', Financial Times, 26 February 2021.

[65] Called 'Regulation 174 approval', see the Human Medicines Regulations 2012, Regulation 174.

[66] European Medicines Agency, 'Comirnaty' (www.ema.europa.eu/en/medicines/human/EPAR/comirnaty accessed 22 November 2022).

marketing,[67] it did not actually receive its marketing authorisation for Great Britain until May 2022, nine months after the USA's Food and Drug Administration had approved it.[68] Moreover, Belzutifan does not yet have National Institute for Health and Care Excellence (NICE) approval to be used in the NHS: this is expected for May 2023.[69] And it is not currently authorised for Northern Ireland – so even if there are benefits for patients based in Great Britain, these apparently will not be shared with patients in Northern Ireland.

In the medium term, it is therefore quite difficult to tell what the UK's approach for Great Britain will be. The Medicines and Medical Devices Act 2021 gives sweeping powers to make changes to depart from the EU's regulatory positions, but these have been little used as yet. The extent of the powers granted has also been criticised, as likely to lead to suboptimal regulations because of the lack of oversight involved. The Conservative Peer Lord Blencathra described the Act as 'absolutely atrocious' in its structure, and 'an affront to parliamentary democracy'.[70] More sweepingly, the Act has been criticised by Laura Downey and colleagues for paying almost no attention to the criticisms of the current situation reported in the independent Cumberlege Review,[71] a review of high profile regulatory failings in vaginal mesh, a hormonal pregnancy test called Primodos, and sodium valproate, published in July 2020.[72] The Act does almost nothing to respond to the significant deficiencies in the UK's (and EU's) current approaches:[73] it is, in short, a missed (Brexit) opportunity.

VII. CONCLUSIONS

Overall, the worst possible outcomes in terms of supply of products to the NHS were avoided by the Withdrawal Agreement and EU-UK TCA. But avoiding 'No Deal' Brexit does not mean that this was a good outcome for product supply, or for the regulatory environment that protects patients and at the same time seeks to encourage global bioscience industries to develop new health technologies, new medicines and vaccines and new treatments, and to supply those to the UK. The UK as a whole is headed towards becoming a small market in global terms. Northern Ireland is headed towards being a tiny market, where uncertainties in the legal rules make continued supply significantly less appealing, or even impossible.

[67] It seems to be undergoing a clinical trial in the EU, see Good Clinical Practice Network, 'Página Nct de ensaios clínicos' (https://ichgcp.net/pt/eu-clinical-trials-registry/trial/2021–003436-92/BG accessed 22 November 2022).

[68] US Food and Drug Administration, 'FDA Approves Belzutifan for Cancers Associated with Von Hippel-Lindau Disease', 1 February 2022 (www.fda.gov/drugs/resources-information-approved-drugs/fda-approves-belzutifan-cancers-associated-von-hippel-lindau-disease).

[69] National Institute for Health and Care Excellence, 'Belzutifan for Treating Clear-Cell Renal Carcinoma Caused by Von Hippel-Lindau disease [ID3932]' (www.nice.org.uk/guidance/indevelopment/gid-ta10817 accessed 22 November 2022).

[70] 'Medicines and Medical Devices Bill', Hansard, HC Vol 805, cols 415–16 (2 September 2020).

[71] Independent Medicines and Medical Devices Safety Review, *First Do No Harm*, July 2020.

[72] H Haskell, 'Cumberlege Review Exposes Stubborn and Dangerous Flaws in Healthcare' (2020) 370 *British Medical Journal* m3099.

[73] L Downey et al, 'The Medicines and Medical Devices Act 2021 & Uncertain Regulatory Futures' (www.birmingham.ac.uk/research/perspective/medical-devices-act-regulation.aspx accessed 22 November 2022).

This outcome is far from what the people we talked with in the street in Northern Ireland and the north of England want for the NHS. Their aspirations are for a world-class health system, and they often describe the NHS as the best in the world,[74] although under-resourced. Many people we talked with responded to the bus picture by talking about the NHS. Nearly four in 10 of those conversations involved the person expressing a positive reaction to the NHS. A similar proportion of people stated they want more resources for the NHS. Only 2 per cent stated they wanted fewer resources. As one white, middle aged local in Derry/Londonderry commented '"I agree with that". More money for the NHS would be good. More GPs and nurses.'[75] The specific funding amount was particularly resonant: one participant said when asked what's the first thing that came to mind: 'money'. This was because '"If we could get money back from where we're sending it and put it in" the NHS that would be "so important". Doctors, hospitals are stretched and stressed'.[76] Others reflected this feeling with strong emotional attachment. One woman said that 'she was very passionate about the NHS'.[77] It seems to us that the photo pulled people emotionally in two directions. On the one hand, their instinctive reaction was to call the picture 'lies' or 'bullshit',[78] but on the other hand they used the rest of the conversation to discuss how the NHS might secure more funding for everything they perceive that it needs.

From the point of view of the health policy community, a strong theme in our interviews, and also in the available public record, is that everyone loses from the outcomes of Brexit in this context. The EU loses, because it can no longer draw on the UK's considerable regulatory capacities, experience and global reputation in terms of medicines and devices regulation.

The UK loses by becoming disconnected from the larger EU market. For sure, in some instances, the UK can adopt a regulatory position that is an improvement on the EU's position – after all, the EU is far from perfect in terms of the detail of how it protects patients and ensures that the products used to treat them are safe. The Poly Implant Prothèse breast implant affair, in which industrial rather than medical grade silicon was used in hundreds of thousands of breast implants, is an example of the failures of EU law in this context.[79] The UK's MHRA may, for example, be able to grant marketing authorisations to new medicines more quickly than the European Medicines Agency, as the examples of the COVID-19 vaccines in December 2020, and of Belzufatin in May 2022 show. But if these particular examples are to become the norm, the MHRA will need to be significantly better resourced, especially if it is really to offer faster-track approvals than the USA's Food and Drug Administration, so as to compete in the global marketplace. And an MHRA marketing authorisation is insufficient – if novel treatments are to reach patients in the UK, the National Institute

[74] Newry 25A; Rochdale 70A.
[75] Derry 139B.
[76] Derry 147B.
[77] Newry 40A.
[78] I Antova et al, 'Calling out "Bullshit" in "Left Behind" Britain', SPERI, 16 September 2019 (http://speri.dept.shef.ac.uk/2019/09/16/calling-out-brexit-bullshit-in-left-behind-britain/).
[79] T Hervey and J McHale, *European Union Health Law: Themes and Implications* (Oxford, Oxford University Press, 2015), 3–6, 371–78, 548–49.

for Health and Care Excellence (NICE) must assess the treatments as available on the NHS. Overall, then, the ideological drive to 'burn' or 'tear up' EU regulation ignores the economic realities of the relative sizes of the UK and EU markets, and the Brussels effect: an undeniable fact that is reported only sparingly in the British press.[80] The disconnects between the governmental narratives of regulatory freedom and the realities on the ground for the NHS are strongly evident in the context of supply of medicines, medical devices and equipment to the NHS.

[80] P Stephens, 'After Brexit the Tories Still Cannot Escape EU Red Tape', Financial Times, 1 August 2022.

9

Biomedical Research

I. INTRODUCTION

In late March 2019, Hervey and Wood attended a meeting with Zoe Martin, policy manager, and some of her colleagues at Cancer Research UK. Formed in 2002, Cancer Research UK is the world's largest independent cancer research charity. Its work is wide-ranging, and includes significant support for cancer research activities. The purpose of our meeting was to scope out whether we could collaborate on legal or policy analysis to assist Cancer Research UK with its Brexit-related engagements, like the analysis we did with the much smaller charity, Kidney Care UK, discussed in chapter five.

March 2019 was a time of huge uncertainty in the Brexit process. The original Brexit date had been set for 29 March 2019, but on 20 March 2019, PM Theresa May requested an extension, which was granted by the EU on 21 March 2019. As it turned out, several further extensions were requested and granted, each resulting in new possible Brexit dates, until the eventual date of 30 January 2020 on which the UK formally left the EU, and 1 January 2021, when EU law ceased to apply in Great Britain.[1]

Looking back on the interview (in winter 2022), it is a perfect reflection of a specific instance of one part of the health policy community in the UK seeking to navigate an extremely tricky situation. A large and international charity, Cancer Research UK enjoys close relationships with the UK government, with the European Commission, with research entities like universities and hospitals across the UK and beyond, and with the global life sciences industry. As we see it, the understandable desire to keep those relationships cordial made it exceptionally difficult for Cancer Research UK to position itself in the national debate about the form that Brexit should take. The charity is also reliant on a huge number of voluntary supporters from across the whole UK population, a high proportion of whom are likely to have been Leave voters.

As a matter of practical reality, the UK was deeply embedded in the EU across a range of core activities for Cancer Research UK, especially clinical trials of new cancer treatments, and 'European Reference Groups' for rare diseases, bringing together specialists for unusual cancers across different EU Member States and

[1] N Walker, *Brexit Timeline: Events Leading to the UK's Exit from the European Union*, Briefing Paper Number 7960, 6 January 2021.

granting them dedicated EU funding for their work, conditional on collaborative research endeavours. As Cancer Research UK pointed out in 2017, collaborative trials were the most common type of clinical trials conducted in the UK, France, Germany, Italy, the Netherlands, Poland and Spain.[2] International collaboration is particularly important when investigating rare diseases and children, because a single country often does not have sufficient patients for a viable trial. In general, future biomedical research was (and still is) expected to become more international, because of the emerging practice of grouping trial patients in accordance with a specific and rare genetic profile.

As a matter of political ideology, though, the May government was articulating a desire to leave the EU's single market, but occupy a new space in the EU's relationships with its trading partners: a 'deep and special relationship', because of having been an EU Member State, in Europe but not in the EU.[3] At the same time, as a matter of its political ideology, the EU, and especially the European Commission, was articulating a rigid interpretation of its single market rules, encapsulated in the phrase 'a non-member of the Union, that does not live up to the same obligations as a member, cannot have the same rights and enjoy the same benefits as a member'.[4] According to this aspect of the EU's negotiating position, there is no legal category of 'departing EU Member State' or 'ex-EU Member State'. Once outside the EU, the UK could either be treated as a state which accepts the disciplines of the internal market and its law (like Norway); or as an ordinary 'third country' (like Canada, Japan or any other country with which the EU has one or more trade agreements). The EU's position had been captured neatly in a PowerPoint slide which became known as the 'steps of doom'. The EU's chief negotiator Michel Barnier set out the possible EU trade relationships, arrayed in a series of downward steps, beginning with EEA membership (the 'Norway' model), and showing how the UK was rejecting each possible model and therefore would end up with an ordinary free trade agreement (the 'Canada' model), which by definition did not offer any special access to the EU's single market.

When we spoke with them in 2019, and in a follow-up meeting in January 2020 as the EU-UK Trade and Cooperation Agreement (EU-UK TCA) was agreed, Cancer Research UK were concerned about several overlapping aspects of biomedical research, and how they would feature in the UK's future relationship with the EU. Cancer Research UK sought to understand how cross-border clinical trials involving

[2] P Vernai et al, The *Impact of Collaboration: The Value of UK Medical Research to EU Science and Health* (Technopolis Group, 2017), 14.

[3] Prime Minister's Office, 10 Downing Street, Department for Exiting the European Union, and Theresa May MP, 'Lancaster House Speech', 17 January 2017; 'Florence Speech', 22 September 2017; 'Mansion House Speech', 2 March 2018.

[4] European Council, Guidelines following the United Kingdom's notification under Article 50 TEU EUCO XT 20004/17, 29 April 2017; European Council, Guidelines (Article 50) EUCO XT 20001/18, 23 March 2018; and see, eg C Barnard and S Butlin, 'Free Movement vs Fair Movement: Brexit and Managed Migration' (2018) 55 *(Special Issue) Common Market Law Review* 203; S Bulmer and L Quaglia, 'The Politics and Economics of Brexit' (2018) 25(8) *Journal of European Public Policy* 1089; D Phinnemore, 'UK Withdrawal from EU Membership: The Quest for Cake' in S Gstöhl and D Phinnemore (eds), *The Proliferation of Privileged Partnerships between the European Union and its Neighbours* (Abingdon, Routledge, 2019). For critique, see, eg, Editorial Comment, 'Is the "Indivisibility" of the Four Freedoms a Principle of EU Law?' (2019) 56(5) *Common Market Law Review* 1.

UK patients and research partners (hospitals, universities) alongside EU patients and research partners would be able to continue. Would data still be able to be shared in those cross-national research teams? Would UK researchers be able to access the EU's new online clinical trials register, which was coming into effect soon, and would be a single portal for research data, the use of which portal would be required in all applications for marketing authorisations for successful new treatments to be marketed in the EU? All of these matters are categorised as part of single market law by the EU. Would researchers in the UK continue to have access to European funding for biomedical research? Would they be able to be part of the 'European Reference Networks' for rare diseases, bringing together specialists and patients suffering from rare cancers, where there are insufficient UK-based patients to investigate new medicines? These concerns were shared by many across the health policy sector.[5]

We also heard in our interviews[6] about concerns that the UK would become a less attractive place for a career in biomedicine. In 2016, the UK had attracted nearly 25 per cent of all migrant researchers within the Marie Curie scheme, which supports mobility across the EU and associated countries.[7] As we have seen in chapter seven, after Brexit, the new 'hostile environment' in terms of the UK's immigration rules meant that non-UK, non-Irish people would be treated as 'outsiders' in a way that EU-26 nationals were not, when their EU citizenship was recognised in UK law and policy.

II. BEFORE THE WITHDRAWAL AGREEMENT

The position here will be familiar from previous chapters. Before the UK and EU reached agreement on the terms of withdrawal, there was a genuine risk of chaos, and threat to patient safety, associated with 'No Deal' Brexit. In the context of biomedical research, the key threat was to patients involved in cross-national research projects. On a 'No Deal' Brexit, a major problem that would have arisen immediately was that it would have become illegal overnight for EU-based researchers to share data with UK-based researchers. This is because the UK would instantly, from one day to the next, have become a place where the EU did not recognise data protection law as 'adequate'. The practical reality, that the UK was planning to 'roll over' the EU's data protection law into domestic law as 'retained EU law' under the European Union (Withdrawal) Act 2018 was not legally relevant to the EU. Without protections associated with internal market law, especially oversight from the EU's Court of Justice and

[5] N Fahy et al, 'How Will Brexit Affect Health and Health Services in the UK? Evaluating Three Possible Scenarios Against the WHO Health System Building Blocks' (2017) 390(10107) *The Lancet* 2110; N Fahy et al, 'How Will Brexit Affect Health and Health Services in the UK? An Updated Evaluation' (2019) 393(10174) *The Lancet* 949; N Fahy et al, 'Assessing the Potential Impact on Health of the UK's Future Relationship Agreement with the EU: Analysis of the Negotiating Positions' (2021) 16(3) *Health Economics, Policy and Law* 290.

[6] Interview with Sarah Wollaston, March 2019; Interview with Philippa Whitford, February 2019.

[7] European Commission, 'Marie Skłodowska-Curie Actions' (https://marie-sklodowska-curie-actions.ec.europa.eu/ accessed 23 November 2022), cited in N Fahy et al, 'How Will Brexit Affect Health and Health Services in the UK?', above n 5, fn 30.

national courts, mere unilateral regulatory alignment on the UK's part would not have been enough.

The effects of this uncertainty were beginning to show in the biomedical research sector. A report by the global economic analysts Fitch – unfortunately not in the public domain, but reported by Reuters in October 2018[8] – showed that just under 600 clinical trials had been initiated in the UK in 2017, compared to an annual average of just over 800 from 2009–16: a 25 per cent decrease. The US-based life sciences company Recardio attracted national news coverage in October 2018 when it decided not to go ahead with recruiting patients to an exploratory trial of dutogliptin, used alongside filgrastim, in hospitals in Glasgow, Exeter and Leeds.[9] The 'Phase II' research, which went ahead in several EU Member States,[10] was to investigate whether dutogliptin might help with cardiac muscle regeneration after certain types of heart attack. The firm cited general uncertainties about the form Brexit would take and in particular lack of clarity in terms of future relations with the European Medicines Agency, as the reasons for its decision. Sheuli Porkess, the deputy chief scientific officer at the Association of the British Pharmaceutical Industry confirmed that this was not an isolated incident: Brexit uncertainties were impeding decisions about whether to commence clinical trials in the NHS across the sector.[11] In response to the Recardio decision, Jane-Claire Judson, from the charity Chest Heart & Stroke Scotland, expressed a view which had become familiar to us: she was 'seriously concerned at the lack of priority and focus given to providing detailed solutions to the health ramifications of Brexit'.[12]

As we have already seen, though, the Withdrawal Agreement and EU-UK TCA avoided these potentially chaotic effects of Brexit, also in the context of biomedical research.

III. THE WITHDRAWAL AGREEMENT, EU-UK TCA AND AFTER 1 JANUARY 2021

For data sharing between the EU and UK, the Withdrawal Agreement secured continuity until 1 January 2021, and the EU-UK TCA[13] gave a 'grace period' of up to six months, within which the UK[14] and the EU[15] were able to take decisions to deem each

[8] B Hirschler and L Heavens, 'UK Clinical Trials Fall as Brexit Clouds Drug Approval Process', Reuters, 9 October 2018.

[9] G Campbell, 'Heart Drug Trials Halted Over Brexit Fears', BBC, 3 October 2018.

[10] D von Lewinski et al, 'Protocol for a Phase 2, Randomised, Double-Blind, Placebo-Controlled, Safety and Efficacy Study of Dutogliptin in Combination with Filgrastim in Early Recovery Post-Myocardial Infarction' (2020) 21 *Trials* 744.

[11] Hirschler and Heavens, 'UK Clinical Trials Fall', above n 8.

[12] J Persuad, 'Recardio Ceases UK Drug Trials, Blaming Brexit', Pharaphorum, 3 October 2018 (https://pharmaphorum.com/news/recardio-ceases-uk-drug-trials-blaming-brexit/).

[13] Article 782 EU-UK TCA.

[14] Department for Digital, Culture, Media and Sport, 'International Data Transfers: Building Trust, Delivering Growth and Firing Up Innovation', 26 August 2021 (www.gov.uk/government/publications/uk-approach-to-international-data-transfers/international-data-transfers-building-trust-delivering-growth-and-firing-up-innovation).

[15] Commission Implementing Decision (EU) 2021/1772 of 28 June 2021 pursuant to Regulation (EU) 2016/679 of the European Parliament and of the Council on the adequate protection of personal data by the United Kingdom (notified under document C(2021)4800) [2021] OJ L 360/1.

other compliant with their respective data protection laws. As things currently stand in winter 2022, therefore, data may lawfully flow in either direction between the UK and the EU, without the need for the expensive 'alternative measures' foreseen in the EU's General Data Protection Regulation[16] for those countries which the EU does not regard as having 'adequate' data protection. One of the topics we worked on with Cancer Research UK[17] was what those 'alternative measures' might look like in the context of biomedical research – fortunately, this costly and complex policy response did not, in the end, have to be deployed. For the future, the EU-UK TCA does include a general 'right to regulate' digital trade clause,[18] for public interest reasons, including public health protection, safety, privacy and data protection. If the UK were to diverge from the EU too significantly in the future, it is possible that the EU would cease to recognise the UK in terms of data protection: another reason for continued 'dynamic regulatory alignment' (as we described in chapter eight) being desired by people in the health policy sector when asked for their views on legitimate post-Brexit health futures.

The EU-UK TCA confirms that the UK had been able to negotiate participation in the EU's flagship research funding programmes, which have been called different things over the years, the one running from 2021 being called 'Horizon Europe'. The UK is – in principle – an 'associate' in Horizon Europe, which means UK-based research entities may not only participate in, but also lead, research projects.[19] This decision was greeted enthusiastically by the science community in January 2021, for example with Catherine Guinard of the Wellcome Trust describing it on Twitter as 'a symbol of hope and solidarity'.[20] We were also pleased – and a little surprised – by the news. Unfortunately, however, by October 2021, it became clear that the EU would not allow the UK to participate in Horizon Europe until the political disagreements over the Ireland/Northern Ireland Protocol had been resolved.[21]

Research participation is one of only two health-related areas of detailed continued substantive cooperation between the UK and the EU found in the EU-UK TCA – the other being reciprocal healthcare discussed in chapter five. Cooperation does not include the EU's health-specific funding programmes, such as EU4Health or the 'European Reference Networks' for rare diseases; or the Erasmus programme which supports student and academic staff mobility (including biomedical researchers); or

[16] Regulation (EU) 2016/679 of the European Parliament and of the Council of 27 April 2016 on the protection of natural persons with regard to the processing of personal data and on the free movement of such data, and repealing Directive 95/46/EC (General Data Protection Regulation) [2016] OJ L 119/1 ('GDPR').

[17] S McCloskey and T Hervey, *Cooperative Relationships for Bio-Medical Science Post-Brexit: The Legal Landscape*, Cancer Research UK Briefing Note, 2020 (www.sheffield.ac.uk/media/9926/download accessed 23 November 2022).

[18] Articles 198 and 199 EU-UK TCA.

[19] European Commission, 'Q&A on the UK's Participation in Horizon Europe' (https://ec.europa.eu/info/sites/default/files/research_and_innovation/strategy_on_research_and_innovation/documents/ec_rtd_uk-participation-in-horizon-europe.pdf accessed 23 November 2022).

[20] E Gibney, 'What the Landmark Brexit Deal Means for Science' (2021) 589 *Nature* 179.

[21] F Zubaşcu, 'Gabriel Confirms UK Can't Join Horizon Europe Until Row Over Northern Ireland Protocol is Settled', Science Business, 14 October 2021 (https://sciencebusiness.net/news/gabriel-confirms-uk-cant-join-horizon-europe-until-row-over-northern-ireland-protocol-settled); N Mitchell, 'As Hopes Fade, UK Unveils Alternative to Horizon Europe', University World News, 23 July 2022 (www.universityworldnews.com/post.php?story=20220723095556503).

the EU's 'cohesion' funding which has been used to support some health research infrastructure projects, like building clinics, in deprived regions. The details on the cost to the UK of participation were hammered out in the TCA itself. So in principle, what would have been a significant detriment to biomedical science in the UK had been avoided. The UK had been a net beneficiary of EU research funding, attracting more funding than it contributed as an EU Member State.[22] The continued ability to participate in Horizon Europe research would mean that UK-based biomedical research would be more likely to be able to maintain its global position, and indeed to attract clinical trial sponsors and inward investment in the global bioscience sector. One lesson learned from the COVID-19 pandemic is the value of collaborative research in the health domain, so as to promote the isomorphic learning that flows from comparisons between countries.

That is the position in principle. But in fact, as Nick Fahy and others reported in 2022,[23] during the years 2016–20, there had been a substantial shift away from inclusion of UK-based research in comparison to projects funded up to 2016 under 'FP7' and 'Horizon 2020', the precursors to Horizon Europe. The UK and Germany had been the countries attracting the most research funding from the EU from 2008–16; then the UK fell to fifth place by 2020. Compared to Germany, Mike Galsworthy of Scientists for EU told us in 2021,[24] the UK had lost around £1.5 billion of research funding since 2017. We have heard from colleagues and friends about how Brexit has impacted inclusion of UK-based researchers in Horizon Europe funding bids. Flear spoke with one of his colleagues (who preferred not to be named) in autumn 2022, asking for an update on where things stand in universities in Northern Ireland:

> Post-Brexit there was much anecdotal commentary around no longer being viewed as a viable lead on applications and sometimes not even a useful partner because of potential negativity of associating with UK scientists … I've heard very little recently – maybe as folk have reorientated schemes they consider.

The Johnson government's March 2021 budget initially did not include specific funding for the UK's participation in Horizon Europe, leaving a gap of around £2 billion a year to be found from core research and development budgets in UK universities.[25] Then by April 2021, funding at least for the first year became available, but in an arrangement described as 'opaque' by the President of the Royal Society, Adrian Smith.[26] At the same time as articulating a narrative of 'global Britain', the Johnson government had also cut the UK's overseas aid budget from 0.7 per cent to 0.5 per cent of gross national income. This funding inter alia supports international biomedical research. The global science journal *Nature* ran an article describing the effects of the

[22] Fahy et al, 'How Will Brexit Affect Health and Health Services in the UK?', above n 5, 2116.

[23] N Fahy et al, 'Impact on the NHS and Health of the UK's Trade and Cooperation Relationship with the EU, and Beyond' (2022) 17(4) *Health Economics, Policy and Law* 471.

[24] Email correspondence on file with Hervey.

[25] E Kelly, 'UK Budget Offers a Few Crumbs for Research, But No Horizon Europe Money', Science Business, 4 March 2021 (https://sciencebusiness.net/framework-programmes/news/uk-budget-offers-few-crumbs-research-no-horizon-europe-money).

[26] E Kelly, 'UK Announces €250M Towards Horizon Europe Participation Cost Following Scientist Revolt', Science Business, 2 April 2021 (https://sciencebusiness.net/framework-programmes/news/uk-announces-eu250m-towards-horizon-europe-participation-cost-following).

reduction on research into coronaviruses at the University of Oxford.[27] The reputational damage to UK science – including biomedical science – is a matter that several of our collaborators in the health policy sector continued to be concerned about.[28]

Moreover, and more seriously, although the UK has negotiated 'in principle' participation in Horizon Europe, the European Commission has blocked the UK's participation until the impasse over the Ireland/Northern Ireland Protocol is resolved.[29] Kwasi Kwarteng, the then UK Secretary of State for Business, Energy and Industrial Strategy responded in July 2022, with what UK Research and Innovation, the arms-length body that administers scientific research in UK universities, describes as a 'new package of transitional measures to ensure the stability and continuity of funding for researchers'.[30] The package is supposed to come into effect if the impasse with the European Commission over Horizon Europe is not resolved.[31] The approach is accompanied by narratives that resonate with the post-Brexit 'cutting red tape' or 'bonfire of regulations' tropes: 'we aim to … ensure we improve the schemes where we can, for example by making proposals less bureaucratic …'.[32] It is too soon to measure whether this policy and budgetary intervention will have the desired effect: the reputational damage and the decline in engagement with UK-based bioscience from researchers based in the EU may need more than funding and administrative simplification to counteract.

IV. EUROPEAN REFERENCE NETWORKS ON RARE DISEASES

One of the elements of its work that particularly concerned Cancer Research UK was the 'European Reference Networks' on rare diseases. Launched in 2017, and supported by EU funding, 24 European Reference Networks bring together into a virtual network specialists in rare low-prevalence complex diseases.[33] The coordinators of

[27] H Else, 'Key COVID Research Hit by Cut to UK Foreign-Aid Budget' (2021) 593 *Nature* 20.

[28] Interview with Philippa Whitford, February 2019; interview with Mark Heffernan and others, March 2019.

[29] B Fox, 'UK Prepares for Life Without Horizon Europe Ahead of "Last Round of Talks"', Euroactiv, 8 June 2022 (www.euractiv.com/section/uk-europe/news/uk-prepares-for-life-without-horizon-europe-ahead-of-last-round-of-talks/).

[30] UK Research Office Brussels, 'UK Participation in EU Programmes for Research, Innovation and Higher Education' (www.ukro.ac.uk/Documents/UK_EU_factsheet.pdf accessed 23 November 2022).

[31] Department for Business, Energy and Industrial Strategy, 'Government Publishes Proposals for Package of Transitional Measures to Support Research and Innovation Sector Affected by Horizon Europe Delays', 20 July 2022 (www.gov.uk/government/news/government-publishes-proposals-for-package-of-transitional-measures-to-support-research-and-innovation-sector-affected-by-horizon-europe-delays); Department for Business, Energy and Industrial Strategy, 'Supporting UK R&D and Collaborative Research Beyond European Programmes', 20 July 2022 (www.gov.uk/government/publications/supporting-uk-rd-and-collaborative-research-beyond-european-programmes).

[32] Department for Business, Energy and Industrial Strategy, 'Supporting UK R&D and Collaborative Research Beyond European Programmes' (www.gov.uk/government/publications/supporting-uk-rd-and-collaborative-research-beyond-european-programmes/supporting-uk-rd-and-collaborative-research-beyond-european-programmes accessed 23 November 2022).

[33] European Commission, 'European Reference Networks' (https://health.ec.europa.eu/european-reference-networks/overview_en accessed 23 November 2022). Legislation relevant to the operation of the European Reference Networks (ERNs) includes: Directive 2011/24/EU of the European Parliament and of the Council of 9 March 2011 on the application of patients' rights in cross-border healthcare [2011] OJ

each network convene virtual advisory panels of medical specialists, using the 'clinical patient management system', an online tool available to participants, to diagnose and treat patients suffering from such rare diseases.[34] Data sharing is covered by EU law. The benefits of European Reference Networks are to bring together a critical mass of clinical experts, to offer healthcare to patients who otherwise would not be able to access it from the national health system in their EU Member State. Before 2016, the UK was hugely over-represented in these networks, particularly in their leadership: we learned that originally six of the 24 networks were led from the UK, based on peer review in an open and merit-based application process. Dozens of UK-based hospital and research teams were part of European Reference Networks. Every Network but one had at least one UK member.[35] By August 2019, no network was led from the UK,[36] and by summer 2022 no clinical centre based in the UK was a full or affiliated member of a European Reference Network.[37] Poignantly, one European Reference Network website listed UK university hospitals as past members, perhaps to show what expertise had been lost.[38]

The treatment of European Reference Groups turned out to be a situation where the practical realities were not enough to drive what would otherwise have been rational decisions by the EU to diverge from its ideologically-driven negotiating position. Consequently, the EU lost leadership and research expertise of some of the world's best biomedical scientists. For example, Professor Jill Clayton-Smith of Manchester University NHS Foundation Trust set up the European Reference Group for patients with rare malformation syndromes and rare intellectual and other

L 88/45; Commission Delegated Decision 2014/286/EU of 10 March 2014 setting out criteria and conditions that European Reference Networks and healthcare providers wishing to join a European Reference Network must fulfil [2014] OJ L 147/71; Annex to the Commission Delegated Decision 2014/286/EU setting out criteria and conditions that European Reference Networks and healthcare providers wishing to join a European Reference Network must fulfil C(2014) 1408 final; Commission Implementing Decision 2014/287/EU of 10 March 2014 setting out criteria for establishing and evaluating European Reference Networks and their Members and for facilitating the exchange of information and expertise on establishing and evaluating such Networks [2014] OJ L 147/79; Annexes to the Commission Implementing Decision 2014/287/EU setting out criteria for establishing and evaluating European Reference Networks and their Members and for facilitating the exchange of information and expertise in relation to the establishment and evaluation of such Networks C(2014) 1411 final; Commission Implementing Decision (EU) 2019/1269 of 26 July 2019 amending Implementing Decision 2014/287/EU setting out criteria for establishing and evaluating European Reference Networks and their Members and for facilitating the exchange of information and expertise on establishing and evaluating such Networks [2019] OJ L 200/35. The ERN initiative receives support from several EU funding programmes, including those viewable at, eg, European Commission, 'Health Programme' (https://health.ec.europa.eu/funding_en accessed 23 November 2022); European Commission, 'Connecting Europe Facility' (https://ec.europa.eu/info/funding-tenders/find-funding/eu-funding-programmes/connecting-europe-facility_en accessed 23 November 2022); European Commission, 'Horizon 2020' (https://research-and-innovation.ec.europa.eu/funding/funding-opportunities/funding-programmes-and-open-calls/horizon-2020_en accessed 23 November 2022).

[34] European Commission, 'Work of the ERNs' (https://health.ec.europa.eu/european-reference-networks/work-erns_en accessed 23 November 2022).

[35] Interview with Kate Ling, March 2019.

[36] European Commission, 'European Reference Networks' (https://ec.europa.eu/health/ern/networks_en accessed 24 November 2022). For discussion see, T Hervey et al, 'Health "Brexternalities": The Brexit Effect on Health and Healthcare Outside the EU' (2021) 46(1) *Journal of Health Politics Policy and Law* 177.

[37] European Commission, 'European Reference Networks', above n 36.

[38] European Reference Network – Eye Diseases (ERN-EYE), 'Home' (www.ern-eye.eu/ern-eye-hcps-members-full-affiliated accessed 24 November 2022).

neurodevelopmental disorders of genetic, genomic/chromosomal or environmental origin in 2017, following a peer reviewed application to do so, and built the network from then on.[39] In 2019, she was required to hand over leadership of the network to Prof Alain Verloes in France, and the three UK members are no longer part of the network. We heard from a leading UK-based biomedical scientist, who preferred not to be named, that one of the Networks had experienced extreme difficulty in finding a non-UK based expert to take over leadership.

Only six of the 24 European Reference Networks – ERN Lung on rare respiratory diseases,[40] EuroBloodNet on rare blood diseases,[41] ERN GENTURIS on rare genetic tumour risk syndromes,[42] MetabERN on hereditary metabolic disorders,[43] ERN Rare-Liver on rare liver diseases,[44] and ERN RITA for rare immunological disorders[45] – now include staff and patients in just a handful of UK hospitals. ERN Lung's website describes 'supporting partnership' as a unique special arrangement, covering 'centres which have relevant specialist clinical expertise, even if they may not meet all formal criteria to become a full Member of an ERN'. The legal modalities of this (which work through the Network byelaws, not EU law per se) are such that the NHS hospital or university clinic cannot be a member of the Network, only the clinicians and other care team members themselves. Partners have no voting rights, and only guest access to the online clinical patient management system.[46] Both EuroBloodNet's and ERN RITA's websites explicitly refer to Brexit.[47] The Italian-based coordinator of MetabERN, Professor Maurizio Scarpa, emailed us in summer 2022 confirming that the UK partners are no longer full members, but also saying 'we are working with the UK providers, we do not care about Brexit political problems'.[48] ERN GENTURIS includes just five named individual clinicians, not even the hospitals in which they are based, suggesting a rather temporary and precarious situation. The arrangement for including UK expertise in this way was apparently

[39] ERN-ITHACA, 'Who We Are' (https://ern-ithaca.eu/about-us/who-we-are/ accessed 24 November 2022).

[40] European Reference Network – ERN-LUNG, 'Welcome to ERN-LUNG' (https://ern-lung.eu/supporting-partners-members/ accessed 24 November 2022).

[41] ERN – EuroBloodNet, 'Who We Are' (www.eurobloodnet.eu/eurobloodnet/who-we-are/ accessed 24 November 2022).

[42] European Reference Network – Genetic Tumour Risk Syndromes (ERN GENTURIS), 'Home' (www.genturis.eu/l=eng/Home.html accessed 24 November 2022).

[43] European Reference Network – MetabERN (European Reference Network for Hereditary Disorders), 'About Us' (https://metab.ern-net.eu/about-us-3/#whoweare accessed 24 November 2022).

[44] European Reference Networks – Hepatological Diseases (ERN RARE-LIVER), 'Members and Partners of the Network' (https://rare-liver.eu/about/members-and-partners-of-the-network accessed 24 November 2022).

[45] ERN-RITA – Rare Immunological Disorders, 'Latest News and Events' (https://ern-rita.org/hcps/ accessed 24 November 2022).

[46] ERN-LUNG, 'Overview Different Roles of ERN-LUNG Membership' (https://public.3.basecamp.com/p/KKWJQK5wzT5koMduWS3CaeaY accessed 24 November 2022).

[47] ERN – EuroBloodNet, 'Supporting Partners' (www.eurobloodnet.eu/supporting-partners/ accessed 24 November 2022); ERN-RITA – Rare Immunological Disorders, 'Reference Centers' (https://ern-rita.org/hcps/ accessed 24 November 2022).

[48] Email correspondence on file with Hervey.

made possible by a communication from the European Commission in June 2018, which does not appear to be in the public domain.[49]

To put this specific example into the context of the general political and legal narratives on Brexit, the UK has gone from being a collaborative 'rule-maker', offering leadership in the biomedical sphere, to being a 'rule-taker'. We could not find any trace of news reporting of the 'supporting partner' legal workaround, suggesting that it took place very much under the political radar. This would have been necessary both for the EU, where the general narrative was that there could be no selective access to anything concerning EU membership, and for the UK, because of the lack of 'control' associated with supporting partner status.[50]

From 1 January 2021, patients suffering from rare low-prevalence complex diseases not only in Great Britain, but across the EU, ended up worse off because of the Brexit settlement reached on European Reference Networks. Patients in Northern Ireland accessing all-island shared healthcare, for instance through Children's Health Ireland, will continue to be able to access the care provided by relevant European Reference Networks with members based in Ireland,[51] although Northern Ireland-based hospitals are no longer able to be members of the Networks.

V. REGULATING CLINICAL TRIALS

Turning to the regulation of biomedical research, as opposed to its funding, another of the key concerns expressed by Cancer Research UK when we worked with them in 2019–2020 was whether UK research entities would be able to continue to participate in the regulatory structures and associated online infrastructure supporting collaborative cross-border clinical trials with entities based in the EU. Although some aspects of clinical trials regulation are internationally determined,[52] others are not,

[49] The statement says: 'It is proposed to use the term Supporting Partner as a generic term to define healthcare providers, medical societies, and any other entity or individual which, without having a commercial relation with the ERNs and their Full Members or Affiliated Partners, or with the European Commission, contribute in different ways to the work of the networks. When using the term Supporting Partner it shall be clear that it refers to a collaboration with entities and individuals which are neither Full Members nor Affiliated Partners' – see, European Reference Network – Genetic Tumour Risk Syndromes (ERN GENTURIS), 'Supporting Partners (Our Experts)' (www.genturis.eu/l=eng/Search.html#searchText=supporting%20partners accessed 24 November 2022); and European Reference Network – eUROGEN (Urogenital Diseases), 'Supporting Partners' (https://eurogen-ern.eu/who-is-involved/supporting-partners/ accessed 24 November 2022).

[50] Note – EURACAN, TransplantChild and MetabERN also list UK members, but we believe the websites have not been updated since December 2020. Hervey emailed their contact people on 4 August 2022 to ask, but did not receive a reply.

[51] Department of Health, 'Minister Donnelly Welcomes Approval for Irish Hospitals to Join European Reference Networks on Rare Diseases' (www.gov.ie/en/press-release/fb5a2-minister-donnelly-welcomes-approval-for-irish-hospitals-to-join-european-reference-networks-on-rare-diseases/# accessed 24 November 2022).

[52] Core technical requirements for clinical trials ('Good Clinical Practice') have been agreed by the International Council for Harmonisation of Technical Requirements for Pharmaceuticals for Human Use (commonly known as the ICH) and as such have a common global reference point. For discussion of the ICH see, ML Flear, 'A Roadmap Towards Membership and Formal Voice in Global Bioethics Standard-Setting: Health Research and the Case of the International Council on Harmonisation' (2018) 18(2–3) *Medical Law International* 157; ML Flear, 'Expectations as Techniques of Legitimation? Imagined

and the EU's 'Brussels effect', discussed in chapter eight, is active in this context as much as in regulation of the marketing of medicines, medical devices and equipment. Outside the EU's single market, entities based in the UK but seeking access for the products that came from successful clinical trials would be required to show compliance with EU clinical trials law. This would involve a significant 'double regulatory burden', especially in the instances where to comply with EU law, an entity would need to be legally established within the EU. We worked with Cancer Research UK to see whether we could find 'legal workarounds' (or 'near precedents' as we called them in our work) to support continuity in relationships between the MHRA and the European Medicines Agency, in terms of their oversight of clinical trial permissions, protocols and data.[53] This was extremely frustrating (and painstaking) work, and we did not have any success in finding any legal or policy solutions which came into effect.

The EU's Clinical Trials Regulation, which replaces an earlier EU Directive,[54] was adopted in 2014[55] but did not come into effect until 31 January 2022. The delay arose from the technical difficulties in bringing in a new database – the Clinical Trials Information System – to support clinical trials information sharing and decision-making at EU level. The Regulation covers some – but not all – aspects of some types of clinical trials. Trials falling within the scope of the Regulation are unlawful in the EU unless authorised. The EU specifies the structures and information required to secure authorisation, the process for submitting authorisation requests, and the bodies which make the decision. For example, there must be a formal trial 'sponsor', that is legally responsible for the trial, and for compliance with the Regulation. The EU also specifies how transparent trial data must be, a question related to public confidence in novel health technologies. We have seen how important it is for the public to feel that new medicines are safe in the context of the rollout of the COVID-19 vaccines from late 2020 onwards. Compliance with the EU's Clinical Trials Regulation is necessary to secure an EU-wide marketing authorisation for new medicines.[56]

Clinical trials regulation is not covered anywhere in the EU-UK TCA. The UK is therefore formally a 'third country' when it comes to collaboration between UK-based entities and EU-based entities conducting clinical trials. Access by entities in the UK to the Clinical Trials Information System is therefore very limited, essentially to access for international partners on a trial-by-trial basis. In a multi-state clinical trial involving the EU, researchers in non-EU Member States must have a legal

Futures through Global Bioethics Standards for Health Research' (2021) 8(2) *Journal of Law and the Biosciences* lsaa086.

[53] McCloskey and Hervey, above n 17.

[54] Directive 2001/20/EC of the European Parliament and of the Council of 4 April 2001 on the approximation of the laws, regulations and administrative provisions of the Member States relating to the implementation of good clinical practice in the conduct of clinical trials on medicinal products for human use [2001] OJ L 121/34.

[55] Regulation (EU) No 536/2014 of the European Parliament and of the Council of 16 April 2014 on clinical trials on medicinal products for human use, and repealing Directive 2001/20/EC [2014] OJ L 158/1.

[56] ML Flear, 'The EU Clinical Trials Regulation: Key Priorities, Purposes and Aims and the Implications for Public Health' (2016) 42(3) *Journal of Medical Ethics* 192; T Hervey and J McHale, *European Union Health Law* (Cambridge, Cambridge University Press 2015), ch 12.

representative established somewhere in the EU. That legal representative is responsible for compliance.[57]

Because the Regulation was not in force on 1 January 2021, it was not automatically part of 'retained EU law' in the UK. However, even if the UK unilaterally decided to align with every aspect of the Regulation, that would not be sufficient to secure access to the EU's system – and all that flows from it, including potentially eventual marketing authorisation – as if the UK were still an EU Member State. The UK unilaterally recognised EU clinical trials sponsors, but the EU did not reciprocate. We suggested that an inter-agency agreement between the European Medicines Agency and the MHRA could be explored, giving UK-based research entities access to the Clinical Trials Information System. However, there are no obvious provisions in the EU-UK TCA that would support such an agreement, and no 'near precedents' either. No other EU agency database provides such access to 'third countries'.

The more obvious workaround, which we believe has been taken and will increasingly be taken, is for UK-based biomedical research entities to set up establishments in EU Member States. As early as 2018, Price Waterhouse Cooper was suggesting UK-based biosciences companies should consider mergers with or acquisitions of EU-based companies.[58] Setting up a company in the EU was, apparently, UK government advice from the Department for International Trade in January 2021.[59]

While this may be an option for private companies, it is, however, not so easy for NHS-based research entities. Cancer Research UK's submission to the House of Lords EU Environment Sub-Committee Inquiry in February 2021 pointed out that the cost of having an EU-based legal representative was around a minimum of £20,000 per year, and could be up to £300,000 per year. It would be impossible in practice for non-commercial entities, like universities, to access this kind of resource. With four in 10 of all UK cancer research trials having a non-commercial sponsor, this means that UK-based cancer research was disadvantaged by the settlement in the EU-UK TCA. Cancer Research UK warned that the UK's reputation as a world leader in cancer research, especially rare and children's cancer research, was in jeopardy. The mutual recognition of clinical trial sponsorship which Cancer Research UK sought was not part of the EU-UK TCA. No additional UK funding to offset these costs has been offered.

The post-Brexit position for biomedical research, in short, adds up to a weakened UK and also EU biomedicine sector, and reduced access for UK-based patients to clinical trials. To return to the trial of dutogliptin, from which UK patients were excluded in 2018, the next phase of that trial went ahead in the USA, EU and China, with approval by the USA's Food and Drug Administration and the European Medicines Agency.[60]

[57] Article 74(1), Regulation 536/2014, above n 55.

[58] PriceWaterhouseCoopers, *Brexit: Implications for Pharma and Life Sciences Companies*, 2018 (www.pwc.co.uk/pharmaceuticals-life-sciences/assets/brexit-for-pharma-and-is-global-flyer.pdf accessed 24 November 2022).

[59] L Behrend, 'Consequences of Brexit for Clinical Trials in Europe', Applied Clinical Trials, 14 October 2021 (www.appliedclinicaltrialsonline.com/view/consequences-of-brexit-for-clinical-trials-in-europe); T Helm, 'Move to EU to Avoid Brexit Costs, Firms Told', The Guardian, 23 January 2021.

[60] 'Recardio and FDA Reach Agreement on Pivotal Phase 3 Trial Design', Diagnostic and Interventional Cardiology, 1 June 2022 (www.dicardiology.com/content/recardio-and-fda-reach-agreement-pivotal-phase-3-trial-design).

VI. BIOMEDICAL STAFF

There are consequent implications for staffing in the biomedicine sector too. In 2019, Paul Nurse, the Director of the Francis Crick Institute, the largest biomedical research facility in a single location in Europe, expressed concern about the fact that one quarter of the lab technicians on which the Institute relies are from EU Member States.[61] The points that we made in chapter seven, about NHS staffing, apply just as much to staffing in the biomedicine sector. Laboratory technicians are part of the Skilled Worker Visa scheme.[62] Potential staffing shortages have not deterred some investors, as the new campus at Canary Wharf, announced in March 2022,[63] shows. This Dutch-backed project aims to be the largest commercially focused life science lab space in Europe by 2026.

What we do not yet know, of course, is how all these interlocking phenomena will play out in the medium to longer term. Here is Dr Philippa Whitford on the subject, when we interviewed her in 2019:

> MPs … think it's all about trade. But I think it's kind of looking at what we've had from the EU, and what we do *with* the EU, that is all going to have to be replaced. So a simple one, that is almost the epitome of the EU, is the European Medicines Agency. By working as 28 countries together, having a single licensing system, we have sped up how things get from the bench-top to patients. Because drugs companies, when they get a drug, go through one process, and it can then be marketed right across the EU. So that makes it attractive. A population of 500 million makes it attractive, so drugs launch in the EU and America at very similar times. If you look at Canada and Australia, it's 6 months to a year later, because it's a smaller market. So we're likely to have access to new drugs later.
>
> So, now it takes a long time for an expensive new drug to get into the NHS. But – they are licensed, and therefore you can put in an individual patient request, or you can be part of trials taking them forward. If we start to fall behind – all research trials are the best current versus the new – now, if we're not using the best current, we can't even be part of future trials. So, the more we fall behind, the more we start to drift out of medical research.

The UK government response is to reposition the life sciences sector as an aspect of what the government describes as 'global Britain'. The Department for Business Energy and Industrial Strategy announced its long-term UK Innovation Strategy in July 2021.[64] There is also a specific 'Life Sciences Vision'.[65] These are part of the Treasury's March 2021 'Build Back Better' plan for growth[66] as the world emerges

[61] R Hurley, 'Brexit Could Spell Trouble for Unsung Heroes of UK Biomedical Research' (2019) 364 *British Medical Journal* 1868.

[62] UK Visas and Immigration, 'Skilled Worker Visa: Shortage Occupations' (www.gov.uk/government/publications/skilled-worker-visa-shortage-occupations/skilled-worker-visa-shortage-occupations accessed 24 November 2022).

[63] O Williams-Grut, 'Canary Wharf Announces £500 Million Project to Build Europe's Biggest Commercial Lab', Evening Standard, 30 March 2022.

[64] Department for Business, Energy and Industrial Strategy, 'UK Innovation Strategy: Leading the Future by Creating It' (www.gov.uk/government/publications/uk-innovation-strategy-leading-the-future-by-creating-it/uk-innovation-strategy-leading-the-future-by-creating-it-accessible-webpage accessed 24 November 2022).

[65] Department for Business, Energy and Industrial Strategy and Office for Life Sciences, 'Life Sciences Vision' (www.gov.uk/government/publications/life-sciences-vision accessed 24 November 2022).

[66] HM Treasury, 'Build Back Better: Our Plan for Growth' (www.gov.uk/government/publications/build-back-better-our-plan-for-growth accessed 24 November 2022).

from the COVID-19 pandemic. Early assessments of the government's plans point out the ambition of the strategy, its links to the 'better regulation'/ 'less red tape' post-Brexit narratives, and its reliance on private finance, as well as a public funding input of 2.4 per cent of GDP by 2027.[67] As we write in winter 2022, the Bank of England is predicting a recession in which the UK economy will shrink throughout 2023 and into 2024.[68] In March 2022, the BioIndustry Association, the main trade association for biosciences in the UK, pointed to the need to grow international collaboration in the sector, especially after leaving the EU, and stressed the importance of continued association with Horizon Europe as essential for keeping up international collaborations.[69] Overall, the bioscience industry seems to be taking a 'wait and see' approach.[70]

VII. CONCLUSIONS

Mark Heffernan, EU Public Affairs Manager at Cancer Research UK, summarised the position very nicely in March 2019. While the EU was insisting that negotiations could only be about the EU's exit, the issues that the biomedical research community wanted to influence were all future EU-UK relationship issues. The desired outcomes were 'probably only possible under the EEA, but we [the UK] are not even thinking about that'. He wanted to be in a position to influence the future relationship negotiations to say 'this is how we can achieve what we want …; this is where the UK position might need to shift, this is where we might need to exert some pressure in Brussels; and trying to … forge a path to as close proximation to our state of policy goals as we can'.[71] The policy goals, in effect, were as much continuity as possible with the position when the UK was an EU Member State. These were incompatible with the overall negotiating positions of the UK and the EU.

We did not hear anything about biomedicine in our street conversations, and that is not a surprise, given the conversational prompts of the photo of the Brexit bus. What we did hear, though, was a desire for the NHS to be, remain, or become, the best in the world.[72] This is consistent with current governmental policy narratives: it is far from clear that the practical steps necessary to make that a reality will follow. The insiders and policy experts we worked with from 2019–22 were clear that they did not want to lose the UK biomedicine sector's close relationship with its EU-based partners.

Where matters have ended up is not the desired policy outcome from the point of view of insiders in the biomedical research sector, but it is not the worst possible

[67] H Balfour, 'UK Life Sciences Sector: Do You Have the Vision for Innovation?', European Pharmaceutical Review, 30 August 2021 (www.europeanpharmaceuticalreview.com/article/161361/uk-life-sciences-sector-do-you-have-the-vision-for-innovation/).

[68] Bank of England, 'Monetary Policy Report – November 2022' (www.bankofengland.co.uk/monetary-policy-report/2022/november-2022 accessed 24 November 22).

[69] BioIndustry Association (BIA), 'Written evidence (STS0077)' (https://committees.parliament.uk/writtenevidence/107761/html/ accessed 24 November 2022).

[70] Balfour, 'UK Life Sciences Sector', above n 67.

[71] Interview with Mark Heffernan and others, March 2019.

[72] Newry 25A; Rochdale 70A.

outcome either. The worst outcomes, associated with a No Deal Brexit, were avoided. The UK is still aligned in practice on many aspects of regulation of biomedical research, and recognises the EU's regulatory decisions in some respects, even though that alignment is not recognised by the EU. Data protection law is sufficiently close to the EU's to secure the European Commission's data adequacy decision, allowing data to flow between the EU and UK. In principle, and subject to the huge proviso of compliance with the Ireland/Northern Ireland Protocol, the UK could still be part of Horizon Europe.

But comparatively speaking, the UK is worse off – and so is the EU – because of the change in the UK's relationship with its nearest collaborators in biomedicine entities in the EU. Decades of interpersonal relationships, carefully built up over time, will not be easily replaced with new ones, however 'global' Britain becomes in its policy orientations. Similarly to the position with regulation of medicines, devices and equipment, the UK does have the potential to gain benefits from regulatory independence. But it would need to resource the MHRA sufficiently to benefit from these. In fact, although there is plenty of articulation of policy intention, there are very few concrete legal changes.[73] Perhaps this is because there is little agreement on what the overall governance environment should be for biomedical research in the UK.

[73] M Dayan et al, 'Parallel, Divergent or Drifting? Regulating Healthcare Products in a Post-Brexit UK' (2023) *Journal of European Public Policy* https://doi.10.1080/13501763.2023.2213721.

10

The UK's Trade Relationships, the NHS and Health

I. INTRODUCTION

The May, Johnson, Truss and Sunak governments have all articulated a new post-Brexit approach to trade policy. Put simply, the UK's trade position is now, at least in theory, more open to free trade than previously. Here is PM Johnson on the subject on 3 February 2020, shortly after the UK formally left the EU:

> We have the opportunity, we have the newly recaptured powers, we know where we want to go, and that is out into the world. … We are re-emerging after decades of hibernation as a campaigner for global free trade.[1]

The Sunak government is said to be 'pragmatic' in terms of trade, but entering into trade agreements is also very much part of its agenda.[2]

It is common to think of trade and health as totally separate. This way of thinking is very much reflected in the conversations we had in the street with people in towns in the north of England and Northern Ireland during 2019. In the majority of the conversations where people talked about the NHS or health in response to the picture of the Brexit bus (nearly 300 of our conversations), even when we prompted them to do so, people either made no link between the UK's trade relationship with the EU and the NHS or health, or they actively denied such a link exists.[3] We have already seen, as reflected in the views of MPs Sarah Wollaston and Philippa Whitford, discussed in chapters four and eight, that many people in parliament and government

[1] Prime Minister's Office, 10 Downing Street and Boris Johnson MP, 'PM Speech in Greenwich', 3 February 2020. See also, eg Department for International Trade and Elizabeth Truss MP, 'Policy Exchange Speech: Liz Truss Sets Out Britain's New Trade Policy', 14 September 2021 (www.gov.uk/government/speeches/policy-exchange-speech-liz-truss-sets-out-britains-new-trade-policy). Sunak's position is less clear, although he has been keen on freeports for years: R Sunak MP, *The Free Ports Opportunity* (London, Centre for Policy Studies, 14 November 2016).

[2] DR Chaudhury, '"Pragmatic" Rishi Sunak May Iron Creases Out of Trade Deal with India', Economic Times, 26 October 2022; P Adnett, 'Sunak Enters Number 10 – Five Stances the New PM Has Had on International Trade', Institute of Export and International Trade, 24 October 2022 (www.export.org.uk/news/620231/Sunak-enters-Number-10--five-stances-the-new-PM-has-had-on-international-trade.htm).

[3] M Wood et al, 'What Do "Left Behind Communities" Want? A Qualitative Study in the United Kingdom using Photo Elicitation' (2023) *American Political Science Review* (first view doi: 10.1017/S0003055422001186).

also think this way. Indeed the way that the UK government is structured reflects an assumed separation between trade and health: the Department of Health and Social Care has no say in the work of the Department for International Trade, or vice versa.

In this chapter we show that there *are* important links between trade and health, and we explore what they mean for health governance in the UK post-Brexit. We do this in part by explaining our work with the Faculty of Public Health. As we have in other chapters, we outline the situation while the UK was a member of the EU, so that the key relevant aspects of the post-Brexit position can be understood. Then we consider the position under the Withdrawal Agreement and the EU-UK Trade and Cooperation Agreement (EU-UK TCA). As the EU is still the UK's largest trading partner,[4] the EU-UK TCA is the most important of the UK's free trade agreements when it comes to effects on health and the NHS across the UK. Finally, we look at trade *within* the UK, especially the position in Scotland and Wales, where devolved powers have allowed for the development of bespoke public health laws for those populations. How does the post-Brexit governance position affect those powers? First of all though, we show how trade and health are linked.

II. LINKS BETWEEN TRADE AND HEALTH

As Deborah Gleeson and Roland Labonté explain,[5] the relationship between trade and health is ambivalent. Trade can be good for health, in that it can stimulate growth. The argument is that new wealth generated through trade translates into tax revenue which can be invested in health, and also that the new wealth generated through trade reduces poverty. It would seem, at least, that if active measures are taken to redistribute wealth within a country, this would reduce poverty, and consequently improve overall health. There is a measurable link between how wealthy a population is, and the overall health of that population.[6]

But free trade can also be bad for health in multiple ways. The ways in which free trade can be detrimental to public health, and consequently may affect the kinds of treatment that a national health system needs to offer to its patients, were underlined to us by Mark Weiss, from the Faculty of Public Health, when we interviewed him in February 2019. In the logic of free trade agreements, as we have already mentioned in chapters four, eight and nine, 'non-tariff barriers to trade' are *undesirable*. Free trade agreements seek to reduce, or even eliminate, such barriers. But, Weiss observed,

[4] Office for National Statistics, 'UK Trading Partners and Trade Relationships: 2020' (www.ons.gov.uk/businessindustryandtrade/internationaltrade/articles/uktradingpartnersananalysisoftraderelationships/2020 accessed 28 November 2022). See also, Office for National Statistics, '09 Geographical Breakdown of the Current Account, The Pink Book' (www.ons.gov.uk/economy/nationalaccounts/balanceofpayments/datasets/9geographicalbreakdownofthecurrentaccountthepinkbook2016 accessed 28 November 2022).

[5] D Gleeson and R Labonté, *Trade Agreements and Public Health* (London, Palgrave Macmillan, 2020).

[6] Ibid, 2, 139. The correlation between poverty and health is not a perfect or direct one, but many studies show that poverty is a key indicator for poor health. Poverty both causes and is a result of poor health. For some global research see, eg, World Bank, *Dying For Change: Poor People's Experience of Health and Ill-Health* (Geneva, World Bank, 2001).

if you look at the USA's annual reports on non-tariff barriers to trade,[7] these are 'almost like a wish-list of all the things that us working in public health might *actually want* … things like sugar taxation on … [soft] drinks'. The USA free trade reports list, as undesirable non-tariff barriers, many rules about matters such as food safety; food additives, especially sugar and salt; food labelling, for example nutrition labelling; alcohol content restrictions; contents of tobacco products, and tobacco labelling – all rules that protect people from ill-health in various ways.

These kinds of laws protect people from both communicable and non-communicable diseases. Communicable diseases[8] – also known as infectious diseases – are caused by microorganisms like bacteria, viruses or parasites that can be spread either directly or indirectly between people. One way of becoming infected is by eating contaminated food. Food can also harbour chemicals or other toxins: these do not cause communicable diseases, but can be harmful to health, as in the infamous 2008 incident where infant formula milk in China was contaminated with the chemical melamine.[9] The main types of non-communicable disease include heart diseases, like heart attacks or strokes; cancers; respiratory diseases, like asthma; and diabetes.[10] Non-communicable diseases – also known as chronic diseases – are caused by a mix of genetic, physiological and environmental factors, as well as human behaviour.[11] According to the World Health Organization, non-communicable diseases are on the increase, mainly because of decreased physical activity, unhealthy diets, alcohol misuse and tobacco use.[12]

Reducing both communicable and non-communicable disease is therefore a critical part of a national health strategy: a national health system will be better able to cope with the health needs of its population if the incidence of diseases in that population is lower because of public health interventions, such as these kinds of laws and policies. Food safety laws protect people from communicable diseases that are passed on through the food chain, where food is unsafe because of the presence of toxins, or disease-bearing micro-organisms. Laws on food additives, sugar taxes, or food labelling, seek to protect people from various non-communicable diseases, like heart disease, by informing them to make better choices when they consume foods. Alcohol and tobacco labelling laws, and laws about alcohol content, and the contents of tobacco products, seek to protect people from the non-communicable diseases that arise from tobacco use or alcohol misuse.

[7] Reports from 2022 back to 1990s are available here, Foreign Trade and Information System, 'Information on the United States of America' (www.sice.oas.org/ctyindex/usa/USANatlDocs_e.asp accessed 28 November 2022).

[8] World Health Organization, 'Communicable Diseases' (www.afro.who.int/health-topics/communicable-diseases accessed 28 November 2022).

[9] Y Huang, 'The 2008 Milk Scandal Revisited', Forbes, 16 July 2014; X Pei et al, 'The China Melamine Milk Scandal and its Implications for Food Safety Regulation' (2011) 36(3) *Food Policy* 412.

[10] World Health Organization, 'Noncommunicable Diseases' (www.who.int/health-topics/noncommunicable-diseases#tab=tab_1 accessed 28 November 2022).

[11] World Health Organization, 'Noncommunicable Diseases. Key Facts' (www.who.int/news-room/fact-sheets/detail/noncommunicable-diseases#:~:text=Noncommunicable%20diseases%20(NCDs)%2C%20also,physiological%2C%20environmental%20and%20behavioural%20factors accessed 28 November 2022).

[12] World Health Organization, 'Noncommunicable Diseases', above n 10.

But seen from the point of view of free trade, all of these kinds of measures are undesirable 'non-tariff barriers' because they restrict trade between countries. Free trade agreements seek to reduce barriers to trade, in particular by mutually recognising different standards, in effect allowing market access for products that do not meet the same standards as those made in the home market.

Rules about safety of medicines, medical devices and equipment, that are used in national health systems across the world, are also potentially 'non-tariff barriers to trade'. We have already discussed this in chapter eight, where we showed how the UK government faces a choice between aligning with the EU (or another large trading bloc), or becoming a place where its different rules create a disincentive to firms supplying the NHS across England, Scotland and Wales. (Northern Ireland, at least according to the law as set out in the Withdrawal Agreement, remains within the EU's product standards rules, so is in a different position.) Under the Trump administration, the USA even considered that rules on how much a national health system *pays* for medicines could count as non-tariff barriers to trade. President Trump described these rules as 'unfair' on US-based producers of medicines, because foreign governments were able to 'extort' 'unreasonably low prices'[13] from those US firms.[14]

Taking this line of thought even further, not allowing foreign firms to supply products or healthcare services within national health systems can also be seen as a non-tariff barrier to trade. The EU's public procurement laws seek to prevent EU Member States from giving valuable public contracts for goods or services to national companies only. The reasoning is that by allowing firms access to the whole EU market, greater efficiencies will be created. But in the context of the NHS, these rules resulted in inefficient behaviours, where contracts were carved up so as to fall below the threshold values at which EU law applied. The decision in NHS England for some service provision to be made from the private sector has opened up the market to firms established outside the UK. The vast majority of this service is not patient-facing: it involves matters such as patient records, IT infrastructure support or staff development.[15] Although some healthcare services, like some elective surgeries, are commissioned from the private sector, this remains a minority of patient-facing services. Provision is different in dentistry and social care, where the majority of providers of care are in the private sector.[16] The NHS is organised differently in Northern Ireland, Scotland and Wales. For example, in Scotland, national policy since 2008 has been to bring services in-house 'wherever possible'.[17] However,

[13] 'Remarks by President Trump on Delivering Lower Prescription Drug Prices for All Americans', Trump White House, 20 November 2020 (https://trumpwhitehouse.archives.gov/briefings-statements/remarks-president-trump-delivering-lower-prescription-drug-prices-americans/).

[14] H Jarman et al, 'Health, Transatlantic Trade and President Trump's Populism: What "American Patients First" Has to Do with Brexit and the NHS' (2018) 392(10145) *The Lancet* 447.

[15] NHS England, 'Accredited Supplier Lists' (www.england.nhs.uk/hssf/supplier-lists/ accessed 28 November 2022).

[16] 'What NHS Care Has Been Outsourced?', NHS For Sale? (www.nhsforsale.info/overview/what-nhs-care-has-been-outsourced/ accessed 28 November 2022); P Russell, 'Doctors Put NHS Privatisation and Outsourcing on the UK Map', Medscape UK (www.medscape.co.uk/viewarticle/doctors-put-nhs-privatisation-and-outsourcing-uk-map-2022a1001wvr accessed 28 November 2022).

[17] S Bell, 'Unison Hails Victory Over Hospital Outsourcing in Wishaw', The National, 9 June 2022. See, eg, this policy statement from 2008, Health Finance Directorate, 'Outsourcing of Soft Facilities Management Services in NHS Scotland' (www.sehd.scot.nhs.uk/mels/cel2008_46.pdf accessed 28 November 2022).

there are some private providers of some services, as the interactive map provided by the campaigning organisation EveryDoctor[18] shows.[19] International trade agreements may require compensation to be given to private providers when their services are no longer needed because of renationalisation. This explains the 'hands off our NHS' trope which characterises opposition to free trade agreements from some sectors of the health policy community[20] and also characterised the EU referendum debates. However, it is quite wrong to assume that EU membership means that a NHS could not be 'renationalised': EU law recognises the special position of healthcare services in EU Member States,[21] and the European Parliament in particular will oppose any trade agreements that do not exclude national healthcare systems from their scope.[22]

Overall, therefore, free trade agreements can be detrimental for health, and for national health systems, if they have the effect of removing the kinds of legal controls over human behaviour that seek to reduce disease, or the values associated with having a nationally owned NHS, but are seen as non-tariff barriers to trade. Free trade agreements can also be indirectly detrimental for a national health system, in that they may make it more difficult to tackle diseases in a population, or make it less easy to supply the products that are needed in a national health system at prices that are sustainable from the public purse.

III. TRADE AND HEALTH WITHIN THE EU

EU Member States have agreed the deepest possible type of free trade agreement between them, especially for goods, but also for services. Of all the free trade agreements in effect globally, the EU's is that which goes the furthest in removing non-tariff barriers to trade. EU law achieves this deep 'integration' of the markets of its Member States through creating the 'single, internal market'. Although the words in the EU Treaties do not necessarily require this, in fact EU Member States have agreed a very wide range of legal, and administrative practical mechanisms to make this 'single market' a reality. They include, above all, a legal system where not only the European Commission, but, crucially, individual traders may take national governments to the courts in their own country if national rules ('non-tariff barriers') are in place that unjustifiably impede trade within the EU. That legal system has oversight from a single EU court, the Court of Justice of the EU, which has power to give the final say

[18] EveryDoctor, 'We Are a Doctor-Led Campaign Organisation Fighting for a Better NHS' (www.everydoctor.org.uk/ accessed 28 November 2022).

[19] EveryDoctor, 'EveryDoctor's Map of NHS Privatisation + Outsourcing' (www.everydoctor.org.uk/nhs-privatisation-map accessed 28 November 2022).

[20] B Cooper, 'How the EU is Making NHS Privatisation Permanent', The New Statesman, 2 December 2013; Keep Our NHS Public, 'Pledge: Hands Off Our NHS' (https://keepournhspublic.com/campaigns/stop-privatisation-of-the-nhs/hands-off-our-nhs/ accessed 28 November 2022).

[21] T Hervey, 'Healthier After Brexit?', UK in a Changing Europe, 22 March 2016 (http://ukandeu.ac.uk/healthier-after-brexit/); T Hervey, 'What Brexit Would Really Mean for the NHS', Health Service Journal, 22 March 2016.

[22] European Parliament resolution of 8 July 2015 containing the European Parliament's recommendations to the European Commission on the negotiations for the Transatlantic Trade and Investment Partnership (TTIP) (2014/2228(INI)).

on interpretation of EU law, and whether EU law has been validly made. Because of all of this depth in terms of removing non-tariff barriers to trade, it might be tempting to assume that EU trade law is extremely bad for health.

This might well have been the case at certain times of the EU's development. For example, in the 1980s–2000s, EU law was used to challenge many national rules that purported to be health protecting, but actually, at least according to the EU's Court of Justice, were protecting national producers. Food regulation was a key subject for this type of litigation. Scores of legal cases about matters such as the rules on alcohol content of certain drinks, additives in certain foods, where certain foods could be sold, and so on, all resulted in EU Member States being required to change their national measures, and open up their markets to food or drinks produced in other EU Member States, with lower, or at least different, health-protecting rules, less attuned to national populations and their health needs or behaviours. In this respect, EU membership was at least potentially detrimental to public health aims. The EU legal structures in effect operated to 'deregulate' health protections – they removed national rules that were seen as non-tariff barriers to trade.[23]

But over time, that deregulatory effect of EU law, operating through its courts, was replaced by EU legislation that set harmonised standards for the whole of the EU.[24] EU legislation is far from perfect, but the EU legislature (the directly elected European Parliament and Council of Ministers representing the governments of EU countries) has made some very important health-supporting decisions, especially in regulation of tobacco,[25] and to a considerable extent in food safety.[26] These provisions

[23] Or 'measures having equivalent effect to quantitative restrictions' in the language of the Article 30 TFEU.

[24] J Zglinski, 'The End of Negative Market Integration: 60 Years of Free Movement of Goods Litigation in the EU (1961–2020)' (2023) *Journal of European Public Policy* (first view doi: 10.1080/13501763.2022.2161603); T Hervey, 'The Role of the European Court of Justice in the Europeanization of Communicable Disease Control: Driver or Irrelevance?' (2012) 37(6) *Journal of Health Politics, Policy and Law* 977.

[25] See R Bertollini et al, 'Tobacco Control in Europe: A Policy Review' (2016) 25(140) *European Respiratory Review* 151; A Gilmore and M McKee, 'Tobacco Policy in the European Union' in EA Feldman and R Bayer (eds), *Unfiltered: Conflicts Over Tobacco Policy and Public Health* (Cambridge MA, Harvard University Press, 2004); A Gilmore and M McKee, 'Tobacco Control policy: The European Dimension' (2002) 2(4) *Clinical Medicine* 335; S Greer et al, *Everything You Always Wanted to Know About European Union Health Policies but Were Afraid to Ask*, 2nd edn (revised) (Copenhagen, European Observatory on Health Systems and Policies, 2019); T Hervey and J McHale, *European Union Health Law* (Cambridge, Cambridge University Press, 2015), ch 15; H Jarman, 'Legalism and Tobacco Control in the EU' (2018) 28(3) *European Journal of Public Health* 26; S Mandal et al, *Block, Amend, Delay: Tobacco Industry Efforts to Influence the EU's Tobacco Products Directive (2001/37/EC)* (SmokeFree Partnership, 2009) (www.smokefreepartnership.eu/images/Reports-and-Position-Papers/EU_TI_TPD_report_May_2012.pdf accessed 3 February 2023); M McKee et al, 'Public Health Policies' in E Mossialos et al, *Health Systems Governance in Europe: The Role of European Union Law and Policy* (Cambridge, Cambridge University Press, 2010); D Studlar, 'Tobacco Control: The End of Europe's Love Affair with Smoking?' in S Greer and P Kurzer (eds), *European Union Public Health Policies: Regional and Global Trends* (Abingdon, Routledge, 2013); L Trubek et al, 'The Construction of Healthier Europe: Lessons from the Fight Against Cancer' (2009) 26(3) *Wisconsin International Law Journal* 804; H Weishaar et al, 'Tobacco Control and Health Advocacy in the European Union: Understanding Effective Coalition-Building' (2016) 18(2) *Nicotine & Tobacco Research* 122; MC Willemsen et al, 'Tobacco Control in Europe: Progress and Key Challenges' *Tobacco Control* (2022) 31 160; and, more generally see A Bradford, *The Brussels Effect: How the European Union Rules the World* (Oxford, Oxford University Press, 2020).

[26] See A Alemanno and S Gabbi (eds), *The Foundations of EU Food Law and Policy: Ten Years of the European Food Safety Authority* (Farnham, Ashgate, 2014); Greer et al, *Everything You Always Wanted*

apply to all products to be traded within the EU, wherever they are made: the 'Brussels effect' we discussed in chapter eight. At the same time, the Court of Justice of the EU became more supportive of national rules that are genuinely needed to protect health. The strongest example of this change of approach is the 2015 Scottish alcohol taxation litigation.[27] The EU Court of Justice accepted that the specific public health needs of the Scottish population justified the rules, which would otherwise have been unlawful non-tariff barriers to trade, and therefore 'disapplied'. Other examples include court decisions upholding Finnish alcohol policy.[28] The EU and EU Member States *share* the competence to regulate the market, including making decisions about public health-protecting rules for products or services circulating in that market.

The EU's internal market goes even further. To support the legislation, and make it a practical reality rather than mere words in a free trade agreement, administrative arrangements at EU level include several agencies, such as the European Food Safety Authority, with powers to take specific decisions about the safety of the food that is sold in the EU from the point of view of human health protection. Decisions are taken by committees of scientific experts, drawn from EU Member States. The relevant committees also collaborate with EU national food safety agencies. These are the 'Brussels bureaucrats' from which the UK seeks to 'take back control' in Brexit political narratives. They – and also the EU's legislature (the Parliament and Council of Ministers, representing EU Member States) – are empowered to draw on experiences of regulation in EU Member States, and where a policy approach is shown to be health protecting, that approach can be adopted for the whole of the EU. This 'regulatory competition' is used for isomorphic policy learning through comparison. The EU also has administrative mechanisms for exchange of information about matters such as medicines pricing, which assist EU Member States to negotiate with medicines suppliers globally. Sometimes, the EU acts as a bloc to purchase medicines, and offers EU countries the chance to participate, as was the case with COVID-19 vaccines.[29]

Legally speaking, since 2009, the EU has been *obliged* by Article 9 of the Treaty on the Functioning of the EU to secure a 'high level of public health' in all its activities. Article 9 TFEU covers the EU's internal activities – when the EU adopts law for the internal market, such as deciding whether a food or medicine is safe, for example. Article 9 also includes the EU's external activities – when the EU enters into trade agreements with other countries. Although this legal obligation on the

to Know, above n 25; T Hervey and J McHale, *European Union Health Law* (Cambridge, Cambridge University Press, 2015), ch 15; S Krapohl, 'Risk Regulation in the EU Between Interests and Expertise: The Case of BSE' (2003) 10(2) *Journal of European Public Policy* 189; E Vos, 'EU Food Safety Regulation in the Aftermath of the BSE Crisis' (2000) 23(3) *Journal of Consumer Policy* 227; M Westlake, '"Mad Cows and Englishmen": The Institutional Consequences of the BSE Crisis' in N Nugent (ed), *European Union 1996: The Annual Review* (London, published in association with the *Journal of Common Market Studies*, 1997); and, more generally Bradford, *The Brussels Effect*, above n 25.

[27] Case C-333/14 *Scotch Whisky Association and Ors v The Lord Advocate and The Advocate General for Scotland* ECLI:EU:C:2015:845.

[28] Case C-434/04 *Criminal proceedings against Jan-Erik Anders Ahokainen and Mati Leppik* ECLI:EU:C:2006:609; C-198/14 *Valev Visnapuu v Kihlakunnansyyttäjä (Helsinki) and Suomen valtio* EU:C:2015:751 and the national constitutional court decision following it ECLI:FI:KKO:2018:49.

[29] European Commission Decision of 15 December 2020 on implementing Advance Purchase Agreements on COVID-19 vaccines COM(2020) 9309 final.

EU institutions to consider the health effects of its laws and policies is not enforceable by private individuals, it is enforceable by the EU institutions (such as the EU's Parliament) and also by the governments of EU Member States. It takes the form of a kind of 'constitutional' limit on what the EU may, and may not, lawfully do. It would not be accurate to overstate its effects as a limitation on the EU's political powers, but it does have some bite in terms of what is seen as politically feasible within the EU, and how the EU's institutions conceptualise the links between free trade and health protection. Article 9 is also used when courts interpret the EU's free trade obligations.

Article 9 has also had an effect on domestic public health law in the UK. In 2015, to comply with EU law,[30] the UK government introduced new regulations on tobacco packaging.[31] These 'standardised packaging' rules limit the information and advertising that tobacco companies may place on tobacco products. The aim is to reduce the ways in which tobacco companies can make their products look appealing or attractive to potential consumers, and thus to reduce tobacco consumption, which is, of course, highly harmful to health. Australia led the world in this kind of regulation, and data suggests that it is an effective public health intervention.[32] The tobacco industry sought to use litigation to challenge these UK Regulations. The industry raised several arguments, including that the Regulations did not balance trade interests correctly with public health interests, and that the Regulations imposed a disproportionate restriction on the industry's freedom to trade. In answering these questions, and finding that the Regulations were lawful, both the High Court[33] and the Court of Appeal[34] referred explicitly to the special protection given in EU law by Article 9 TFEU. Obviously, once the UK left the EU, Article 9 would no longer be a touchstone to help courts resolve litigation where health and trade interests were at odds with one another.

IV. THE WITHDRAWAL AGREEMENT AND EU-UK TCA

Products sold in the UK are produced all over the world, but the EU remains the UK's most important trading partner. The EU accounted for 50 per cent of the UK's imports in 2020–21.[35] In fact, trade with the EU dwarfs all other trade patterns in the UK.

[30] Directive 2014/40/EU of the European Parliament and of the Council of 3 April 2014 on the approximation of the laws, regulations and administrative provisions of the Member States concerning the manufacture, presentation and sale of tobacco and related products and repealing Directive 2001/37/EC [2014] OJ L 127/1.

[31] Standardised Packaging of Tobacco Products Regulations 2015.

[32] *R (British American Tobacco and Ors) v Secretary of State for Health* [2016] EWHC 1169 (Admin), para 5; but see D Underwood et al, 'The Effectiveness of Plain Packaging in Discouraging Tobacco Consumption in Australia' (2020) 4(12) *Nature Human Behaviour* 1273 which shows that causation patterns are complex.

[33] *R (British American Tobacco and Ors)*, above n 32, paras 256, 268, 269, 271, 440.

[34] *R (British American Tobacco UK Ltd and Ors) v The Secretary of State for Health* [2016] EWCA Civ 1182, para 201. Leave to appeal to the Supreme Court was refused – see 'Permission to Appeal' (www.supremecourt.uk/news/permission-to-appeal-decision-12-april-2017.html accessed 28 November 2022).

[35] M Ward, *The Geographical Pattern of UK Trade*, Commons Library Research Briefing 7593, House of Commons Library, 16 December 2021.

The USA comes second, with just 13 per cent of the UK's imports, followed by China with around 10 per cent.[36] This is why the agreements reached between the EU and the UK are by far the most important in terms of health protection in the UK going forward.

Research by the Faculty of Public Health in 2019,[37] and by others such as the Confederation of British Industries,[38] suggests that – like the biomedical research community discussed in chapter nine – most British-based businesses sought a post-Brexit trade relationship that kept the UK closely aligned to the EU's high product standards – including standards concerned with protecting public health.

The EU-UK TCA, therefore, was sub-optimal from that point of view. Rather than being bound by EU standards, like Norway, the UK remains free to depart from them, at least for the laws that apply in England, Scotland and Wales. The Withdrawal Agreement puts Northern Ireland in a different position. Products sold in Northern Ireland will be required to meet EU standards, if the Protocol on Ireland/Northern Ireland comes fully into effect.

Although not all British business stakeholders want to maintain alignment with the EU, the vast majority want to maintain high standards for public health. The Faculty of Public Health's *Blueprint on Negotiating a Healthy Trade Policy for the UK* 2019 found that 94 per cent of the 26 business organisations they talked with, representing over 150,000 people, wanted the UK to enter trade agreements with high public health standards.[39] Rather than thinking of health interests as competing with business interests, the research revealed:

> a strong, shared set of priorities between the business and health communities regarding the negotiation of our post-Brexit trade agreements. As the UK develops an independent trade policy, health and business leaders are clear that competing on quality, not cost, is vital to sustainable economic growth. Underlying this is a shared commitment to the health and wellbeing of the UK's workforce and population. Nearly a third of business leaders agree there is no more important aspect for trade negotiations to focus on.

This position has been replicated in subsequent research. For example, the independent Trade and Agriculture Commission, which reported in 2021, also called for continued high standards for food that reaches the UK market.[40]

From a public health point of view, Brexit removed what could be considered a 'constitutional' commitment to a high level of health protection. While it was an EU Member State, relevant laws and policies applicable in the UK were required to comply with the legal duty to secure a high level of human health protection. When negotiating trade agreements with the rest of the world, which applied to the UK,

[36] Ibid.

[37] Faculty of Public Health, *Negotiating a 'Healthy' Trade Policy for the UK* (London, Faculty of Public Health, April 2019).

[38] S Gordon, 'Majority of Businesses Want Regulatory Alignment After Brexit', Financial Times, 17 January 2018; Confederation of British Industry, 'Views of Industry Trade Associations on EU Rules and Regulations', 30 April 2018 (www.cbi.org.uk/articles/views-of-industry-trade-associations-on-eu-rules-and-regulations/).

[39] Faculty of Public Health, *Negotiating a 'Healthy' Trade Policy for the UK*, above n 37.

[40] Trade and Agriculture Commission, *Final Report* (London, Trade and Agriculture Commission, March 2021).

as an EU Member State, the EU is also bound by this obligation. After 1 January 2021, no such obligation constrains the UK government when negotiating trade agreements with other countries, such as Australia, New Zealand and, crucially, the USA.

Working with the Faculty of Public Health, we developed a proposal seeking to replace such a duty in UK law. The UK does not have a formal written constitution, and the UK parliament is regarded as 'sovereign' in British constitutional theory, therefore legislation is the means through which to achieve this. In early February 2018, while the House of Lords was debating the European Union (Withdrawal) Bill, a cross-party group of peers tabled an amendment[41] to the effect that ministers carrying out duties under the Act should 'have regard to the principle that a high level of human health protection must be ensured in the definition and implementation of all policies and activities.' This proposal, which attracted support from 52 organisations across the public health sector,[42] was one of many which sought to achieve similar effects to prevent regulatory backsliding on a wide range of topics, including the environment and labour standards. None was successful. The government did give assurances, during the debate,[43] that the principle of Article 9 would continue to be respected, but of course this is far from as clear a legal position as enshrining such a duty in the Act would have been.

The research organisation *UK in a Changing Europe* has been tracking regulatory divergence since October 2021.[44] So far, however, there have been few examples of 'active' regulatory divergence overall. In areas related to health, as we described in chapter eight, there has been divergence between EU and UK medical devices standards, because the EU's medical devices rules changed after 1 January 2021. The UK government still recognises EU-approved devices, and has indicated that it will 'broadly reflect'[45] general safety and performance requirements for medical devices, when it brings in new UK Regulations, promised for July 2023. Also, the EU's rules designed to protect patients from falsified medicines no longer apply in Great Britain, because the system of checking the 'unique identifiers' on medicines in the EU is not open to pharmacies or traders in Great Britain.

V. THE POSITION IN SCOTLAND AND WALES

As we saw during the COVID-19 outbreak from early 2020, public health is a devolved matter in the UK.[46] Public health rules not only include responses to pandemics or

[41] European Union (Withdrawal) Bill, Amendments (https://publications.parliament.uk/pa/bills/lbill/2017-2019/0079/18079(a).pdf accessed 28 November 2022), 6; 'European Union (Withdrawal) Bill', Hansard, HC Vol 790, cols 1386–92 (23 April 2018).

[42] Ibid; 'Letters: Brexit Bill Needs 'Do No Harm' Amendment to Protect Public Health', The Guardian, 20 April 2018.

[43] 'European Union (Withdrawal) Bill', Hansard, above n 41.

[44] UK in a Changing Europe, 'UK-EU Divergence Tracker' 4th edn, July 2022. Also see, eg, UK in a Changing Europe, 'UK-EU Divergence Tracker', October 2021; UK in a Changing Europe, 'UK-EU Divergence Tracker' 2nd edn, December 2021.

[45] Medicines and Healthcare Products Regulatory Agency, *Government Response to Consultation on the Future Regulation of Medical Devices in the United Kingdom*, June 2022, 22.

[46] Institute for Government, 'Devolution: Common Frameworks and Brexit' (www.instituteforgovernment.org.uk/explainers/devolution-common-frameworks-brexit accessed 28 November 2022).

other disease outbreaks: they also include laws and policies targeted at reducing non-communicable diseases. Northern Ireland, Scotland and Wales ('the devolveds') have different public health laws and policies from those that apply in England. While the UK was an EU Member State, each of the 'devolveds' was operating within a common framework of EU law. They could adopt food standards, alcohol or tobacco controls, or other non-tariff barriers, so long as these were consistent with the UK's duties as an EU Member State. As we mentioned above, over time, the EU, and especially its Court of Justice, became more attuned to the need for population-specific differences in these kinds of laws and policies, so as to respond to population-specific public health needs.

When various private companies, including the Scotch Whisky Association, challenged Scotland's Alcohol (Minimum Pricing) Act 2012, this awareness of the need for tailored public health-supportive laws and policies was in evidence in the decisions of the relevant courts involved. The EU's Court of Justice was prepared to consider that the minimum pricing policy might constitute a disproportionate restriction on trade,[47] but left the balancing of the evidence to the UK Supreme Court which eventually decided the case under the preliminary reference procedure.[48] Referring to the effects of the policy on the specific public health needs of the Scottish population, the Supreme Court upheld the Act.[49] This example demonstrates how EU law was a place where legal arguments could be made about public health policies across the UK being restrictions on trade, but that EU law allows for specific conditions in the 'devolveds' to be taken into account, when assessing these kinds of arguments. Wales has since followed Scotland's lead on alcohol pricing.[50]

Our interactions with health policy actors across the UK from 2017 to early 2019 (some of which were within our research project, and others within the project led by Jean McHale, in which Flear and Hervey were also involved) revealed significant concerns among the 'devolveds' about the post-Brexit position. For example, one interviewee described the public health sector as 'a little bit fearful about tobacco and sugar'. That interviewee went on to note the ways in which the EU has itself been 'energetic' on those topics, while at the same time giving Wales the freedom to diverge where needed for the Welsh population.[51]

Initial uncertainties about where the powers from the EU would be 'repatriated' (Westminster alone, or also Cardiff, Edinburgh and Belfast) were formally resolved by the UK's Internal Market Act 2020. This Act imposes two rules that create an 'internal market' within the UK: the mutual recognition principle and the non-discrimination principle. The mutual recognition principle requires that goods that have been produced in or imported into one part of the UK, and could lawfully be sold there, should in principle be able to be sold anywhere in the UK, 'free from any relevant requirements that would otherwise apply to the sale'.[52] This principle

[47] Case C-333/14 *Scotch Whisky Association*, above n 27.
[48] Article 267 TFEU.
[49] *Scotch Whisky Association and Ors v The Lord Advocate and another (Scotland)* [2017] UKSC 76.
[50] The Public Health (Minimum Price for Alcohol) (Wales) Act 2018.
[51] J McHale et al, 'Health Law and Policy, Devolution and Brexit' (2020) 55(9) *Regional Studies* 1561.
[52] Section 2, United Kingdom Internal Market Act 2020.

applies to a fixed list of types of measures ('requirements') that have to do with the goods themselves, how they are made, packaged and labelled, and inspected.[53] The non-discrimination principle[54] – that there must be no direct or indirect discrimination between the law that applies to 'incoming' goods and 'local' goods – applies to a different list of measures, which includes how goods are sold and the price of goods.[55]

There are also similar rules concerning services, but the Act contains a blanket exclusion which applies to healthcare services.[56]

The provisions of the Act do not apply at all to some policy areas concerned with public health, essentially policy areas covering communicable disease control.[57] The Act does not apply to reasonable and evidence-based legislation that aims to prevent or reduce the movement of a pest or disease that is a serious threat to human health into part of the UK where that disease is not present or where it is less prevalent than other parts of the UK. This exclusion would cover measures adopted to prevent the spread of a food-borne disease. The mutual recognition principle does not apply to measures excluding unsafe food. The non-discrimination principle does not apply to measures that are a reasonable response to a public health emergency, defined as posing an 'extraordinary threat to human health'. But the provisions of the Act *do apply* to many measures that can be taken against non-communicable diseases.

The rules for each part of the UK apply to goods produced in or imported into that part of the UK, so formally speaking the Act preserves the powers of the 'devolveds', and indeed the obligations in the Ireland/Northern Ireland Protocol. England, Scotland and Wales may set different rules for goods produced in, or imported into, their territories and sold there. The position in Northern Ireland is a bit more complex. The Protocol – if fully brought into effect – applies EU law rules on goods produced in Northern Ireland. The United Kingdom Internal Market Act was amended to secure those obligations, but at the same time to promote the constitutional integrity of the UK, and make sure that companies in Northern Ireland still have unfettered access to markets in Great Britain. Goods for Northern Ireland (that are not merely transiting through Northern Ireland so as to avoid the customs and regulatory controls that apply on the EU-UK border) are known as 'qualifying Northern Ireland goods'.[58] Those goods must be able to be sold in Great Britain, unless, for example, new measures are needed to deal with a threat to biosecurity or food safety.[59] The Northern Ireland Executive may continue to make rules that apply to domestic producers, that are lawful within the scope of EU law.

That is the formal legal position. In practice, though, the UK is not a market made up of four equal regulatory spaces. The market in England is significantly larger than any of the other UK markets.[60] England is responsible for nearly 90 per cent of UK GDP.

[53] Section 3, United Kingdom Internal Market Act 2020.
[54] Section 5, United Kingdom Internal Market Act 2020.
[55] Section 6, United Kingdom Internal Market Act 2020.
[56] Section 18, United Kingdom Internal Market Act 2020 and Schedule 2.
[57] Section 10, United Kingdom Internal Market Act 2020 and Schedule 1.
[58] The Definition of Qualifying Northern Ireland Goods (EU Exit) Regulations 2020.
[59] Section 47, United Kingdom Internal Market Act 2020.
[60] 'The four nations of the UK vary significantly in the size of their populations and economies. Total Gross Domestic Product (GDP) for England in 2019 was £1903 billion compared to £167 billion

Producers in or importers into Wales or Scotland, for instance, are required to comply with the Welsh and Scottish rules, while, because of the mutual recognition principle, producers in England have access to the Welsh and Scottish markets by complying only with English rules. If the Welsh and Scottish rules are more restrictive, and thus less favourable to producers or importers – for example if they require more labelling information about sugar or alcohol content, or reduced salt content, or larger warnings on tobacco products packaging – market forces will mean that products on the Welsh or Scottish markets which comply with the English rules will be cheaper, and therefore more attractive to consumers. In addition, the size of the English market makes it more attractive for firms to operate in, if they have to meet different rules when operating in Scotland or Wales. In these ways, the practical effect of the Act is to reduce the power that the 'devolveds' have to make public health-promoting laws. Where the mutual recognition principle applies, there is no scope in the Act for the Welsh or Scottish governments to argue that the rules are necessary to protect public health interests of their population. Where the non-discrimination principle applies, public health measures could be justified under the Act, but only if the Welsh or Scottish government can show that the measure is necessary to achieve the aim of protecting human health.[61]

The Act sets up a new process for excluding rules from the Act's scope.[62] The power to do this lies with the UK government – with London-based ministers. There is a structure through which the 'devolveds' may request a new exclusion.[63] Exclusions should be reached by consensus. But there is no obligation on the UK government to grant a new exclusion requested by one or more of the 'devolveds'. Nor is there a power for the 'devolveds' to block proposed exclusions. Nor is there any judicial oversight of the process.

As Kenneth Armstrong points out,[64] the UK's Internal Market Act provides for a totally different type of legal settlement from EU law, as to how to manage the different interests of devolved entities, within a single trading space. The governance framework is 'de-constitutionalised' and then 're-constitutionalised'; courts are replaced with ministerial, or UK parliamentary authority; and the legislation is skewed towards the 'economic' rather than balancing economic with 'social' aims as the EU does in its internal market, including for public health protections. The EU's legal structures allow for regulatory diversity where necessary to achieve non-market

in Scotland, £78 billion in Wales and £49 billion in Northern Ireland' – see Competition and Markets Authority and Office for the Internal Market, 'Overview of the UK Internal Market', 22 March 2022 (www.gov.uk/government/publications/overview-of-the-uk-internal-market-report/overview-of-the-uk-internal-market#:~:text=The%204%20nations%20of%20the%20UK%20vary%20significantly%20in%20the,49%20billion%20in%20Northern%20Ireland).

[61] Section 8, United Kingdom Internal Market Act 2020.

[62] Sections 10 and 18, United Kingdom Internal Market Act 2020.

[63] Cabinet Office and Department for Levelling Up, Housing and Communities, 'Process for Considering UK Internal Market Act Exclusions in Common Framework Areas', 10 December 2021 (www.gov.uk/government/publications/process-for-considering-ukim-act-exclusions-in-common-framework-areas/process-for-considering-uk-internal-market-act-exclusions-in-common-framework-areas).

[64] KA Armstrong, 'The Governance of Economic Unionism after the United Kingdom Internal Market Act' (2022) 85(3) *The Modern Law Review* 635.

aims: the United Kingdom Internal Market Act permits much less regulatory diversity, unless it is explicitly permitted by parliament or executive action at Westminster. As Armstrong puts it, 'the authority of courts and constitutionalism is substituted by the authority of the UK parliament and legislation'.[65]

In the short term, the United Kingdom Internal Market Act provides a kind of 'standstill' protection for different rules that existed before 1 January 2021. But research from the Welsh Senedd in March 2022[66] showed that the Act was already having a detrimental effect on law making in Scotland and Wales. Neither the Scottish parliament nor the Welsh Senedd consented to the Act. But, under the Sewel Convention, a principle of UK constitutional law to the effect that the UK parliament does not normally adopt law on devolved topics unless parliaments in the 'devolveds' consent to that law, there is no room for Scotland or Wales to hold the UK parliament to account for that lack of consent by using the courts.[67] We will turn to the lack of judicial oversight of Brexit processes and outcomes in more detail in chapter 11.

VI. CONCLUSION

There is, as yet (winter 2022), a significant gap between the policy aspirations and the number of truly new trade agreements reached by the UK since 1 February 2020.[68] The turn away from the EU has been associated with a desire to strengthen UK trade with the USA, with the 11 states involved in the Trans Pacific Partnership, which includes Japan, New Zealand and Singapore, and with India. The UK political narratives about trade with the rest of the world have already caused some alarm in public health contexts. Fears tend to be focused around meat standards, particularly if the UK secures a trade agreement with the USA where the practices in the meat industry are very different to European approaches.[69] The UK's trade agreements with Australia and New Zealand (neither of which is yet in force) are already controversial because of their expected impacts, for instance on the semi-processed food sector in the UK.[70]

[65] Ibid, 651.

[66] Senedd Research, 'The UK Internal Market Act 2020: What Difference is it Making?' (https://research.senedd.wales/research-articles/the-uk-internal-market-act-2020-what-difference-is-it-making/#:~:text=The%20UK%20Parliament%20passed%20the,market%20access%20principles%E2%80%9D%20in%20law accessed 28 November 2022).

[67] This aspect of the Sewel Convention was confirmed by the UK Supreme Court in *R (Miller) v Secretary of State for Exiting the EU; In re McCord; In re Agnew* [2017] UKSC 5.

[68] The vast majority of the UK's 'new' agreements are actually 'continuity' agreements, where the EU already had an agreement with the relevant country or group of countries, and the UK had to forge a separate agreement to apply once the UK left the EU. The UK has reached new agreements with the EU and Singapore (on digital trade); Australia and New Zealand – the latter are not yet in force, see D Webb, *Progress on UK Free Trade Agreement Negotiations*, Commons Library Research Briefing 9314, House of Commons Library, 8 November 2022.

[69] See, eg, E Millstone et al, 'Food, Brexit and Chlorinated Chicken: A Microcosm of Wider Food Problems' (2019) 90(4) *The Political Quarterly* 645.

[70] G Lanktree, 'UK's Liz Truss was Warned of Blow to Food Sector under Australia and New Zealand Trade Deals', Politico, 12 July 2022.

Yet the patterns of supply suggest that the UK's relationship with the EU continues to be the trade relationship of most practical importance. Deviation from EU regulatory standards has the potential to improve public health in Great Britain: the settlement for the island of Ireland imposes limitations on such regulatory divergence. The implementation of the Protocol on Ireland/Northern Ireland forms an important site of contestation of the UK's independence from EU regulation in the domain of food, while at the same time, the Westminster government has to grapple with the reality of supply routes to Northern Ireland.

The EU-UK TCA binds the UK only to very weak commitments on matters such as food safety, sugar, alcohol or tobacco control. Outside the single market, the UK may lawfully improve or lower these kinds of standards, for Great Britain. Northern Ireland remains, formally speaking, within the single market's product rules. Whatever direction it takes, UK public health law and policy will develop in the context of international standards which set a minimum floor of protection.[71] These standards offer significantly less constraint over the UK's policy choices than EU membership, or a 'Norway' relationship where the whole of the UK is bound by single market rules, would have done.

Attempts to impose health-protecting constraints on UK policy choices through legislation (Brexit should 'do no harm' to public health) or through the constitutional settlement for the 'devolveds' in the UK's market have not been particularly successful. Nor has there been much success in securing parliamentary oversight over negotiation of trade agreements giving access to the market in Great Britain for products meeting public health standards in other countries.[72] The parliaments and executives in Northern Ireland, Scotland and Wales are also excluded from participating in trade negotiations. These aspects of our research resonate with questions about what counts as a legitimate post-Brexit settlement for health governance. We turn more explicitly to this question in the next chapter.

[71] Codex Alimentarius (www.fao.org/fao-who-codexalimentarius/en/ accessed 15 February 2023); WHO Framework Convention on Tobacco Control (https://fctc.who.int/who-fctc/overview access 15 February 2023).

[72] MCI van Schalkwyk et al, 'Brexit and Trade Policy: An Analysis of the Governance of UK Trade Policy and What It Means for Health, and Social Justice' (2021) 17 *Globalization and Health* 61; MCI van Schalkwyk et al, 'Risks to Health and the NHS in the Post-Brexit Era' (2020) 369 *British Medical Journal* m2307.

11

Accountability for Post-Brexit Health Governance

I. INTRODUCTION

'We send the EU £350 million a week. Let's fund our NHS instead' (Message on the 'Brexit bus', spring 2016)

As we already noted in chapter four, the 'Brexit bus' began its tour of England, Scotland and Wales in early May 2016. The image of the bus was also widely circulated through traditional and social media. In our film, Robert (filmed in London in 2019, who did not wish to give his surname) is keen to explain that the £350 million figure is real:

> We know that we make a net contribution to the EU of £10 billion a year. Put that to one side. If we were to go onto World Trade Organization terms, … our companies would pay about £5 billion worth of tariffs, in exporting to the EU. But their exporters to us would pay about £13 billion, because they sell us a lot more than we sell them. And they sell us more goods; we sell them more services, and you don't have tariffs on services. The difference between the £13 billion – which goes direct to the Treasury – and the £ 5 billion is about £8 billion. Add that to the £10 billion I mentioned earlier. £18 billion, divided by 52 weeks, comes to £350 million a week.

Although it seems to us that Robert, and perhaps many more like him, genuinely believed that these numbers added up, we also understand that they were quite wrong. The idea that leaving the EU *only* involves a positive saving of the financial contribution made to the EU, with no further negative economic implications, has now been totally discredited.

This is, of course, not only for the technical reason that the amount of money claimed is not an amount 'we send' to the EU, as it does not take into account the UK's rebate. Robert assumes that the UK would be able to continue to sell services to the EU on the same basis as before, but in fact, trading on what Robert calls 'World Trade Organization terms', which means trading without a trade agreement, involves significant barriers to cross-border trade in services. The trade relationship that the UK eventually negotiated with the EU (the EU-UK Trade and Cooperation

Agreement) involves no tariffs, but this is a more advantageous arrangement for the UK economy than 'No Deal' Brexit ('World Trade Organization terms') would have been.[1] The detrimental effect on the UK economy associated with Brexit,[2] in the form of the EU-UK Trade and Cooperation Agreement (TCA), especially if combined with a low public spending economic policy,[3] make it very difficult, if not impossible, to deliver any kind of 'Brexit NHS dividend'.

What we have seen, in chapters five to 10, is that, across all important aspects of health and the NHS, there is a significant gap between the message of the bus and the post-Brexit realities. The implied promise that Brexit would mean a better NHS is at odds with the reality that all forms of Brexit are, taken in the round, bad for health and the NHS. In this chapter, we focus on the question of who should be accountable for that broken (implied) promise, and how they should be held to account.

II. WHAT DO WE MEAN BY 'HELD TO ACCOUNT'?

Accountability is associated with the ways in which power is exercised within democratic countries. Dawn Oliver, writing in the early 1990s, described accountability as a framework requiring public bodies to justify their actions, to change policies that turn out to be a bad idea, and to 'make amends' for mistakes.[4] This framework could involve political processes, such as governments changing policies to respond to voter preferences, or it could involve legal processes, such as judicial review of public policies, or administrative decisions. Wood, writing with Vivien Schmidt in 2019,[5]

[1] Office for Budget Responsibility, 'Impact of the Brexit Trade Agreement on Our Economy Forecast' (https://obr.uk/box/impact-of-the-brexit-trade-agreement-on-our-economy-forecast/ accessed 29 November 2022); House of Lords EU Goods Sub-Committee, 'Trade in Goods Significantly Harder Under Brexit Deal', 25 March 2021 (https://committees.parliament.uk/committee/445/eu-goods-subcommittee/news/153116/trade-in-goods-significantly-harder-under-brexit-deal/); UK in a Changing Europe, *Cost of a No Deal Revisited* (London, UK in a Changing Europe, 3 September 2018).

[2] A recent analysis shows a 4 per cent long-run reduction in productivity, compared to staying in the EU, see Office for Budget Responsibility, 'Brexit Analysis', 26 May 2022 (https://obr.uk/forecasts-in-depth/the-economy-forecast/brexit-analysis/#assumptions); Office for Budget Responsibility, *Economic and Fiscal Outlook*, CP 648, March 2022, 62–63; Office for Budget Responsibility, *Fiscal Risks and Sustainability Report*, CP 702, July 2022, 63; HM Government, *EU Exit: Long-Term Economic Analysis*, CM 9742, November 2018; A Hantzsche et al, *The Economic Effects of the Government's Proposed Brexit Deal* (London, National Institute of Economic and Social Research, 2018); T Sampson and S Dhingra, 'The Economic Consequences of the Brexit Deal', 29 November 2018 (https://blogs.lse.ac.uk/businessreview/2018/11/29/the-economic-consequences-of-the-brexit-deal-the-case-of-trade/). Of course, Brexit economic effects are difficult to disentangle from COVID-19 pandemic effects, but the OBR's analysis does this.

[3] R Partington, 'Sunak's Government "Going Backwards" on Green Economy, says CBI', The Guardian, 5 December 2022; G Wilkes, 'Early Questions for Sunak's Growth Policy', Institute for Government, 21 November 2022 (www.instituteforgovernment.org.uk/publication/rishi-sunak-growth-policy); W Booth and K Adam, 'Rishi Sunak Budget Seeks to Stabilise UK Economy Rattled by Liz Truss', Washington Post, 17 November 2022.

[4] D Oliver, *Government in the United Kingdom: The Search for Accountability, Effectiveness and Citizenship* (Milton Keynes, Open University Press, 1991), 28.

[5] V Schmidt and M Wood, 'Conceptualizing Throughput Legitimacy: Procedural Mechanisms of Accountability, Transparency, Inclusiveness and Openness in EU Governance' (2019) 97(4) *Public Administration* 727. Also see, eg, M Bovens et al, 'Does Public Accountability Work? An Assessment Tool' (2008) 86(1) *Public Administration* 225; M Bovens et al (eds), *The Real World of EU Accountability* (Oxford, Oxford University Press, 2010); M Bovens et al, 'Public Accountability' in M Bovens et al (eds), *The Oxford Handbook of Public Accountability* (Oxford, Oxford University Press, 2014).

elaborates accountability further. Accountability is where a (political) actor or organisation provides information, which is discussed or deliberated upon, and where there are potentially rewards or sanctions if actors or organisations are guilty of misconduct. Accountability is related to transparency, and to fair and equitable actions that are compliant with public standards of conduct.

In the UK, the main mechanism to hold a government to account for any promises made during a political campaign is at the next election. This is the case for elections to the parliaments/assemblies that form the governments/executives/administrations in Northern Ireland, Scotland and Wales, as well as for elections to the House of Commons. Individuals and political parties who hold power must compete to be re-elected, and that fact gives an incentive to deliver on their campaign promises, because that is the basis on which they have been given power to govern by the electorate.[6]

But, as many scholars[7] point out, accountability through elections does not tell the whole story. Complex states like the UK include multiple other accountability mechanisms. Accountability may be secured through a process whereby elected MPs compel the government to explain its policies and decisions. Expulsion of politicians from office if they are found to have done something illegal or otherwise improper is a form of accountability. The parliaments or governments in the 'devolveds' may request the Westminster government to account for effects of UK-wide policies on Northern Ireland, Scotland and Wales. Accountability also applies to people or institutions with technical administrative powers, for example a decision to authorise a new medicine or vaccine, or a decision that a particular food-stuff is unsafe and may not be sold. Where public entities are required to explain their actions, for instance, when an Ombudsman asks for an explanation of a medical treatment that has gone wrong, that is also an example of accountability.

Courts and tribunals may also be involved in accountability. Where the outcome of a judicial review procedure is that an administrative decision, in a range of areas such as housing, welfare benefits or healthcare, has been incorrectly taken, that decision must be revisited and potentially reversed. In short, accountability concerns those who hold public office being responsible for the consequences of their actions.

The UK parliament and government are responsible for the conduct of referendums, and referendums are seen by the public as obliging the government to deliver the result.[8] In the case of the EU referendum, the government that called the referendum (Cameron's government) was succeeded by the May government, the Johnson government, briefly the Truss government, and now (winter 2022) the Sunak government. The Johnson government 'delivered Brexit' in the sense that the UK formally

[6] C Lord, *Democracy in the European Union* (Sheffield, Sheffield Academic Press, 1998), 80.

[7] C Harlow, *Accountability in the European Union* (Oxford, Oxford University Press, 2002), 8–23; C Harlow, 'Accountability and Constitutional Law' in M Bovens et al (eds), *The Oxford Handbook of Public Accountability* (Oxford, Oxford University Press, 2014); C Scott, 'Accountability in the Regulatory State' (2000) 27(1) *Journal of Law and Society* 38.

[8] 'Lessons Learned from the EU Referendum', *Twelfth Report from the Public Administration and Constitutional Affairs Committee*, HC 496 (2016–17).

left the EU while Johnson was Prime Minister. But as we have seen, especially in the case of Northern Ireland, but also in many other contexts, Brexit is an ongoing process, responsibility for which now (winter 2022) lies with the Sunak government.

In our conversations with people during our work on health governance after Brexit, which took place while Johnson was Prime Minister, we did not impose any particular definition of accountability. Instead, if it was relevant, we let people use whatever meaning of accountability felt right to them.

III. HOPED-FOR ACCOUNTABILITY FOR THE BUS PROMISE?

How do the different people with whom we talked and worked with on Brexit and health think about accountability for the (implied) promise on the bus? Our focus here is not whether people believed the statement on the bus or not, or whether it made a difference in the way people voted in the EU referendum. We have touched on those matters in chapter four. This chapter explores people's views on *whether* someone should be held to account, or should have been held to account, for the statement; and, if so, *who* should be held to account, and *how*.

As we have explained in more detail in chapters two and three, to try to uncover this question, we did not ask people directly about accountability. This was for several reasons. For the people in the health policy community with whom we were working, our focus was on trying to assist them, even in modest ways, to navigate the legal and policy positions as post-referendum futures unfolded. We were not primarily focused on their views about accountability for those futures. When we had conversations with people in the street, we sought to meet people where they were, to try to make sense of their realities, rather than asking them 'academic' or 'political' questions. Asking people to respond to a picture of the bus, however they felt appropriate, was a better method for understanding what already marginalised or 'left behind' people might think, feel or believe, than using questionnaires or focus groups would have been.[9] If people did talk about the implied promise, we steered the conversations towards their views on who was responsible, and how they might be held to account. But not all of the conversations we had took that direction, and we followed the direction that the person we were talking with wanted to take.

So for an insight into what the people with whom we engaged during our research thought about accountability for the promise on the bus, we looked back on our conversations and interactions throughout our work. We focused on anything that they said directly about accountability, or responsibility for delivering on the (implied) promise on the bus. But we also reflected together on the *stories* people told, and the *metaphors* they used, that might shed light on accountability. As we have explained in chapters two and three, those stories and metaphors give us a view onto complex ideas in a way that direct questions do not.

[9] M Wood et al, 'What Do "Left Behind Communities" Want? A Qualitative Study in the United Kingdom using Photo Elicitation' (2023) *American Political Science Review* (first view doi: 10.1017/S0003055422001186).

IV. VIEWS OF HEALTH POLICY 'EXPERTS' ON ACCOUNTABILITY

When we worked with people in the health policy community from 2016 onwards, their focus tended not to be about accountability for the promise on the bus. Indeed, they said very little directly about that promise, except to express frustration at how futile it was to use evidence, or reason, to respond to the 'wall of fake news'[10] that the bus represented. Instead, the 'experts' focused on three related elements, each of which implies something about accountability.

First, they expressed the inter-connections between health, free movement and trade. The most common metaphors used in our interview data concern inter-connection: 'linkage', 'link', 'chain', 'web'. Some of these, such as 'thread', 'unpicked', suggest the interwoven nature of cloth, where the warp and the weft work together seamlessly and invisibly to create the functional whole. This language is used to express both the ways in which health is connected, via multiple points, to trade; and the ways in which the UK's health policy, and the effective functioning of the NHS, are connected to UK membership of the EU. The implication here is that, although the discussions of Brexit seemed to be about esoteric matters of trade, actually, they were *also* about health, and it follows that the government should be as accountable for those as they would be for decisions that affect the NHS, and the health of the UK population, under normal circumstances.

Second, people in the health policy community repeatedly stressed their view that the government(s) did not understand the specific details of what Brexit means for health. Members of the health policy community talked in terms of the unreality and impossibility of what was being promised: 'fantasy', 'unicorns', 'magical thinking', 'cake-and-eat-it'. They talked in terms of superficial 'surface' views and the need to 'dig down' and 'go deeper'. They suggested that broad brush 'big picture' views meant that specifics (like specific patients, such as the people we wrote about in chapters five and six, and their needs) got 'lost'. For the health policy community, accountability meant parliament, and others, being able to make sure that the government understood the very specific consequences of its proposed actions for the NHS, especially the threat of a 'No Deal' Brexit. It meant detailed scrutiny of the different possible courses of action – the different types of Brexit – and what those would mean for specific aspects of the NHS and health. In the context of Northern Ireland, these specific consequences are still unfolding as we write (winter 2022), because the Ireland/Northern Ireland Protocol has never fully come into effect.

Third, the health policy community was concerned about the inadequacy of the public debate on these matters, especially in the UK parliament. They suggested that the government was being immature. We heard the phrase 'fairy tales' several times, and one interview suggested that the May government's Brexit impact papers[11] were 'an almost childlike summary of the issues', and that the government had put 'the whole thing [Brexit's impacts on health] into the "too difficult" box'.[12] Dr Philippa

[10] Interview with Philippa Whitford, February 2019.
[11] G Parker, 'Ministers Agree to Release Secret Brexit Impact Paper', Financial Times, 31 January 2018.
[12] Interview with Sarah Wollaston, March 2019.

Whitford, whom we interviewed in 2019, was particularly colourful on the subject. She described the government as behaving like a toddler in its refusal to engage with the problems for health associated with Brexit:

> So there's been a kind of, like some kid hiding behind their hands going 'you can't see me', you know? 'There isn't a problem, I'm not engaging with anybody' … the idea that we're going to come out of free movement, but somehow can keep all the jelly babies that were attached to it … [the government has to be] dragged kicking and screaming to consider public health …

The implication of all of these views is that accountability should take place through political processes: through the ballot box, through proper scrutiny of the effects of proposed government policies (like 'No Deal' Brexit), and through open and transparent parliamentary debate. In general, except for the unsuccessful 'do no harm' proposal discussed in chapter 10, there is nothing in the views of the health policy community that suggested that any kind of *legal* accountability was expected.

V. VIEWS OF 'ORDINARY PEOPLE' ON ACCOUNTABILITY

The 'ordinary people' we talked with in the street, and who appeared in footage shot for the Shout Out UK film about our project, also thought about political accountability. Many people said that 'the government' or 'politicians', sometimes specifically referring to Stormont, or to Westminster, are responsible for the NHS and what might happen to it after Brexit. Many people specifically stated that Johnson, rather than Cameron, or May, should be held to account, highlighting how closely connected Johnson is to the bus, and its implied promise.

As we have already explained, not all of our conversations covered questions of accountability for the implied promise on the bus. Sometimes, however, the people with whom we talked explicitly said that they were not sure how anyone could be held to account for the promise, or the effects of Brexit on the NHS, or went further and said that it is impossible to hold anyone to account.[13] For example, a woman in Sheffield felt that politicians can get away with saying what people want to hear without checking if the statement is true.[14] Someone in Derry/Londonderry explicitly said that accountability was not possible because the country had become too divided on Leave/Remain lines.[15] A couple of people in Derry/Londonderry felt that politicians misused law to avoid accountability: they are 'crooks on the right side of the law'[16] or have all these 'wriggly laws they can use to get away [from accountability]'.[17] A running metaphorical theme in our conversations was the idea that politicians are 'gangsters', operating outside of any kind of political or legal control.[18]

[13] Sheffield 7A, 8A, 4B; Newry 41A, 47A; Rochdale 66A, 67A, 68A, 74A, 87A, 48B, 53B, 58B; Rotherham 128A, 129A, 136A 137A 138A, 140A, 149A; Derry 180A, 201A; 203A, 228A, 125B, 134B, 145B, 164B, 166B, 173B, 174B; 183B, 188B.

[14] Sheffield 8A.

[15] Derry 180A.

[16] Derry 201A.

[17] Derry 166B.

[18] Rochdale 66A, 41B, 72B; Derry 166A, 171A, 228A, 137B.

But when people were able to imagine accountability, a good number of them talked about political means of accountability. They thought elections,[19] or another referendum,[20] would be a way to hold the government to account for effects of Brexit on the NHS. Some expressed electoral support for populist politicians, especially Nigel Farage who was described as 'making sense' in two separate conversations in Rochdale.[21] 'The people should always vote, and make themselves heard', a young British Asian man in Rochdale told us,[22] and two others were adamant that people should vote to stop English nationalists like Tommy Robinson, whom they described as 'dangerous' because of his frightening 'Kill a Muslim Day' campaign on Facebook, which they showed us on their mobile phones.[23] A couple of people thought about fitness for office: they felt that politicians who lie should be deselected and not allowed to stand for election again.[24] One woman in Derry/Londonderry felt that the Cabinet should be holding Johnson to account.[25] She described Johnson as 'that boy in No 10', resonating with our discussions with health policy 'elites' about how childish the government's behaviour seemed. Another person in Derry/Londonderry suggested, more imaginatively, that, 'people should have a one year training course before going into politics – if you fail it, you don't get in'.[26]

Some people had more discursive modes of accountability in mind. We should ask politicians more questions;[27] politicians should be 'made to present their figures and analysis';[28] Johnson should be 'made to tell the truth and show his papers';[29] someone wanted to ask Nigel Farage 'what happened with that?', meaning the funding promised to the NHS.[30]

Still others wanted politicians, and Johnson in particular, to be faced with the consequences of their decisions for other people on an interpersonal level. A woman in Derry/Londonderry said she would like to be able to make Johnson listen to her.[31] There was a strong sense running through many of our conversations that people felt that those in power have no understanding of what their 'normal' lives are like. People in both Northern Ireland and the north of England said they would like to make Johnson live – and especially to experience the NHS – like an ordinary person.[32] A woman in Rochdale thought that Johnson and Farage should shadow a doctor and a nurse to see where the money is needed.[33]

[19] Sheffield 6B; Rochdale 75A, 91A, 100A+ 101A, 104A, 106A 107A, 135A, 41B; Rotherham 130A, 135A; Derry 173A 132B 155B 157B, 179B, 182B.
[20] Newry 55A, 19B, 30B; Derry 170A, 224A.
[21] Rochdale 104A, 41B.
[22] Rochdale 100; 101A.
[23] Rochdale 106; 107A.
[24] Sheffield 10A; Derry 154B.
[25] Derry 161B.
[26] Derry 132B.
[27] Sheffield 9B.
[28] Newry 165B.
[29] Newry 28A.
[30] Rochdale 63A.
[31] Derry 189A.
[32] Derry 194A; Rochdale 63A.
[33] Rochdale 63A.

Not all of our conversations suggested political, or even peaceful, modes of accountability. Some of them evoked accountability through a 'people's movement',[34] resistance,[35] revolution,[36] riots[37] or violent means. Slapping,[38] ear-pulling,[39] punching in the face,[40] were all suggested – not necessarily entirely seriously, but rather in a joking or sarcastic manner – as suitable accountability mechanisms for Johnson, or politicians in general. Others were more extreme: useless, 'fat and uninterested' politicians should be shot in the head;[41] lined up outside the Town Hall and shot;[42] we should 'bomb' Stormont and kill all politicians;[43] 'do away with' or shoot Johnson;[44] or deport Johnson to the USA where they have the death penalty.[45] Evoking past violence on the island of Ireland, a conversation in Derry/Londonderry was striking:

> Accountability? [looks at me [Wood] straight] 'A Kalashnikov!'.[46]

Someone in Sheffield[47] thought Johnson should be 'nailed to the bus', for his part in perpetuating the lie painted on its side. The language here suggests crucifixion, which in the Christian tradition includes not only a painful death, but also public humiliation.

What was more surprising to us, especially to Hervey as a socio-legal scholar, was how many conversations evoked *legal* responsibility and accountability.

In a few of our conversations,[48] there is a disbelief that no one had been prosecuted for the bus. One woman in Newry had an entirely legal understanding of what holding someone responsible would look like. She argued that the Electoral Commission should build a case against Johnson.[49] Someone in Derry/Londonderry felt there should be a law to remove Johnson 'because he is dangerous'.[50] In one instance, courts are felt to be a good place for discursive accountability: 'Court – take them to court. Make them present their figures and analysis'.[51]

Examples of conversations suggesting some kind of civil legal accountability include the idea of a salary deduction, or reduction in politicians' expenses;[52] or being 'done for false advertising'.[53] The idea of negligent harm, or perhaps an

[34] Derry 186A.
[35] Rochdale 100A, 101A.
[36] Rochdale 68A; Derry 164A.
[37] Rochdale 70A.
[38] Derry 188A.
[39] Derry 189A.
[40] Derry 144B.
[41] Rochdale 94A.
[42] Rochdale 55B.
[43] Derry 214A.
[44] Derry 166A, 173A.
[45] Derry 177A.
[46] Derry 164B.
[47] Sheffield 3A.
[48] Newry 16A; Rochdale 55B; Derry 211A, 175B.
[49] Newry 16A.
[50] Derry 176AA.
[51] Newry 165B.
[52] Newry 51A; Rotherham 142A.
[53] Derry 163B.

insurance claim, is evoked by the conversation in Derry/Londonderry, to the effect that a hard border on the island of Ireland would be 'a proper liability' for the NHS and health.[54]

Criminal legal accountability was a more common idea among our conversations. Criminal prosecutions were mentioned several times.[55] People thought Johnson, or politicians in general, should be jailed for telling so many lies.[56] More than one person evoked the crime of fraud,[57] either using that word directly or calling the bus a 'con'.[58] A man in Derry/Londonderry said he would like to see a 'top lawyer' find Johnson guilty of breaking a law, take him to court, and get him arrested. Another would have liked Johnson to be deported to the USA, where they have the death penalty.[59] People's understanding of how criminal and civil legal processes work may have been muddled, unclear or inaccurate. But what was evident was that they believed – or wanted to believe – in legal processes of accountability.

Here, there is a strong resonance with one of the most powerful interviews in our film, with 'Drillminister', a young black drill rapper who claims to represent 'the voice of young Britain, the one they've forgotten about'.[60] This part of the interview is replete with references to legal forms of accountability: criminal processes, including imprisonment, for stealing, fraud and 'joint enterprise',[61] as well as investigatory processes designed to promote transparency, such as Royal Commissions.

> Interviewer: … Your song *NI Backstop* for me was a song about educating, but also that encapsulated the arguments so well. What made you want to do that?
>
> Drillminister: Because my main ops is government, my main ops is the people that's putting us down. What I'm saying, in certain lines like, um "Before the referendum, did the average Joe know what Brexit was?" – before the referendum, not after, where everybody's saying "Brexit, Brexit, Brexit", saying the buzzword – did they know what Brexit was? No, they didn't. They had no clue, otherwise they wouldn't have been driving around with big buses saying "yeah, 150 million … [corrects himself] 350 million … is going back to the NHS", which is a lie. Which, right now, why is no one in jail for that? Because if I'm a fraud man, and if some Uncle is coming and saying "Yo, I'm putting blah, blah, blah into your account" … you'd be like "Yo, Uncle, you're putting that money in my account, yeah". That man'd be in jail. The minute you say, "This didn't go in my account, you was lying, you took my details, all of a sudden … now more money's going out of my account". That's what's basically happening to us right now – more money's going to be going out of our accounts, not going back in – we're getting robbed. But yet you were able to say 350 million, and got your vote through, and now we're all effed …

[54] Derry 179A.

[55] Newry 39A; Rochdale 55B; Derry 139B, 154B; Rochdale 75A.

[56] Rochdale 90A, 95A; Derry 158B, 172B.

[57] Rochdale 90A; Derry 132B.

[58] Rotherham 148A; Derry 207A.

[59] Derry 177A.

[60] E Edwards, 'Who is Drillminister? This Morning Viewers Divided over London Mayor Candidate's Comments', RealityTitbit, 15 May 2020 (www.realitytitbit.com/celebrity-gossip-and-news/who-is-drillminister).

[61] 'Joint enterprise' is 'a doctrine of common law which has been developed by the courts in cases where more than one person is to be prosecuted for the same offence', see P Williams and B Clarke, *Dangerous Associations: Joint Enterprise, Gangs and Racism*, Centre for Crime and Justice Studies 2016, 5.

> Interviewer: What do you think should happen? Cos obviously the 350 million going back to the NHS, on the big red bus by Boris Johnson, it's been discredited, obviously, it's not true, what do you think should happen to MPs who abuse our trust, and the general public, like that?
>
> Drillminister: Um, to be fair, when you're doing something so important, I know it sounds extreme, you have to do jail time. You have to. Guys are doing jail time for less, on the roads. Just, um, joint enterprise, if you know what that is – that's you was in the wrong place, at the wrong time, you never did anything, you never touched anything, you weren't a part of anything, you were there. So, if you were there, with Boris Johnson, when he's saying 350 million, knowing that there's an old pensioner, who is actually believing in that policy – she actually believes in the NHS, she might have been a retired nurse, and she believes in this country and believes in that – and you misled that woman with 350 million – to then rob from her pension now (because that's how she's going to have to pay that back) – what? You're telling me there's no jail time? There's no joint enterprise? There's nobody investigating that? There was nobody saying "how did that ... ?" ... There was no commissions brought to say how did this even come about?

Drillminister's evocative narrative of the innocent retired nurse pensioner, with her faith in the NHS, and trust in government promises such as that on the bus, being 'robbed' by the results of Brexit, suggests that the criminal law would be a suitable form of post-Brexit accountability for health and the NHS.

VI. IS THERE ANY LEGAL ACCOUNTABILITY FOR POST-BREXIT HEALTH GOVERNANCE?

What are the legal constraints, if any, that applied to the statement on the side of the Brexit bus? In general, the UK's 'political' constitution[62] is weaker than the constitutional arrangements in other European countries, where stronger forms of 'legal' constitutionalism[63] provide accountability through law, courts and especially constitutional courts. We are aware of four possible sources of legal accountability: electoral law; common law offences, especially 'misconduct in public office'; administrative and intellectual property law on the use of the NHS logo; and freedom of information.

[62] R Bellamy, 'Political Constitutionalism and the Human Rights Act' (2011) 9(1) *International Journal of Constitutional Law* 86; JAG Griffith, 'The Political Constitution' (1979) 42(1) *The Modern Law Review* 1; A Tomkins, 'Review: In Defence of the Political Constitution' (2002) 22(1) *Oxford Journal of Legal Studies* 157; M Tushnet, 'The Relation between Political Constitutionalism and Weak-Form Judicial Review' (2013) 14(12) *German Law Journal* 2249.

[63] Associated with Kelsen, see, eg, the contributions to the special issue in *German Law Journal* (2019) 20(3) 'Populist Constitutionalism: Varieties, Complexities and Contradictions'; G de Búrca and JHH Weiler (eds), *The Worlds of European Constitutionalism* (Cambridge, Cambridge University Press, 2012); A Sajó and R Uitz, *The Constitution of Freedom: An Introduction to Legal Constitutionalism* (Oxford, Oxford University Press, 2017); M Tushnet, 'Varieties of Constitutionalism' (2016) 14(1) *International Journal of Constitutional Law* 1. Note that the distinction between political and legal constitutionalism has been criticised, see, eg, A Latham-Gambi, 'Political Constitutionalism and Legal Constitutionalism – an Imaginary Opposition?' (2020) 40(4) *Oxford Journal of Legal Studies* 737.

VII. ELECTORAL LAW

UK electoral law consists of a patchwork of measures, some dating back to the Victorian era. The Political Parties, Elections and Referendums Act 2000 provides the current framework for the conduct of referendums in the UK. The Act requires that parliament adopt enabling legislation before a referendum can be held. For the 2016 EU referendum, this legislation is the European Union Referendum Act 2015. The EU Referendum Act gives ministers power to set out how the referendum is to be conducted, including rules on referendum offences.[64] These rules are set out in Regulations.

The European Union Referendum (Conduct) Regulations 2016[65] detail the rules according to which the EU referendum had to be conducted. The Regulations do this by referring back to the Representation of the People Act 1983. This means that the EU Referendum Act has essentially repeated problems that exist in UK electoral law more generally. These problems include its patchwork nature, complexity, and focus on offences like bribery, treating and undue influence that were highly pertinent in Victorian times, but are less so today. In the Victorian era, violence, intimidation, treating votes as a commodity to be bought or sold, and residual feelings that land-owners could influence elections were significant.[66] Today, we are more concerned with the use of 'big data', and various manipulative activities associated with the creation and promulgation of 'fake news' and 'post-truth politics'.

The Political Parties, Elections and Referendums Act, EU Referendum Act and Regulations set out measures concerning how individuals or groups could lawfully campaign during the referendum. These include rules about how much campaigners were permitted to spend and what donations they were allowed to receive. If someone incurs electoral expenses over the permitted amounts, that is a criminal offence.[67] Only 'permitted participants' were allowed to incur more than £10,000 in 'referendum expenses' during the relevant period.[68] Duly authorised 'permitted participants' could spend up to £700,000.[69] The two designated organisations (Vote Leave Ltd and Britain Stronger in Europe/'The In Campaign Ltd') could spend no more than £7 million, along with designated public funding of £600,000. The Electoral Commission is responsible for overseeing these spending rules, and its decisions are subject to judicial review. But there are no electoral offences that cover making untrue statements to influence the campaign.

[64] Section 4, European Union Referendum Act 2015.

[65] UK SI 2016 No 219.

[66] The Law Commission, Scottish Law Commission, Northern Ireland Law Commission, *Electoral Law: An Interim Report* (London, Edinburgh and Belfast, The Law Commission, Scottish Law Commission, Northern Ireland Law Commission, 4 February 2016).

[67] Section 118(2) and (3), Political Parties, Elections and Referendums Act 2000.

[68] Section 117 (1), Political Parties, Elections and Referendums Act 2000, as modified by the European Union Referendum Act.

[69] Section 118(1) and Schedule 14, Political Parties, Elections and Referendums Act 2000, as amended by European Union Referendum Act, Schedule 1, para 25 (2).

Although there are legal controls over making misleading or untrue statements in broadcast media,[70] these controls do not cover non-broadcast political advertising. As Beth Shiner points out,[71] there are laws allowing individuals to complain about misleading claims in consumer advertising, and in government departmental advertising. But these provisions do not apply to claims in political advertisements. Apart from data protection law,[72] there are no legal controls over the dissemination of the image of the bus through social media. So only the campaign spending rules apply to the implied promises made during the referendum. Electoral law therefore does not provide any basis on which to hold Johnson, or the UK government, to account for implied promises made during the referendum campaign, such as that on the NHS Brexit bus. The Electoral Commission is not a 'Truth Commission'.[73]

As far as we are aware, no one sought to rely on electoral law to hold anyone to account for the implied promise on the bus. There were attempts to hold the Electoral Commission to account for its enforcement of the spending rules in the EU Referendum Act 2015, but these did not focus on the bus. They focused on Darren Grimes, the leader of 'BeLeave', and on Vote Leave paying for advertising services that Grimes had commissioned from AggregateIQ Data Services Ltd.[74] The court took a narrow view on what could be argued in the case, and was keen for the arguments to focus only on the specific points, and not the broader political contexts.

This is not surprising as it reflects a particularly narrow, but very British, sense of political accountability, resting on the idea of 'parliamentary sovereignty', which does not envisage a significant role for courts to check parliamentary powers or responsibilities. There is no sense in UK electoral law that the courts might have any duty to look to the wider picture in responding to the referendum process, or that litigation might be a place for public discussion of the referendum process and who is accountable for claims or promises made during it.

VIII. MISCONDUCT IN PUBLIC OFFICE

A second possible route to legal accountability was a private prosecution,[75] brought in the Westminster Magistrates court, relying on the common law offence of 'misconduct in public office'. This claim enjoyed some initial success in May 2019. The allegation was that Johnson (at the relevant time the Mayor of London and an MP)

[70] Sections 319(2)(g), 321(2), 333, Communications Act 2003.

[71] B Shiner, 'Big Data, Small Law: How Gaps in Regulation are Affecting Political Campaigning Methods and the Need for Fundamental Reform' (2019) (2) *Public Law* 362.

[72] The GDPR and Data Protection Act 1998 make provision on 'processing' of 'personal data'. Online political profiling, so as to target users of social media sites, constitutes such processing, although it is the misuse of the personal data, for example, using it without consent, not the political targeting per se, that is unlawful, see Shiner, ibid.

[73] The Law Commission, Scottish Law Commission, Northern Ireland Law Commission, *Electoral Law*, above n 66; KA Armstrong, *Brexit Time. Leaving the EU – Why, How and When?* (Cambridge, Cambridge University Press, 2017), 67.

[74] *Good Law Project v Electoral Commission* [2018] EWHC 602 (Admin); [2018] EWHC 2414 (Admin); [2018] EWHC 2553.

[75] *Ball and Brexit Justice Ltd v Johnson* (www.judiciary.uk/wp-content/uploads/2019/05/Ball-v-Johnson-FV-290519.pdf accessed 15 February 2023).

had endorsed two misleading statements, one of which was the statement displayed on the NHS Brexit bus, and elsewhere, such as on billboards. During broadcast media interviews, Johnson repeatedly suggested that the UK 'parted weekly with that sum' to the EU. The District Judge, Margot Coleman, found that the ingredients of the offence of misconduct in public office were present in these actions, and thus there was a proper case to issue a summons against Johnson to stand trial in a criminal court.

But in July 2019, the High Court overturned the Magistrates' decision.[76] The High Court held that there is an important distinction between acting *as* a public official and acting *whilst* a public official. 'Misconduct in public office' requires that the person must be acting *as* a public official. Johnson was acting *whilst* a public official. This was not the legal offence of misconduct in public office. If the public wishes to hold the office-holder to account for actions *whilst* a public official, the public must do that through *political* processes only. The criminal law is not an available mechanism of accountability.

IX. USE OF THE NHS LOGO

The NHS logo, as part of the NHS identity, has been legally protected since 1999.[77] As a brand, the NHS is easily recognised and highly trusted. The NHS' own research shows that the logo evokes positive emotional responses of confidence, security and dependability. The NHS identity policy, and associated guidelines, require all NHS entities to use the logo, and to do so only in specific ways. Part of the rationale for these requirements is to ensure high quality healthcare, part of the NHS values and key principles embodied in its Constitution.[78] The use of the NHS brand is therefore one of the ways that the NHS is held to account for its actions,[79] and is a third legal route that could have been used to secure accountability for the use of the logo on the bus.

The term 'NHS' is protected by the Company, Limited Liability Partnership and Business Names (Sensitive Words and Expressions) Regulations 2014. No company may lawfully be incorporated with 'NHS' in its name without the express permission of the Department of Health and Social Care. The NHS logo is a trademark, owned by the Secretary of State for Health and Social Care, who also owns the copyright in the logo. The NHS logo may not lawfully be used without permission.[80] That this matters to at least some NHS patients is demonstrated by the criticism raised by

[76] *Johnson v Westminster Magistrates* [2019] EWHC 1709 (Admin). See also, P Dallison, 'Bid to Prosecute Boris Johnson over Brexit Bus Claim Thrown Out by Court', Politico, 7 June 2019.

[77] NHS England, 'Why It's Important' (www.england.nhs.uk/nhsidentity/why-its-important/ accessed 29 November 2022).

[78] Department of Health and Social Care, 'The NHS Constitution for England' (www.gov.uk/government/publications/the-nhs-constitution-for-england/the-nhs-constitution-for-england accessed 29 November 2022).

[79] NHS England, 'NHS Logo' (www.england.nhs.uk/nhsidentity/identity-guidelines/nhs-logo/ accessed 29 November 2022).

[80] NHS England, 'Who Cannot Use the NHS Identity?' (www.england.nhs.uk/nhsidentity/identity-guidelines/who-cannot-use-the-nhs-identity/ accessed 29 November 2022).

the NGO 'patients4nhs' in 2015. Patients4nhs objected to permission being given to private entities such as Virgin Care Ltd to use the NHS logo when providing services on behalf of NHS England.[81]

One of the public responses to the Brexit bus was to use the NHS logo 'hotline' to register a complaint about the use of the NHS brand by the Leave campaign. The number of people concerned by this may be indicated by the fact that, by early May 2016, the NHS phone number on the relevant website remained unanswered, due to the volume of calls, although an email address continued to receive complaints. Hervey's Facebook entries for the time shows that she was one of the people who emailed, and many of her friends and acquaintances said that they had done this too. Hervey never received any reply.

The Independent[82] and the Observer[83] newspapers reported on 3 and 5 March 2016 that the Department of Health had threatened legal action on behalf of NHS England. Vote Leave was reported by the media as characterising the Department of Health's actions as 'bullying'. Possible remedies discussed in the Observer's news report were an injunction; destroying all leaflets, posters and billboards that infringed the Department of Health's copyright in the logo (which would have included the information on the bus); and damages.

On 16 May 2016, the Huffington Post[84] reported that Heidi Alexander MP, then Shadow Health Secretary, had written to Sir Simon Stevens, the Chief Executive of NHS England, asking him to clearly and explicitly disassociate the NHS from the Vote Leave campaign. Alexander wrote: 'I am concerned that [Vote Leave's] use of the logo is giving voters the misleading impression that their campaign, and its highly dubious claims, is somehow endorsed by the NHS'.

However, despite these actions by members of the public and their elected representatives, no legal action saw the light of day. The Vote Leave campaign continued to use the logo, right up to the end of its campaign. The 'core principles and values' of the NHS Constitution, which justify the legal restrictions on the use of the logo, evidently did not reach sufficiently far to justify further or stronger actions by the Department of Health, to bring to account the Vote Leave campaign for its unauthorised use of the NHS logo. We endeavoured on several occasions to find out who had made this decision in the Department of Health, but we were not successful.

X. FREEDOM OF INFORMATION

We were not the only people seeking to discover this information. Dr Paul Thornton, a GP from Nuneaton, initiated a freedom of information request[85] to discover

[81] Patients 4 NHS, 'Use of the NHS Logo' (www.patients4nhs.org.uk/abuse-of-nhs-logo/ accessed 29 November 2022).

[82] P Gallagher, 'EU Referendum: Department of Health Tells Vote Leave Campaign to Stop Using Official NHS Logo in its Brexit Literature', Independent, 3 March 2016.

[83] D Boffey, 'Brexit Group Warned: Stop Using NHS Logo or We'll Sue', The Observer, 5 March 2016.

[84] G Demianyk, 'Labour Criticises "Brexit" Campaign For "Misleading" Use Of NHS Logo', Huffington Post, 16 May 2016.

[85] What Do They Know, 'Use of NHS logo by Vote Leave' (www.whatdotheyknow.com/request/use_of_nhs_logo_by_vote_leave accessed 29 November 2022).

whether the Department of Health had indeed taken action to prevent the use of the NHS logo by the Vote Leave campaign. A freedom of information request is a fourth aspect of possible legal accountability. Freedom of information laws can be used to hold holders of public office to account *indirectly* for their actions, by members of the public being able to use legal processes to secure transparent information about public office-holders' decisions. Transparency as a mode of accountability fits well with the UK's constitution, where the ballot box is central to holding the government to account.

The information that Dr Thornton tried to find out was not released until 5 October 2016, after an initial refusal was overturned on internal review by the Information Commission, following multiple communications from Dr Thornton. It eventually transpired that the NHS brand and identity team *had indeed* written to Vote Leave:

> I am sure you can appreciate why these people [members of the public who alerted the team to the logo on a campaign leaflet] believed they were receiving communications from the NHS, and then upon further inspection their annoyance and concern which led them to bring this to our attention once they realised that is not NHS resource.[86]

Apparently, the team requested that the Vote Leave remove all uses of the NHS logo or stop their distribution within seven days. But no further information about the decision not to pursue matters further was forthcoming.

The Department of Health did not respond to Dr Thornton's freedom of information request in its entirety, citing its 'commercial interests' and legal professional privilege. The Department of Health response concludes 'we consider that the public interest in withholding the requested information outweighs the public interest in disclosing it'. This response – referring to a dispassionate 'balance', and therefore a proportionate response[87] – neutralises the viewpoint that the Department of Health acted unreasonably and illegitimately. The idea of a balance, as Nicola Lacey puts it, evokes 'harmony, natural (quasi-geometric) order or coherence founded on reason and issuing in fairness, social justice, and limits on power'.[88] It would follow that there was no need to disclose all the information that Dr Thornton was seeking. It is unlikely that we will ever know who took a decision not to pursue the unlawful use of the NHS logo on the bus further, or what the reasons were for that decision.

Overall therefore, none of the possible direct or indirect routes to legal accountability for the (implied) promise on the bus was successful. These outcomes are because courts and litigation are not understood as the place or procedure for holding anyone to account for a referendum claim like the one made on the bus, and for its effects on voter behaviour, or what it means, or should mean, for future NHS or health policies post-Brexit. Even the very indirect accountability route of using legal processes to secure transparent information about why the Department of Health did not rely on its legal rights against Vote Leave, was held to be not in the public interest. Instead, parliament's political power in the UK constitution is put front and centre,

[86] Cited in M McCartney, 'Vote Leave Broke Rules Over NHS Logo' (2016) 355 *British Medical Journal* i5482.

[87] See N Lacey, 'The Metaphor of Proportionality' (2016) 43(1) *Journal of Law and Society* 27.

[88] Ibid, 31.

and no legal oversight from courts or legal processes in general is deemed to be necessary to hold the government to account. As Sinéad Douglas Scott has pointed out, the practical effect of this position is that, despite the power and influence of the message on the bus, there was 'little or no accountability for its inaccuracies'.[89]

XI. CONCLUSIONS

Our research resonates with broader research on how the law was a very limited means to engage with – or seek to reverse – the Brexit process.[90] It is widely recognised now that the (implied) promise on the bus, of £350 million a week more for the NHS, and associated improvements for patients, staff and the country's health as a whole, cannot be kept – or at least cannot be kept as a natural consequence flowing from leaving the EU. What we saw in our conversations in the street, and in our documentary film interviews, is that, while many people could not imagine how Johnson, or subsequent governments, could be held accountable for that broken promise, a significant proportion of people thought that law should be a viable accountability process in this instance. What we have shown in this chapter, is that UK law, as it currently stands, is wholly deficient in that respect.

[89] S Douglas Scott, 'Brexit, Boundaries and the Power of Images' (2019) 13(1) *Pólemos* 63, 74.

[90] See, eg, M Elliott et al (eds), *The UK Constitution after Miller: Brexit and Beyond* (Oxford, Hart Publishing, 2018); C McCorkindale and A McHarg, 'Litigating Brexit' in O Doyle et al (eds), *The Brexit Challenge for Ireland and the United Kingdom* (Cambridge, Cambridge University Press, 2021); V Miller and S de Mars, 'Brexit Questions in National and EU Courts', HC Library Briefing Paper, No. 8415 (1 November 2019); S Peers, 'Litigating Brexit – a Guide to the Case Law', 27 July 2020, http://eulawanalysis.blogspot.com/p/litigating-brexit-guide-to-caselaw.html.

12

Conclusions

I. INTRODUCTION

IN KEEPING WITH the narrative tradition in socio-legal studies that frames this book at its very outset (in chapter one), we end it just how we began – with a story. Only this time it is a continuation of Flear's earlier story about (sometimes difficult) conversations with his blood family about Brexit, and keeping open the lines of communication (in chapter two):

> I had a chat with my mother recently (winter 2022) about how things are with the NHS in our respective places of residence within the UK: Northern Ireland and England. The prompt for our chat was how much the NHS in both places is struggling and how that is impacting on access to care. We both agreed that Brexit hasn't helped matters. For instance, there doesn't appear to be enough staff to treat everyone who is waiting for care. We both also had concerns about my ability to access essential medicines due to the operation of the Ireland/Northern Ireland Protocol. While the latter may have been resolved, for now at least, the former remains a pressing problem. We both see reports of the queues outside hospitals, and have relatives waiting to access care, seemingly because of the strain on the NHS this winter. But the politicians don't appear to be sorting out the problem now or in the long term.
>
> On top of that, we also agreed that beginning by recounting our stories was helpful as we sought to understand each other's positions on Brexit (which were – and are – mixed for both of us). My mother commented that stories – saying what's going on in our lives and how Brexit seems to relate – 'allows us to make a connection between our lives and leaving the EU, something that not even the politicians seemed to know much about or don't seem able to explain clearly'. Storytelling gives us a 'chance to understand that [the consequences of Brexit]' and to have 'some empathy for one another'. We laughed at that!
>
> We agreed that just having conversations like this seemed impossible a few years ago, and that exchanging stories, from a position of time and distance from Brexit Day, and from different locations in the UK, gave us both an opportunity to stand back, develop empathy and reflexivity. We were both emphatic that this is vital for getting through all manner of shared problems, and that there are so many of them to resolve, large and small, public and private. Mum said, 'Now, wouldn't that be a good thing!'.

This concluding chapter draws together the threads across the book, most of which are present in this opening story, to summarise and underscore our main findings. First, we reflect back, from the vantage point of winter 2022, initially, on what we have learned about the effects of Brexit on the NHS and health; and on how, and in what ways, governance, law and policy have changed or are changing in health contexts.

We bring together our observations on the significance of those changes, in terms of public understandings of what a legitimate post-Brexit NHS and health governance settlement might look like, across the UK, and of the accountability mechanisms that are felt appropriate to secure such legitimacy. To what extent do 'expert' and 'ordinary' understandings of legitimate and accountable health governance align with the constitutional settlement for health in the UK, as a state now independent from the EU? Overall, and more broadly, we reflect on what the future might hold in terms of legitimate post-Brexit health governance. In terms of our specific contribution to substantive knowledge and understanding, we also summarise what we did not cover, what we found that was expected, and what we found that is new or surprising.

From there, we round out the book's discussions on methodology, by explaining how, in addition to helping us to understand post-Brexit health governance, its (lack of) legitimacy, and who might be held to account for its deficiencies, the stories that we heard and retell in this project lead us to reflect on what a methodology and narrative methods such as ours can bring to the study of law, legal text and socio-legal studies. Here, we come full circle to underscore the observation we made at the very outset of the book: by explaining how we contribute towards the strong narrative tradition in socio-legal scholarship. More than that, now, we are able to point out how our contribution also helps to reinvigorate the potential for socio-legal studies to not just resonate, but also make a difference, by adding to knowledge and understanding both across and outwith the academy.

Finally, and in keeping with our methodology and research design, which centres our identities, positionality and reflexivity as researchers, we also use this concluding chapter to present some of our key reflections on what we have learned and continue to learn.

II. A SUMMARY OF OUR OVERALL FINDINGS

As regards our first set of questions, looking across all the 'building blocks' of a health system (as we laid it out in chapter four), in summary, what have we learned about the main effects of leaving the EU, on the basis of the Withdrawal Agreement and EU-UK Trade and Cooperation Agreement (TCA), and where are we now in terms of health governance?

Using legal and socio-legal methods (outlined in chapters two and three), we have been able to explain how the UK and EU's choice of the *type* of Brexit has had important effects on health and the NHS, especially in Northern Ireland, but also in general across the UK. Our temporal scope, through interpretative analyses of the unfolding legal texts, over the time period 2016–22, coupled with the general policy context, our interview data with 'experts', and the co-produced scenario analyses which we developed with and for those interlocutors in the health policy sector, allow us not only to make general observations in this regard, but also to offer specific granularity to Brexit effects on an important aspect of the UK's social, economic, and public life: health and the NHS. Our engagement with health policy actors, especially from London, Belfast and Dublin, allows us to understand what the unfolding law means in practice, not just to interpret the legal text in the abstract. Our geographic or spatial scope, including a focus on the island of Ireland, allows us to draw out implications for the NHS in the different parts of the UK, especially in Northern Ireland.

The 'steps of doom' options (described in chapter nine) led the EU and UK to a trade relationship, embodied in the Withdrawal Agreement and EU-UK TCA, that leaves the UK less closely integrated with the EU than could have been the case. That choice of relationship has implications for the people (chapters seven and nine), and the products (chapters eight and nine), that the NHS and health sector need, in order to operate effectively. Some parts of the UK, especially Northern Ireland, stand in a precarious position, as the legal settlement – particularly concerning product supply – is still unfolding and yet to be fully implemented. The Withdrawal Agreement and EU-UK TCA have implications for patients who might need healthcare in another country (as we have explained in chapters five and six). Again, these implications are different for patients in Northern Ireland, as compared to the rest of the UK.

Overall, the effects of Brexit on the NHS, and health, across the UK, are detrimental, but not as devastating as they would have been if the UK had left on a 'No Deal' basis. Furthermore, as we have shown (especially in chapters eight, nine and ten), the EU has *also* lost out in terms of health protection. Without the UK, important biomedical and regulatory expertise has been lost from the EU's law-making processes; from its ability to negotiate with the global bioscience industry (for example, to secure new vaccines at a fair price); and from its investment in biomedical scientific research.

Turning to our second set of questions, looking across our project data as a whole, what would constitute a 'legitimate' post-Brexit health governance settlement for the UK and its constituent parts, and who should be held to account for (lack of) delivery of such a governance settlement?

As we explained (in chapters two, three and eleven), we are able to go further than an elaboration beyond the 'law in the books' of the post-Brexit health governance settlement. To do this, we draw on the stories that people working in the health policy sector told us, as we worked together. Interrogating the metaphorical language they used, we have not only enriched an understanding of the specific implications of more general legal texts, and the ways in which law and policy interact, as the post-Brexit health governance settlement unfolds. From these socio-legal encounters, we learned not only something about what was (and is) taking place, but also about how key health policy actors felt (and feel) in response to these changing EU-UK relationships. Although we did not ask directly about legitimacy or accountability, we were able to infer views on these matters when we looked back at our interview data and recalled our policy collaborations. We have told the story/ies of these collaborations throughout the book.

As we have explained (in chapter 11), the views of health policy 'experts' on the links between health and trade, on the superficiality of government understandings of the difficulties and challenges different aspects of various forms of Brexit meant for health and the NHS, and on the inadequacies of public debates on these matters, meant that they expected ordinary modes of political accountability in the UK constitution to apply. Overall, our health policy community collaborators – representing the 'expert' view – did not expect any forms of legal accountability for post-Brexit health governance. Further, they found that accountability through political mechanisms (elections, parliamentary scrutiny, honest and factually-informed public debate) was profoundly lacking. This conclusion, specific to the (very important) health policy sector and the NHS, makes us wonder whether it could and should be generalised to the UK's system of political accountability more generally.

What about the views of 'ordinary people', non-experts? Here, we need to be careful not to overclaim. Our street conversation and film data was gathered in particular places and at particular moments in time. It provides a snapshot of what nearly 500 'ordinary people', mainly in the North of England and Northern Ireland, chose to tell us, and the film crew, that they thought and felt, on specific dates in 2019 (some of which were significant for the Brexit process). Furthermore, while we have been careful to distinguish between direct reporting of the statements that those people made to us (captured in the film data, or in our handwritten notes taken immediately after each conversation), and our impressions of the conversations and what they meant, we do not claim to directly represent the views expressed to us. Our methods (detailed in chapters two and three) involve elements of ethnographically-inspired research, where we, as researchers, become instruments of data collection and interpretation, key instruments of *knowing*. Our positionality (shaped in part by space, place and time), and our understanding of the ethical obligations on us as reflexive researchers, limits the extent to which we claim to understand the perspectives of those whose epistemologies (how people know what they know) and ontologies (how people perceive what they perceive to be reality) are borne of experiences that are very different from our own.

Within those limitations, we understand from our encounters with 'ordinary people' that many of them expect not only political and discursive modes of accountability, but also *legal* modes of accountability, to apply to the post-Brexit health governance settlement. We have explained how we interpreted the stories people told us, and the metaphors they used in response to the photograph of the Brexit bus, throughout the book. 'Lies', and even 'bullshit', many people said. But the ways in which they described the NHS suggest they are concerned for its future. People talked of the NHS as if it were a building or physical structure about to collapse, or a human being on the verge of a critical (mental) illness. The NHS is 'struggling';[1] 'stressed';[2] 'under too much pressure';[3] 'strained';[4] 'a big gaping hole';[5] 'in trouble';[6] being 'run into the ground';[7] 'running down';[8] or 'on its knees'.[9] The NHS should be 'cherished';[10] is a 'brilliant institution' needing more funding;[11]

[1] Newry 30A, 36A, 39A, 58A; Rochdale 64A, 75A, 91A; Rotherham 115B; Derry 164A.
[2] Rochdale 61B; Derry 125B, 147B, 189B.
[3] Newry 36A, 44A, 45A.
[4] Newry 36A; Derry 213A.
[5] Sheffield 2A.
[6] Newry 54A.
[7] Rochdale 97A.
[8] Rochdale 98A.
[9] Derry 189B.
[10] Rochdale 63A.
[11] Rochdale 66A.

needing 'protection'.[12] Some people talked more broadly too, about their town having 'fallen behind';[13] being 'left behind' (compared to the South of England), which is 'skyrocketing';[14] having 'lost all sense of community';[15] 'used to be a model town';[16] 'heart taken out of [it]';[17] or broader still, the country 'going backwards' and 'in chaos';[18] 'jumping off a cliff';[19] being 'in dire straits';[20] or Brexit bringing 'havoc'.[21] A few conversations linked the two: Brexit will 'cripple' the NHS;[22] 'if we lose the NHS [as a consequence of Brexit], we lose everything'.[23] The implied promise on the Brexit bus, to the effect that leaving the EU would mean improvements in their experience of the NHS, has not been kept. Implicitly, therefore, legal – as well as political – consequences should follow for those who made the promise, and – again implicitly – for those who perpetuate it. There is, therefore, a significant gap between 'expert' and 'ordinary' understandings of legitimate and accountable health governance post-Brexit. However, as we will see below, this is not quite the gap that is represented in some of the more general literature on Brexit.

III. WHAT WE DID NOT COVER

There is much more we could have discussed. For example, although we have touched on the COVID-19 pandemic in various places in this book, we have not reflected on the ways in which the COVID-19 pandemic affected us, our work, and the post-Brexit landscape in which the UK now finds itself. We recall a meme, circulating on social media in spring 2020, that read: 'remember when all we used to talk about was Brexit?'. That meme encapsulated how much energy the pandemic took over, in both public life, and in people's private lives. Brexit receded into the background in terms of news reporting, but also in terms of where attention was focused, including in the NHS (obviously), in health policy spaces, and also in universities. When EU law finally ceased to apply in Great Britain, on 1 January 2021, press reaction was distinctly muted, because so many people were pinning their hopes on an effective COVID-19 vaccine being rolled out across the population as soon as possible, to allow a full reopening of schools and workplaces, and a 'return to normality'.[24]

Nor have we written in detail about how difficult it is to disentangle Brexit effects on the NHS and health from COVID-19 effects. We are working with the *Health Foundation* and the *Nuffield Trust*, for at least the next three years, on a project that

[12] Rochdale 69B.
[13] Rochdale 85A.
[14] Rotherham 137A.
[15] Rochdale 75A.
[16] Rotherham 124A.
[17] Rotherham 117B.
[18] Rochdale 105A.
[19] Derry 170A.
[20] Rotherham 132A.
[21] Derry 201A.
[22] Derry 220A.
[23] Rotherham 148A.
[24] 'Newspaper Headlines: New Year Hope and Campaign for "Jabs Army"', BBC, 1 January 2021.

seeks to do exactly that: to track effects on health and the NHS of the UK's changing relationships with the EU and the rest of the world. So far, much of our effort in that project has concerned the situation in Northern Ireland. There, we have heard about real fears for continued supply of medicines, and ongoing frustration at the political impasse arising from the Johnson, Truss, and now Sunak governments' approaches to the Ireland/Northern Ireland Protocol, and the practical effects on the people of Northern Ireland of the lack of functioning executive in Stormont.[25]

IV. WHAT WE FOUND THAT WAS EXPECTED

Our exploration confirms much existing knowledge. First, there are no convincing simple narratives about 'why' Brexit happened (which was not our research agenda in any event), nor what Brexit means for the future of (any aspect of) the governance of the UK. From our point of view, anyone who is offering a single narrative or explanation is over-simplifying what are very complex phenomena. We would suggest that such a person is probably also not being as attentive to how Brexit is affecting people, or institutions, across different parts of the UK, as we have tried to be, even though our main focus is Westminster, the north of England and Northern Ireland.

Second, we also show how – in the context of health and the NHS at least – Brexit is not 'done'. The disentangling of the UK from EU membership was always going to be a process, not a moment, despite political narratives to the contrary. The UK has formally left the EU. But the legacies of previous EU membership remain. To give just one example, as we completed this manuscript, the future of the Retained EU Law (Revocation and Reform) Bill, which seeks to remove all vestiges of EU law from the British statute book by 31 December 2023, remained opaque. If the Bill comes into effect, a range of legal entitlements, for instance, the basic employment conditions under which people work in the NHS, will no longer be guaranteed by law that originated in the EU. At present (winter 2022), we do not yet know what their replacements might be.

Some aspects of health law and policy in Great Britain, such as the clinical trial standards for new medicines, may be slowly diverging from the EU's position, but there is no clear picture of direction of travel, or of the extent of *actual legal divergence*, as opposed to a *political discussion* of divergence, at all. There are undoubtedly potential benefits from Great Britain departing from the EU's standards for regulation of medicines, medical devices or equipment, for example, to try to incentivise companies in the global bioscience industry to launch new products in Great Britain, or to make products used in the NHS safer. There would be benefits from aligning decision-making about whether a new product is not only safe and effective enough to sell, with decision-making about whether that product is also available to patients within the NHS. But the benefits of departing too far from the regulatory standards

[25] M McCarey et al, *Health and Brexit: Six Years On* (London, Nuffield Trust, 2022).

that apply in the much bigger, proximate market of the EU would need to be weighed against the potential downsides. If safety or efficacy standards for medicines or medical devices and equipment depart too far from EU standards, especially if they become more difficult to meet, it will become more difficult for the NHS to source products at good prices, because the industry will be supplying a much smaller market in Great Britain. These decisions would also need to take account of whatever is decided for supply of the NHS in Northern Ireland. At the moment, as we see things, the UK is unable even to have a measured discussion in the health policy community about these trade-offs, because the narratives of post-Brexit 'freedom', and 'global Britain', have stifled that kind of debate.[26]

Third, in the context of the NHS, our research confirms how much at odds an ideological focus on 'freedom' associated with leaving the EU is with a focus on the ways that the UK interacts in practice with the rest of the world. For example, the supposed benefits of the UK developing an independent approach to immigration law are difficult to discern, when the NHS must attract staff from outside the UK for the foreseeable future. The health policy people with whom we worked understand this well, and they would like the UK to be able to attract migrant labour to the NHS workforce.

But the experience and feelings of many ordinary people we talked with were not consistent with this understanding. James Saunders, proudly wearing a West Ham football shirt, whom Shout Out UK interviewed in London in 2019, for the film about our project, explains how he sees things:

> Well, I think we have to ask ourselves what is the impact of the NHS going on in England now. Me personally, if I want to book a doctor's appointment, I'm left on a waiting list for three or four weeks. Some time ago, I booked an emergency appointment, because I had a lung infection. It took me two weeks to even be seen by a doctor.
>
> I feel like the NHS is backlogged, and I think the reason why that is, is because the British government has overflooded this country with immigrants. I feel like this country is losing its identity. I think it's losing its loyalty, I think it's losing its pride, to be honest with you. …
>
> I feel like the NHS is understaffed, as well. …
>
> I feel like there is an element of betrayal from the establishment. I feel, personally, very hurt, betrayed, upset, and slightly angry about the way that the establishment have not really taken into consideration the 17.4 million people that voted to leave the EU.

James was disappointed, even betrayed,[27] that the UK had not yet left the EU. It seems to us that his perception was that, from the moment that the UK had left the EU, that change would naturally and logically result in an improvement in his NHS experience, because there would be fewer 'immigrants', 'flooding' into the country and using NHS services. As we understand it though, the sad irony of James' position includes that the doctor who (eventually) treated his lung infection *was an EU national*. Although of course it is difficult to disaggregate effects of the COVID-19

[26] M Dayan et al, 'Parallel, Divergent or Drifting? Regulating Healthcare Products in a Post-Brexit UK' (2023) *Journal of European Public Policy* https://doi.10.1080/13501763.2023.2213721.

[27] The idea of 'betrayal' also appeared in our street conversations, eg, Rotherham 158A.

pandemic from those of Brexit, waiting times to access a GP in England have not significantly improved.[28]

Another example of a disconnect between the UK government's ideologies and the ways in which the UK interacts with the rest of the world in practice concerns the UK's global power. The May, Johnson, Truss and Sunak governments all articulated the idea of 'global Britain', freed from the 'shackles' of EU membership. But in practice, the EU was a space through which the UK exercised global power. One instance (discussed in chapter nine), is the ways in which the UK now no longer leads European Research Networks at the cutting edge of biomedical research into rare diseases. Another instance is the regulation of medicines, devices and equipment where (as we saw in chapter eight), the EU's standards reach beyond the EU, because companies in other countries comply with them so as to be able to access the EU market. The UK, while an EU Member State, had played a strong role in determining those standards. Outside the EU, the UK is no longer able to use that route to exercise global influence.

V. WHAT WE FOUND THAT IS NEW OR SURPRISING

Our focus on the NHS and health governance, seen through the lenses of our sources of information, reveals interesting and important connections and disconnections between governments/administrations, policy 'experts' and 'ordinary people'. It does so in four main ways.

First, our data confounds the perception that a deep disconnection between 'experts' and 'ordinary people' characterises the post-Brexit UK. While our street conversations, and the other data on which we draw to understand the views of 'ordinary people', sometimes suggest what to us are quite profound misunderstandings about how the NHS is funded or functions, or how health and the NHS intersect with migration or trade, or indeed how global trade operates in practice, those views are not, on closer investigation, as naïve as some of the 'expert' narratives suggest. This evidence aligns with recent political opinion data that shows growing general agreement across demographic groups that leaving the European Union was a mistake.[29]

One example is that our data does not show that 'ordinary people' believed the message on the Brexit bus in an unquestioning or simplistic way. Instead, as we explained (for example in chapters four and eight), the photograph of the bus evoked many responses that suggested a complex and bifurcated position of *both* understanding that the bus message was 'lies' or 'bullshit',[30] *and at the same time* a hope that somehow the referendum vote might prompt an unspecified process through which the NHS might secure more funding and thus provide better services. Further,

[28] Nuffield Trust, 'Access to GP Services' (www.nuffieldtrust.org.uk/resource/access-to-gp-services#background accessed 29 November 2022).

[29] J Larik et al, 'Will Support for Brexit Become Extinct?', 30 November 2022 (https://ukandeu.ac.uk/will-support-for-brexit-become-extinct/).

[30] I Antova et al, 'Calling out "Bullshit" in "Left Behind" Britain', SPERI, 16 September 2019 (http://speri.dept.shef.ac.uk/2019/09/16/calling-out-brexit-bullshit-in-left-behind-britain/).

many of our conversations suggest that 'ordinary people' see little, or no, connection between Brexit and the NHS. Their desires or ambitions for the NHS were expressed as unrelated to the UK's relationships with the EU, or indeed the rest of the world.[31]

Another example concerns migration. Sometimes, we heard stories based on nostalgia for an imagined past where things were perceived to be better, and greater openness to the world, associated with EU membership, especially to human migration, was implicitly assumed to be the causal factor responsible. These are consistent with survey data, which shows anxiety about migration, and a desire for greater investment in healthcare.[32] Often we heard blatant racism, sometimes expressed apologetically ('no offence to you, love'), in a narrative where England (that is where the words were spoken, rather than in Northern Ireland) implicitly took a wrong turn in its labour supply policies (including to the NHS), not only through EU membership, but also through openness to Britain's former colonies. An instance in our conversations where this seemed to be the case is the conversation we recounted (in chapter seven), in which the woman with whom we talked felt that her anti-immigration views were so far from 'elite' views such as ours that it would 'get her arrested'. Here, as we explained, we experienced significant epistemological and ontological distance from our own position, as well as a gap between the position of the 'ordinary people' with whom we had conversations and the position of the health policy community, which is that the NHS needs inward migration, and EU, or at least single market, membership is valuable in that respect.

But our research suggests that understanding the referendum vote as 'ordinary people' in 'left behind' places seeking to prevent 'elite-supported' liberal policies on migration to the UK is far too simplistic.[33] Anti-immigration views were not the only types of stories we heard where people talked about migration in response to the photograph of the Brexit bus. We also heard many more complex understandings about migration of labour, especially where people had experienced care in the NHS from people they perceived to be 'not British'. Assumptions that a link may be drawn between demands for increased NHS investment, or public sector investment more generally, and support for populist policies like Brexit, is prevalent in the kinds of communities labelled as 'left behind',[34] are deficient. On the

[31] M Wood et al, 'What Do "Left Behind Communities" Want? A Qualitative Study in the United Kingdom using Photo Elicitation' (2023) *American Political Science Review* (first view doi: 10.1017/S0003055422001186).

[32] See, eg, S Becker et al, 'Who Voted for Brexit? A Comprehensive District-Level Analysis' (2017) 32(92) *Economic Policy* 601; M Hameleers and D Schmuck, 'It's Us against Them: A Comparative Experiment on the Effects of Populist Messages Communicated via Social Media' (2017) 20(9) *Information, Communication & Society* 1425; D Goodhart, *The Road to Somewhere: The Populist Revolt and the Future of Politics* (Oxford, Oxford University Press, 2017).

[33] Others have also pointed out the deficiencies of this simplistic narrative see, eg, GK Bhambra, 'Brexit, Trump, and "Methodological Whiteness": On the Misrecognition of Race and Class' (2017) 68(1) *British Journal of Sociology* S214.

[34] J Goldstone and L Diamond, 'Demography and the Future of Democracy' (2020) 18(3) *Perspectives on Politics* 867; M Goodwin and O Heath, *Brexit Vote Explained* (London, Joseph Rowntree Foundation, 2016); M Watson, 'Brexit, the Left Behind and the Let Down: The Political Abstraction of "the Economy" and the UK's Brexit Referendum' (2018) 13(1) *British Politics* 17.

island of Ireland, especially, there was no sense that people from Ireland providing healthcare in Northern Ireland were perceived as somehow 'other', as EU citizens. 'Experts' and 'ordinary people' there shared a complex understanding of the island of Ireland as a fragile, but functioning, debordered space, and expressed fear that this precious and precarious way of life would be lost as the UK's relationships with the EU unfolded.

Second, we heard of distrust of the May and Johnson governments from both the stories told by 'ordinary people' and from our interactions with health policy 'experts'. But distrust of government was not restricted to those specific governments, or to the Conservative Party in general. On the island of Ireland, although we did hear of distrust of Westminster, we also heard of distrust of Stormont. A strong theme in our street conversations was the common trope found in western liberal democracies to the effect that politicians of all political persuasions are untrustworthy.[35] We heard stories based on a perception that 'politicians' do not understand or care about the NHS because they probably do not rely on its services, but instead use their privilege to escape to the private sector. There is scant evidence that this view is based on reality,[36] if we look at all elected MPs in Westminster and the parliamentary entities in Northern Ireland, Scotland and Wales, but it is quite pervasive in our conversations. It is also reflected in some online petitions[37] from around 2016, one of which was still attracting signatures in winter 2022. This insight makes it difficult to imagine post-Brexit (health) governance futures that are regarded as legitimate, if we continue with the current political system of accountability. It follows that a legitimate (health) governance system must find ways of supporting public decision-making that is perceived to be less self-serving of those in power.

Third, we regret that the UK – at least so far – seems to be missing out on one of the most significant potential benefits of leaving the EU, in the context of health law and policy. The EU's health law and policy is constrained by the EU's formal competences in health, and by the way that health is institutionally spread across the EU's structures (as explained in chapter four). Often, the EU takes regulatory decisions that affect human health in the context of its powers to regulate the EU's market, or develop its economy, in contrast to decision-making processes, assumptions, or values that typify a national health ministry. Put simply, the EU's exercise of its health competences can result in the wrong people being 'in the room': there is

[35] C Hay, *Why We Hate Politics* (Cambridge, Polity Press, 2007).

[36] See, eg, D Penna, 'Rishi Sunak Ducks Question on Private Health Insurance as Labour Attacks His Wealth', The Telegraph, 9 November 2022; What Do They Know, 'Should MPs Declare Private Health Insurance in Registers of Interest?' (www.whatdotheyknow.com/request/should_mps_declare_private_healt accessed 2 February 2023); J Burman, 'SCANDAL: MPs Get Free VIP Service at NHS Hospital to Protect Them from Members of Public', The Express, 1 September 2015; Independent Parliamentary Standards Authority, 'Details of any MPs with Private Medical Insurance', 18 July 2012 (www.theipsa.org.uk/freedom-of-information/2012-13/foi2012-a055).

[37] 38Degrees, 'Make British Politicians and MPs Use the NHS Instead of Private Healthcare' (https://you.38degrees.org.uk/petitions/make-british-politicians-and-mps-use-the-nhs-instead-of-private-healthcare accessed 2 February 2023); Petitions, UK Government and Parliament, 'MPs Who Use Private Healthcare Should be Barred from Voting on the NHS', 5 August 2016 (https://petition.parliament.uk/archived/petitions/118632).

insufficient engagement with stakeholders and experts in health matters when the EU makes its health law and policy. The EU has sought to redress this phenomenon, but its efforts in this regard – most recently, the supposed 'European Health Union'[38] – are incomplete at best.

Outside the EU, the UK is now empowered to make health law and policy decisions that centre human health – rather than the market or the economy. The UK may draw on strong engagement with *all* health policy stakeholders, and secure robust scrutiny of its laws and policies.[39] Given the devolved settlement for health in the UK, such decision-making may centre expertise and evidence-driven policy making at the level of England, Northern Ireland, Scotland and Wales, rather than being a 'one size fits all' Westminster-driven approach. But as we have seen across a range of health law and policy areas, the UK has yet to capitalise on these opportunities.

There is scope, outside the EU, for the UK government, and the governments or administrations of its devolved nations, to take many actions which would improve the NHS, and health, and bring it closer to the way the 'ordinary people' with whom we interacted say they would like it to be. Much of that competence lay with the UK even when it was an EU Member State: it is enhanced now that the UK is not. The UK's devolved nations, especially England which has gone further than Northern Ireland, Scotland or Wales in this respect, could reorganise their National Health Systems to be less managerial, with fewer such roles and more clinical and other frontline caring roles. These were desires for the NHS that we heard repeatedly in our conversations in the street.[40] The English NHS could reverse the approach to private ownership of infrastructure and contracting out of provision to private entities that has prevailed over the last several governments. Again, we heard examples of opposition to this model for the NHS from both our 'expert' collaborators and from our street conversations.[41]

There are aspects of domestic law and policy which, freed from EU regulatory approaches, could take the UK down a path towards better health of the UK population, and better health systems within the UK. The UK could, for example, invest in its domestically-educated health and biomedical workforce, free from the obligation to treat EU national students, and staff, in the same way. Less inward migration plus pay increments for NHS staff, particularly those at the lower end of the pay scale, might fill staffing gaps and encourage greater staff retention. Even with its lower GDP than if it had remained an EU Member State, the UK could adopt a tax and spend policy which resulted in significantly greater human (and non-human) resource for the NHS.

[38] For discussion of some of the limitations, see F Biedermann, 'European Health Union One Step Closer' (2022) 400(0360) *The Lancet* 1294.

[39] For discussion on how all stakeholders know things in different ways and may thus usefully contribute towards legal and regulatory decision-making, see ML Flear, *Governing Public Health: EU Law, Regulation and Biopolitics* (Oxford, Hart Publishing, 2015 hb, 2018 pb (revised)). For discussion of how expertise is, and might best be, incorporated in policy-making see M Wood, *Hyper-Active Governance: How Governments Manage the Politics of Expertise* (Cambridge, Cambridge University Press, 2019).

[40] For example, Sheffield 3A, 12B; Newry 19B, 29B, 33B, 38B; Derry 162A, 142B, 153B, 163B, 181B; Rochdale 54B, 61A; Rotherham 110A, 114A, 127A.

[41] For example, Sheffield 7A; Newry 39A, 56A, 27B; Rochdale 62A, 70A, 71A, 92A, 74B; Rotherham 127A, 128A, 140A; Derry 160A, 172A, 173A, 174A, 175A, 176AA, 177A, 185A, 198A, 200A, 208A, 225A, 148B, 175B, 182B.

The UK could adopt a biomedical strategy to encourage greater inward investment, and open up opportunities for scientific collaboration with the whole world which were previously skewed towards Europe. The UK could integrate licensing of novel health technologies more directly with value for money within the NHS, rather than having health technology assessment separate from marketing decisions based only on quality, efficacy and safety.

We have scant evidence of these desired approaches being adopted. As we completed our manuscript (winter 2022), the Financial Times was reporting that people in the UK have the worst access to healthcare in Europe, with one in six UK adults reporting a pressing need to access healthcare, but being unable to do so.[42] But a post-Brexit reset of the NHS across the UK remains a possible hope for the future.

Fourth, and finally, our focus on the NHS and health sharpens broader socio-legal and political understandings of the dysfunctional UK constitution.[43] We suggest this is the case in at least two respects. Most obviously, we see dysfunctionality in terms of allocation of powers within and between the UK's constituent nations, governments or administrations: 'the devolveds' (Northern Ireland, Scotland and Wales), and Westminster. On a very simple level, the Scottish electorate and the Northern Irish electorate voted to remain in the EU, but the Scottish and Northern Irish government/administration do not have power to respect that decision and keep Scotland or Northern Ireland within the EU.[44] The consequences that flow for the NHS in those parts of the UK cannot therefore be said to be legitimately 'chosen' by the electorate in Northern Ireland or Scotland. Neither are there obvious ways for the 'devolveds' to hold Westminster to account for the post-Brexit health governance settlement.

Perhaps more subtly, one of the roles for law, in a legitimate and accountable governance system, is to 'hold the ring' between competing visions of policy or indeed society. Here we find that the post-Brexit settlement for health and the NHS is far from even a basic model of legal legitimacy and accountability. Despite popular belief in law and legal process, legal strategies, especially litigation, fall woefully short of providing spaces for governance according to the law, both in terms of sharing power between the centre and the 'devolveds' in the UK, and in terms of fostering confidence

[42] J Burn-Murdoch, 'Britons Now Have the Worst Access to Healthcare in Europe, and it Shows', Financial Times, 4 November 2022.

[43] There is a significant literature on the effects of Brexit on the UK constitution. See, eg, V Bogdanor, *Beyond Brexit: Towards a British Constitution* (London, Bloomsbury, 2019); P Craig, 'Brexit and the UK Constitution' in J Jowell and C O'Cinneide (eds), *The Changing Constitution* (Oxford, Oxford University Press, 2019); M Dougan, *The UK's Withdrawal from the EU: A Legal Analysis* (Oxford, Oxford University Press, 2021); M Elliott et al (eds), *The UK Constitution After Miller: Brexit and Beyond* (London, Hart Publishing, 2018); F Fabbrini (ed), *The Law and Politics of Brexit* (Oxford, Oxford University Press, 2017); F Fabbrini (ed), *The Law and Politics of Brexit II: The Withdrawal Agreement* (Oxford, Oxford University Press, 2020); F Fabbrini (ed), *The Law and Politics of Brexit III: The Framework of new UK-EU Relations* (Oxford, Oxford University Press, 2021); F Fabbrini (ed), *The Law and Politics of Brexit IV: The Protocol on Ireland/Northern Ireland* (Oxford, Oxford University Press, 2022); J Murkens, 'Democracy as the Legitimating Condition in the UK Constitution' (2018) 38(1) *Legal Studies* 42; S White, 'Brexit and the Future of the UK Constitution' (2022) 43(3) *International Political Science Review* 359.

[44] *R (Miller) v Secretary of State for Exiting the EU; In re McCord; In re Agnew* [2017] UKSC 5.

that UK governments (of any political persuasion) are taking decisions within properly informed, transparent, and defined processes. Legal spaces and processes could be one way of having a difficult conversation about the laws and policies that the UK should adopt: in the UK's constitution, they are not available for those discussions as much as they could be. The UK's 'political constitution' is thus failing to provide legitimacy to post-Brexit health governance.

One of the biggest surprises in our data is the trust both 'ordinary people' and the health policy 'experts' with whom we worked place in law and legal process. The health policy community was keen to understand the unfolding legal position, even while they engaged on a political or policy level with Brexit. The people we talked with in the street did not always suggest legal mechanisms of accountability – often they referred to political processes, especially elections, and sometimes they referred to violence. But many expressed a belief, or at least a hope and expectation, that law would hold the government to account: either through criminal or civil process, or by requiring transparency ('Johnson should be made to tell the truth and show his papers').[45] As socio-legal and cross-disciplinary scholars, this faith in law represents a profound challenge to our habits of scepticism and our deep awareness of the limitations of law. Hervey, in particular, has been encouraged to revisit her position, and to reconnect with strategies for legitimation of governance that include legal processes, especially litigation.

VI. WHAT OUR METHODOLOGY AND OUR NARRATIVE METHODS BRING TO SOCIO-LEGAL STUDIES

Overall, we make two broad contributions to socio-legal studies. The first concerns the spatial and temporal; the second concerns narration. Both rely on how we understand researcher positionality in socio-legal studies.

In our attempts to foreground the broader methodological implications of the metaphorical and narrative detail of our data, we are responding to calls such as those by Sally Wheeler, who urges socio-legal scholars to make more of the empirical findings in their studies.[46] Our response comes not only through our substantive contribution in illuminating the gap in understandings of the consequences of Brexit for health and the NHS. To use our own metaphor, in attempting to achieve this aim, we had to strike out on our own path. In order to navigate our terrain, and reach our destination, we had to be creative about how we went about our expedition. In other words, we needed to develop the methodology (explained in chapters two and three): a methodology which we believe is innovative and novel in socio-legal studies, as well as in political science, and probably even wider still.

First, in terms of our methodological contributions, our approach and analysis extends and may even usefully disrupt socio-legal discussions in law and geography.

[45] Newry 28A.

[46] S Wheeler, 'Socio-Legal Studies in 2020' (2020) 47(S2) *Journal of Law and Society* S209, S215.

It does so by helping to reduce the dislocation between the two disciplines that the 'and' between them implies, and encouraging interdisciplinarity through the study of legal technicality. Our research provides clearer insight than much general Brexit literature, or public policy narratives, into how legal technicality applies and operates at and across multiple scales and levels of governance, going from the UK level to jurisdictions (England and Wales (one jurisdiction) and Northern Ireland) which overlap with the regions that form our focus (north of England and Northern Ireland – respectively, less contiguous and precisely contiguous with their (legal) constructs as jurisdictions). In this regard, it is important to re-emphasise our own positionality as researchers – especially the various kinds of distance between us and our interlocutors in our research. Conscious of the latter, one aspect of our methodology involves foregrounding the spatial elements of epistemology: put simply, the idea that where you are feeds into what you know. This is why we needed to go further than the 'ordinary' modes of socio-legal research that interface with political science and policy studies. Methods like surveys and focus groups have their place, but we bring something different by going to our interlocutors (both 'experts' and 'ordinary people') *where they were*, and drawing them into conversations on their own terms.

Our methodology also underscores the importance of understanding our research as occurring at a particular time (what Kenneth Armstrong has called 'Brexit time').[47] Time matters here, in constituting space and place, even as legal technicality may leverage the timelessness of law, and thus have the sheen of appearing to be naturally occurring, rather than highly contingent on political, institutional and wider social context, including time(s).[48] Our research provides a specific example of this process. Structurally speaking, many of the chapters in the latter half of the book (chapters five to 10) distinguish between different phases of 'Brexit time', technically defined (before the Withdrawal Agreement; after transition, etc). But those legal formalities are disrupted by the knowledges from both our 'elite' interlocutors and our conversations with 'ordinary people', whose realities did not (and, in some cases, especially in Northern Ireland, do not yet) map to legal technicalities. In doing so we echo the legal sociologist Roger Cotterrell, who makes an explicit link between the meanings of law and legal technicality for the people who engage with them, and time and place. Cotterell points out that most of the key theoretical questions about law are actually very timely and context related, and they and the meanings of law, are not independent of place and time.[49]

So – applying these insights to our research – we have shown that questions of legitimacy of post-Brexit health governance (and who is accountable for it) are not understood as having 'natural', technical or a-historical answers.[50] Historicisation

[47] KA Armstrong, *Brexit Time. Leaving the EU – Why, How and When?* (Cambridge, Cambridge University Press, 2017).

[48] P Ewick and SS Silbey, *The Common Place of Law* (Chicago, University of Chicago Press, 1998), 94–96.

[49] R Cotterrell, 'Socio-Legal Studies, Law Schools, and Legal and Social Theory', *Legal Studies Research Paper* No 126/2012 (London, Queen Mary University of London School of Law, 2012), 2.

[50] A 'law in the books' constitutional or administrative law response to that question would be different.

brings a necessary, but not sufficient, analytical frame, in that attention to the past is important, but attention to the present and future matters too. Our data does pay attention to the past, but it is also attentive to other temporalities: to present and immediate fears, hopes and fantasies; and to hoped for/dreamed of or feared and dreaded futures. In this regard, by showing multiple perspectives, our research in the legal technicalities of 'Brexit time' builds on socio-legal and other scholarship that centres time.

But we also centre space and place. The locations and venues within them where we engaged with our interlocutors and gathered data through conversations and other interactions with them are an important facet of our research design, and our overall claims. In fact, we go further by showing how the time and space/place are not separate or separable concepts, in terms of our methodology, but rather are co-constitutive as space/place/time (and thus cannot be fully understood separately). In this way, we are inspired by literatures outwith socio-legal studies, including anthropology (from which we also draw our ethnography-inspired methods).[51] We also add to and extend recent contributions within socio-legal studies that seek to de-reify space and place as stable concepts, and to correct the privileging of the spatial over the temporal,[52] which is still seen in attempts to transcend the 'and' in law and geography scholarship.[53]

[51] We are particularly influenced here by the various time-related insights from human geography, especially: D Harvey, *Justice, Nature and the Geography of Difference* (Oxford, Blackwell Publishers, 1996); SM Low and D Lawrence-Zúñiga, *The Anthropology of Space and Place* (Oxford, Blackwell Publishing, 2003); D Massey, *For Space* (London, Sage, 2005); N Thrift, 'Space: The Fundamental Stuff of Human Geography' in N Clifford et al (eds), *Key Concepts in Geography*, 2nd edn (London, Sage, 2009). We are also influenced by the rich vein of discussion in anthropology, especially: DM Engel, 'Litigation across Space and Time: Courts, Conflict, and Social Change' (1990) 24(2) *Law & Society Review* 333; J Fabian, *Time and the Other: How Anthropology Makes Its Object* (Chichester, Columbia University Press, 2004); CJ Greenhouse, *A Moment's Notice: Time Politics across Cultures* (Ithaca NY, Cornell University Press, 1996); CJ Greenhouse, 'Time's Up, Timed Out: Reflections on Social Time and Legal Pluralism' (2014) 46(1) *Journal of Legal Pluralism and Unofficial Law* 141; JB Richland, 'Sovereign Time, Storied Moments: The Temporalities of Law, Tradition, and Ethnography in Hopi Tribal Court' (2008) 31 *PoLAR: Political and Legal Anthropology Review* 8; JB Richland, 'Perpetuities Against Rules: Law, Ethnography and the Irresolution of Inheritance' (2013) 8(3) *Law Culture and the Humanities* 433.

[52] The importance of extending discussion on space, place and time as a general concern of socio-legal studies is underlined in D Cowan et al (eds), 'Introduction: Celebrating Phil Thomas at 80' (2020) 47(S2) *Journal of Law and Society* S187. For specific contributions, see I Braverman et al (eds), *The Expanding Spaces of Law: A Timely Legal Geography* (Stanford, Stanford University Press, 2014) and several chapters therein, especially those by von Benda-Beckmann and von Benda-Beckmann and Valverde; T Chowdhury, *Time, Temporality and Legal Judgment* (Abingdon, Routledge, 2020); D Cowan and D Wincott (eds), *Exploring the 'Legal' in Socio-Legal Studies* (London, Palgrave Macmillan, 2016); ML Flear and et al (eds), *Socio-Legal Studies of Epistemic Injustice and Spaces and Places* (London, Palgrave Macmillan, 2024 forthcoming); W Grabham and S Beynon-Jones, *Law and Time* (Abingdon, Routledge, 2019); J Harrington, 'Time and Space in Medical Law: Building on Valverde's *Chronotopes of Law*' (2015) 23(3) *Feminist Legal Studies* 361; A Layard, 'Reading Law Spatially' in N Creutzfeldt et al (eds), *Routledge Handbook of Socio-Legal Theory and Methods* (Abingdon, Routledge, 2020); R Mawani, 'Law as Temporality: Colonial Politics and Indian Settlers' (2014) 4 *University of California Irvine Law Review* 65; K McNeilly and B Warwick, *The Times and Temporalities of International Human Rights Law* (Abingdon, Routledge, 2022); M Valverde, *Chronotopes of Law: Jurisdiction, Scale and Governance* (Abingdon, Routledge, 2015), ch 2 on 'Theorising the Space and Time of Law'.

[53] Including in attempts to innovate and overcome the limitations of the 'and' (noted above), including through the formulation of novel nouns, such as 'nomicity' and 'nomosphere' that highlight space/place as at once discursive and material, and performative: D Delaney, *The Spatial, the Legal and the Pragmatics of World-Making: Nomospheric Investigations* (Abingdon, Routledge, 2010).

As such, despite the way in which our research design limits the generalisability of claims we might make, we are able to generate and bring to light detailed specific knowledges and understandings, always grounded in particular spatial and temporal situations and relations. Put differently, forms of knowledge, and the meanings they carry and with which they interact, have spatial, place-based and temporal dimensions. By highlighting these dimensions throughout this book about our project on legitimate health governance after Brexit, and who is accountable for it, we develop broader discussions both within and outwith socio-legal studies.[54]

Second, we make a methodological contribution to socio-legal studies – and broader studies – of narration.[55] Our use of *stories* to frame the book, right at its outset in the introductory chapter, as threaded across the whole book, and in our conclusions, is deliberate. Stories do not describe the truth, in the way that a natural science experiment or equation might be understood to describe the truth about the natural world. But stories *express* truths – they help us to make sense of complex and hard-to-describe phenomena and emotions. There are indeed wolves in the woods, Red Riding Hood, and beware of those who pose as grandmothers! Beauty is only skin deep, and once Beauty understands that, she can see someone's true identity, including that a Beast could be a bibliophile. The omnipotent ruler of the universe born as a baby in a barn, who has to flee for his safety to a foreign land, teaches us about how early Christians understood (and contemporary Christians still understand) the nature of divinity, and of humanity.

Realising that stories express truths underscores the importance of positionality and reflexivity to our research methods and overarching methodology, in that it shows how seriously we take it that knowledges, and related meanings and understandings, are always situational and relational, instead of reflecting some objective reality outside and independent of the persons producing them. We do, as explained (in chapter two), adopt a more 'realist' understanding of 'the law' as being determined by interpretative practices in a legal system, and therefore not open to more than a limited number of legally acceptable interpretations. But, overall, we adhere to a constructivist methodology to the effect that the *broader significance, implications* and *meaning* of post-Brexit health governance are only understandable from the point of view of specific situational and temporal relations. That is why we have foregrounded those relations (with 'experts' and 'ordinary people') in the stories on which we rely throughout the book.

In doing so, we also seek to extend our pursuit of epistemic justice, and thereby contribute to growing discussion in socio-legal scholarship,[56] which recognises, following Miranda Fricker, the possibility of multiple interpretations, each with equal

[54] For related discussion within legal and socio-legal scholarship, see Cowan and Wincott (eds), *Exploring the 'Legal' in Socio-Legal Studies*, above n 52; Flear et al (eds), *Socio-Legal Studies of Epistemic Injustice and Spaces and Places*, above n 52 (with further discussion of the relations between space, place and time).

[55] On the relations between the two, see, eg A Nurse, 'Law, the Environment and Narrative Storytelling' in N Creutzfeldt et al (eds), *Routledge Handbook of Socio-Legal Theory and Methods* (Abingdon, Routledge, 2020); and L Wolff, 'Let's Talk about Lex: Narrative Analysis as Both Research Method and Teaching Technique in Law' (2014) 35(1) *Adelaide Law Review* 3.

[56] Flear et al, *Socio-Legal Studies of Epistemic Injustice and Spaces and Places*, above n 52.

valid title to truth, since there is no way to determine whose interpretation is 'Truth'.[57] This attention to epistemic justice aligns the book, and the centrality of reflexivity and positionality (space, place and time) to its methods and methodology, with wider work in socio-legal studies that adopts a similar – and explicit – ethical stance in seeking to reveal truths rather than 'Truth'. As Mariana Valverde puts it, assuming this kind of position, which is not the same as a theory, would help to achieve reflexivity as a requirement for ethical conduct and politics.[58]

To improve understanding of how to achieve a legitimate settlement for health governance in the post-Brexit world, who should be held to account for it, and how, through our methodology and its specific research methods, we have sought to bring the diverse perspectives of our interlocutors into dialogue. In doing so, we also seek to bring their particular underpinning epistemologies and ontologies to light, but in such a way as to ensure each remains valued. In this sense, our book makes its central contribution by, as Patricia Ewick and Susan Silbey put it, 'collecting stories' and 'having conversations'.[59] Moreover, our approach shares some similarities with other genres of stories, especially the modern novel, including Brexit literature such as Ali Smith's *Seasonal Quartet*.[60] As discussed by Mikhail Bakhtin, and summarised by Mariana Valverde, such texts use a variety of perspectives and narratives or 'heteroglossia', which serves to underscore that multiplicity of (equally valuable) views.[61]

One way stories express truths is through the metaphors that they use. Wherever we find metaphorical language, or narratives, those are doing a job of communicating meaning, truths, about how the speaker or writer sees the phenomenon described or discussed. Listening to and retelling these stories, as we have done in this book, allows us to understand something(s) about how those people whose conversations with us we record and reflect on see the post-Brexit world, by interrogating the metaphors that they use and the stories that they tell.

Metaphor and narratives (which operate as extended metaphors), and related terms,[62] are central to our approach, as they are replete with information about how people make sense of the world and themselves. A metaphor involves a resonance of meaning from its literal context to another context: one thing is regarded as representative or symbolic of something else. Metaphors are not just a matter of pure words: cognitive linguists[63] have shown that human thought processes are largely metaphorical, because thinking about abstract concepts (such as politics or society, or the NHS) is easier if one thinks in terms of more concrete concepts (such as buildings

[57] M Fricker, *Epistemic Injustice: Power and the Ethics of Knowing* (Oxford, Oxford University Press, 2007), 170.

[58] M Valverde, *Law's Dream of a Common Knowledge* (Princeton NJ, Princeton University Press, 2003), 8. Emphasis added.

[59] Ewick and Silbey, *The Common Place of Law*, above n 48, xii.

[60] A Smith, *Autumn* (London, Penguin Books, 2017); *Winter* (London, Penguin Books, 2018); *Spring* (London, Penguin Books, 2020); *Summer* (London, Penguin Books, 2021).

[61] Valverde, *Chronotopes of Law*, above n 52, 7.

[62] For law-led discussion, see ML Flear and R Ashcroft (eds), 'Law, Biomedical Technoscience and Imaginaries' (2021) 8(2) (Special Issue) *Journal of Law and the Biosciences*.

[63] G Lakoff and M Johnson, *Metaphors We Live By* (London, University of Chicago Press, 1980); Z Kövecses, *Metaphor: A Practical Introduction* (Oxford, Oxford University Press, 2010).

or the human body).[64] Metaphors structure our thought, in ways that escape our conscious reasoning, and that conceptual system plays a central role in defining everyday realities.

Metaphors and stories both reveal and obfuscate, enable and constrain. The way metaphors highlight some aspects of the phenomenon being talked about also means that they hide other aspects.[65] Metaphors are replete with information about how people make sense of the world, themselves and their relations with others. Metaphors operate as framing devices, expressing what is seen as possible and impossible, likely and out of the ordinary. By extension, they are mirrors onto epistemology and ontology.[66] Thinking about narratives, argues Kalypso Nicolaidis, also helps researchers to adopt a critical distance from the stories that we tell ourselves 'by placing question marks around our collective self-righteousness'.[67]

We suggest that the metaphors and narratives that are used in (rarely) and of (much more often) *legal* language are revealing too.[68] Metaphors in legal language become accepted without question, and preclude alternative ways of understanding legal relationships, stultifying and capturing the way a field of law is understood.[69] In this regard, our approach aligns with a deep vein of socio-legal scholarship, which has long attended to interactions between the legal and the political, social or cultural. A more recent turn in such scholarship considers the 'technicalities' of law, and was flagged (in chapter two) as adopting a neutral position in social science metatheory relating to epistemology and ontology. This socio-legal literature underlines how what might be seen as 'extra-legal' realities (political, social, cultural understandings) are instead encapsulated in the technicalities of legal text.[70] This is a point broadly shared by Valverde.[71] Socio-legal questions – like our research

[64] Lakoff and Johnson ibid; Master Metaphor List (http://araw.mede.uic.edu/~alansz/metaphor/METAPHORLIST.pdf accessed 8 February 2023). See also A Deignan, *Collins Co-Build English Guides 7: Metaphor* (London, Collins, 1995).

[65] Lakoff and Johnson, *Metaphors We Live By*, above n 63, 10.

[66] E Goffman, *Frame Analysis: An Essay on the Organization of Experience* (Cambridge MA, Harvard University Press, 1974); M LeBaron, 'Is the Blush off the Rose? Legal Education Metaphors in a Changing World' (2016) 43(1) *Journal of Law and Society* 144; M Rein and D Schön, 'Problem Setting in Policy Research' in C Weiss (ed), *Using Social Research in Public Policy Making* (Lexington MA, Lexington Books, 1977); G Sammut et al (eds), *The Cambridge Handbook of Social Representations* (Cambridge, Cambridge University Press, 2015).

[67] K Nicolaidis, *Exodus, Reckoning, Sacrifice: Three Meanings of Brexit* (London, The Unbound Press, 2019), 182. For an example of 'collective self-righteousness' about the Leave vote, see McGarvey's account of the anguished Guardian readers' responses to the 'crisis' of the referendum vote, D McGarvey, *Poverty Safari* (Edinburgh, Luath Press, 2017).

[68] J Boyd White, *The Legal Imagination* (Chicago, Chicago University Press, 1973); P Brooks, 'Narrative in and of the Law' in J Phelan and PJ Rabinowitz (eds), *A Companion to Narrative Theory* (Hoboken NJ, Wiley-Blackwell, 2005); D Gurnham, 'Law's Metaphors: Introduction' (2016) 43(1) *Journal of Law and Society* 1; M Hanne and R Weisburg (eds), *Narrative and Metaphor in the Law* (Cambridge, Cambridge University Press, 2018); Nurse, 'Law, the Environment and Narrative Storytelling', above n 55; AA Tait and L Norris, 'Narrative and the Origins of Law' (2011) 5(1) *Law and Humanities* 11.

[69] D Cowan et al, *Reconciling Owning and Renting in Shared Ownership Housing: Moving Forward* (Bristol, University of Bristol/York, University of York, 2015); Cowan and Wincott (eds), *Exploring the 'Legal' in Socio-Legal Studies*, above n 52; A Philippopoulos-Mihalopoulos, 'The Flesh of the Law: Material Legal Metaphors' (2016) 43(1) *Journal of Law and Society* 45.

[70] A Riles, 'A New Agenda for the Cultural Study of Law: Taking on the Technicalities' (2005) 63(4) *Buffalo Law Review* 973.

[71] M Valverde, 'Jurisdiction and Scale: Legal "Technicalities" as Resources for Theory' (2009) 18(2) *Social & Legal Studies* 139.

agenda in this book – can thus be understood through material, institutional and ideational aspects of reality (whatever one's understanding of 'reality' – broadly social constructivist or realist). A focus on how the law constrains or enables agency; constructs or works through institutions; *and* 'frames', embodies and perpetuates or excludes ideas involves close attention to legal text and the language it uses.[72] Our project is inspired by and contributes to this literature. Indeed, much existing work on law and metaphor concerns litigation and judicial reasoning. It often discusses criminal processes.[73] Deploying this approach in the context of civil justice/administrative law and of legislation/treaty law, as in this book, is relatively unusual, though not entirely untrodden territory.[74] Some work on the metaphorical nature of law concerns health law broadly speaking.[75] There is, however, very little work in this vein on EU law,[76] and relatedly the law of Brexit.[77]

We believe this book makes a contribution to these literatures. It does so by considering the language used in and about the law, by 'elites', and the law and policy documentation that they produce, and what that reveals. We examine both the effects of the post-Brexit 'law in practice' (in classical socio-legal mode), and the perceptions and understandings of those 'elites' and 'elite' discourses about the effects of post-Brexit health governance and its (lack of) legitimacy. We compare that with the language used by 'ordinary people' in our street conversations, and film, and the stories that explain understandings of legitimate post-Brexit health governance from those perspectives. Bringing those sets of narratives together across this book allows us to present a rich and nuanced analysis of the gap[78] between legal, 'elite' and public understandings of the post-Brexit world, who is responsible for it, and how they should be held to account. Any attempt to close such a gap in understandings goes well beyond what we can accomplish in a single book. Instead, the more modest aspiration of this book is to reveal and analyse the nature of the gap, showing that assumptions about its nature may often be misplaced. We offer this analysis as a first step in beginning to close the gap, and to develop an idea of what legitimate post-Brexit health governance might look like to its various interlocutors, and what might characterise the process(es) towards such a post-Brexit future.

This analysis is made possible by our methodological innovations. In particular, positionality and reflexivity, both integral to ethical comportment, underscore the

[72] Cowan and Wincott (eds), *Exploring the 'Legal' in Socio-Legal Studies*, above n 52, 3–4.

[73] See examples in Brooks, 'Narrative in and of the Law', above n 68; Gurnham, 'Law's Metaphors: Introduction', above n 68; Hanne and Weisburg (eds), *Narrative and Metaphor in the Law*, above n 68; N Lacey, 'The Metaphor of Proportionality' (2016) 43(1) *Journal of Law and Society* 27.

[74] See some contributors to Cowan and Wincott (eds), *Exploring the 'Legal' in Socio-Legal Studies*, above n 52.

[75] Harrington, 'Time and Space in Medical Law', above n 52, drawing on Valverde, *Chronotopes of Law*, above n 52.

[76] PJ Cardwell and T Hervey, 'Bringing the Technical into the Socio-Legal: The Metaphors of Law and Legal Scholarship of a Twenty-First Century European Union' in D Cowan and D Wincott (eds), *Exploring the 'Legal' in Socio-Legal Studies* (London, Palgrave Macmillan, 2016); T Hervey, 'Realism, Empiricism and Doctrine in EU Legal Studies: Views from a Common Law Perspective' in R Nielsen and U Neergaard (eds), *European Legal Method: Towards a New European Legal Realism* (Copenhagen, DJØF, 2013).

[77] S Douglas-Scott, 'Brexit, Boundaries and the Power of Images' (2019) 13(1) *Pólemos* 63.

[78] For discussion of 'socio-legal gap studies', see J Gould and S Barclay, 'Mind the Gap: The Place of Gap Studies in Sociolegal Scholarship' (2012) 8(1) *Annual Review of Law and Social Science* 323.

vital importance of humility, especially when it is understood as meaning that there are limits to what we can think, do, and achieve alone or from any single perspective. We believe – or, consistent with humility, at least hope – that our book demonstrates the importance of humility as a value in itself within the research process (and as an aspect of 'ethical comportment', see chapter three), and through it the production of (ethically grounded) findings (new or improved knowledge and understanding such as that set out across the preceding chapters and summarised in the current chapter). The dissemination of humility throughout the academy (the research enterprise and teaching), and across society, holds out the promise of common benefit.

This is especially clear in respect of highly fraught issues such as health (and indeed other areas of) governance after Brexit. Humility relates closely to empathy – and stories help with both.[79] Indeed, empathy may even be prior to humility, for if we seek to understand others, their positions on key questions and what goes into them, we might then adopt humility as a posture for approaching others and our discussions and negotiations with them. For instance, humility is vital in respect of (still) ongoing negotiation within the UK, between the various levels of governance, and within England, Northern Ireland, Scotland and Wales, about what a legitimate post-Brexit settlement might look like, who should be held to account for its delivery, and how that should happen. This is something that will take time: humility should prompt us to *take the time* necessary to have the necessary (and time-consuming) discussions between different and sometimes (apparently) conflicting perspectives, while also recognising exigencies (health and even life) mean time cannot be an indulgence. But this is another aspect of humility: recognising when to give way in order to achieve the things we all want to see realised. Humility is ultimately, then, also central to achieving legitimate (health and wider forms of) governance after Brexit, as the process continues to unfold across its multiple and various spaces and places, now and into the future.

VII. WHAT WE HAVE LEARNED AND CONTINUE TO LEARN

Finally, we outline some thoughts on what we have learned and continue to learn. It is a truism that hindsight is a wonderful thing. With the benefit of hindsight and reflection, including on the significant published work on Brexit, Hervey has come to understand some of the reasons why the efforts she, and many others, made to inform the referendum were 'not enough' (see chapter one) to result in a Remain vote. Membership of the EU is not simply a rational economic choice, or a matter where accurate information could ever have won 'hearts and minds'.[80] For the UK voting public, in June 2016, it was also a matter of feelings, identities and, frankly, fantasies.

[79] Nurse, 'Law, the Environment and Narrative Storytelling', above n 55, 304, citing C Love, 'The Value of Narrative in Legal Scholarship and Teaching' (1998) 2(1) *Journal of Gender, Race, and Justice* 92.

[80] Although note that education was one indicator of a likely Leave vote, see, eg, SO Becker et al, 'Who Voted for Brexit? A Comprehensive District-Level Analysis' (2017) 32(92) *Economic Policy* 601; E Alabrese et al, 'Who Voted for Brexit? Individual and Regional Data Combined' (2019) 56 *European Journal of Political Economy* 132.

No amount of expertise would be effective in changing that kind of emotion-based decision-making.

For Hervey, as perhaps for others in universities, the ways in which 'experts' were depicted by the media as untrustworthy became impossible to ignore. Hervey had been struck by how the referendum brought out academic generosity: in Twitter conversations, emails, Facebook, videos, infographics and in face-to-face encounters – many people, across disciplines and career stages, gave up their time and energy to inform and assist. Everyone was still doing their 'day jobs' – teaching students, marking their work, writing papers, running laboratories, engaging with collaborators, going to meetings. But, it seemed to Hervey at least, no one was 'too busy' or 'too important' to opt out. And in all of this, the disciplinary distinctions that sometimes beset universities became much less relevant than before.

And yet, in the public discourses, research scientists, economists, academics from all disciplines were branded as equivalent to power-driven politicians. As Hervey's former colleague Rebecca Sanders observed via Facebook, it is hugely insulting to assert that the general public are not interested in the views of 'experts', or too stupid to understand those views. So one thing the EU referendum has taught Hervey is that the claim of authority that comes from the kind of knowledge built on deep reflection and learning, (that perhaps used to be) valued in the UK, is much more fragile than she hoped.

Antova's experience of not being able to vote in the referendum, coupled with growing anxiety about her own life after the referendum, led her initially to disconnect from the topic altogether. Her academic work on disability and austerity did not lend itself to research on Brexit easily at the first instance, until Antova had time to reflect that there are multiple connections, narratives and realities that surrounded the Brexit referendum that were familiar to her, for example responsibilisation (of health).[81] The referendum result was expected, yet had a profound impact on much of Antova's life, including personal relationships with colleagues. What followed the referendum was at times emotional indifference as a protective reaction, swiftly replaced by a frantic (ultimately successful) attempt to secure a settled status prior to one of the Brexit deadlines.

Her work on the *Health Governance after Brexit* project for Antova has meant an invaluable opportunity to strengthen pre-existing research interests and to expand knowledge and experience in a new field (Brexit, EU health law). Antova shares Hervey's disdain for the practice of crude simplification of carefully thought out and substantiated positions on EU membership and what it means for the everyday reality of people. In Antova's case, this refers to a 'Lexit' position: a view from the political left that EU membership is not a good idea. Antova also notes with regret that the 'Left' could have done more to articulate better a position Antova believes in, but continues to struggle with aspects of, much like many of the people we spoke with throughout the project.

[81] See, for example I Antova, 'Taking Back Control (of Our Health): The Responsibilised Citizen and Post-Brexit Health Governance', conference paper at the *Critical Legal Conference* 2019, University of Perugia, on file with authors.

Wood's work, which has in large part been about the study of 'expert' agencies and commissions, led him to a more nuanced view than Hervey's about expertise. Wood's book *Hyper-Active Governance*[82] was written in large part in the summer after the referendum, and is about how 'expert' authority is politically mediated. Wood was already aware that expertise was fragile and had to be claimed and approved rather than holding de facto legitimacy, and the book began with the famous Michael Gove quote about people having 'had enough of experts'. But the joke was on Gove when he subsequently became Secretary of State for the Environment and Rural Affairs, and claimed to need scientific expertise to do his job properly. It has also been shown in the COVID-19 pandemic that it is still essential for politicians to rely on scientific expertise when faced with a seemingly intractable crisis.

Wood reflects:

> I found the referendum result to be traumatic, yes, and it led to something of a moral panic within the academy about the expertise and authority of social scientists in particular, and 'experts'/scientists more generally. It led us to feel insecure, and you can still see those ripple effects even now.
>
> Personally, Brexit led me to question my own research methods. How can we really know what people think about the EU, about 'the law' as an apparently solid and stable embodiment of political will, about health and how people feel about their access to good healthcare, and how they interrelate? This led me to start thinking that ethnographically inspired methods might help us shore up (or challenge/problematise) some of the grand claims made in quantitative studies.

Flear's work, which focuses on the integration of 'expert' and 'non-expert' knowledge in legal and regulatory decision-making, especially in *Governing Public Health*,[83] and increasingly epistemic injustice (ie injustice to people in their status as knowers), such as that which may be experienced by the people in the left behind communities engaged in this book,[84] led him to appreciate Hervey and Wood's individual views on expertise. Similar to Hervey, Flear was – and remains – troubled by how quickly 'experts' and their expertise can be undermined. But, similar to Wood, he is now more acutely aware of how 'experts' and their knowledges derive authority through various processes, and how they gain traction in decision-making in part through claims to authority that are, perhaps unfortunately, more politically mediated than he had once appreciated.

Flear reflects:

> As I have said, the referendum result was not surprising to me. My abiding feeling after the referendum was, and continues to be, about how disconnected 'expert' and non-expert views and knowledges can be, and may continue to be, around the subject of the UK's relationships with the EU. I see how many fellow academics have tried to spread 'the facts'. This is praiseworthy and essential for democratic life. But, less acknowledged, but quite often voiced quietly, is how there may sometimes be a tendency among academics to advance a particular position through 'the facts', as though by shedding light on them there

[82] Wood, *Hyper-Active Governance*, above n 39.
[83] Flear, *Governing Public Health*, above n 39.
[84] Flear et al, *Socio-Legal Studies of Epistemic Injustice and Spaces and Places*, above n 52.

logically, or even naturally, follows a given position on a particular topic like Brexit. And that's usually a stance in opposition to it. The facts are viewed through a particular set or prism of values. Yet, those values are not necessarily shared by everyone; even if they are, they may not fit together in the same way for everyone, particularly those outside a given social and professional milieu or epistemic community.

Sometimes prejudices reveal themselves in interesting ways, and often without question, including among academics. Here I do not take myself out of the frame – but my point is not about my own views, but rather the views of academics as a whole, and the importance of honesty and integrity in our research practices. So, I shall continue with my reflection. I remember attending an academic conference not long after the referendum result. A senior (white, probably straight (he's married to a woman)) male colleague was chairing and commented approvingly on his daughter's words: the result was down to those up north (in England). Many in the audience seemed to agree.

I felt quite detached from what seemed to me to be a smug and self-satisfied chorus of approval: sitting there among people, many of whom grew up in or were employed or based in the south of England, unlike me, I felt very uncomfortable and separate. This was not least because it felt as though people I know and love, but with whom the referendum had made things very difficult (mostly my blood family), were being blamed and scapegoated. I could not quite express this at the time without facts about voting patterns and tendencies. And even if I could have, that was neither the time nor place to express my view, not least because I would be seen as embarrassing one of the leading scholars. Timing, it seems, is everything.

But I had a hunch – a real gut feeling – that the complexity of the views of those who voted for Brexit was being sidelined and ignored. Negative stereotypes about people 'up north' – poorer, less well educated, certainly less cosmopolitan and insular – may have been at play. The focus on English politics was also myopic: Brexit (an inaccurate but catchy acronym) was about the people(s) of the whole United Kingdom. Not just those in England – or the English. We know now that this view about who is 'to blame' is not (entirely) true: rich white people in the south of England had far more weight in the referendum result.[85] There is also much research on why people voted the way they did – and the views are understandable, at least when we try to stand in the positions of those people and reflect on what their lives might be like. People who feel – are – disenfranchised, and who feel – are – let down by the government and see little to lose, may indeed be less likely to vote for more of the same, and may even want others to feel some of their pain. When nothing else seems to work, a vote for Brexit may seem like a very rare and fleeting way to get heard by those who seldom think about them.

Back to timing. It might now be the right time to raise questions brought about by that nagging feeling. It seems obvious to me that public discourse around the effects of Brexit remains stubbornly limited and cries out for more focus on facts, on what is actually happening. These limitations are not all down to academics of course – there's a sense of a need to move on from Brexit, at least among a sizable portion of the electorate, perhaps more in some parts of the UK than others. Still, one of my big 'take aways' from Brexit is actually quite a difficult one to hold within the academy, not least because others may point at me.

[85] 'EU Referendum: The Result in Maps and Charts', BBC, 8 June 2021. See, eg, K Swales, *Understanding the Vote to Leave* (London, National Centre for Social Research, 2016).

> But I am not trying to point at others and avoid questions about my own practice. Instead, I see a need for honesty and reflexivity among academics, me included, about whatever views we hold, how they shape our research questions and findings, and attempts to get those findings out there and understood.

We hope that, at least in a modest way, this book shows how we might have these kinds of conversations, from a position of honest reflection, imbued with a sense of humility that flows from an attention to positionalities (including those pertaining to space, place and time) and epistemic justice. We hope that we have shown that – far from being peripheral to larger and more esoteric Brexit debates about trade, tariffs, regulatory divergence, sovereignty or 'freedom' – health and the NHS have been, and continue to be, a central part of the Brexit process. Perhaps it is time to stop sacrificing health and the NHS to those larger political aims.

A process of discovering and moving towards a legitimate post-Brexit governance settlement (for health) will certainly involve (legal – as well as economic and political) technical knowledge and expertise. But it will also involve those in relatively empowered positions learning from those who do not share that power and from whom they may learn, and probably adopting a posture of humility in order to do so, just as we aim or at least hope to do, particularly after all we have learned through this project. Indeed, as we have shown, one mode of learning is to (really) hear (and reflect on) the stories that (other) people tell. A key part of that process entails trying to understand where people are coming from – in all its complexity. That is our main offering from this book. It applies both to the question of post-Brexit futures for health and the NHS, and to the question of the contribution of socio-legal studies, in its interdisciplinary contexts, to more fully understanding and (re)making relations between the different parts of the UK, and between the UK and Ireland, in these islands, within our shared continent, and indeed, shared world.

Appendix

Table 1 Project Partners

Organisation	People	Date of first meeting in context of this project	Place of first meeting in context of this project
British Medical Association, London	Paul Laffin	22 May 2019	London
Cancer Research UK, London	Mark Heffernan, Zoe Martin, Duncan Sim, Angeliki Yiangou, Oliver Buckley-Mellor, Prof Pamela Kearns	26 March 2019	London
Cooperation and Working Together, Belfast and Dublin	Bernie McCrory	16 April 2019	Belfast
CORU, Health and Social Care Professional Regulators, Dublin	Margaret Hynds O'Flannagan	29 May 2019	Dublin
Faculty of Public Health, London	Mark Weiss	12 February 2019	London
Health and Social Care Committee of the House of Commons, London	Dr Sarah Wollaston, MP Dr Philippa Whitford, MP	11 March 2019 26 February 2019	London London
Health Information and Quality Authority, Dublin	Phelim Quinn	3 May 2019	Belfast/Dublin
Kidney Care UK, Alton, Hants, England	Fiona Loud	28 February 2019	Alton, Hants
NHS Confederation/ Brexit Health Alliance, Brussels, Leeds and London	Kate Ling	15 March 2019	Leeds
Royal College of Midwives, Belfast	Karen Murray	3 May 2019	Belfast

Table 2.1 Contributors to the Film *Brexit, Health & Me*, per Credits

Anand Menon	UK in a Changing Europe, London
Femi Oluwole	Our Future, Our Choice, London
DrillMinister	Political Drill Music Artist
Paul Blomfield MP	Shadow Minister for Exiting the EU 2016–2019, MP for Sheffield Central
Layla McCay	NHS Confederation, UK
Seamus Murphy	Brexitborder.com, Newry
Raymond Jackson	Confederation of Community Groups, Newry
Steven Shepperd 'Shep'	Pub owner, Gleadless, Sheffield
Priscilla Nkwenti	Black Health Agency for equality in health and social care, Manchester
Anonymous NHS employee A	
Anonymous NHS employee B	

Participants are represented by the name they chose to give, whether that was full name, or only called name. Several students were included, because Shout Out UK's focus is young people.

Connor	Belfast
Stephen	Belfast
Angela	Belfast
Chris	Student, Belfast
Szilvia	Student, Sheffield
Wilkister	Student, Sheffield
Aaron	Newry
Rainbow George	London
James Saunders	London
Jane	London
Justyna	London
Philip	Student from Derby, interviewed in London
Callum	Student from Derby, interviewed in London
Robert	London
Mike	London

Table 2.2 Filming Dates

Date	Location(s)
23 March 2019	London (Westminster)
Spring 2019	London various
25–27 March 2019	Belfast, Newry, Irish border
29 March 2019	Sheffield
30 March 2019	Manchester
1 May 2019	Westminster
10 September 2019	Rotherham

Table 3 Dates and Locations of Street Conversations

	Sheffield (pilot)	**Newry**	**Rochdale**	**Rotherham**	**Derry**
Dates	20–22 March 2019	25–29 March 2019	19–24 May 2019	10–14 June 2019	19–23 August 2019
Brexit event		First cancelled withdrawal date	2019 European Parliament elections	Conservative Party leadership contest begins	Leaked 'No Deal' preparations published in *The Times*
Specific locations	The Moor shopping precinct	Buttercrane Shopping Center	Yorkshire Street	Rotherham Market	Richmond Shopping Centre/ Lisnagelvin Shopping Centre
Accommodation		Belmont Hall	Flying Horse pub/ Broadfield park hotel	Carlton Park hotel	Maldron Hotel

Source: M Wood et al, 'What Do "Left Behind Communities" Want? A Qualitative Study in the United Kingdom using Photo Elicitation' (2023) *American Political Science Review* (first view doi: 10.1017/S0003055422001186).

Table 4 'Left Behind Communities'

Districts and Boroughs Chosen as Field Sites and Indicators of Their LBC Status				
Indicators of LBC status*	**Newry, Mourne and Down District**	**Derry City and Strabane District**	**Rochdale Metropolitan Borough**	**Rotherham Metropolitan Borough**
Population of district/borough (ONS 2019)	180,012	150,680	220,001	264,671
'Satellite' to city	Belfast	Belfast	Manchester	Sheffield
Areas with high multiple deprivations**	10% (8) of SOAs	27% (20) of SOAs	Balderstone and Kirkholt, Smallbridge and Firgrove, West Heywood, West Middleton	Maltby, Valley, Wingfield
Local hospital	Daisy Hill Hospital	Altnagelvin Hospital	Rochdale Infirmary	Rotherham General Hospital

*Compiled from: Office of National Statistics (ONS), Northern Ireland Statistics and Research Agency (NISRA), and Oxford Consultants for Social Inclusion (OCSI).

**Wards classed as left behind in UK towns (OCSI 2019) and percentage of Super Output Areas (SOAs) in 100 most deprived in Northern Ireland (NISRA 2017, 8).

Table 5 Summary of Conversation Data

Location	**N participants**	**% of total**
Sheffield (pilot)	25	5.11
Newry	84	17.18
Rochdale	103	21.06
Rotherham	112	22.9
Derry	165	33.74
Northern Ireland	249	50.92
North of England	240	49.08

Source: M Wood et al, 'What Do "Left Behind Communities" Want? A Qualitative Study in the United Kingdom using Photo Elicitation' (2023) *American Political Science Review* (first view doi: 10.1017/S0003055422001186).

Table 6 Descriptive Statistics of Participants, as Perceived by Researchers

		N
	Young (18–30)	104
Perceived age	Middle aged (30–60)	169
	Elderly/retired (60 and above)	129
	Female	268
Perceived gender	Male	205
	Neither	0
Perceived disability		26
	White	375
Perceived race	Black	14
	Asian	20
	Other	7

Source: M Wood et al, 'What Do "Left Behind Communities" Want? A Qualitative Study in the United Kingdom using Photo Elicitation' (2023) *American Political Science Review* (first view doi: 10.1017/S0003055422001186).

Figures 1 and 2 The Street conversations Set Up

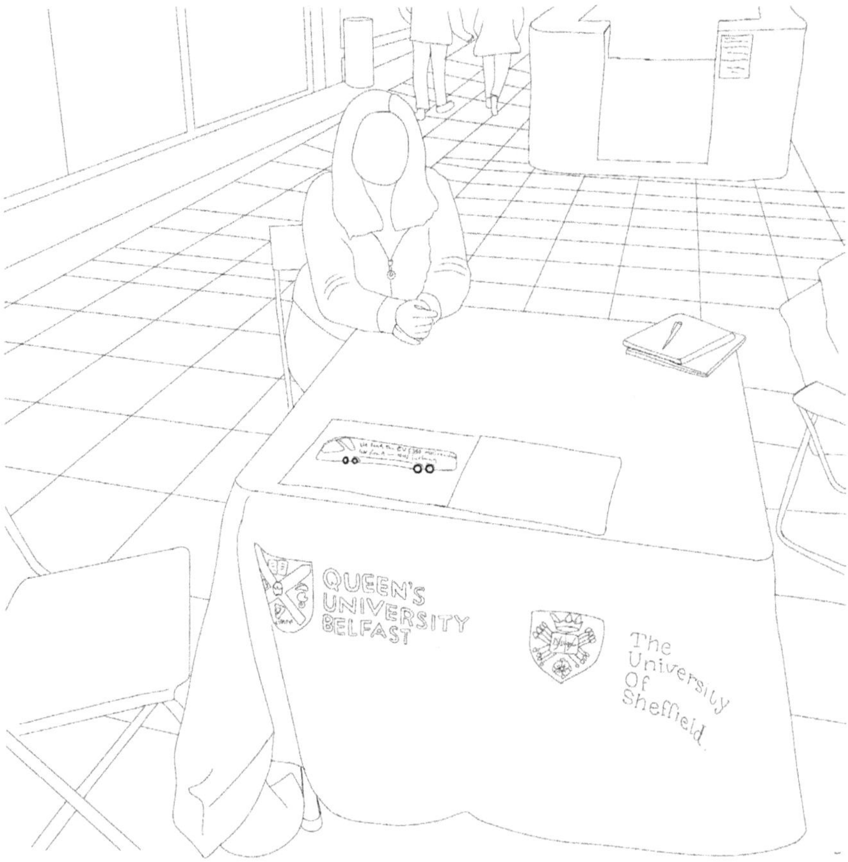

Credit: Sally Birrell @s.sketches.b.

Further information on materials related to the research, including records of fieldnotes, are available from the authors and the UK Data Archive (www.data-archive.ac.uk/).

Bibliography

A

Adnett, P, 'Sunak Enters Number 10 – Five Stances the New PM Has Had on International Trade', Institute of Export and International Trade, 24 October 2022 (www.export.org.uk/news/620231/Sunak-enters-Number-10--five-stances-the-new-PM-has-had-on-international-trade.htm)

Ainsley, C, *The New Working Class* (Bristol, Policy Press, 2018)

Alabrese, E et al, 'Who Voted for Brexit? Individual and Regional Data Combined' (2019) 56 *European Journal of Political Economy* 132

Alemanno, A and S Gabbi (eds), *The Foundations of EU Food Law and Policy: Ten Years of the European Food Safety Authority* (Farnham, Ashgate, 2014)

Alter, K, 'The European Court's Political Power' (1996) 19(3) *West European Politics* 452

Anderson, B et al, 'Modes of Uncertainty and Futures in an Impasse' (2020) 45(2) *Transactions of the Institute of British Geography* 256

Ansell C and J Torfing (eds), *Handbook on Theories of Governance*, 2nd edn (Cheltenham, Edward Elgar, 2022)

Antova, I et al, 'Calling Out "Bullshit" in "Left Behind" Britain', SPERI, 16 September 2019 (http://speri.dept.shef.ac.uk/2019/09/16/calling-out-brexit-bullshit-in-left-behind-britain/)

Antova, I, 'Taking Back Control (of Our Health): The Responsibilised Citizen and Post-Brexit Health Governance', conference paper at the *Critical Legal Conference* 2019, University of Perugia

Armstrong, KA, *Brexit Time. Leaving the EU – Why, How and When?* (Cambridge, Cambridge University Press, 2017)

Armstrong, KA, 'Regulatory Alignment and Divergence After Brexit' (2018) 25(8) *Journal of European Public Policy* 1099

Armstrong, KA, 'The Governance of Economic Unionism after the United Kingdom Internal Market Act' (2022) 85(3) *The Modern Law Review* 635

B

Baker, C, *NHS Staff from Overseas: Statistics*, Commons Library Research Briefing 7783, House of Commons Library, 20 September 2021

Balfour, H, 'UK Life Sciences Sector: Do You Have the Vision for Innovation?', European Pharmaceutical Review, 30 August 2021 (www.europeanpharmaceuticalreview.com/article/161361/uk-life-sciences-sector-do-you-have-the-vision-for-innovation/)

Bank of England, 'Monetary Policy Summary and Minutes of the Monetary Policy Committee Meeting Ending on 15 December 2021', 16 December 2021 (www.bankofengland.co.uk/-/media/boe/files/monetary-policy-summary-and-minutes/2021/december-2021.pdf)

Bank of England, 'Monetary Policy Report – November 2022' (www.bankofengland.co.uk/monetary-policy-report/2022/november-2022)

Barber, NW, 'Legal Pluralism and the European Union' (2006) 12(3) *European Law Journal* 306

Barbulescu, R et al, *Class, Race and Inequality in Northern Towns* (London, Runnymede Trust, 2019)

Barnard, C and S Butlin, 'Free Movement vs Fair Movement: Brexit and Managed Migration' (2018) 55 (Special Issue) *Common Market Law Review* 203

Barnard, C and A Ludlow, *Unravelling and Reimagining the UK's Relationship with the EU: Public Engagement about Brexit in the East of England* (Cambridge and London, University of Cambridge and UK in a Changing Europe, 2017)

Barnard, C et al, 'The Changing Status of European Union Nationals in the United Kingdom Following Brexit: The Lived Experience of the European Union Settlement Scheme' (2022) 31(3) *Social & Legal Studies* 365

Barnier, M, *My Secret Brexit Diary: A Glorious Illusion* (Cambridge, Polity Press, 2021)

Becker, S et al, 'Who Voted for Brexit? A Comprehensive District-Level Analysis' (2017) 32(92) *Economic Policy* 601

Beech, J et al, *Closing the Gap. Key Areas for Action on the Health and Care Workforce* (London, The Health Foundation, The King's Fund, Nuffield Trust, March 2019)

Behrend, L, 'Consequences of Brexit for Clinical Trials in Europe', Applied Clinical Trials, 14 October 2021 (www.appliedclinicaltrialsonline.com/view/consequences-of-brexit-for-clinical-trials-in-europe)

Bell, S, 'Unison Hails Victory Over Hospital Outsourcing in Wishaw', The National, 9 June 2022

Bellamy, R, 'Political Constitutionalism and the Human Rights Act' (2011) 9(1) *International Journal of Constitutional Law* 86

Berger, R, 'Now I See It, Now I Don't: Researcher's Position and Reflexivity in Qualitative Research' (2015) 15(2) *Qualitative Research* 219

Bertollini, R et al, 'Tobacco Control in Europe: A Policy Review' (2016) 25(140) *European Respiratory Review* 151

Beukers, T et al (eds), *Constitutional Change through Euro-Crisis Law* (Cambridge, Cambridge University Press 2017)

Bevir, M, *Governance: A Very Short Introduction* (Oxford, Oxford University Press, 2012)

Bhambra, GK, 'Brexit, Trump, and "Methodological Whiteness": On the Misrecognition of Race and Class' (2017) 68(1) *British Journal of Sociology* S214

Bianchi, A, 'Epistemic Communities' in J d'Aspremont and S Singh, *Concepts for International Law* (Abingdon, Routledge, 2019)

Biedermann, F, 'European Health Union One Step Closer' (2022) 400(0360) *The Lancet* 1294

Bierbach, JB, 'The "Person of Northern Ireland": A Vestigial Form of EU Citizenship?' (2021) 17(2) *European Constitutional Law Review* 232

Bix, B, *Law, Language and Legal Determinacy* (Oxford, Oxford University Press, 1995)

Boffey, D, 'Brexit Group Warned: Stop Using NHS Logo or We'll Sue', The Observer, 5 March 2016

Bogdanor, V, *Beyond Brexit: Towards a British Constitution* (London, Bloomsbury, 2019)

Bolton, M et al, 'England's Overlooked Neighbourhoods: Defining, Understanding and Regenerating "Left Behind" Communities' (2019) 13(2) *Journal of Urban Regeneration and Renewal* 116

Booth, W and K Adam, 'Rishi Sunak Budget Seeks to Stabilise UK Economy Rattled by Liz Truss', Washington Post, 17 November 2022

Border People, 'Brexit: The Complex New Boundaries Between Different Groups of Citizens in Northern Ireland', 14 January 2019 (https://borderpeople.info/media_news/brexit-the-complex-new-boundaries-between-different-groups-of-citizens-in-northern-ireland)

Border People, 'Healthcare for Frontier Workers – EU Rights (Withdrawal Agreement)', 7 December 2021 (https://borderpeople.info/a-z/healthcare-for-frontier-workers-eu-rights-withdrawal-agreement.html)

Bovens, M et al, 'Does Public Accountability Work? An Assessment Tool' (2008) 86(1) *Public Administration* 225

Bovens, M et al (eds), *The Real World of EU Accountability* (Oxford, Oxford University Press, 2010)

Bovens, M et al, 'Public Accountability' in M Bovens et al (eds), *The Oxford Handbook of Public Accountability* (Oxford, Oxford University Press, 2014)

Boyd White, J, *The Legal Imagination* (Chicago, Chicago University Press, 1973)

Bradford, A, *The Brussels Effect: How the European Union Rules the World* (Oxford, Oxford University Press, 2020)

Braithwaite, J and P Drahos, *Global Business Regulation* (Cambridge, Cambridge University Press, 2000)

Braverman, I et al (eds), *The Expanding Spaces of Law: A Timely Legal Geography* (Stanford, Stanford University Press, 2014)

British Medical Association, *Brexit Briefing: The Medical Workforce and Future Immigration Policy*, London, 2018

Briddick, C, 'Fortress Europe: Cause or Consequence of Europe's "Migrant Crisis"', The London School of Economics and Political Science, 28 August 2015 (http://blogs.lse.ac.uk/eurocrisispress/2015/08/28/fortress-europe-cause-or-consequence-of-europes-migrant-crisis/)

Brooks, P, 'Narrative in and of the Law' in J Phelan and PJ Rabinowitz (eds), *A Companion to Narrative Theory* (Hoboken NJ, Wiley-Blackwell, 2005)

Browning, C, 'Brexit Populism and Fantasies of Fulfilment' (2019) 32(3) *Cambridge Review of International Affairs* 222

Buchan, J et al, *Health Professional Mobility in a Changing Europe*, Observatory Study Series 32 (Copenhagen, European Observatory on Health Systems and Policies, 2014)

Bulmer, S and L Quaglia, 'The Politics and Economics of Brexit' (2018) 25(8) *Journal of European Public Policy* 1089

Burley, AM and W Mattli, 'Europe Before the Court: A Political Theory of Legal Integration' (1993) 47(1) *International Organization* 41

Burman, J, 'SCANDAL: MPs Get Free VIP Service at NHS Hospital to Protect Them from Members of Public', The Express, 1 September 2015

Burn-Murdoch, J, 'Britons Now Have the Worst Access to Healthcare in Europe, and it Shows', Financial Times, 4 November 2022

Bush, C and R Hawley, *Standing at the Sky's Edge* (London, Nick Hern Books, 2022)

C

Cabinet Office and Department for Levelling Up, Housing and Communities, 'Process for Considering UK Internal Market Act Exclusions in Common Framework Areas', 10 December 2021 (www.gov.uk/government/publications/process-for-considering-ukim-act-exclusions-in-common-framework-areas/process-for-considering-uk-internal-market-act-exclusions-in-common-framework-areas)

Campbell, G, 'Heart Drug Trials Halted Over Brexit Fears', BBC, 3 October 2018

Cardwell, PJ and T Hervey, 'Bringing the Technical into the Socio-Legal: The Metaphors of Law and Legal Scholarship of a Twenty-First Century European Union' in D Cowan and D Wincott (eds), *Exploring the 'Legal' in Socio-Legal Studies* (London, Palgrave Macmillan, 2016)

Carolan, E and A O'Neill, 'Ireland: Legal Response to Covid-19' in J King and O LM Ferraz et al (eds), *The Oxford Compendium of National Legal Responses to Covid-19* (Oxford, Oxford University Press, 2021)

Carraway, C, *Skint Estate* (London, Penguin Random House, 2019)

Carreras, M et al, 'Long-Term Economic Distress, Cultural Backlash, and Support for Brexit' (2019) 52(9) *Comparative Political Studies* 1396

Centre for Inequality and Levelling Up, *Funding Levelling Up: The Story So Far* (London, University of Westminster, 2021)

Charlesworth, A, 'Staff Shortages Left the NHS Vulnerable to the COVID-19 Storm', The Health Foundation, 21 January 2021 (www.health.org.uk/news-and-comment/blogs/staff-shortages-left-the-nhs-vulnerable-to-the-covid-19-storm?gclid=Cj0KCQjwz96WBhC8ARIsAATR250x15tuNYQqejXo6Zr7emv2tZX9JC7ZDeCkpb7GKsAVwQbFqJPG98YaAtdfEALw_wcB)

Chaudhury, DR, '"Pragmatic" Rishi Sunak May Iron Creases Out of Trade Deal with India', Economic Times, 26 October 2022

Chicowski, R, *The European Court and Civil Society: Litigation, Mobilization and Governance* (Cambridge, Cambridge University Press, 2009)

Chowdhury, T, *Time, Temporality and Legal Judgment* (Abingdon, Routledge, 2020)

Christie, B, 'Scotland's New Staffing Plan is Criticised for Failing to Tackle Retention Problems' (2022) 376 *British Medical Journal* o674

Clarke, H et al, *Brexit: Why Britain Voted to Leave the European Union* (Cambridge, Cambridge University Press, 2017)

Clarke, N et al, *The Good Politician: Folk Theories, Political Interaction, and the Rise of Anti-Politics* (Cambridge, Cambridge University Press, 2018)

Clarke-Ezzidio, H, 'A Message to the New Health Secretary: Don't Scrap the Health Inequalities Review', The New Statesman, 28 October 2022

Competition and Markets Authority and Office for the Internal Market, 'Overview of the UK Internal Market', 22 March 2022 (www.gov.uk/government/publications/overview-of-the-uk-internal-market-report/overview-of-the-uk-internal-market#:~:text=The%204%20nations%20of%20the%20UK%20vary%20significantly%20in%20the,49%20billion%20in%20Northern%20Ireland)

Confederation of British Industry, 'Views of Industry Trade Associations on EU Rules and Regulations', 30 April 2018 (www.cbi.org.uk/articles/views-of-industry-trade-associations-on-eu-rules-and-regulations/)

Cook, C, 'How Immigration Changed Boston, Lincolnshire', BBC, 10 May 2016

Cooper, B, 'How the EU is Making NHS Privatisation Permanent', The New Statesman, 2 December 2013

Cooper, L and C Cooper, '"Get Brexit Done': The New Political Divides of England and Wales at the 2019 Election' (2020) 91(4) *The Political Quarterly* 751

Copeland, P and P Diamond, 'From EU Structural Funds to Levelling Up: Empty Signifiers, Ungrounded Statism and English Regional Policy' (2022) 37(1–2) *Local Economy* 34

Cotterrell, R, 'Socio-Legal Studies, Law Schools, and Legal and Social Theory', *Legal Studies Research Paper* No 126/2012 (London, Queen Mary University of London School of Law, 2012)

Cowan, D et al (eds), 'Introduction: Celebrating Phil Thomas at 80' (2020) 47(S2) *Journal of Law and Society* S187

Cowan, D et al, *Reconciling Owning and Renting in Shared Ownership Housing: Moving Forward* (Bristol, University of Bristol/York, University of York, 2015)

Cowan, D and D Wincott (eds), *Exploring the 'Legal' in Socio-Legal Studies* (London, Palgrave Macmillan, 2016)

Cox, E and S Longlands, *City Systems* (Manchester, Institute for Public Policy Research North, 2016)

Craig, P, 'Constitutions, Constitutionalism and the European Union' (2001) 7(2) *European Law Journal* 125

Craig, P, 'Brexit and the UK Constitution' in J Jowell and C O'Cinneide (eds), *The Changing Constitution* (Oxford, Oxford University Press, 2019)

Cremona, M, 'The Treaties that Created Europe' in G Amato et al (eds), *The History of the European Union: Constructing Utopia* (London, Hart Publishing, 2019)

Creutzfeldt, N, 'Traditions of Studying the Social and the Legal' in N Creutzfeldt et al, *Routledge Handbook of Socio-Legal Studies* (Abingdon, Routledge, 2020)

Cryer, R et al, *Research Methodologies in EU and International Law* (Oxford, Hart Publishing, 2011)

Cummings, D, 'On the Referendum #21: Branching Histories of the 2016 Referendum and "the Frogs Before the Storm"', 9 January 2017 (https://dominiccummings.com/2017/01/09/on-the-referendum-21-branching-histories-of-the-2016-referendum-and-the-frogs-before-the-storm-2/)

D

Dallison, P, 'Bid to Prosecute Boris Johnson over Brexit Bus Claim Thrown Out by Court', Politico, 7 June 2019

David, C, 'Nurse Says She "Dreads" Coming into Work Due to Staff Shortages Which Are Putting Patients at Risk', Cymru Online, 8 June 2022 (www.walesonline.co.uk/news/wales-news/nurse-says-dreads-coming-work-24158222)

Dawson, M, *New Governance and the Transformation of European Law: Coordinating EU Social Law and Policy* (Cambridge, Cambridge University Press, 2011)

Dawson, M and F de Witte, 'Constitutional Balance in the EU After the Euro-Crisis' (2013) 76(5) *The Modern Law Review* 817

Dawson, M and F de Witte, 'Self-Determination in the Constitutional Future of the EU' (2015) 21(3) *European Law Journal* 371

Dawson M and F de Witte, *EU Law and Governance* (Cambridge, Cambridge University Press, 2022)

Dayan, M, 'The Facts: EU Immigration and Pressure on the NHS', Nuffield Trust and Full Fact, 15 June 2016 (www.nuffieldtrust.org.uk/resource/the-facts-eu-immigration-and-pressure-on-the-nhs)

Dayan, M, 'How Will Brexit Affect the Supply of Drugs to UK Patients? A Q&A', Nuffield Trust, 16 November 2020 (www.nuffieldtrust.org.uk/news-item/how-will-brexit-affect-the-supply-of-drugs-to-uk-patients)

Dayan, M et al, *Understanding the Impact of Brexit on Health in the UK*, Nuffield Trust, December 2020

Dayan, M et al, 'Medicines' in UK in a Changing Europe, *UK Regulation After Brexit Revisited* (London, UK in a Changing Europe, 19 October 2022)
Dayan, M and T Hervey, 'Breaking the Northern Ireland Protocol Would Create Problems for Health and Care' (2022) 378 *British Medical Journal* o1673
Dayan, M et al, 'Boosterism Blinds Us to the Possible Benefits of Brexit', Nuffield Trust, 3 March 2022 (www.nuffieldtrust.org.uk/news-item/boosterism-blinds-us-to-the-possible-benefits-of-brexit)
Dayan, M et al, 'Protocol Politics Mean Hard Times Ahead for Health in Northern Ireland', Nuffield Trust, 6 July 2022
Dayan, M et al, 'Parallel, Divergent or Drifting? Regulating Healthcare Products in a Post-Brexit UK' (2023) *Journal of European Public Policy* https://doi.10.1080/13501763.2023.2213721
de Búrca G and J Scott (eds), *New Governance and Constitutionalism in the EU and the US* (Oxford, Hart Publishing, 2006)
de Búrca, G and JHH Weiler (eds), *The European Court of Justice* (Oxford, University Press, 2002)
de Búrca, G and JHH Weiler (eds), *The Worlds of European Constitutionalism* (Cambridge, Cambridge University Press, 2011)
de Mars, S, 'Economically Inactive EU Migrants and the NHS: Unreasonable Burdens Without Real Links?' (2014) 39(6) *European Law Review* 770
de Mars, S et al, *Bordering Two Unions: Northern Ireland and Brexit* (Bristol, Policy Press, 2018)
de Mars, S et al, *Continuing EU Citizenship 'Rights, Opportunities and Benefits' in Northern Ireland after Brexit* (Dublin and Belfast, Irish Human Rights and Equality Commission and Northern Ireland Human Rights and Equality Commission, March 2020)
de Mars, S and C Murray, 'With or Without EU? The Common Travel Area After Brexit' (2020) 21(5) *German Law Journal* 815
de Ruijter, A, *EU Health Law & Policy: The Expansion of EU Power in Public Health and Health Care* (Oxford, Oxford University Press, 2019)
de Witte, B, 'The European Union as an International Legal Experiment' in G de Búrca and JHH Weiler (eds), *The Worlds of European Constitutionalism* (Cambridge, Cambridge University Press, 2012)
de Witte, B, 'Structure and Evolution of Union law' in PJ Kuijper et al (eds), *The Law of the European Union*, 5th edn (Alphen aan der Rijn, Wolters Kluwer, 2018)
de Witte, B, 'Direct Effect, Primacy and the Nature of the Legal Order' in P Craig and G de Búrca (eds), *The Evolution of EU Law*, 3rd edn (Oxford, Oxford University Press, 2022)
de Witte, B, 'Guest Editorial: EU Emergency Law and Its Impact on the EU Legal Order' (2022) 59(1) *Common Market Law Review* 3
Deignan, A, *Collins Co-Build English Guides 7: Metaphor* (London, Collins, 1995)
Delaney, D, *The Spatial, the Legal and the Pragmatics of World-Making: Nomospheric Investigations* (Abingdon, Routledge, 2010)
Demianyk, G, 'Labour Criticises "Brexit" Campaign For "Misleading" Use Of NHS Logo', Huffington Post, 16 May 2016
Department of Health, ' Minister Donnelly Welcomes Approval for Irish Hospitals to Join European Reference Networks on Rare Diseases' (www.gov.ie/en/press-release/fb5a2-minister-donnelly-welcomes-approval-for-irish-hospitals-to-join-european-reference-networks-on-rare-diseases/#)
Department of Health and Social Care, 'The NHS Constitution for England' (www.gov.uk/government/publications/the-nhs-constitution-for-england/the-nhs-constitution-for-england)
Department of Health and Social Care, *NHS Bursary Reform*, Policy Paper, 27 January 2017
Department of Health and Social Care, Foreign and Commonwealth Office, and Foreign, Commonwealth and Development Office, 'Healthcare for UK Nationals Living in Ireland' (hwww.gov.uk/guidance/healthcare-in-ireland)
Department of Health and Social Care, 'EEA-Qualified and Swiss Healthcare Professionals Practising in the UK', 31 December 2020 (www.gov.uk/guidance/eea-qualified-and-swiss-healthcare-professionals-practising-in-the-uk)
Department of Health and Social Care and Steve Barclay MP, 'NHS Staff to Receive Pay Rise', 19 July 2022 (www.gov.uk/government/news/nhs-staff-to-receive-pay-rise)
Department of Health (Northern Ireland), 'Release of Northern Ireland Inpatient, Day Case and Outpatient Hospital Statistics for 2019/20', 6 August 2020 (www.health-ni.gov.uk/news/release-northern-ireland-inpatient-day-case-and-outpatient-hospital-statistics-201920)

Department for Business, Energy and Industrial Strategy, 'Guidance: Using the UKCA Marking', 31 December 2020, updated 14 November 2022

Department for Business, Energy and Industrial Strategy, 'Placing Manufactured Products on the Market in Great Britain' (hwww.gov.uk/guidance/placing-manufactured-goods-on-the-market-in-great-britain)

Department for Business, Energy and Industrial Strategy, 'Government Publishes Proposals for Package of Transitional Measures to Support Research and Innovation Sector Affected by Horizon Europe Delays', 20 July 2022 (www.gov.uk/government/news/government-publishes-proposals-for-package-of-transitional-measures-to-support-research-and-innovation-sector-affected-by-horizon-europe-delays)

Department for Business, Energy and Industrial Strategy, 'Supporting UK R&D and Collaborative Research Beyond European Programmes', 20 July 2022 (www.gov.uk/government/publications/supporting-uk-rd-and-collaborative-research-beyond-european-programmes)

Department for Business, Energy and Industrial Strategy, 'Supporting UK R&D and Collaborative Research Beyond European Programmes' (www.gov.uk/government/publications/supporting-uk-rd-and-collaborative-research-beyond-european-programmes/supporting-uk-rd-and-collaborative-research-beyond-european-programmes)

Department for Business, Energy and Industrial Strategy, 'UK Innovation Strategy: Leading the Future by Creating It' (www.gov.uk/government/publications/uk-innovation-strategy-leading-the-future-by-creating-it/uk-innovation-strategy-leading-the-future-by-creating-it-accessible-webpage)

Department for Business, Energy and Industrial Strategy and Office for Life Sciences, 'Life Sciences Vision' (www.gov.uk/government/publications/life-sciences-vision)

Department for Digital, Culture, Media and Sport, 'International Data Transfers: Building Trust, Delivering Growth and Firing Up Innovation', 26 August 2021 (www.gov.uk/government/publications/uk-approach-to-international-data-transfers/international-data-transfers-building-trust-delivering-growth-and-firing-up-innovation)

Department for International Trade and Elizabeth Truss MP, 'Policy Exchange Speech: Liz Truss Sets Out Britain's New Trade Policy', 14 September 2021 (www.gov.uk/government/speeches/policy-exchange-speech-liz-truss-sets-out-britains-new-trade-policy)

Department for International Trade, 'Framework Agreement Between the Government of India and the Government of the United Kingdom of Great Britain and Northern Ireland for Collaboration on Health Care Workforce', 21 July 2022 (www.gov.uk/government/publications/uk-and-india-collaboration-on-healthcare-workforce-framework-agreement/framework-agreement-between-the-government-of-india-and-the-government-of-the-united-kingdom-of-great-britain-and-northern-ireland-for-collaboration-o)

Department for Levelling Up, Housing and Communities and HM Government, *White Paper: Levelling Up the United Kingdom*, CP 604, 2 February 2022

Department for Levelling Up, Housing and Communities and HM Government, *Levelling Up the United Kingdom: Missions and Metrics Technical Annex*, CP 604, 2 February 2022

Department for Levelling Up, Housing and Communities, HM Government, *Levelling Up – Delivering for All Parts of the UK*, 2 February 2022

Dougan, M, 'The "Brexit" Threat to the Northern Irish Border: Clarifying the Constitutional Framework' in M Dougan (ed), *The UK After Brexit* (Cambridge, Intersentia, 2017)

Dougan, M, *The UK's Withdrawal from the EU: A Legal Analysis* (Oxford, Oxford University Press, 2021)

Douglas Scott, S, 'Brexit, Boundaries and the Power of Images' (2019) 13(1) *Pólemos* 63

Downey, L et al, 'The Changing Face of Medical Devices Regulation? A Consultation & Expected New Regulations', 11 April 2022 (blog.bham.ac.uk/everydaycyborgs/2022/04/11/the-changing-face-of-medical-devices-regulation-a-consultation/)

Doyle, O et al (ed), *The Brexit Challenge for Ireland and the United Kingdom: Constitutions Under Pressure* (Cambridge, Cambridge University Press, 2021)

Duneier, M, 'How Not to Lie with Ethnography' (2011) 41(1) *Sociological Methodology* 1

Dworkin, R, 'Law as Interpretation' (1982) 9(1) *Critical Inquiry* 179

E

Edgar, B, 'Rishi Sunak Commits to Levelling Up in First PMQs', The Northern Echo, 26 October 2022

Editorial, 'Is the Indivisibility of the Four Freedoms a Principle of EU Law?' (2019) 56 *Common Market Law Review* 1
Edwards, E, 'Who is Drillminister? This Morning Viewers Divided over London Mayor Candidate's Comments', RealityTitbit, 15 May 2020 (www.realitytitbit.com/celebrity-gossip-and-news/who-is-drillminister)
Edwards, N, 'The GP Crisis We Have Long Feared is Arriving', Nuffield Trust, 14 July 2022 (www.nuffieldtrust.org.uk/news-item/the-gp-crisis-we-have-long-feared-is-arriving)
Ellard-Gray, A et al, 'Finding the Hidden Participant: Solutions for Recruiting Hidden, Hard-to-Reach and Vulnerable Populations' (2015) 14(5) *International Journal of Qualitative Methods* 1
Ellickson, R, *Order Without Law: How Neighbours Settle Disputes* (London, Harvard University Press, 1994)
Elliott, M et al (eds), *The UK Constitution after Miller: Brexit and Beyond* (Oxford, Hart Publishing, 2018)
Else, H, 'Key COVID Research Hit by Cut to UK Foreign-Aid Budget' (2021) 593 *Nature* 20
Engel, DM, 'Litigation across Space and Time: Courts, Conflict, and Social Change' (1990) 24(2) *Law & Society Review* 333
Engle Merry, S, *Getting Justice and Getting Even: Legal Consciousness among Working-Class Americans* (London, University of Chicago Press, 1990)
Epilepsy Society, 'Brexit Contingency Plans for Epilepsy Medication' (https://epilepsysociety.org.uk/contingency-plans-epilepsy-medications-case-no-deal-brexit)
Erikson, T, *Small Places, Large Issues: An Introduction to Social and Cultural Anthropology*, 2nd edn (London, Pluto Press, 2001)
ERN – EuroBloodNet, 'Who We Are' (www.eurobloodnet.eu/eurobloodnet/who-we-are/)
ERN – EuroBloodNet, 'Supporting Partners' (www.eurobloodnet.eu/supporting-partners/)
ERN-ITHACA, 'Who We Are' (https://ern-ithaca.eu/about-us/who-we-are/)
ERN-LUNG, 'Overview Different Roles of ERN-LUNG Membership' (https://public.3.basecamp.com/p/KKWJQK5wzT5koMduWS3CaeaY)
ERN-RITA – Rare Immunological Disorders, 'Latest News and Events' (https://ern-rita.org/hcps/)
ERN-RITA – Rare Immunological Disorders, 'Reference Centers' (https://ern-rita.org/hcps/)
European Commission, 'Residence Rights of UK Nationals and Their Family Members Under the Citizens' Rights Part of the Withdrawal Agreement – Overview of Implementation' (https://ec.europa.eu/info/sites/default/files/overview_ms_residence_rights.pdf)
European Commission, 'Commission Launches Infringement Proceedings Against the UK for Breaking International Law and Provides Further Details on Possible Solutions to Facilitate the Movement of Goods Between Great Britain and Northern Ireland' (https://ec.europa.eu/commission/presscorner/detail/en/IP_22_3676)
European Commission, 'Q&A on the UK's Participation in Horizon Europe' (https://ec.europa.eu/info/sites/default/files/research_and_innovation/strategy_on_research_and_innovation/documents/ec_rtd_uk-participation-in-horizon-europe.pdf)
European Commission, 'European Reference Networks' (https://health.ec.europa.eu/european-reference-networks/overview_en)
European Commission, 'Work of the ERNs' (https://health.ec.europa.eu/european-reference-networks/work-erns_en)
European Commission, 'Health Programme' (https://health.ec.europa.eu/funding_en)
European Commission, 'Connecting Europe Facility' (https://ec.europa.eu/info/funding-tenders/find-funding/eu-funding-programmes/connecting-europe-facility_en)
European Commission, 'Horizon 2020' (https://research-and-innovation.ec.europa.eu/funding/funding-opportunities/funding-programmes-and-open-calls/horizon-2020_en)
European Health Union Initiative and Manifesto, 'European Health Union Initiative and Manifesto', European Health Forum Gastein (www.ehfg.org/projects-events/europeanhealthunion)
European Medicines Agency, 'Comirnaty' (www.ema.europa.eu/en/medicines/human/EPAR/comirnaty)
European Reference Network – eUROGEN (Urogenital Diseases), 'Supporting Partners' (https://eurogen-ern.eu/who-is-involved/supporting-partners/)
European Reference Network – Eye Diseases (ERN-EYE), 'Home' (www.ern-eye.eu/ern-eye-hcps-members-full-affiliated)
European Reference Network – Genetic Tumour Risk Syndromes (ERN GENTURIS), 'Home' (www.genturis.eu/l=eng/Home.html)

European Reference Network – Genetic Tumour Risk Syndromes (ERN GENTURIS), 'Supporting Partners (Our Experts)' (www.genturis.eu/l=eng/Search.html#searchText=supporting%20partners)
European Reference Networks – Hepatological Diseases (ERN RARE-LIVER), 'Members and Partners of the Network' (https://rare-liver.eu/about/members-and-partners-of-the-network)
European Reference Network – ERN-LUNG, 'Welcome to ERN-LUNG' (https://ern-lung.eu/supporting-partners-members/)
European Reference Network – MetabERN (European Reference Network for Hereditary Disorders), 'About Us' (https://metab.ern-net.eu/about-us-3/#whoweare)
EveryDoctor, 'We Are a Doctor-Led Campaign Organisation Fighting for a Better NHS' (www.everydoctor.org.uk/)
EveryDoctor, 'EveryDoctor's Map of NHS Privatisation + Outsourcing' (hwww.everydoctor.org.uk/nhs-privatisation-map)
Ewick, P and SS Silbey, *The Common Place of Law: Stories from Everyday Life* (Chicago and London, University of Chicago Press, 1998)

F

Fabbrini, F (ed), *The Law and Politics of Brexit* (Oxford, Oxford University Press, 2017)
Fabbrini, F (ed), *The Law and Politics of Brexit II: The Withdrawal Agreement* (Oxford, Oxford University Press, 2020)
Fabbrini, F (ed), *The Law and Politics of Brexit III: The Framework of New UK-EU Relations* (Oxford, Oxford University Press, 2021)
Fabbrini, F (ed), *The Law and Politics of Brexit IV: The Protocol on Ireland/Northern Ireland* (Oxford, Oxford University Press, 2022)
Fabian, J, *Time and the Other: How Anthropology Makes Its Object* (Chichester, Columbia University Press, 2004)
Faculty of Public Health, *Negotiating a 'Healthy' Trade Policy for the UK* (London, Faculty of Public Health, April 2019)
Fahy, N et al, 'How Will Brexit Affect Health and Health Services in the UK? Evaluating Three Possible Scenarios Against the WHO Health System Building Blocks' (2017) 390(10107) *The Lancet* 2110
Fahy, N et al, 'How Will Brexit Affect Health and Health Services in the UK? An Updated Evaluation' (2019) 393(10174) *The Lancet* 949
Fahy, N et al, 'Assessing the Potential Impact on Health of the UK's Future Relationship Agreement with the EU: Analysis of the Negotiating Positions' (2021) 16(3) *Health Economics, Policy and Law* 290
Fahy, N et al, 'Impact on the NHS and Health of the UK's Trade and Cooperation Relationship with the EU, and Beyond' (2022) 17(4) *Health Economics, Policy and Law* 471
Favell, A and R Barbulescu, 'Brexit, "Immigration" and Anti-Discrimination' in P Diamond et al (eds), *The Routledge Handbook of the Politics of Brexit* (Abingdon, Routledge, 2018)
Fella, S et al, *UK-EU Withdrawal Agreement: Implementation of Citizens' Rights* Briefing Paper Number 9657, House of Commons Library, 2 November 2022
Ferguson, D et al, *Will Free Movement end from 31 October 2019?* (London, House of Commons Library, 2019)
Fernández-Reino, M, 'The Health of Migrants in the UK', The Migration Observatory, 21 August 2020 (https://migrationobservatory.ox.ac.uk/resources/briefings/the-health-of-migrants-in-the-uk/)
Ferrara, M, *The Boundaries of Welfare. European Integration and the New Spatial Politics of Social Protection* (Oxford, Oxford University Press, 2005)
Fichera, M and O Pollicino, 'The Dialectics Between Constitutional Identity and Common Constitutional Traditions: Which Language for Cooperative Constitutionalism in Europe?' (2019) 20(8) *German Law Journal* 1097
Flear, ML, 'Developing Euro-Biocitizens Through Migration for Healthcare Services' (2007) 14(3) *Maastricht Journal of European and Comparative* Law 239
Flear, ML, '"Together for Health"? How EU Governance of Health Undermines Active Biological Citizenship' (2008) 26(3) *Wisconsin International Law Journal* 868

Flear, ML et al, *European Law and New Health Technologies* (Oxford, Oxford University Press, 2012)

Flear, ML, *Governing Public Health: EU Law, Regulation and Biopolitics* (Oxford, Hart Publishing, 2015 hb, 2018 pb (revised))

Flear, ML, 'The EU Clinical Trials Regulation: Key Priorities, Purposes and Aims and the Implications for Public Health' (2016) 42(3) *Journal of Medical Ethics* 192

Flear, ML, 'A Roadmap Towards Membership and Formal Voice in Global Bioethics Standard-Setting: Health Research and the Case of the International Council on Harmonisation' (2018) 18(2–3) *Medical Law International* 157

Flear, ML, 'Expectations as Techniques of Legitimation? Imagined Futures through Global Bioethics Standards for Health Research' (2021) 8(2) *Journal of Law and the Biosciences* lsaa086

Flear, ML and R Ashcroft (eds), 'Law, Biomedical Technoscience and Imaginaries' (2021) 8(2) (Special Issue) *Journal of Law and the Biosciences*

Flear, ML and et al (eds), *Socio-Legal Studies of Epistemic Injustice and Spaces and Places* (London, Palgrave Macmillan, 2024 forthcoming)

Flood, C et al (eds), *Borders and Pandemics* (Abingdon, Routledge, 2023)

Ford, S, 'Unions Sign Unique Deal Designed to "Brexit Proof Midwives"', The Nursing Times, 22 January 2018

Foreign and Commonwealth Office, 'UK Introduces Health Surcharge' (www.gov.uk/government/news/uk-introduces-health-surcharge)

Foreign Trade and Information System, 'Information on the United States of America' (www.sice.oas.org/ctyindex/usa/USANatlDocs_e.asp)

Foster, P, 'UK Extends Northern Ireland "Grace Periods" for Third Time', Financial Times, 6 September 2021

Foster, D and T Hervey, *Kidney Dialysis Patients Seeking Care in Selected EU Member States Following Brexit: The Expected Legal Position Under the Withdrawal Agreement and 'No Deal'*, Kidney Care UK Briefing Note, 2019 (www.sheffield.ac.uk/media/9187/download)

Foster, P et al, 'UK Workers' Rights at Risk in Plans to Rip Up EU Labour Market Rules', Financial Times, 14 January 2021

Foster, P, 'Medical Devices Industry Tests UK plans for Post-Brexit Divergence', Financial Times 18 July 2021

Fox, B, 'UK Prepares for Life Without Horizon Europe Ahead of "Last Round of Talks"', Euroactiv, 8 June 2022 (www.euractiv.com/section/uk-europe/news/uk-prepares-for-life-without-horizon-europe-ahead-of-last-round-of-talks/)

Frankfurt, HG, *On Bullshit* (Oxford, Princeton University Press, 2005)

Frantziou, E and C Murray, 'C-247/20 *VI v The Commissioners for Her Majesty's Revenue & Customs* and the Implications of Preliminary References During the Transitional Period: A Case Study in Legal Complexity', 17 March 2022 (https://europeanlawblog.eu/author/colinmurray/)

Fricker, M, *Epistemic Injustice: Power and the Ethics of Knowing* (Oxford, Oxford University Press, 2007)

Friedman, LM, *The Roots of Justice* (Chapel Hill, University of North Carolina Press, 2017)

Fritz, T, *CETA and TTIP: Potential Impacts on Health and Health Services* (Brussels, European Public Service Union, 2016)

G

Gallagher, P, 'EU Referendum: Department of Health Tells Vote Leave Campaign to Stop Using Official NHS Logo in its Brexit Literature', Independent, 3 March 2016

Gamble, A, 'The Brexit Negotiations and the Anglosphere' (2021) 92(1) *The Political Quarterly* 108

Garben, S et al (eds), *Critical Reflections on Constitutional Democracy in the European Union* (Oxford, Hart Publishing, 2019)

Gates-Lincoln, A, 'Granting Indefinite Leave to Remain to Migrant NHS Workers', Federal Trust, 12 March 2021 (https://fedtrust.co.uk/granting-indefinite-leave-to-remain-to-migrant-nhs-workers/)

Geertz, C, *The Interpretation of Cultures: Selected Essays* (New York, Basic Books, 1973/2017)

Gershlick, B and A Charlesworth, *Health and Social Care Workforce: Priorities for the New Government* (London, The Health Foundation, 2019)

Gibney, E, 'What the Landmark Brexit Deal Means for Science' (2021) 589 *Nature* 179

Gilmore, A and M McKee, 'Tobacco Policy in the European Union' in EA Feldman and R Bayer (eds), *Unfiltered: Conflicts Over Tobacco Policy and Public Health* (Cambridge MA, Harvard University Press, 2004)

Gilmore, A and M McKee, 'Tobacco Control policy: The European Dimension' (2002) 2(4) *Clinical Medicine* 335

Gleeson, D and R Labonté, *Trade Agreements and Public Health* (London, Palgrave Macmillan, 2020)

Goffman, E, *Frame Analysis: An Essay on the Organization of Experience* (Cambridge MA, Harvard University Press, 1974)

Goldstone, J and L Diamond, 'Demography and the Future of Democracy' (2020) 18(3) *Perspectives on Politics* 867

Gonzales, R and N Sigona, 'Mapping the Soft Borders of Citizenship' in R Gonzales and N Sigona (eds), *Within and Beyond Citizenship* (Abingdon, Routledge, 2017)

Good Clinical Practice Network, 'Página Nct de ensaios clínicos' (https://ichgcp.net/pt/eu-clinical-trials-registry/trial/2021-003436-92/BG)

Goodfellow, M, *Hostile Environment: How Immigrants Became Scapegoats* (London, Verso, 2019)

Goodhart, D, *The Road to Somewhere: The Populist Revolt and the Future of Politics* (Oxford, Oxford University Press, 2017)

Goodwin, M and O Heath, 'The 2016 Referendum, Brexit and the Left Behind: An Aggregate-level Analysis of the Result' (2016) 87(3) *The Political Quarterly* 323

Goodwin, M and O Heath, *Brexit Vote Explained* (London, Joseph Rowntree Foundation, 2016)

Goodwin, M and C Milazzo, 'Taking Back Control? Investigating the Role of Immigration in the Vote for Brexit' (2017) 19(3) *The British Journal of Politics and International Relations* 450

Goodwin, M et al, 'For and Against Brexit: A Survey Experiment of the Impact of Campaign Effects on Public Attitudes Toward EU Membership' (2018) 50(2) *British Journal of Political Science* 481

Gordon, S, 'Majority of Businesses Want Regulatory Alignment After Brexit', Financial Times, 17 January 2018

Gould, J and S Barclay, 'Mind the Gap: The Place of Gap Studies in Sociolegal Scholarship' (2012) 8(1) *Annual Review of Law and Social Science* 323

Gower, M, *The Immigration Health Surcharge*, Number CBP 7274, House of Commons Library, 18 June 2020

Grabham, W and S Beynon-Jones, *Law and Time* (Abingdon, Routledge, 2019)

Green, A, 'Speaking Bullshit to Power: Populism and the Rhetoric of Bullshit' (2019) *SSRN*

Greenfields, M et al, *The Impact of Migration in the Fenland Area: A Scoping Report*, Rosmini Centre, Wisbech, UK, 31 October 2019 (https://arro.anglia.ac.uk/id/eprint/704980/)

Greenhouse, CJ, *A Moment's Notice: Time Politics across Cultures* (Ithaca NY, Cornell University Press, 1996)

Greenhouse, CJ, 'Time's Up, Timed Out: Reflections on Social Time and Legal Pluralism' (2014) 46(1) *Journal of Legal Pluralism and Unofficial Law* 141

Greer, SL et al, *Everything You Always Wanted to Know About European Union Health Policies but Were Afraid to Ask*, 2nd edn (revised) (Copenhagen, European Observatory on Health Systems and Policies, 2019)

Grey, C, *Brexit Unfolded: How No One Got What They Wanted (and Why They Were Never Going to)* (London, Biteback Publishing, 2021)

Griffith, JAG, 'The Political Constitution' (1979) 42(1) *The Modern Law Review* 1

Griller, S and J Ziller (eds), *The Lisbon Treaty: EU Constitutionalism Without a Constitutional Treaty?* (Berlin, Springer, 2008)

Grimm, D, 'Does Europe Need a Constitution?' (1995) 1(3) *European Law Journal* 282

Grzelak, A, 'Are the EU Member States Still Masters of the Treaties? The European Rule of Law Concept as a Means of Limiting National Authorities' in T Drinóczi and A Bień-Kacała (eds), *Rule of Law, Common Values, and Illiberal Constitutionalism: Poland and Hungary Within the European Union* (Abingdon, Routledge, 2020)

Gurnham, D, 'Law's Metaphors: Introduction' (2016) 43(1) *Journal of Law and Society* 1

H

Haas, PB, *Epistemic Communities, Constructivism, and International Environmental Politics* (Abingdon, Routledge 2015)
Haas, PB, 'Epistemic Communities' in L Rajamani and J Peel (eds), *The Oxford Handbook of International Environmental Law* (Oxford, Oxford University Press, 2021)
Halliday S and P Schmidt, *Conducting Law and Society Research* (Cambridge, Cambridge University Press, 2009)
Ham, C, 'The General Election, the NHS, and Social Care' (2017) 357 *British Medical Journal* j2840
Hameleers, M and D Schmuck, 'It's Us against Them: A Comparative Experiment on the Effects of Populist Messages Communicated via Social Media' (2017) 20(9) *Information, Communication & Society* 1425
Handley, L, *Respectable* (London, Penguin Random House, 2016)
Hanne, M and R Weisburg (eds), *Narrative and Metaphor in the Law* (Cambridge, Cambridge University Press, 2018)
Hantzsche, A et al, *The Economic Effects of the Government's Proposed Brexit Deal*, National Institute of Economic and Social Research, London, 2018
Hargen, G, 'Concern Over "Dangerous Staffing Levels" in NI Health System with Thousands of Nursing and Social Work Vacancies', Belfast Telegraph, 11 August 2021
Harlow, C, *Accountability in the European Union* (Oxford, Oxford University Press, 2002)
Harlow, C, 'Accountability and Constitutional Law' in M Bovens et al (eds), *The Oxford Handbook of Public Accountability* (Oxford, Oxford University Press, 2014)
Harper, D, 'Talking about Pictures: A Case for Photo Elicitation' (2002) 17(1) *Visual Studies* 13
Harper, D, 'People and Places' in C Jerolmack and S Kahn (eds), *Approaches to Ethnography* (Oxford, Oxford University Press, 2018)
Harrington, J, 'Time and Space in Medical Law: Building on Valverde's *Chronotopes of Law*' (2015) 23(3) *Feminist Legal Studies* 361
Harris, J, 'They Say After Brexit There'll Be Food Rotting in the Fields. It's Already Started', The Guardian, 5 August 2017
Harrison, AK, *Ethnography: Understanding Qualitative Research* (Oxford, Oxford University Press, 2018)
Harvey, D, *Justice, Nature and the Geography of Difference* (Oxford, Blackwell Publishers, 1996)
Haskell, H, 'Cumberlege Review Exposes Stubborn and Dangerous Flaws in Healthcare' (2020) 370 *British Medical Journal* m3099
Hatzopoulos, V, '*Killing* National Health and Insurance Systems but *Healing* Patients? The European Market for Health Care Services After the Judgments of the ECJ in *Vanbraekel* and *Peerbooms*' (2002) 39(4) *Common Market Law Review* 683
Hawkins, N, 'Please Don't Take Away My EHIC Card', 31 August 2018 (www.kidneycareuk.org/news-and-campaigns/news/please-dont-take-away-my-ehic-card/)
Hay, C, *Why We Hate Politics* (Cambridge, Polity Press, 2007)
Hayward, K, 'Northern Ireland: Demographics and Divisions' in F Fabbrini (ed), *The Law & Politics of Brexit: Volume IV. The Protocol on Ireland/Northern Ireland* (Oxford, Oxford University Press, 2022)
Hayward, K, 'Northern Ireland: Demographics and Divisions' in F Fabbrini (ed), *The Law and Politics of Brexit Vol IV* (Oxford, Oxford University Press, 2022)
Health Finance Directorate, 'Outsourcing of Soft Facilities Management Services in NHS Scotland' (www.sehd.scot.nhs.uk/mels/cel2008_46.pdf)
Helm, T, 'Move to EU to Avoid Brexit Costs, Firms Told', The Guardian, 23 January 2021
Hervey, T, 'The European Union and the Governance of Health Care' in G de Búrca and J Scott (eds), *New Governance and Constitutionalism in the EU and the US* (Oxford, Hart Publishing, 2006)
Hervey, T, 'The European Union's Governance of Health Care and the Welfare Modernization Agenda' (2008) 2(1) *Regulation & Governance* 103
Hervey, T, '"Adjudicating in the Shadow of the Informal Settlement"?: The Court of Justice of the European Union, "New Governance" and Social Welfare' (2010) 63 *Current Legal Problems* 92
Hervey, T, 'The Role of the European Court of Justice in the Europeanization of Communicable Disease Control: Driver or Irrelevance?' (2012) 37(6) *Journal of Health Politics, Policy and Law* 977

Hervey, T, 'Realism, Empiricism and Doctrine in EU Legal Studies: Views from a Common Law Perspective' in R Nielsen and U Neergaard (eds), *European Legal Method: Towards a New European Legal Realism* (Copenhagen, DJØF, 2013)

Hervey, T, 'Healthier After Brexit?', UK in a Changing Europe, 22 March 2016 (http://ukandeu.ac.uk/healthier-after-brexit/)

Hervey, T, 'What Brexit Would Really Mean for the NHS', Health Service Journal, 22 March 2016

Hervey, T, 'Letter to NHS Identity Helpline', 11 May 2016 (ablendedlifeblog.wordpress.com/2016/06/23/letter-to-nhs-identity-helpline-may-2016/)

Hervey, T, 'NHS Safer Within EU', 22 June 2016 (ablendedlifeblog.wordpress.com/2016/06/22/nhs-safer-within-eu/)

Hervey, T, 'EU Health Law' in C Barnard and S Peers (eds), *European Union Law* (Oxford, Oxford University Press, 2023)

Hervey, T, 'Analysis 1 of the Brexit Deal: Healthcare Entitlements in the EU-UK Trade and Cooperation Agreement', 29 December 2020 (http://eulawanalysis.blogspot.com/2020/12/analysis-1-of-brexit-deal-healthcare.html)

Hervey, T et al, 'Health "Brexternalities": The Brexit Effect on Health and Healthcare Outside the EU' (2021) 46(1) *Journal of Health Politics Policy and Law* 177

Hervey, T, *Brexit, Health and its Potential Impact on Article 2 of the Ireland/Northern Ireland Protocol* (Belfast, Northern Ireland Human Rights Commission, 2022)

Hervey, T and J McHale, *European Union Health Law: Themes and Implications* (Oxford, Oxford University Press, 2015)

Hervey, T and EM Speakman, 'The Immediate Futures of EU Health Law in the UK after Brexit: Law, "Alegality" and Uncertainty' (2018) 18(2–3) *Medical Law International* 65

Hervey, T and L Trubek, 'Freedom to Provide Health Care Services Within the EU: An Opportunity for Hybrid Governance' (2007) 13(3) *Columbia Journal of European Law* 623

Hirschler, B and L Heavens, 'UK Clinical Trials Fall as Brexit Clouds Drug Approval Process', Reuters, 9 October 2018

Hix, S et al, 'UK Voters, Including Leavers, Care More about Reducing Non-EU Than EU Migration', The London School of Economics and Political Science, 30 June 2017 (https://blogs.lse.ac.uk/europpblog/2017/05/30/uk-voters-including-leavers-care-more-about-reducing-non-eu-than-eu-migration/)

HM Government, *EU Exit: Long-Term Economic Analysis*, CM 9742, November 2018

HM Government, *The Benefits of Brexit: How the UK is Taking Advantage of Leaving the EU*, January 2022

HM Government Home Office, *Media Factsheet: EU Citizens and Freedom of Movement* (https://homeofficemedia.blog.gov.uk/2019/08/19/media-factsheet-eu-citizens-and-freedom-of-movement/)

HM Revenue and Customs, 'Explanatory Notes' (www.gov.uk/government/publications/uk-trade-tariff-customs-duty-relief-on-pharmaceutical-products/explanatory-notes)

HM Treasury, 'Build Back Better: Our Plan for Growth' (www.gov.uk/government/publications/build-back-better-our-plan-for-growth)

Homer, A, 'Growth in NHS Recruits from Abroad Prompts Concern About Over-Reliance', BBC, 5 August 2022 (www.bbc.co.uk/news/uk-61230287)

Hooghe, L and G Marks, *Multilevel Governance and European Integration* (Oxford, Rowman & Littlefield, 2001)

Hopkin, J and B Rosamond, 'Post-Truth Politics, Bullshit and Bad Ideas: "Deficit Fetishism" in the UK' (2018) 23(6) *New Political Economy* 641

Huang, Y, 'The 2008 Milk Scandal Revisited', Forbes, 16 July 2014

Hurley, R, 'Brexit Could Spell Trouble for Unsung Heroes of UK Biomedical Research' (2019) 364 *British Medical Journal* l868

Hymas, C, 'All Foreign NHS Staff Should Be Offered Chance of UK Citizenship After Serving on Frontline in Covid-19 Pandemic, Say MPs', The Telegraph, 14 June 2020

I

Iacobucci, G, '"Levelling Up" Plan Needs More Funding and a Focus on Health Inequalities, Say Experts' (2002) 376 *British Medical Journal* o303

Independent Medicines and Medical Devices Safety Review, *First Do No Harm*, July 2020

Independent Parliamentary Standards Authority, 'Details of any MPs with Private Medical Insurance', 18 July 2012 (www.theipsa.org.uk/freedom-of-information/2012-13/foi2012-a055)

Institute for Government, 'Devolution: Common Frameworks and Brexit' (www.instituteforgovernment.org.uk/explainers/devolution-common-frameworks-brexit)

J

Jardine, C, ' The Government Must Take on My Bill to Give NHS Heroes the Right to Live in the UK', Liberal Democrats, 14 January 2021 (www.libdems.org.uk/nhs-heroes-at-risk)

Jarman, H et al, 'Health, Transatlantic trade and President Trump's Populism: What "American Patients First" Has to do with Brexit and the NHS' (2018) 392(10145) *The Lancet* 447

Jarman, H, 'Legalism and Tobacco Control in the EU' (2018) 28(3) *European Journal of Public Health* 26

Jerolmack, C and S Kahn (eds), *Approaches to Ethnography* (Oxford, Oxford University Press, 2018)

Jones, H, 'UK Immigration Policy in a Hostile Environment' in B Jones et al (eds), *Politics UK*, 10th edn (Abingdon, Routledge, 2022)

Joyce, R et al, 'The Cost of Living Crunch', Institute for Fiscal Studies, 12 January 2022 (https://ifs.org.uk/publications/15905?gclid=Cj0KCQjwxIOXBhCrARIsAL1QFCZhPYRswNKkwkA011T54QS-ViNCKg1bfEb7qyKRoIJVH2bguTjm0RUaAq5_EALw_wcB)

K

Kagan, R, *Regulatory Justice* (New York, Russell Sage Foundation, 1978)

Kahneman, D, *Thinking, Fast and Slow* (London, Allen Lane, 2011)

Keep Our NHS Public, 'Pledge: Hands Off Our NHS' (https://keepournhspublic.com/campaigns/stop-privatisation-of-the-nhs/hands-off-our-nhs/)

Kelly, E, 'UK Budget Offers a Few Crumbs for Research, But No Horizon Europe Money', Science Business, 4 March 2021 (https://sciencebusiness.net/framework-programmes/news/uk-budget-offers-few-crumbs-research-no-horizon-europe-money)

Kelly, E, 'UK Announces €250M Towards Horizon Europe Participation Cost Following Scientist Revolt', Science Business, 2 April 2021 (https://sciencebusiness.net/framework-programmes/news/uk-announces-eu250m-towards-horizon-europe-participation-cost-following)

Kettell, S and P Kerr, 'The Brexit Religion and the Holy Grail of the NHS' (2021) 20(2) *Social Policy and Society* 282

Klabbers, J, 'Volkerrechtsfreundlich? International Law and the Union Legal Order' in P Koutrakos (ed), *European Foreign Policy: Legal and Political Perspectives* (Cheltenham, Edward Elgar, 2011)

Kövecses, Z, *Metaphor: A Practical Introduction* (Oxford, Oxford University Press, 2010)

Krapohl, S, 'Risk Regulation in the EU Between Interests and Expertise: The Case of BSE' (2003) 10(2) *Journal of European Public Policy* 189

L

Lacey, N, 'The Metaphor of Proportionality' (2016) 43(1) *Journal of Law and Society* 27

Lakoff, G and M Johnson, *Metaphors We Live By* (London, University of Chicago Press, 1980)

Lanktree, G, 'UK's Liz Truss was Warned of Blow to Food Sector under Australia and New Zealand Trade Deals', Politico, 12 July 2022

Larik, J, et al, 'Will Support for Brexit Become Extinct?', 30 November 2022 (https://ukandeu.ac.uk/will-support-for-brexit-become-extinct/)

Latham-Gambi, A, 'Political Constitutionalism and Legal Constitutionalism – an Imaginary Opposition?' (2020) 40(4) *Oxford Journal of Legal Studies* 737

Layard, A, 'Reading Law Spatially' in N Creutzfeldt et al (eds), *Routledge Handbook of Socio-Legal Theory and Methods* (Abingdon, Routledge, 2020)

LeBaron, M, 'Is the Blush off the Rose? Legal Education Metaphors in a Changing World' (2016) 43(1) *Journal of Law and Society* 144

Leibfried, S and P Pierson, *European Social Policy: Between Fragmentation and Integration* (Washington DC, Brookings Institute Press, 1995)

Lévi-Strauss, C, *The Savage Mind* (Chicago, Chicago University Press, 1966)

Lezotre, P-L, *International Cooperation, Convergence and Harmonization of Pharmaceutical Regulations* (London, Academic Press, 2014)

Lintern, S, 'Exclusive: "Crash" in EU Nurses Working in UK Since Brexit Referendum', Health Service Journal, 12 June 2017

Lock FK, and D Carrieri, 'Factors Affecting the UK Junior Doctor Workforce Retention Crisis: An Integrative Review' (2022) 12 *British Medical Journal Open* e059397

Lock, T, 'A Common Travel Area? Brexit and the New (Northern) Irish' in C McCrudden (ed), *The Law and Practice of the Protocol on Ireland/Northern Ireland* (Cambridge, Cambridge University Press, 2022)

Lord Ashcroft, 'How the United Kingdom Voted on Thursday … and Why', 24 June 2016 (https://lordashcroftpolls.com/2016/06/how-the-united-kingdom-voted-and-why/)

Lord, C, *Democracy in the European Union* (Sheffield, Sheffield Academic Press, 1998)

Lorenz, LS, 'A Way into Empathy: A "Case" of Photo-Elicitation in Illness Research' (2011) 15(3) *Health* 259

Loudon, C, 'NHS at "Crisis Point" as Funding on Temporary Staff Reaches £423m', STV News, 12 June 2022

Love, BL, 'Complex Personhood of Hip Hop & the Sensibilities of the Culture that Fosters Knowledge of Self & Self-Determination' (2016) 49(4) *Equity & Excellence in Education* 414

Low, SM and D Lawrence-Zúñiga, *The Anthropology of Space and Place* (Oxford, Blackwell Publishing, 2003)

Lubet, S, *Interrogating Ethnography: Why Evidence Matters* (Oxford, Oxford University Press, 2018)

M

Madeley, P, 'Rishi Sunak Pressed Over Commitment to Levelling Up in the West Midlands', Express & Star, 27 October 2022

MacCormick, N, 'Democracy, Subsidiarity, and Citizenship in the "European Commonwealth"' (1997) 16(4) *Law and Philosophy* 331

MacCormick, N, *Questioning Sovereignty* (Oxford, Oxford University Press, 1999)

Maddox, D, 'Major Leak from Brussels Reveals NHS Will be "KILLED OFF" if Britain Remains in the EU', Express, 3 May 2016

Maduro, M, 'Contrapunctual Law' in N Walker (ed), *Sovereignty in Transition* (Oxford, Hart Publishing, 2003)

Maduro, M and L Azoulai (eds), *The Past and Future of EU Law: The Classics of EU Law Revisited on the 50th Anniversary of the Rome Treaty* (Oxford, Hart Publishing, 2010)

Magni, G, 'Economic Inequality, Immigrants and Selective Solidarity: From Perceived Lack of Opportunity to In-Group Favouritism' (2021) 51(4) *British Journal of Political Science* 1357

Mandal, S et al, *Block, Amend, Delay: Tobacco Industry Efforts to Influence the EU's Tobacco Products Directive (2001/37/EC)* (SmokeFree Partnership, 2009) (www.smokefreepartnership.eu/images/Reports-and-Position-Papers/EU_TI_TPD_report_May_2012.pdf)

Mancini, F, 'The Making of a Constitution for Europe' (1989) 26(4) *Common Market Law Review* 595

Marsh, S and F Ryan, 'Revealed: UK Patients Stockpile Drugs in Fear of No-Deal Brexit', The Guardian, 18 January 2019

Martill, B and U Staiger, 'Negotiating Brexit: The Cultural Sources of British Hard Bargaining' (2021) 59(2) *Journal of Common Market Studies* 261

Mason, M, 'On Objectivity and Staying "Native": Researching LGBTQI+ Lawyers as a Queer Lawyer' in N Creutzfeldt et al (eds), *Routledge Handbook of Socio-Legal Theory and Methods* (Abingdon, Routledge, 2020)

Massey, D, *For Space* (London, Sage, 2005)

Mawani, R, 'Law as Temporality: Colonial Politics and Indian Settlers' (2014) 4 *University of California Irvine Law Review* 65

McCarey, M et al, *Health and Brexit Six Years On* (London, The Nuffield Trust, 2022)

McCartney, M, 'Vote Leave Broke Rules Over NHS Logo' (2016) 355 *British Medical Journal* i5482

McCloskey, S and T Hervey, *Cooperative Relationships for Bio-Medical Science Post-Brexit: The Legal Landscape*, Cancer Research UK Briefing Note, 2020 (www.sheffield.ac.uk/media/9926/download)

McCorkindale, C and A McHarg, 'Litigating Brexit' in O Doyle et al (eds), *The Brexit Challenge for Ireland and the United Kingdom* (Cambridge, Cambridge University Press, 2021)

McCormack, J, 'Brexit: How the Irish Border Issue Was Viewed During Campaigning', BBC, 12 October 2019

McCrudden, C (ed), *The Law and Practice of the Ireland/Northern Ireland Protocol* (Oxford, Oxford University Press, 2022)

McGarvey, D, *Poverty Safari* (Edinburgh, Luarth Press, 2017)

McHale, J et al, 'Health Law and Policy, Devolution and Brexit' (2021) 55(9) *Regional Studies* 1561

McKay, L, 'Left Behind People, or Places? The Role of Local Economies in Perceived Community Representation' (2019) 60(1) *Electoral Studies* 102046

McKee, M et al, 'Public Health Policies' in E Mossialos et al, *Health Systems Governance in Europe: The Role of European Union Law and Policy* (Cambridge, Cambridge University Press, 2010)

McKee, D and M McKee, 'What Might Brexit Mean for British Tourists Travelling to the Rest of Europe?' (2018) 48(2) *Journal of the Royal College of Physicians of Edinburgh* 134

McKeever, G, 'Brexit, the Irish Border and Social Security Rights' (2018) 25(1) *Journal of Social Security Law* 34

Mckenzie, L, 'The Class Politics of Prejudice: Brexit and the Land of No-Hope and Glory' (2017) 68(S1) *The British Journal of Sociology* S265

Mckenzie, L, '"It's Not Ideal": Reconsidering "Anger" and "Apathy" in the Brexit Vote Among an Invisible Working Class' (2018) 21(3) *Competition & Change* 199

McNeilly, K and B Warwick, *The Times and Temporalities of International Human Rights Law* (Abingdon, Routledge, 2022)

Medicine and Healthcare Products Regulatory Agency and S Javid MP (Secretary of State for Health and Social Care), *Consultation on the Future Regulation of Medical Devices in the United Kingdom*, 16 September 2021

Medicines and Healthcare Products Regulatory Agency, *Government Response to Consultation on the Future Regulation of Medical Devices in the United Kingdom*, June 2022

Medicines and Healthcare Products Regulatory Agency, 'The Northern Ireland MHRA Authorised Route (NIMAR)' (www.gov.uk/government/publications/the-northern-ireland-mhra-authorised-route-nimar/the-northern-ireland-mhra-authorised-route-nimar)

Medicines and Healthcare Products Regulatory Agency, 'Supplying Authorised Medicines to Northern Ireland' (www.gov.uk/guidance/supplying-authorised-medicines-to-northern-ireland)

Medicines and Healthcare Products Regulatory Agency, 'Regulating Medical Devices in the UK' (www.gov.uk/guidance/regulating-medical-devices-in-the-uk)

Medicines and Healthcare Products Regulatory Agency, 'Approved Bodies for Medical Devices' (www.gov.uk/government/publications/approved-bodies-for-medical-devices)

Medicines and Healthcare Products Regulatory Agency, 'Great Britain Marketing Authorisations (MAs) for Centrally Authorised Products (CAPs)' (www.gov.uk/government/publications/great-britain-marketing-authorisations-mas-for-centrally-authorised-products-caps)

Medicines and Healthcare Products Regulatory Agency, 'European Commission (EC) Decision Reliance Procedure' (www.gov.uk/guidance/european-commission-ec-decision-reliance-procedure)

Medicines and Healthcare Products Regulatory Agency, 'Regulatory approval of Pfizer/BioNTech vaccine for COVID-19' (www.gov.uk/government/publications/regulatory-approval-of-pfizer-biontech-vaccine-for-covid-19#)

Medicines and Healthcare Products Regulatory Agency, 'Oxford University/AstraZeneca COVID-19 Vaccine Approved' (www.gov.uk/government/news/oxford-universityastrazeneca-covid-19-vaccine-approved)

Medicines and Healthcare Products Regulatory Agency, 'The MHRA Innovative Licensing and Access Pathway is Open for Business' (www.gov.uk/government/news/the-mhra-innovative-licensing-and-access-pathway-is-open-for-business)

Menéndez, AJ, 'A European Union in Constitutional Mutation' (2014) 20(2) *European Law Journal* 127

Miller, V and S de Mars, 'Brexit Questions in National and EU Courts', HC Library Briefing Paper, No. 8415 (1 November 2019)

Millstone, E et al, 'Food, Brexit and Chlorinated Chicken: A Microcosm of Wider Food Problems' (2019) 90(4) *The Political Quarterly* 645

Mitchell, N, 'As Hopes Fade, UK Unveils Alternative to Horizon Europe', University World News, 23 July 2022 (www.universityworldnews.com/post.php?story=20220723095556503)

Moorhead, H and M Fitzsimons, 'Securing the Health and Wellbeing of Our Population 2022-2027: Informing the Public Debate Ahead of the May 2022 Northern Ireland Assembly Elections', NHS Confederation, 22 April 2022

Morries, M, *What Does the UK-EU Deal Mean for Workers' Rights?* (London, Institute for Public Policy Research, January 2022)

Mossialos E, et al (eds), *Health Systems Governance in Europe: The Role of EU Law and Policy* (Cambridge, Cambridge University Press, 2010)

Murkens, J, 'Democracy as the Legitimating Condition in the UK Constitution' (2018) 38(1) *Legal Studies* 42

N

National Institute for Health and Care Excellence, 'Belzutifan for Treating Clear-Cell Renal Carcinoma Caused by Von Hippel-Lindau disease [ID3932]' (www.nice.org.uk/guidance/indevelopment/gid-ta10817)

Neville, A et al, *Implementation of the Withdrawal Agreement: Financial Provisions, Citizens Rights and the Northern Ireland Protocol* (Brussels, European Parliament Research Service, January 2022)

Neville, S, 'Cancer Drug is First to Begin Fast-Track UK Approval Process', Financial Times, 26 February 2021

Newdick, C, *Who Should We Treat? Rights, Rationing and Resources in the NHS*, 2nd edn (Oxford, Oxford University Press, 2004)

Newdick, C, 'Citizenship, Free Movement and Health Care: Cementing Individual Rights by Corroding Social Solidarity' (2006) 43(6) *Common Market Law Review* 1645

NHS Confederation, 'Reciprocal Healthcare Arrangements in a No Deal Brexit Scenario: Overview of the Reciprocal Healthcare Arrangements within the Context of the UK Exiting the EU' (www.nhsconfed.org/regions-and-eu/nhs-european-office/brexit-and-the-nhs/brexit-implications-for-health-and-care/reciprocal-healthcare)

NHS England, 'Accredited Supplier Lists' (www.england.nhs.uk/hssf/supplier-lists/)

NHS England, 'NHS Logo' (www.england.nhs.uk/nhsidentity/identity-guidelines/nhs-logo/)

NHS England, 'Who Cannot Use the NHS Identity?' (www.england.nhs.uk/nhsidentity/identity-guidelines/who-cannot-use-the-nhs-identity/)

Nicolaïdis, K, *Exodus, Reckoning, Sacrifice: Three Meanings of Brexit* (London, The Unbound Press, 2019)

Norris, P and R Inglehart, *Cultural Backlash: Trump, Brexit, and Authoritarian Populism* (Cambridge, Cambridge University Press, 2019)

Northern Ireland Human Rights Commission and Equality Commission for Northern Ireland, *Joint NIHRC / ECNI Briefing Paper on the Modern Slavery and Human Trafficking and Electronic Travel Authorisation provisions in the Nationality and Borders Bill*, 27 January 2022

Nuffield Trust, 'Brexit and Health and Social Care' submitted to the Health Select Committee Inquiry, November 2016 (www.nuffieldtrust.org.uk/files/2017-05/brexit-submission-to-health-select-committee-formatted-final.pdf)

Nuffield Trust, 'NHS Staffing Tracker' (www.nuffieldtrust.org.uk/nhs-staffing-tracker)

Nuffield Trust, 'The NHS Workforce in Numbers (www.nuffieldtrust.org.uk/resource/the-nhs-workforce-in-numbers)

Nuffield Trust, 'Number of EU and Non-EU Nurse Registrations, UK, 1990/91 to 2020/21' (www.nuffieldtrust.org.uk/chart/number-of-eu-and-non-eu-nurse-registrations-uk-1990-91-to-2017-18)

Nuffield Trust, 'Access to GP Services' (www.nuffieldtrust.org.uk/resource/access-to-gp-services#background)

Nurse, A, 'Law, the Environment and Narrative Storytelling' in N Creutzfeldt et al (eds), *Routledge Handbook of Socio-Legal Theory and Methods* (Abingdon, Routledge, 2020)

O

O'Brien, C, *Unity in Adversity* (Oxford, Hart Publishing, 2017)

O'Brien, C, 'Between the Devil and the Deep Blue Sea: Vulnerable EU Citizens Cast Adrift in the UK Post-Brexit' (2021) 58(2) *Common Market Law Review* 431

O'Dwyer, M, 'The Intersectional Politics of Bullshit' (2018) 1(3) *European Journal of Politics and Gender* 405

Office for Budget Responsibility, 'Brexit Analysis', 26 May 2022 (https://obr.uk/forecasts-in-depth/the-economy-forecast/brexit-analysis/#assumptions)

Office for Budget Responsibility, *Economic and Fiscal Outlook*, CP 648, March 2022

Office for Budget Responsibility, *Fiscal Risks and Sustainability Report*, CP 702, July 2022

Office for Budget Responsibility, 'Impact of the Brexit Trade Agreement on Our Economy Forecast' (https://obr.uk/box/impact-of-the-brexit-trade-agreement-on-our-economy-forecast/)

Office for Budget Responsibility, 'Brexit Analysis', 26 May 2022 (https://obr.uk/forecasts-in-depth/the-economy-forecast/brexit-analysis/#assumptions)

Office for National Statistics, 'Consumer Price Inflation, UK: September 2022' (www.ons.gov.uk/economy/inflationandpriceindices/bulletins/consumerpriceinflation/september2022)

Office for National Statistics, 'Inflation and Price Indices' (www.ons.gov.uk/economy/inflationandpriceindices)

Office for National Statistics, 'UK Trading Partners and Trade Relationships: 2020' (www.ons.gov.uk/businessindustryandtrade/internationaltrade/articles/uktradingpartnersananalysisoftraderelationships/2020)

Office for National Statistics, '09 Geographical Breakdown of the Current Account, The Pink Book' (www.ons.gov.uk/economy/nationalaccounts/balanceofpayments/datasets/9geographicalbreakdownofthecurrentaccountthepinkbook2016)

Okwonga, M, 'The Ungrateful Country' in N Shukla (ed), *The Good Immigrant: 21 Writers Reflect on Race in Contemporary Britain* (London, The Unbound Press, 2017)

Oliver, D, *Government in the United Kingdom: The Search for Accountability, Effectiveness and Citizenship* (Milton Keynes, Open University Press, 1991)

Ortner, S, 'Resistance and the Problem of Ethnographic Refusal' (1995) 37(1) *Contemporary Studies in Society and History* 173

Oxford Consultants for Social Inclusion, *Left Behind? Understanding Communities on the Edge* (London, Oxford Consultants for Social Inclusion, 2019)

P

Pachirat, T, *Among Wolves: Ethnography and the Immersive Study of Power* (Abingdon, Routledge, 2018)

Palmer, B, 'Failure to Adequately Plan for Workforce Putting Patient Care at Risk', Nuffield Trust, 25 July 2022 (www.nuffieldtrust.org.uk/news-item/failure-to-adequately-plan-for-workforce-putting-patient-care-at-risk)

Parker, G, 'Ministers Agree to Release Secret Brexit Impact Paper', Financial Times, 31 January 2018

Parker, G et al, 'How Two Decades of EU Migration Went into Reverse', Financial Times, 1 April 2021

Partington, R, 'Sunak's Government "Going Backwards" on Green Economy, says CBI', The Guardian, 5 December 2022

Paterson, A, *The Law Lords* (London, Palgrave Macmillan, 1982)

Patients 4 NHS, 'Use of the NHS Logo' (www.patients4nhs.org.uk/abuse-of-nhs-logo/)

Pavone, T and RD Kelemen, 'The Evolving Judicial Politics of European Integration: The European Court of Justice and National Courts Revisited' (2019) 25(4) *European Law Journal* 352

Pedreschi, L, *Public Services in EU Trade and Investments Agreements* (Asser Press, The Hague, 2020)

Peers, S, 'Litigating Brexit – a Guide to the Case Law', 27 July 2020, http://eulawanalysis.blogspot.com/p/litigating-brexit-guide-to-caselaw.html

Pei, X et al, 'The China Melamine Milk Scandal and its Implications for Food Safety Regulation' (2011) 36(3) *Food Policy* 412

Penna, D, 'Rishi Sunak Ducks Question on Private Health Insurance as Labour Attacks His Wealth', The Telegraph, 9 November 2022

Peretz, G and X Borrás, 'A Case of Unforeseen Adverse Side-Effects? The Ireland/Northern Ireland Protocol and Medicines Regulation' (2021) 5(4) *European Pharmaceutical Law Review* 175

Persuad, J, 'Recardio Ceases UK Drug Trials, Blaming Brexit', Pharaphorum, 3 October 2018 (https://pharmaphorum.com/news/recardio-ceases-uk-drug-trials-blaming-brexit/)

Pezzola, A and CM Sweet, 'Global Pharmaceutical Regulation: The Challenge of Integration for Developing States' (2016) 12 *Global Health* 85

Philippopoulos-Mihalopoulos, A, 'The Flesh of the Law: Material Legal Metaphors' (2016) 43(1) *Journal of Law and Society* 45

Phillips, A and T Hervey, 'Brexit and Biobanking: GDPR Perspectives' in S Slokenberga et al (eds), *GDPR and Biobanking. Individual Rights, Public Interest and Research Regulation Across Europe* (Charn, Switzerland, Springer, 2021)

Phillips, M, Welsh NHS Confederation response to the Legislation, Justice and Constitution Committee on the Retained EU Law (Revocation and Reform) Bill, 17 November 2022 (www.nhsconfed.org/publications/wnhsc-response-retained-eu-law-revocation-and-reform-bill)

Phinnemore, D, 'UK Withdrawal from EU Membership: The Quest for cake' in S Gstöhl and D Phinnemore (eds), *The Proliferation of Privileged Partnerships between the European Union and its Neighbours* (Abingdon, Routledge, 2019)

Phinnemore, D, 'Northern Ireland – A "Place Between" in UK-EU Relations?' (2020) 25(4) *European Foreign Affairs Review* 631

Phinnemore, D and K Hayward, *UK Withdrawal ('Brexit') and the Good Friday Agreement* (Brussels, European Parliament Policy Department for Citizens' Rights and Constitutional Affairs, 2017)

Piris, J-C, 'Does the European Union Have a Constitution? Does It Need One?' (1999) 24(6) *European Law Review* 557

Pound, R, 'Law in Books and Law in Action' (1910) 44(1) *American Law Review* 12

Powell, T, *Healthcare (International Arrangements) Bill 2017-2019*, Briefing Paper Number 08435, House of Commons Library, 17 January 2019

PriceWaterhouseCoopers, *Brexit: Implications for Pharma and Life Sciences Companies*, 2018 (www.pwc.co.uk/pharmaceuticals-life-sciences/assets/brexit-for-pharma-and-is-global-flyer.pdf)

Proctor, K et al, 'Tory MPs Call for End to "Immoral" Surcharge for Migrant Health Workers', The Guardian, 21 May 2020

Q

Quigley, M and L Downey, 'Integrating the Biological and the Technological: Time to Move Beyond Law's Boundaries' in E Dove and N Nic Shuibne (eds), *Law and Legacy in Medical Jurisprudence: Essays in Honour of Graeme Laurie* (Cambridge, Cambridge University Press, 2021)

R

Raz, J, *Between Authority and Interpretation: On the Theory of Law and Practical Reason* (Oxford, Oxford University Press, 2009)

Rein, M and D Schön, 'Problem Setting in Policy Research' in C Weiss (ed), *Using Social Research in Public Policy Making* (Lexington MA, Lexington Books, 1977)

Rhodes, RAW, *Understanding Governance: Policy Networks, Governance, Reflexivity and Accountability* (Oxford, Oxford University Press, 1997)

Rhodes, RAW, *Everyday Life in British Government* (Oxford, Oxford University Press, 2011)

Richardson, L et al, 'Responsible Citizens and Accountable Service Providers? Renegotiating the Contract Between Citizen and State' (2014) 46(7) *Environment and Planning A* 1716

Richardson, L, 'Engaging the Public in Policy Research: Are Community Researchers the Answer?' (2014) 2(1) *Politics and Governance* 32

Richardson, L and EA St Pierre, 'Writing: A Method of Inquiry' in N Denzin and Y Lincoln (eds), *The Sage Handbook of Qualitative Research*, 5th edn (London, Sage, 2018)

Richland, JB, 'Sovereign Time, Storied Moments: The Temporalities of Law, Tradition, and Ethnography in Hopi Tribal Court' (2008) 31 *PoLAR: Political and Legal Anthropology Review* 8

Richland, JB, 'Perpetuities Against Rules: Law, Ethnography and the Irresolution of Inheritance' (2013) 8(3) *Law Culture and the Humanities* 433

Riles, A, 'A New Agenda for the Cultural Study of Law: Taking on the Technicalities' (2005) 63(4) *Buffalo Law Review* 973

Rogers, S, 'NHS Bursary', Complete University Guide, 16 November 2022 (www.thecompleteuniversityguide.co.uk/student-advice/finance/nhs-bursary#NHSbursaryandfundingfornursingandalliedhealthprofessionsinEngland)

Rosas, A and L Armati, *EU Constitutional Law* (Oxford, Hart Publishing, 2012)

Royal College of Nursing, 'RCN Wales Publishes Nursing in Numbers 2021 Report Revealing Current Workforce Statistics', 23 November 2021 (www.rcn.org.uk/news-and-events/news/w-rcn-wales-publishes-nursing-in-numbers-2021-report-revealing-current-workforce-statistics-231121)

Royal College of Nursing, *Nursing Workforce in Scotland Report*, 29 March 2022

Royal College of Physicians, 'A Lack of NHS Staff Will Continue to Limit COVID-19 Recovery Plans', 22 April 2022 (www.rcplondon.ac.uk/news/lack-nhs-staff-will-continue-limit-covid-19-recovery-plans)

Ruffert, M and P Leino-Sandberg, 'Next Generation EU and Its Constitutional Ramifications: A Critical Assessment' (2022) 59(2) *Common Market Law Review* 433

Ruhs, M and B Anderson (eds), *Who Needs Migrant Workers? Labour Shortages, Immigration and Public Policy* (Oxford, Oxford University Press, 2010)

Russell, P, 'Doctors Put NHS Privatisation and Outsourcing on the UK Map', Medscape UK (www.medscape.co.uk/viewarticle/doctors-put-nhs-privatisation-and-outsourcing-uk-map-2022a1001wvr)

Ryan, B, 'The Common Travel Area between Britain and Ireland' (2003) 64 *The Modern Law Review* 855

S

Sajó, A and R Uitz, *The Constitution of Freedom: An Introduction to Legal Constitutionalism* (Oxford, Oxford University Press, 2017)

Sammut, G et al (eds), *The Cambridge Handbook of Social Representations* (Cambridge, Cambridge University Press, 2015)

Sampson, T and S Dhingra, 'The Economic Consequences of the Brexit Deal', 29 November 2018 (https://blogs.lse.ac.uk/businessreview/2018/11/29/the-economic-consequences-of-the-brexit-deal-the-case-of-trade/)

Sandu, M, *The Economics of Belonging: A Radical Plan to Win Back the Left Behind and Achieve Prosperity for All* (Oxford, Princeton University Press, 2020)

Sanjek, R (ed), *Fieldnotes: The Makings of Anthropology* (London, Cornell University Press, 1990)

Savage, M et al, *Social Class in the 21st Century* (London, Penguin Random House, 2015)

Scheingold, SA, *The Rule of Law in European Integration* (New Haven CT, Yale University Press 1965)

Schmidt, V and M Wood, 'Conceptualizing Throughput Legitimacy: Procedural Mechanisms of Accountability, Transparency, Inclusiveness and Openness in EU Governance' (2019) 97(4) *Public Administration* 727

Schorkopf, F, 'The European Union as an Association of Sovereign States: Karlsruhe's Ruling on the Treaty of Lisbon' (2009) 10(8) *German Law Journal* 1219

Shukla, N (ed), *The Good Immigrant: 21 Writers Reflect on Race in Contemporary Britain* (London, The Unbound Press, 2017)

Schymyck, A, 'How Does Brexit Affect Irish Citizens in the UK?' (https://freemovement.org.uk/how-will-brexit-affect-irish-citizens/)

Scott, C, 'Accountability in the Regulatory State' (2000) 27(1) *Journal of Law and Society* 38

Scott J and DM Trubek, 'Mind the Gap: Law and New Approaches to Governance in the European Union' (2002) 8(1) *European Law Journal* 1

Scottish Government, *The Contribution of Non-UK EU Workers in the Social Care Workforce in Scotland*, June 2018

Senedd Research, 'The UK Internal Market Act 2020: What Difference is it Making?' (https://research.senedd.wales/research-articles/the-uk-internal-market-act-2020-what-difference-is-it-making/#:~:text=The%20UK%20Parliament%20passed%20the,market%20access%20principles%E2%80%9D%20in%20law)

Shiner, B, 'Big Data, Small Law: How Gaps in Regulation are Affecting Political Campaigning Methods and the Need for Fundamental Reform' (2019) (2) *Public Law* 362

Shipman, T, *All Out War* (London, William Collins, 2016)

Siles-Brügge, G, 'Bound by Gravity or Living in a "Post Geography Trading World"? Expert Knowledge and Affective Spatial Imaginaries in the Construction of the UK's Post-Brexit Trade Policy' (2019) 24(3) *New Political Economy* 422

Smith, A, *Autumn* (London, Penguin Books, 2017)

Smith, A, *Winter* (London, Penguin Books, 2018)

Smith, A, *Spring* (London, Penguin Books, 2020)

Smith, A, *Summer* (London, Penguin Books, 2021)

Smith, B, 'MPs Demand Answers on "Scrapped" Health Inequalities paper', Civil Service World, 19 October 2022

Smith, C, 'Key Covid Medicine Agency Cuts Drug Assessor Staff by a Third', The Times, 25 October 2021

Smyth, L, 'Pay Rise for Northern Ireland Healthcare Staff Looks Set to be Delayed', Belfast Telegraph, 20 July 2022

Snell, J, '"European Constitutional Settlement", and Ever-Closer Union, and the Treaty of Lisbon: Democracy or Relevance?' (2008) 33(5) *European Law Review* 619

Sobolewska, M and R Ford, *Brexitland: Identity, Diversity and the Reshaping of British Politics* (Cambridge, Cambridge University Press, 2020)

Sorace, M and S Hobolt, 'A Tale of Two Peoples: Motivated Reasoning in the Aftermath of the Brexit Vote' (2021) 9(4) *Political Science Research and Methods* 675

Special Issue in *German Law Journal* (2019) 20(3) 'Populist Constitutionalism: Varieties, Complexities and Contradictions'

Springford, J, 'What Can We Know About the Cost of Brexit So Far?', Centre for European Reform, 9 June 2022 (www.cer.eu/publications/archive/policy-brief/2022/cost-brexit-so-far)

Stein, E, 'Lawyers, Judges, and the Making of a Transnational Constitution' (1981) 75(1) *American Journal of International Law* 1

Stephens, P, 'After Brexit the Tories Still Cannot Escape EU Red Tape', Financial Times, 1 August 2022

Stoker, G et al, 'Fast Thinking: Implications for Democratic Politics' (2016) 55(1) *European Journal of Political Research* 3

Stuart, F, 'Reflexivity: Introspection, Positionality, and the Self as Research Instrument – Toward a Model of Abductive Reflexivity' in C Jerolmack and S Kahn (eds), *Approaches to Ethnography* (Oxford, Oxford University Press, 2018)

Studlar, D, 'Tobacco Control: The End of Europe's Love Affair with Smoking?' in S Greer and P Kurzer (eds), *European Union Public Health Policies: Regional and Global Trends* (Abingdon, Routledge, 2013)

Sunak, R, *The Free Ports Opportunity* (London, Centre for Policy Studies, 14 November 2016)

Swales, K, *Understanding the Vote to Leave* (London, National Centre for Social Research, 2016)

T

Tait, AA and L Norris, 'Narrative and the Origins of Law' (2011) 5(1) *Law and Humanities* 11

Tamanaha, B, *Realistic Socio-Legal Theory: Pragmatism and a Social Theory of Law* (Oxford, Clarendon Press, 1997)

Taylor, MJ et al, 'United Kingdom: Transfers of Genomic Data to Third Countries' (2018) 137(8) *Human Genetics* 637

The Kings Fund, 'Big Election Questions: the Brexit Workforce', May 2017

The Law Commission, Scottish Law Commission, Northern Ireland Law Commission, *Electoral Law: An Interim Report* (London, Edinburgh and Belfast, The Law Commission, Scottish Law Commission, Northern Ireland Law Commission, 4 February 2016)

The Policy Institute, IPSOS Mori and UK in a Changing Europe, *The Public's Brexit Misperceptions*, October 2018 (www.kcl.ac.uk/policy-institute/assets/brexit-misperceptions.pdf)

The Royal Society, *UK Research and the European Union: The EU Role in International Research Collaboration and Researcher Mobility* (London, The Royal Society, 2016)

Thornton, E, 'Withholding of Health-Inequalities White Paper "Tough to Swallow" says Bishop of London', Church Times, 12 October 2022

Thrift, N, 'Space: The Fundamental Stuff of Human Geography' in N Clifford et al (eds), *Key Concepts in Geography*, 2nd edn (London, Sage, 2009)

Tischkowitz, M et al, 'A No-Deal Brexit will be Detrimental to People with Rare Diseases' (2021) 397(10268) *The Lancet* 20

Timmermans, F, 'The Constitutionalization of the European Union' (2002) 21(1) *Yearbook of European Law* 1

Tomkins, A, 'Review: In Defence of the Political Constitution' (2002) 22(1) *Oxford Journal of Legal Studies* 157

Trade and Agriculture Commission, *Final Report* (London, Trade and Agriculture Commission, March 2021)

Trubek, L et al, 'The Construction of Healthier Europe: Lessons from the Fight Against Cancer' (2008) 26(2) *Wisconsin International Law Journal* 868

Tuori, K and S Sankari (eds), *The Many Constitutions of Europe* (Abingdon, Routledge, 2016)

Tushnet, M, 'The Relation between Political Constitutionalism and Weak-Form Judicial Review' (2013) 14(12) *German Law Journal* 2249

Tushnet, M, 'Varieties of Constitutionalism' (2016) 14(1) *International Journal of Constitutional Law* 1

U

UK in a Changing Europe, *Cost of a No Deal Revisited* (London, UK in a Changing Europe, 3 September 2018)

UK in a Changing Europe, *No Deal Brexit: Issues, Impacts, Implications* (London, UK in a Changing Europe, 4 September 2019)

UK in a Changing Europe, 'UK-EU Divergence Tracker' (London, UK in a Changing Europe, October 2021, December 2021, July 2022)

UK in a Changing Europe, *UK Regulation After Brexit Revisited* (London, UK in a Changing Europe, 19 October 2022)

UK Research Office Brussels, 'UK Participation in EU Programmes for Research, Innovation and Higher Education' (www.ukro.ac.uk/Documents/UK_EU_factsheet.pdf)

UK Visas and Immigration, 'National Pay Scales for Eligible Healthcare Occupation Codes' (www.gov.uk/government/publications/national-pay-scales-for-eligible-healthcare-jobs/national-pay-scales-for-eligible-healthcare-occupation-codes)

UK Visas and Immigration, 'Pay for UK Healthcare as Part of Your Immigration Application' (www.gov.uk/healthcare-immigration-application/who-needs-pay)

UK Visas and Immigration, 'Skilled Worker Visa: Eligible Healthcare and Education Jobs' (www.gov.uk/government/publications/skilled-worker-visa-eligible-healthcare-and-education-jobs/skilled-worker-visa-eligible-healthcare-and-education-jobs)

UK Visas and Immigration, 'Skilled Worker Visa: Shortage Occupations' (www.gov.uk/government/publications/skilled-worker-visa-shortage-occupations/skilled-worker-visa-shortage-occupations)

UK Visas and Immigration, 'Skilled Worker Visa: Shortage Occupations for Healthcare and Education' (www.gov.uk/government/publications/skilled-worker-visa-shortage-occupations-for-health-and-education/skilled-worker-visa-shortage-occupations-for-healthcare-and-education)

Underwood, D et al, 'The Effectiveness of Plain Packaging in Discouraging Tobacco Consumption in Australia' (2020) 4(12) *Nature Human Behaviour* 1273

US Food and Drug Administration, 'FDA Approves Belzutifan for Cancers Associated with Von Hippel-Lindau Disease', 1 February 2022 (www.fda.gov/drugs/resources-information-approved-drugs/fda-approves-belzutifan-cancers-associated-von-hippel-lindau-disease)

V

Valverde, M, *Law's Dream of a Common Knowledge* (Woodstock, Princeton University Press, 2003)

Valverde, M, 'Jurisdiction and Scale: Legal "Technicalities" as Resources for Theory' (2009) 18(2) *Social & Legal Studies* 139

Valverde, M, *Chronotopes of Law: Jurisdiction, Scale and Governance* (Abingdon, Routledge, 2015)

Valverde, M, 'Class and Economic Equality' in M Valverde et al (eds), *The Routledge Handbook of Law and Society* (Abingdon, Routledge, 2021)

Valverde, M et al, 'Contested Laws, Contested Societies' in M Valverde et al (eds), *The Routledge Handbook of Law and Society* (Abingdon, Routledge, 2021)

van Schalkwyk, MCI et al, 'Brexit and Trade Policy: An Analysis of the Governance of UK Trade Policy and What It Means for Health, and Social Justice' (2021) 17 *Globalization and Health* 61

van Schalkwyk, MCI et al, 'Risks to Health and the NHS in the Post-Brexit Era' (2020) 369 *British Medical Journal* m2307

Vernai, P et al, *The Impact of Collaboration: The Value of UK Medical Research to EU Science and Health* (Technopolis Group, 2017)

Verschueren, H, 'The Complex Social Security Provisions of the Brexit Withdrawal Agreement, to be Implemented for Decades' (2021) 23(1) *European Journal of Social Security* 7

von Bogdandy, A et al, 'Guest Editorial: A Potential Constitutional Moment for the European Rule of Law – The Importance of Red Lines' (2018) 55(1) *Common Market Law Review* 983

von Lewinski, D et al, 'Protocol for a Phase 2, Randomised, Double-Blind, Placebo-Controlled, Safety and Efficacy Study of Dutogliptin in Combination with Filgrastim in Early Recovery Post-Myocardial Infarction' (2020) 21 *Trials* 744

Vos, E, 'EU Food Safety Regulation in the Aftermath of the BSE Crisis' (2000) 23(3) *Journal of Consumer Policy* 227

W

Wakisaka, D and PJ Cardwell, 'Exploring the Trajectories of Highly Skilled Migration Law and Policy in Japan and the UK' (2021) 9(1) *Comparative Migration Studies* 43

Walford, G, 'The Practice of Writing Ethnographic Fieldnotes' (2009) 4(2) *Ethnography and Education* 117

Walker, N, 'The Idea of Constitutional Pluralism' (2002) 65(3) *The Modern Law Review* 317

Walker, N, *Sovereignty in Transition* (Oxford, Hart Publishing, 2003)

Walker, N, 'Beyond Boundary Disputes and Basic Grids: Mapping the Global Disorder of Normative Orders' (2008) 6(3–4) *International Journal of Constitutional Law* 373

Walker, N et al (eds), *Europe's Constitutional Mosaic* (Oxford, Hart Publishing, 2011)

Walker, N, *Brexit Timeline: Events Leading to the UK's Exit from the European Union*, Briefing Paper Number 7960, 6 January 2021

Ward, I, *A Critical Introduction to European Union Law* (Cambridge, Cambridge University Press, 2009)

Ward, M, *The Geographical Pattern of UK Trade*, Commons Library Research Briefing 7593, House of Commons Library, 16 December 2021

Watson, M, 'Brexit, the Left Behind and the Let Down: The Political Abstraction of "the Economy" and the UK's Brexit Referendum' (2018) 13(1) *British Politics* 17

Weatherill, S, 'Interpreting the Protocol' in C McCrudden (ed), *The Law and Practice of the Ireland/Northern Ireland Protocol* (Cambridge, Cambridge University Press, 2022)

Weatherill, S, 'The Protocol on Ireland/Northern Ireland: Protecting the EU's Internal Market at the Expense of the UK's' (2020) 45(2) *European Law Review* 222

Weatherill, S, 'The Protocol on Ireland/ Northern Ireland: What It Says Is Not What It Does', 17 March 2020 (http://eulawanalysis.blogspot.com/2020/03/the-protocol-on-ireland-northern.html)

Webb, D, *Progress on UK Free Trade Agreement Negotiations*, Commons Library Research Briefing 9314, House of Commons Library, 8 November 2022

Weiler, JHH, 'The Transformation of Europe' (1991) 100(8) *Yale Law Journal* 2403

Weiler, JHH, 'A Quiet Revolution' (1994) 26(4) *Comparative Political Studies* 510

Weishaar, H et al, 'Tobacco Control and Health Advocacy in the European Union: Understanding Effective Coalition-Building' (2016) 18(2) *Nicotine & Tobacco Research* 122

Westlake, M, '"Mad Cows and Englishmen": The Institutional Consequences of the BSE Crisis' in N Nugent (ed), *European Union 1996: The Annual Review* (London, published in association with the *Journal of Common Market Studies*, 1997)

What Do They Know, 'Use of NHS logo by Vote Leave' (www.whatdotheyknow.com/request/use_of_nhs_logo_by_vote_leave)

What Do They Know, 'Should MPs Declare Private Health Insurance in Registers of Interest?' (www.whatdotheyknow.com/request/should_mps_declare_private_healt)

Wheeler, S, 'Socio-Legal Studies in 2020' (2020) 47(S2) *Journal of Law and Society* S209

White, S, 'Brexit and the Future of the UK Constitution' (2022) 43(3) *International Political Science Review* 359

Wilkes, G, 'Early Questions for Sunak's Growth Policy', Institute for Government, 21 November 2022 (www.instituteforgovernment.org.uk/publication/rishi-sunak-growth-policy)

Williams, P and B Clarke, *Dangerous Associations: Joint Enterprise, Gangs and Racism*, Centre for Crime and Justice Studies 2016

Williams-Grut, O, 'Canary Wharf Announces £500 Million Project to Build Europe's Biggest Commercial Lab', Evening Standard, 30 March 2022

Willemsen, MC et al, 'Tobacco Control in Europe: Progress and Key Challenges' *Tobacco Control* (2022) 31 160

Wise, J, 'Patient Satisfaction in GP Services Falls Sharply in Latest Survey' (2022) 378 *British Medical Journal* o1764

Wolff, L, 'Let's Talk about Lex: Narrative Analysis as Both Research Method and Teaching Technique in Law' (2014) 35(1) *Adelaide Law Review* 3

Wood, M, *Hyper-Active Governance: How Governments Manage the Politics of Expertise* (Cambridge, Cambridge University Press, 2019)

Wood, M, *Post-Brexit Trade Negotiations and Health Governance* (London, UK in a Changing Europe, 28 July 2020)

Wood, M, 'The Political Ideas Underpinning Political Distrust: Analysing Four Types of Anti-Politics' (2022) 2(58) *Representation* 27

Wood, M et al, 'What Do "Left Behind Communities" Want? A Qualitative Study in the United Kingdom using Photo Elicitation' (2023) *American Political Science Review* (first view doi: 10.1017/S0003055422001186)

World Bank, *Dying For Change: Poor People's Experience of Health and Ill-Health* (Geneva, World Bank, 2001)

World Health Organization, *Everybody's Business: Strengthening Health Systems to Improve Outcomes* (Geneva, World Health Organization, 2007)

World Health Organization, 'Communicable Diseases' (www.afro.who.int/health-topics/communicable-diseases)

World Health Organization, 'Noncommunicable Diseases' (www.who.int/health-topics/noncommunicable-diseases#tab=tab_1)

World Health Organization, 'Noncommunicable Diseases. Key Facts' (www.who.int/news-room/fact-sheets/detail/noncommunicable-diseases#:~:text=Noncommunicable%20diseases%20(NCDs)%2C%20also,physiological%2C%20environmental%20and%20behavioural%20factors)

World Nuclear Association, 'Radioisotopes in Medicine' (https://world-nuclear.org/information-library/non-power-nuclear-applications/radioisotopes-research/radioisotopes-in-medicine.aspx)

Wuthnow, R, *The Left Behind: Decline and Rage in Small-Town America* (Princeton, NJ, Princeton University Press, 2019)

Y

York, S, *The Impact of UK Immigration Law: Declining Standards of Public Administration, Legal Probity and Democratic Accountability* (London, Palgrave Macmillan, 2022)

Yusufi, H et al, 'The NHS in Northern Ireland Post-Brexit: The Legal Position on Product Supply' 2021 29(2) *European Journal of Health Law* 165

Yuval-Davis, N et al, 'Everyday Bordering, Belonging and the Reorientation of British Immigration Legislation' (2018) 52(2) *Sociology* 228

Z

Zubaşcu, F, 'Gabriel Confirms UK Can't Join Horizon Europe Until Row Over Northern Ireland Protocol is Settled', Science Business, 14 October 2021 (https://sciencebusiness.net/news/gabriel-confirms-uk-cant-join-horizon-europe-until-row-over-northern-ireland-protocol-settled)

Zainzinger, V, 'Budget Cuts at UK Medicines Regulator Raise Eyebrows', Chemistry World, 25 August 2021

Zglinski, J, 'The End of Negative Market Integration: 60 Years of Free Movement of Goods Litigation in the EU (1961–2020)' (2023) *Journal of European Public Policy* (first view doi: 10.1080/13501763.2022.2161603)

Index